# Children, War & Propaganda

**Mediating American History**

David Copeland
*General Editor*

Vol. 6

The Mediating American History series is part of the Peter Lang
Media and Communication list.
Every volume is peer reviewed and meets
the highest quality standards for content and production.

PETER LANG
New York • Washington, D.C./Baltimore • Bern
Frankfurt • Berlin • Brussels • Vienna • Oxford

Ross F. Collins

# Children, War & Propaganda

PETER LANG
New York • Washington, D.C./Baltimore • Bern
Frankfurt • Berlin • Brussels • Vienna • Oxford

Library of Congress Cataloging-in-Publication Data

Collins, Ross F.
Children, war and propaganda / Ross F. Collins.
p. cm. — (Mediating American history; v. 6)
Includes bibliographical references and index.
1. Children and war—United States—History—20th century.
2. Propaganda, American—History—20th century. I. Title.
HQ784.W3C646   303.6'6—dc22   2010035246
ISBN 978-1-4331-0382-7
ISSN 0085-2473


Bibliographic information published by **Die Deutsche Nationalbibliothek.**
**Die Deutsche Nationalbibliothek** lists this publication in the "Deutsche
Nationalbibliografie"; detailed bibliographic data is available
on the Internet at http://dnb.d-nb.de/.

*For children condemned to know war*

# Table of Contents

# PREFACE

A troubling development of the brutal century recently passed has been the growing use of children for war. Before the twentieth century children may have served as valets or messengers. They may have played with war toys, or dreamed of becoming soldiers someday. Sometimes they may have actually fought, lying about their age to reach the battlefields. But children were not generally expected to participate in any organized way. As the Great War of 1914-1918 changed world societies in so many ways, it also changed expectations for children during wartime. World War I was the first "total war," so designated by the belligerent nations. "Total" was determined to mean that everyone needed to be involved, not only those in the armies. In total war, war on an immense, world-wide scale, everyone worked. Including children of all ages.

But we have often ignored the wartime contributions of children. What were they expected to do? How did it contribute to the war? How did it affect their lives? This history attempts to respond to these questions, by examining activities of children in the United States during World Wars I and II. Modern propaganda helped to draw children into those wars. A variety of authorities participated, in the school, on the playground, at work or at home. They promoted military ideals and activities in hopes these might reduce fear, build character, prepare for service, and even tangibly help the war effort. In doing so, authorities brought war themes to children on a day to day basis, a militarization of American childhood. This research takes a look at how they did that.

Chapter one considers methods used to encourage the transformation, the development of propaganda. The idea of propaganda had been debated in some detail throughout the last century, both as a negative and positive force in modern society. Also considered here is how United States Government propaganda offices operated in both world wars.

Chapter two examines the many methods authorities used to militarize American childhood through both wars, and the challenges they faced. Children were encouraged to accept war values as a way to virtuous character, both physical and mental. Paid war work could be a viable alternative to school work, while children could show their patriotism in many volunteer activities.

Chapter three considers the single most important focus of authorities working to militarize childhood, the schools. Schools could serve as clearinghouses for a child's war education and activities. Children could also be counted on to bring wartime messages from the classroom to their parents at home. If parents were away doing war work or in the service, the schools could help children take on wartime roles to avoid delinquency.

Chapter four describes the most significant jobs children were expected to undertake for war services, and how those jobs were coordinated. Food production in particular would be a focus for children, as well as scavenging for material of use on the battlefields, and selling war bonds. The High School Victory Corps was the largest of many formal programs governments relied on to coordinate children's war work.

Chapter five considers the non-governmental groups interested in bringing children into war. These ranged from private values-building groups such as the Boy Scouts and the Red Cross, to marketing appeals and war toys.

Chapter six devotes attention to the juvenile press, editors of quality children's publications interested in presenting the war to their readers and parents.

Chapter seven examines how American children responded to war, and how they responded as later adults. It considers the role of children in war around the world, and how that role has changed since World War II. It concludes that child participation in war has evolved through the century from a militarized home life to actual combat.

At the beginning of the twenty-first century, nearly one-quarter of the world's armies recruited adolescents; almost one-fifth drafted children under twelve. Two million children died in wars during the last decade of the twentieth century. War of the new millennium was not only being fought for the children; it was being fought by the children. This seemed to be a logical progression after it became acceptable to recruit children for wartime needs. As the world seems to be more and more indifferent to mass death, war becomes a natural part of everyday life.

# ACKNOWLEDGMENTS

The genesis for this study of children during world war belongs to Sté-phane Audoin-Rouzeau. The French historian examined in disturbing detail the extremes to which French authorities during World War I were willing to reach in an attempt to draw children into a military frame of mind.

The late George Mosse's penetratingly sad analysis of the last century's grow-ing brutality included a discussion of militarization of childhood in Europe. His ideas served as an overarching principle guiding my research.

Jay M. Winter, one of the world's leading World War I historians, was the advisor during my graduate work who introduced me to these great scholars, and set a standard of quality for historical research that I have tried to emulate. As for setting a standard of quality in the written word, no one could surpass the influence of my mother, Dorothy Collins, a reporter and editor for a half century. I wish she were still here to guide and correct my efforts that, I fear, still fall far short of her example.

The librarians behind North Dakota State University's interlibrary loan desk scoured the country for obscure documents and so saved me an enormous amount of time and money in archival research. Series editor David Copeland liked my idea and gave me a chance to pursue it. And my wife, Kanako Kabaki, put up with the sometimes tiresome chatter from the kind of person who loves to explore times past.

# INTRODUCTION

In hippie-era America torn by the war in Vietnam, an angry artist drew an impressionistic sunflower. Words hanging from its leaves, the poster declared, "War Is Not Healthy for Children and Other Living Things." Artist Lorraine Schneider's simple statement became part of American culture. In 2010 it was still available through the California peace group formed in the 1960s to protest a war long ended.[1] Perhaps the commonsense statement resonated through decades because the violence and hatred of war seem particularly anathema to the innocence of childhood. Yet people have to be reminded of that, why? Because war is too often fought by children, for children, and in spite of children.

While children certainly have always suffered in war, it was not until the total wars of the last century that they would be made a prime focus of the conflict, and be involved as prime actors. The involvement began in World War I. This total war, as children were repeatedly reminded, was fought for them, for the children, for the future. More than that, if this war were to set children free from tyranny of the enemy, they would have to do their share. Children were not exempt from the rest of society in expectation to report for duty. That duty might be spinning socks or selling bonds, or a dozen other things. For the older, and the boys, it might be training and preparing for their turn to serve. But always, in world wars I and II, children in enthusiasm and by exhortation joined the home front. In doing that, the children found all sorts of opportunities to work together scrapping for Uncle Sam, to learn a trade for better employment, to get fit, or to get hard, physically and mentally. Maybe the poster was wrong.

Certainly for America's children, war had its healthy aspects.

At least that is what the wars' propagandists might have intended. Because the propaganda that has become such a well-known feature of total war certainly was part of the child's world as it was part of the adult's. Yet we know little about war propaganda as it affected children's lives when the world was at total war. Scholars during the last century almost never directly addressed propaganda as it related to children, even as they debated it extensively as it related to adults. This is surprising, given the strong and growing interest in child welfare and education throughout the twentieth century. Sociologists have seldom examined children and propaganda. Historians seldom have considered the experiences of American children during these wars. Children have been mostly seen as inconsequential to the history of the American home front, particularly during World War I. Even high-circulation, quality publications for children, such as *Boys' Life* and *Jack and Jill*, have seldom been taken seriously as primary sources. Children's periodicals were not systematically archived, and so today even some that circulated in the millions are difficult to find. A compiler of juvenile literature lamented that research libraries did not generally compile collections of children's periodicals; even the Library of Congress had shown limited interest.[2] The kids just didn't seem to matter.

Yet they did. In examining how adults brought children into these wars, we are also examining adult values and ideals. "We can discern the main patterns in adult thinking about children—what adults thought should be done to and with children," observed two scholars of childhood. "They, too, were historical actors who had their own subjective experience and who influenced adults as well.... Simply put, much more of the past becomes understandable when we focus on children."[3] Values, ideas, hopes of one generation for a future one flow through children's literature, noted Hamilton, who added during war children's periodicals may lose some of their independent character to become "a vehicle for national and political propaganda."[4] It is in that vehicle that we will ride through this study. We will examine children's periodicals, but more. We will examine propaganda directed at children from government authorities, private and corporate authorities, educational authorities, religious authorities, and others whose charge was to occupy their time in presenting a world during war to a generation of innocents.

## Scope and Approach

This study uses traditional historical research methods in an examination of the militarization of American childhood during both world wars. By historical methods we mean a considered interpretation of events in the past based mainly on primary sources from the past, and construction of a narrative based on that interpretation. By militarization we mean how authorities tried to create a wartime culture for American children using propaganda: what they wanted children to think, what they hoped children would learn, what they intended children to do, what they expected children to accomplish, and what they believed children should not know.

A child here is anyone under eighteen. We recognize, of course, that young children will respond differently than near-adults, and that authorities will often use different approaches and have different expectations for different age groups. But no child was left behind from service during the world wars. Even toddlers under five, during World War I organized into the "Khaki Babes."[5]

We will learn mostly about Caucasian children; authorities examined here almost never considered special appeals to African Americans, Native Americans, Hispanic Americans, or other minorities. One would expect this during World War I; the emphasis was on "Americanization," not separation by race, class or "hyphen." World War II authorities spoke little of Americanization, but their sensitivity toward children of races other than that of the dominant culture did not seem to change much from that of 1918, at least as reflected in these sources. We do know that popular culture was pervasively racist, particularly in World War II.[6] World wars means the wars during the time the United States was participating, from about 1917-1918, and about 1941-1945. The definition of propaganda is controversial; here propaganda has been accepted in its neutral sense as persuasion neither good nor bad, although to be noted is the troubling notion that children most of the time were manipulated through this material.

The grooming process to militarize American children was undertaken primarily by four groups. These are the groups we mean when we generally refer to "the authorities": government, educators, private children's organizations and industries, and juvenile media. The last three took cues from the first, as of course in both wars it was the U.S. Government which declared and directed war policies. But despite the almost universal underlying belief in the correctness of the government's choice to go to war, groups and individuals displayed a variation in concept and philosophy of how children should be brought into wartime culture. Differences existed in the approaches taken during World War

I and World War II. But in common was agreement over positive values and skills children could gain from living through a total war. War was a disaster in principle. But in practice it could be a good opportunity to build a child's character on the home front.

We rely on documents designed for consumption by children themselves, or by their adult charges such as teachers and scout leaders, that is, those whose main interest was to serve as guides for the journey through childhood. This focus suggests some primary sources on the pop culture periphery are excluded from study. In fact, it is acknowledged that child media consumption during the world wars extended beyond children's publications. Movies were enormously popular during both wars; by 1918 they already attracted 10 million viewers a day.[7] By World War II, radio had grown to the point where three-fourths of Americans used it as their major source for war information.[8] Obviously children made up a share of this audience, and some programs appealed directly to them. It is also obvious that children consumed adult-aimed media. A World War II study showed children as young as ten already had a reasonably good knowledge of the war, presumably based in part on their consumption of adult-aimed radio and publications.[9] By World War II, as well, comic books had become popular; more than 90 percent of younger children read them regularly.[10] But these media were not generally under direct control of authorities as we have defined them, and they presented themes of pure entertainment and popular culture more insistently than the children's publications considered here. The publications examined presumed a more literary and instructional tone, perhaps slightly preachy. Clearly editors of children's publications such as *Boys' Life* and *American Girl* were interested in values-based education, and so deserve a place in a study of authorities, their propaganda, and militarization of American childhood. It is presumed that movies, radio, and comics cared more about "low-brow" entertainment, although the author will quickly agree that this was not always true, and that it does not mean these should not be the focus of a future study. In direct quotations from primary sources, obvious spelling anomalies of the period have been updated (e.g., to-day/today). Other grammar and usage patterns have been preserved, even if they do not conform to contemporary practice.

## Notes

1. "History," Another Mother for Peace, http://www.anothermother.org.

2. R. Gorden Kelly, ed., Children's Periodicals of the United States (Westport, CT: Greenwood, 1984), ix.

3. Joseph M. Hawes and N. Ray Hiner, American Childhood. A Research Guide and Historical Hand-

book (Westport CT: Greenwood Press, 1985), x.

4. Karen L. Hamilton, "St. Nicholas at War: The Effects of the Great War on a Prominent Children's Magazine, 1914-1919" (Master's thesis, University of Minnesota, 1972), 1.

5. Florence Woolston, "Billy and the World War," New Republic, January 25, 1919, 369-371; reprinted in David F. Trask, ed., World War I at Home. Readings on American Life, 1914-1920 (New York: John Wiley, 1970), 92.

6. W. Linwood Chase, Wartime Social Studies in the Elementary School (Washington, DC: The National Council for the Social Studies, 1943), 12.

7. Emma Gary Wallace, "Moving Pictures—The Fifth Dimension," Child-Welfare Magazine (became PTA), August 1918, 262.

8. William M. Tuttle, Jr., "Daddy's Gone to War." The Second World War and the Lives of America's Children (New York and Oxford: Oxford University Press, 1993), 150.

9. Robert William Kirk, Earning Their Stripes. The Mobilization of American Children in the Second World War (New York: Peter Lang, 1994), 15.

10. Tuttle, "Daddy's Gone to War." The Second World War and the Lives of America's Children, 159.

# 1

## Children Meet Propaganda

Whe know little about war propaganda as it related to the children's culture when the world was at war. Historians have not extensively considered wartime propaganda and children. A large library of propaganda literature actually reflects uncertainly over the precise definition of propaganda. Is it a great evil, something pretty good, or maybe some of both? The historiography of propaganda has reached all the way back to the 1600s, when the term was first employed by the Roman Catholic Church in its Counter-Reformation. The *congregatio de propaganda fide* aimed to re-establish Roman Catholic primacy in a Europe splitting into Protestant shards, a propaganda strictly religious, a congregation for the propagation of the faith. The word slipped into general meaning through centuries of use, so that by the time of the U.S. Civil War Lincoln's Gettysburg Address could be called a powerful piece of propaganda, meaning a strong argument. Propaganda suggested no negative connotation at that time.

Some propaganda historians have suggested that the word gained negative connotations based on anti-Protestant activities by the Roman Catholic Church.[1] But as late as 1917, many writers still considered propaganda an activity neutral in nature. For example, even as war reached the United States in April 1917, an editor of a parent/teacher publication could write under the title, "A Propaganda for Better Obstetrics," that he would "devote an occasional page of the journal to a propaganda for better obstetrics."[2] Propaganda, in its early meaning, for most people simply meant persuasion. World War I would change this definition so that it was not so simple, and bring in its wake a century of scholarly disagreement.

## World War I and After: The Beginning of Modern Propaganda

All World War I belligerent nations moved to control bad news, first, and promote good news later as it became clear the war would involve everyone, everywhere. In the golden age of print media it became possible to reach the masses like never before. Realization that home front morale would be required to sustain a military force in the millions drove governments to become formal propagandists. In France, the operation morphed into a thatch of press control and persuasion touching every single mass communication from newspapers to music. In Britain, Wellington House produced a blizzard of publications. Germany's World War I domestic operation began as piecework. But it, as all Europe's nations at war, worked overseas for the biggest neutral prize: the United States. Germany's propaganda in the United States was directed by German ambassador Johann von Bernstorff, who oversaw the New York-based German Information Service. Supposedly Germany spent $38 million trying to woo America, much of it in secret subsidies to friendly German-American organizations. Among the four hundred titles that inundated American libraries were *Warlike England as Seen by Herself*, and *Germany's Just Cause*.[3] But Germany's propaganda in the United States suffered from haphazard coordination and uncontrolled private agitators such as George Sylvester Viereck, who insisted on self-publishing offensive tirades against the Allies in his *Fatherland*.

Britain worked as covertly as Germany, circulating to American libraries propaganda that gave no clue regarding its origins. But its propaganda "was much more thorough, sophisticated and effective than the German effort." It also realized its suffering and occupied ally France could convince more readily, and so widely distributed pro-France and other titles, 204 by 1916.[4] Some historians have credited British propaganda not only with driving the United States into war, but with teaching Germany to refine its methods for the next world war. When the United States itself joined, Woodrow Wilson realized the powerful force that domestic propaganda had become in Europe. He immediately set to establishing a focus for propaganda in the United States, and one week after the war declaration the Committee on Public Information was established. George Creel, a former reporter, brought what he believed were Wilsonian Progressive American ideals to propagandistic activities. Censorship would be voluntary, and not administered through a propaganda bureau, as it was in France.

Focus would be on promulgating the truth. "We did not call it 'propaganda,' for that word, in German hands, had come to be associated with lies and corruptions," Creel said in 1920. "Our work was educational and informative only, for we had such confidence in our case as to feel that only fair presentation of its facts was needed."[5] Those facts as the CPI saw them paved all corners of the country in paper; 6,000 press releases, 75,000 pamphlets, 1,438 drawings, a daily newspaper, films, advertisements, an enormous output. "Despite general opinion, the Committee on Public Information was not an agency of censorship," declared Creel, "nor was the press of the United States at any time under any compulsion of statute in the sense that the European press was curbed and supervised."[6] Creel's work reflected an earnest belief that war could open the opportunity to create positive good in America, and the CPI could foster that through propaganda. Thrift, health, conservation, civic virtue—these and more could flow from a truthful and honest propaganda. "The CPI reflected their naive faith in the integrity of the American government and its leaders and in the power of ideas to transform men and society," observed a historian of the CPI.[7]

Creel's detractors were more cynical. In response to Creel's argument that his CPI provided facts and education, a recent scholar reflected the skepticism of many. He called Creel's claim that Germany, not America, had besmirched the good name of propaganda "a stunning bit of propaganda, as it bluntly reconfirms the Manichaean plot that Creel & Co. had hammered home throughout the war: Germans always lie, Americans always tell the truth."[8] But Creel wrote in 1920, when the white-hot hatred of the enemy had little cooled. The CPI itself during the war did try to tell the truth and avoid the worst of German hate-mongering that so swept away the decent sense of many non-governmental pro-war groups.[9]

Passions passed but the world's problems remained, and grew darker. Former adversaries sought to find blame for universal disillusionment in the 1920s. Both found a scapegoat in the extensive propaganda campaigns that defined the first war's home fronts. Hitler's stab-in-the-back argument credited Allied propaganda for demoralizing German troops and civilians into surrender. In the United States and its allies, many criticized the propagandists for building unreasonable expectations while misleading the public into believing war aims more noble than possible. Propaganda was determined to be necessary because United States citizens would not see a direct threat, and so needed winning over. "To win the war the popular will had to be attracted and mobilized, and dissenting opinion suppressed," concluded Brumberg, while Kennedy noted the dramatic end to a century of United States isolation from world politics

required persuasive forces of the CPI's magnitude.[10] Certainly government authorities believed this. In 1939 a CPI history concluded, "Every item of war news
they saw—in the country weekly, in magazines or in the city daily picked up occasionally in the general store— was not merely officially approved information
but precisely the same kind that millions of their fellow citizens were getting
at the same moment."[11] But an extensive reading of World War I publications
in 1916 and early 1917 casts doubt on the presumption that Americans would
oppose joining the war, or that government authorities had to do much to mobilize emotions and ideas.[12] Those were already in ample supply, pushing up
from below, not bequeathed from above. By February 1917 the Zimmermann
Telegram incident would be the last straw in a series of events perpetrated by
an obviously insensitive Germany that angered the American public. The sinking of the *Lusitania* and other civilian ships, the atrocity stories, the invasion of
neutral Belgium—all this was what outraged Americans. What Wilson had to
do after the war declaration was to sustain and direct this popular wellspring
of emotion to organize the immense task of joining full-force into a world war.
While a few straws in the wind still voiced opposition to the United States' joining the war, these were slender and generally not credible, because they came
from mostly the socialist left and not from mainstream America. During the
interwar years the war's detractors argued that these voices were essentially correct, that the United States Government was wrong in joining World War I, and
that propaganda was to blame. But in April 1917 hardly anybody thought the
United States was incorrect in declaring war. It had been attacked in essence
if not in fact by German actions. The mood of the country as evidenced in its
journalism—public opinion polling did not exist—seemed in outrage to match
that after the World Trade Center attacks of September 11, 2001. Then even if
President George W. Bush had wanted to do nothing, that was politically impossible. Public opinion sought revenge; the president had to act, though later
analysis showed some of that action probably to be misguided. Similarly, in 1917
President Wilson, who had tried mightily to avoid war in the face of sometimes
obnoxious political hawkishness, could not have stopped the American cascade
into war even if he wanted to. And there's some evidence to show that he did
want to.

Still, many interwar revisionists determined that war had come to an America that should have stayed out, and propaganda could be taken to task for the
perfidy. Creel never agreed, but found himself on the defensive. Some of the
most outrageous propaganda, the stories of shocking German atrocities that
helped tip the United States into war, were debunked in postwar research by

Arthur Ponsonby and others.[13] Although the CPI had repeatedly tried to avoid spreading atrocity stories, the group still took the blame for the falsehoods, some of which, it must be acknowledged, later historians have found to be true after all. But no war lacks stories of atrocity, from either side. "The propaganda itself was viewed as too boisterous, too exuberant for a world that had hardly been made safe for democracy," wrote one contemporary historian to explain the interwar vilifying of the propagandist's efforts. "Creel had oversold his product."[14]

Particularly significant in pulling propaganda to the darker side of persuasion was Harold Lasswell. Lasswell became one of the last century's most influential sociologists on the momentum of his 1927 book, *Propaganda Technique in the World War.*[15] "Propaganda is concerned with the management of opinions and attitudes by the direct manipulation of social suggestion," he explained. While propaganda could be used to promote bond sales and conservation, "by far the most potent role of propaganda is to mobilize the animosity of the community against the enemy, to maintain friendly relations with neutrals and Allies, to arouse the neutrals against the enemy."[16] Propaganda gained such strength in World War I, stressed Lasswell, because the extent of world conflict required "the mobilization of the civilian mind." He said civilians oppose war, and so "the intentional circulation of ideas by propaganda helps to overcome the psychic resistances to whole-hearted participation in war." Because people have a normal "psychological resistance" to war, the propagandist must teach them to hate the enemy, and must find a focus for that hate in an evil leader. "If the propagandist is to mobilize the hate of the people, he must see to it that everything is circulated which establishes the sole responsibility of the enemy." While Lasswell agreed with a congressman who found "great danger" in propaganda bureaus such as the CPI, "there is no question but that government management of opinion is an unescapable corollary of lrge-scale modern war. The only question is the degree to which the government should try to conduct its propaganda secretly, and the degree to which it should conduct it openly."[17] Americans learned even more about the dark side of propaganda from H. C. Peterson, whose 1939 examination of World War I British propaganda drew the conclusion that the United States had been hoodwinked into war by its scheming ally working from Wellington House in London.[18] "Critics resented the ways techniques of mass persuasion were used, and their arguments colored attitudes about similarly manipulative propaganda."[19]

From propaganda children were not exempt, critics observed after World War I. The propagandist's tools worked primarily through the country's educational system. Lasswell observed during World War I, "certain American educators took advantage of the war to gather steam behind their pet projects of educational reform."[20] But much of the propaganda flowing through the educational system came from the CPI itself, particularly interested in reaching children and their parents with the enthusiastic support of teachers and administrators.[21]

As some influential writers in the 1920s were busy recasting the practice of propaganda into a far more sinister role based on wartime experiences, others hoped to maintain a view more objective. Edward Bernays, the century's most well-known publicist and promoter of ethical public relations, found that propaganda in itself was not as evil as detractors such as Lasswell would have liked to think. "I am aware that the word propaganda carries to many minds an unpleasant connotation," he argued in 1928. "Yet whether, in any instance, propaganda is good or bad depends upon the merit of the cause urged, and the correctness of the information published."[22] Bernays, inventor of modern American public relations, clearly considered propaganda to be a part of his craft. He noted that while the country might run more efficiently if "wise men" dictated citizen choice, "we have chosen the opposite method, that of open competition. We must find a way to make free competition function with reasonable smoothness. To achieve this society has consented to permit free competition to be organized by leadership and propaganda."[23] As Americans do not have time to make informed choices about everything in modern society, Bernays argued an "invisible government which dictates our thoughts, directs our feelings, and controls our actions."[24] That was okay, though, as "there is no means of human communication which may not also be a means of deliberate propaganda, because propaganda is simply the establishing of reciprocal understanding between an individual and a group."[25]

## World War II: Propaganda Made Disreputable

Reframing propaganda into a simple public relations tool, however, did not capture the imagination of many detractors, Franklin Roosevelt among them. The president apparently agreed with those who said Creel's powerful committee had whipped up hate and so had engendered the arrests and deportations that came to embarrass interwar critics.[26] Still, Roosevelt knew modern war required propagandists. How that was operationalized depended on the president in World War II, as it had in World War I. Wilson let his propagandists take over. Roosevelt did not. "He had no intention of allowing a formal government bureau the same latitude the CPI had enjoyed."[27]

While the CPI sprang to life a week after the war declaration, World War II's Office of War Information sputtered into existence more than six months after Pearl Harbor, by order of a recalcitrant Roosevelt. Like Creel, director Elmer Davis was a journalist. He was more widely known nationally, however, perhaps based on his radio commentary work. Davis was also more hesitant than Creel had been. He had complained publicly on radio of the government's poor coordination of wartime communication. He "recognized the confusion in the government's information program and the effect it was having on the effort to mobilize support for the war."[28] But while well-regarded journalists and authors such as E. B. White urged Davis to make improvements as head of a new agency, Davis agreed to serve out of a sense of wartime obligation more than profound admiration for the power of persuasion, as Creel had shown. His reluctance proved prescient; Davis spent considerable time defending an agency neither respected by the military nor defended by the commander-in-chief.

Secretary of War Henry Stimson would not support OWI's attempts to coordinate military communication, while Roosevelt let other agencies continue to operate independent public relations offices. This reflected Roosevelt's interest in dividing propaganda activities and so limiting the power of the OWI. "The War Department had indicated that it still held the upper hand in determining what news might be released," observed an OWI historian.[29] Roosevelt's approach to the war was less idealistic than Wilson's had been; Roosevelt did not speak of saving the world for democracy, but of simply winning the war. That pragmatism disappointed idealists behind the OWI. In particular Archibald MacLeish, Librarian of Congress and anti-fascist, thought an American propaganda office could bring America's ideals to the world: "Through propaganda, they wanted to communicate what they considered the basic American values of freedom and democracy to friends and foes alike in all corners of the earth."[30] MacLeish had been director of the Office of Facts and Figures, Roosevelt's euphemistically named propaganda bureau predating Pearl Harbor. After it was eclipsed in favor of the OWI, MacLeish stayed on as assistant director. But his reputation for liberal politics put him at odds with powerful federal figures such as FBI director J. Edgar Hoover, who investigated him for purported Communist ties.[31] Some congressmen so strongly distrusted the OWI that when Davis in 1944 asked for legislative appropriation to continue his work, he faced widespread skepticism at the Capitol. Davis was under personal suspicion, and his agency also was criticized by Republicans for supposedly promoting Democrat Roosevelt's fourth term. At the same time, Roosevelt declined to come to the rescue of an office he supported only modestly to begin with. The House voted to abolish the OWI, one representative calling its domestic activities "a stench to the nostrils of a democratic people." The Senate did not take such an extreme step, but conference committee work left OWI with a budget of about $2.7 million, not enough to do much, according to Davis, and demanded the agency work with others to generate material.[32] President Harry Truman abolished the OWI on August 31, 1945, and lauded it for its work, but in fact, other agencies were responsible for the most famous of this period's propaganda. Frank Capra's "Why We Fight" series was produced outside the OWI, and the famous poster of Rosie the Riveter, entitled "We Can Do It!" was produced by J. Walter Thompson agency.[33]

Despite its struggles for legitimacy, OWI was credited with considerable work aimed toward American children. The agency reached to the American Library Association in an agreement with school libraries, and in 1942 created a "library liaison unit to interpret OWI to libraries and libraries to OWI...in an institute on war problems for librarians in that area."[34] While many librarians agreed to set up what were called War Information Centers using OWI and other materials, they did not agree to calling their role one of propaganda. "The library must make available valid interpretations of current facts and events," declared the ALA in a 1942 statement. "Manipulations of the truth for any reason, public hysteria or indifference, overconfidence or despair, will impair the national war effort."[35] As well, OWI material joined the avalanche from the federal Office of Education's own efforts to reach children, reflecting Roosevelt's determination to dilute the efforts of a department devoted exclusively to propaganda.

During World War II, the old interwar distrust of propaganda grew to disgust as Nazi Germany claimed the word in its totalitarian control of media. Writers interested in children considered teachers to be potential propagandists, and so warned against choosing approaches found feasible during World War I. "After all, the teacher must be a propagandist," declared one educator in 1942. "Surely he must advocate something! It might even be said that the good teacher is the good propagandist.... He is a propagandist for truth as he understands it.[36] "There stands grimly before us the danger that American education, in the wrong hands, might easily degenerate into a mere agency of political propaganda," warned a junior college dean.[37] Since propaganda was "a deliberate effort to 'influence the minds of other people,' all teachers will recognize themselves as strained propagandists in the sense that they continually advocate 'a philosophy of man's mind and how to use it,'" wrote Albert J. George of Syracuse University in 1942. In World War I, said George, "skilled writers mixed fact and fancy in doses calculated to force people to adopt the desired thought patterns by making them revolt against the perpetrators of heinous crimes." But post-war disillusionment as atrocity stories were found to be false made such techniques less effective by World War II. George observed that totalitarian propaganda had persuaded entire populations by perverting language. Slogans and non-sequiturs replaced reason. "The individual must be subservient and, to this end, he is showered with such phrases as 'in the hand of fate,' 'driven by an invisible power,' 'seized by the spirit....' Consequently totalitarian propaganda contains abstractions and facts that are never connected." The teacher's responsibility, George concluded, was to help children understand how propaganda rested on twisted use of language. "And their instruction will help ward off not only foreign propaganda, but also the domestic variety which can and does use the same methods."[38]

George's caution against World War I-style atrocity propaganda campaigns to encourage hate was echoed by OWI guidelines, just as it had been by the World War I CPI. In both cases, however, privately produced propaganda promulgated through the media seldom heeded prudent official admonitions. During World War II stories trickled out claiming Nazis were perpetrating heinous atrocities in Jewish concentration camps. They met with skeptical response. After all, people distrustful of the first war's propaganda were not about to be duped a second time.

The propaganda instruction advocated by George obviously was aimed at older students. But World War II elementary school children too needed education to avoid dangers of propaganda. In a book describing best practices for elementary school wartime study, W. Linwood Chase suggested, "Discuss in school ways of detecting propaganda. Ask, What is the source of a statement? Who is responsible for it? Whom will it help, us or the enemy?"[39]

World War II-era writers who took a broader look at propaganda, however, found difficulty coming to a definition as have scholars throughout the century. Propaganda "is said to be able to determine the behavior of the most obscure citizen, and at the same time to settle the destinies of the great nations," F. C. Bartlett observed in 1940. "It is at work to fashion the education of the child, and ambitions of youth, the activities of the prime of life, and it pursues the aged to the grave." Such a definition means propaganda in itself may not always be nefarious. "Propaganda is an attempt to influence opinion and conduct—especially social opinion and conduct—in such a manner that the persons who adopt the opinions and behavior indicated do so without themselves making any definite search for reasons," he observed. But teachers also do that. They must, because children at first must be taught before they can learn to reason. "The early stages of education must come very near to the characteristic forms of propaganda. But there is a vital distinction between a propaganda which is designed to fix people forever at its own level, and a propaganda which is designed to lead those to whom it is directed through the necessary preliminary steps to education."[40]

"If one assumes that propaganda is a method utilized for influencing the conduct of others on behalf of predetermined ends, it appears that every articulate person with a purpose is a propagandist," concluded the leaders of the Institute for Propaganda Analysis, also in 1940. "From this viewpoint it would hence be more fair to state that ours is an age of competing propagandas. The task of the thoughtful citizen, who still believes that it is his responsibility to formulate the principal ends of life, then becomes that of distinguishing and choosing between rival propagandas."[41]

The Institute for Propaganda Analysis had been founded in 1937 in an effort to establish cognitive tools Americans could use to evaluate propaganda. Its seven techniques have become classic devices used repeatedly in propaganda, ideas that resonate to the present:[42]

> Name-calling: Finding a label for an idea so that people will reject the idea without considering factual evaluation.
> Glittering generality: Finding a positive word to attach to a concept and so avoid examining the concept.
> Transfer/testimonial: Adding prestige of a person or idea of gain acceptance, or disrepute of a person/idea to gain rejection.
> Plain folks: Gaining acceptance by acting like a part of the common people.
> Card-stacking: Selecting facts or statements to skew idea to best or worst case.
> Bandwagon: Suggesting an idea or group is good because others have accepted it.

It is obvious that all these techniques saw hard use among authorities in their attempts to persuade children to join the home front. Those who didn't participate were "slackers" or "traitors." Those who did were "patriots." Wilson and Roosevelt offered repeated letters of support. Generals and politicians wrote directly to children's publications to urge acceptance. Ulterior motivations behind recruitment of minors for the home front—to keep them off the streets and money out of circulation—were downplayed. Youngsters were urged to join the many groups in school and out working for the war effort because it's what their friends and neighbors were doing. In addition, the wartime themes that crept through curricula, using, for example, numbers of warships or speed of bombers in arithmetic word problems, could fall under the umbrella of propaganda. Weaving the war into apparently unrelated coursework served to "endorse the system, legitimate it, and suggest that it is the natural and normal way."[43] Writing years before propaganda became a topic for organized study, a Columbia University vocational education professor concluded in 1918, "propaganda set forth by settlements, women's clubs, the YMCA, the Boy Scouts, the National Security League, the Women's Patriotic Service League, and a score of other organizations...put a psychological persuasion into the situation which was hard for school authorities and school children to resist."[44]

Still, the idea that these techniques and propaganda generally could "infect" a group like a "hypodermic needle" through media promotion already was under scrutiny by the eve of World War II. The hypodermic needle or "magic bullet" theory as suggested by Lasswell's early work proposed that the right message through the right channel could be presumed to have the desired effect if constructed correctly. Paul Lazarsfeld in 1940 set out to test the power of the media to influence American voters. He selected an Ohio county as focus of his study. Results from that and later studies began to discredit the magic bullet theory; "In sum," he concluded, "the media had minimal effects on the 1940 presidential election campaign."[45]

**Post-war America: Power of Propaganda in Question**

By the late 1940s the magic bullet theory had slid into discredit. Empirical research based on surveys not available to Lasswell indicated to researchers that effective propaganda depended on circumstances. The old interwar fear that people could be easily manipulated by skilled propaganda eased, as research showed propagandistic persuasion was not that simple. Bernard Cohen in 1963 concluded famously that the media "may not be successful much of the time in telling people what to think, but it is stunningly successful in telling its readers what to think about."[46] Scholars begin reconsidering the dark definitions of propaganda established before World War II, accepting that its techniques and its effects must be nuanced. But while research seemed to indicate persuasion through the media did not necessarily have the sinister power it was presumed to have, propaganda as a concept had become associated in popular wisdom with Nazi Germany, and war. Even in the twenty-first century, "This is a testament to the especially negative connotation the term propaganda has acquired in our society and to the persistent and somewhat troublesome strength of Nazi mythology and imagery."[47] Some leading scholars of propaganda and persuasion have tried to move beyond that bleak image now antiquated. "It is my contention that such assumptions should be challenged and that propaganda in and of itself is not necessarily evil," emphasized a contemporary scholar.[48]

In doing that, it is necessary to disentangle propaganda from its sprawling entirety into discrete strands based on method and goal. Many contemporary researchers divide propaganda by shade: white, black, or gray. These divisions are based on persuasive techniques and openness of sources. White propaganda is designed to persuade using mostly factual evidence from a known source. For example, the United States used the Voice of America radio network as propaganda aimed at Communist countries, freely disclosing its source and telling the truth, although a truth as interpreted by Washington. United States television station coverage proudly featuring American Olympic athletes also could be considered white propaganda. Under this definition, both CPI and OWI materials were white propaganda. Black propaganda tries to persuade using unethical techniques such as the Nazi "big lie," and usually does not disclose its source. Much war propaganda is black, and not only from disreputable sources such as Hitler's Germany. British propaganda disseminated to the United States to encourage participation in both world wars often included no evidence of its true source; neither did Allied propaganda designed to disrupt morale of its enemies. Black propaganda is what people generally think of first when considering propaganda. Gray propaganda is somewhere in between, sometimes identifying sources, sometimes providing accurate material. "In the 1940s and 50s, the Truman and Eisenhower administrations used gray propaganda by furnishing texts to newspapers, and favoring journalists who cooperated. In this way they covertly disseminated information to a domestic audience."[49]

Propaganda may also be examined in the context of a larger definition of persuasion. Some scholars have defined propaganda in such a way that just about every kind of persuasive speech might be included; others have specifically tied it to government entities and disreputable ends. "Propaganda is often associated with the influencing of behavior by governments rather than by private individuals," noted an advertising scholar, but "a state of confusion still exists in the definitive approach for this term."[50] Jowett and O'Donnell defined it as "the deliberate, systematic attempt to shape perceptions, manipulate cognitions, and direct behavior to achieve a response that furthers the desired intent of the propagandist."[51] This brings propaganda beyond the typical government source. It could be any entity willing to set up systematic operations, from city get-out-the-vote campaigns to non-profit blood drives. Advertising is systematic, so is also propaganda under this definition. Also films which include product placement, corporations which distort statistics, semi-postal stamps issued to raise money, or televangelists stumping for God, "who keep the money they solicit for religious causes."[52] This contrasts propaganda with persuasion. Persuasion suggests an interaction: I try to convince you because I need your support. For example, a politician will try to persuade colleagues to vote for a bill she is sponsoring. This also contrasts with education. Persuasion of children also can be defined as propaganda. But usually it is not.

Scholars of propaganda have seldom examined these techniques as applied to children during a world war. They have considered education as propaganda. Totalitarian governments in particular view education as propaganda of the highest level; the Soviet Union considered them to be the same thing. But contemporary scholars have concluded education and propaganda are clearly separate. Education, noted Cull, Culbert and Welch, tells students how to think; propaganda tells students what to think. Education sets out to broaden student perspectives; propaganda sets out to close student minds.[53] Jowett and O'Donnell suggested education uses informative communication, designed to create mutual understanding of data. Propaganda goes further, using information to promote "a partisan or competitive cause in the best interest of the propagandist but not necessarily in the best interest of the recipient. The recipient, however, may believe that the communication is merely informative."[54]

The goal of propaganda as defined in education, then, is manipulative rather than informative. This means that the efforts of most authorities, most of the time, during both world wars, can be defined as propaganda. As a World War II educator observed, "a teacher is a propagandist in peace and in war.... In time of war, our country must rely on the teacher for the maintenance of excellence in national morale."[55] Although some scholars have concluded "propaganda in and of itself is not necessarily evil,"[56] the word "manipulation" does have a somewhat negative connotation. It seems clear we are examining a vast field comprising dozens of authorities and dozens of wartime programs that undertook what can be defined as propaganda aimed at American children. Whether that was a bad thing can be debated; recent scholars hoping to examine propaganda under a fairer light have concluded propaganda is amoral, ubiquitous, and necessary in society. Still, manipulating children for wartime needs can but give us pause.

Children during these wars weren't always on the receiving end of propaganda. They also could be manipulators, and so can be thought also to be propagandists. Authorities encouraged World War I children to gang together in parades to promote preparedness, patriotism, and purchase of war bonds. They complied, over and over; 25,000 assembled in New York on short notice after the war declaration in a "Wake Up America" parade to inspire patriotism.[57] Children during both wars who excelled in public speaking were encouraged to approach the adult public beyond the school with wartime messages designed by authorities, usually promoting war bond sales. During World War I, thousands joined a formal speech-making propaganda circuit through the Junior Four Minute Men. "Here were young Americans teaching their parents the principles of democracy," observed a federal reserve officer, pleased at the children's persuasive speaking ability. "The effort of these children sold the county's quota of Victory Loan Bonds. The selling of the bonds was important, but the lessons learned and taught by these children of a foreign-born population were worth more to our national life than could be well measured in money."[58] Propaganda messages fashioned by children usually were intended for speeches. But not always. A New York sixteen-year-old wrote to *American Boy* in 1918 showing pride for his work as a propaganda copy writer. "Newspaper publicity is the backbone of recruiting, and I wrote up the recruiting campaigns in our city," declared Del Dunning in a letter for the magazine's writing contest. "I got so I could write recruiting 'copy' by the yard, and it was all good 'dope.'"[59] The editor was apparently impressed with children's efforts as propagandists, as he encouraged children to continue: "It looks as if boys had been about everything since the war started, but now they have a chance to be propagandists—not the German kind who circulated insidious lies, but the American kind who stand for the truth.... You have influence. Make use of it!"[60]

Less publicly, children in that war were the kind of magic bullets that could target the hearth, carrying the message of the war into the homes. Authorities primed children by training their teachers into patriotic fervor; the message passed from teacher to child, who carried it home. Authorities thought this particularly effective in immigrant homes. The country's enormous population of new Americans during World War I was hard to reach. Many did not speak English. Many distrusted authorities, based on experiences that often led originally to their immigration. But most could be presumed to have a soft spot for their children, and teachers might be more credible than politicians or police. "Just because of this fact, therefore, it is important that the war should receive systematic treatment in the schools," declared the CPI sponsored *National School Service*. "Such teaching will not merely stimulate the patriotism of the child and aid the various war services imposed upon the schools. It will react upon the homes, and powerfully promote a sound civilian morale."[61] While World War II children were not pressed into service as obviously to propagandize for authorities, presumption seemed to be that they were to serve on the team. Writing shortly after the war, Kandel described activities of the High School Victory Corps, including "participation in parades and other community ceremonies—all these were elements in developing consciousness of participation in the war effort."[62] American children in the world wars became the propagandizers and the propagandized, even as American society debated merits and demerits of that propaganda.

## Notes

1. Garth S. Jowett and Victoria O'Donnell, *Propaganda and Persuasion*, 4th ed. (Thousand Oaks, CA: Sage Publications, 2006), 2.

2. Editor's note, J. Whitridge Williams, "A Propaganda for Better Obstetrics," *Child-Welfare Magazine* (became PTA), April 1917, 227.

3. Wayne A. Wiegand, "An Active Instrument for Propaganda," *The American Public Library During World War I* (New York and Westport, CT: Greenwood Press, 1989), 13.

4. Ibid., 17.

5. United States Committee on Public Information (George Creel), *The Creel Report. Complete Report of the Chairman of the Committee on Public Information 1917: 1918: 1919* (New York: DaCapo Press, 1972, reprint edition), 1.

6 Ibid., 3-4, 10.

7. Stephen Vaughn, *Holding Fast the Inner Lines. Democracy, Nationalism, and the Committee on Public Information* (Chapel Hill: University of North Carolina Press, 1980), xii-xiii.

8. Mark Crispin Miller, introduction to Edward Bernays, *Propaganda* (New York: Ig Publishing, 2005, reprint of 1928 edition), 14.

9. Ross F. Collins and Patrick S. Washburn, *The Greenwood Library of American Reporting Volume 5, World War I and World War II, the European Theater*, David A. Copeland, general ed. (Westport, CT and London: Greenwood Press, 2005), 154.

10. Stephan F. Brumberg, Brooklyn College, "New York City Schools March Off to War. The Nature and Extent of Participation of the City Schools in the Great War, April 1917-June 1918," *Urban Education* 24, no. 4 (1990), 441; David M. Kennedy. *Over Here. The First World War and American Society* (Oxford and New York: Oxford University Press, 1980), xii-xiii.

11. James R. Mock and Cedric Larson, *Words that Won the War. The Story of the Committee on Public Information* (Princeton, NJ: Princeton University Press, 1939), 6.

12. Collins, *The Greenwood Library of American Reporting Volume 5*; Ross F. Collins, *World War I. Primary Documents from 1914 to 1919* (Westport, CT: Greenwood Press, 2008).

13. Arthur Ponsonby, *Falsehood in Wartime* (New York: E.P. Dutton, 1928).

14. Allan M. Winkler, *The Politics of Propaganda* (New Haven and London: Yale University Press, 1978), 3.

15. Harold D. Lasswell, *Propaganda Technique in the World War* (New York: Alfred A. Knopf, 1927).

16. Ibid., 10.

17. Ibid., 11-12, 14-15, 47.

18. H. C. Peterson, *Propaganda for War. The Campaign against American Neutrality, 1914-1917* (Norman: University of Oklahoma Press, 1939).

19. Winkler, 4-5.

20. Lasswell, *Propaganda Technique in the World War.*, 75.

21. Kennedy, 100-101.

22. Bernays, 48.

23. Ibid., 39.

24. Ibid., 82.

25. Ibid., 161.

26. Martin Folly, *The United States and World War II: The Awakening Giant* (Edinburgh: Edinburgh Uni-

versity Press, 2002), 50.

27. Winkler, *The Politics of Propaganda*, 5.

28. Ibid., 33.

29. Ibid., 48.

30. Ibid., 6.

31. "Archibald MacLeish," Spartacus Educational, http://www.spartacus.schoolnet.co.uk/USAmacleish. htm.

32. Winkler, *The Politics of Propaganda*, 70–71.

33. Folly, 51; "Women in War Jobs—Rosie the Riveter, 1942-1945," Historic Campaigns, The Ad Council, http://www.adcouncil.org/default.aspx?id=128.

34. "The ALA Allies Itself with the OWI," *School and Society*, October 24, 1942, 376.

35. *Education for Victory*, March 3, 1942, 15.

36. Raymond L. Hightower, Kalamazoo (Michigan) College, "Propaganda and the Teacher," *School and Society*, May 26, 1942, 558.

37. Tyrus Tillway, dean of the evening college, Hillyer Junior College, Hartford, Connecticut, "America's Educational Dilemma," *Education*, November 1943, 168.

38. Albert J. George, "Propaganda and the Modern-Language Teacher," *School and Society*, December 12, 1942, 568–569.

39. W. Linwood Chase, *Wartime Social Studies in the Elementary School. Curriculum Series No. 3* (Washington, DC: The National Council for the Social Studies, 1943), 12.

40. F. C. Bartlett, "The Aims of Political Propaganda" (1940), in *Public Opinion and Propaganda. A Book of Readings* (New York: Dryden Press, 1954), 463-464.

41. Eduard C. Lindeman, president, and Clyde R. Miller, executive secretary, Institute for Propaganda Analysis, in Harold Lavine and James Wechsler, *War Propaganda and the United States* (New Haven: Yale University Press, Published for the Institute for Propaganda Analysis, 1940), vii.

42. Jack Rosenberry and Lauren A. Vicker, *Applied Mass Communication Theory* (Boston: Pearson, 2009), 103.

43. Jowett and O'Donnell, *Propaganda and Persuasion*, 31.

44. Arthur R. Dean, professor of vocational education, teachers college, Columbia University, and supervising officer, Bureau of Vocational Training, New York State Military Training Commission, *Our Schools in War Time—and After* (Boston: Ginn and Company, 1918), 139-140.

45. Rosenberry and Vicker, *Applied Mass Communication Theory*, 111.

46. Ibid., 150.

47. Jowett and O'Donnell, *Propaganda and Persuasion*, xiii.

48. David Welch, in Nicholas J. Cull, David Culbert, and David Welch, *Propaganda and Mass Persuasion. A Historical Encyclopedia, 1500 to the Present* (Santa Barbara, CA: ABC-CLIO, 2003), xv.

49. Jowett and O'Donnell, *Propaganda and Persuasion*, 20.

50. Irvin Graham, *Encyclopedia of Advertising*, 2nd ed. (New York: Fairchild Publications, Inc., 1969), 339, 341.

51. Jowett and O'Donnell, *Propaganda and Persuasion*, 7.

52. Ibid., 21.

53. Cull, Culbert, and Welch, *Propaganda and Mass Persuasion*, xix.

54. Jowett and O'Donnell, *Propaganda and Persuasion*, 30.

55. Hightower, "Propaganda and the Teacher," 558.

56. Welch, in Cull, Culbert and Welch, *Propaganda and Mass Persuasion*, xv.

57. Stephan F. Brumberg, "New York City Schools March Off to War. The Nature and Extent of Participation of the City Schools in the Great War, April 1917-June 1918." *Urban Education* 24, no. 4 (1990), 456.

58. John H. Puelicher, government director of savings, Seventh Federal Reserve District, Milwaukee, Wisconsin, "The New World and the Demand that It Will Make upon Public Education. A. Manufacturing and Commercial Interests," *National Education Association, Addresses and Proceedings, Fifty-Seventh Annual Meeting, Milwaukee, Wisconsin, June 28-July 5, 1919*, (Washington, DC: NEA, 1919), 50-51.

59. Del Dunning, "Third Prize Letter," *American Boy*, January 1918, 34.

60. "Friendly Talks with the Editor. Be a Propagandist," *American Boy*, March 1919, 3.

61. "Why the War Should Be Studied In Schools," *National School Service*, September 1, 1918, 5.

62. I. L. Kandel, *The Impact of the War upon American Education* (Chapel Hill: University of North Carolina Press, 1948), 92.

# 2

# HOW WAR CAN MAKE BETTER CHILDREN

Children in the United States were not asked to participate in their government's war in Korea. They did not receive a call for help during the Vietnam War. They were not drafted into service during engagements in Panama, Granada, Kosovo, Iraq one and two, or Afghanistan. In fact, if American children wanted to do their bit for the troops during these conflicts, they had to do it vicariously through their G.I. Joes, plastic F-4 fighters, or model Huey helicopters. No government leader, no educational authority, no parent—at least officially—called out to America's children to serve their country in a war fought for them, for the next generation.

This would seem reasonable. Real war is frightful. Real war is brutal. Real war does not reflect the values we want to encourage among children.

Or does it? In fact, while the United States has not seen its children lately participating in war, it certainly did during the two world wars. In both World War I and World War II, children were intensive participants on the home front. They were part of almost every activity considered important to the war effort. This included a wide swath of activities ostensibly open to children as volunteers, as well as paid jobs. It included school work, home work, hobbies, management of money, sports, and play. During the world wars, American children found out what "total war" meant—and to them, it meant a whole lot. Adults of the era believed the country was fighting expressly for the children. "Our boys and girls will inherit the world that emerges from this war," wrote the author of a World War II booklet suggesting war studies in the elementary curriculum.[1]

"And this, as all boys and girls should know, is peculiarly *their* war–a war waged for the sake of the years to come," the editor reminded readers of *St. Nicholas*, a well-known World War I children's magazine.[2]

Authorities during the world wars believed the country could not wait for the children to motivate themselves to join the home front. The war had to be brought to them. "Bring the war into the schools," affirmed one educator.[3] They believed the war was a children's war for an obvious reason: it was the children who would inherit the outcome. And because the world wars were thought nearly universally to be critical tests of democratic ideals and free-world values, American children would be forced to live with the victorious philosophy. The philosophy must not be that of the enemy.

Based on the unifying principle that children had a stake in the outcome of world war—in fact, that they may have had the largest stake—it was obvious that children also had a responsibility to become part of the culture of total war. Total war, as the phrase took shape in World War II, "involves entire populations, military and civilian, adults and youth," explained a World War II educator. "It involves them not only as victims of dislocation, injury and death, but as contributors to the national effort. Except for invasion or bombing, war has never before so affected the lives of entire populations, nor has the contribution of the average citizen been so significant."[4] Total war demanded "total participation."[5] World War I, the "war to end all wars," was declared to be a critical crossroads with world tyranny, so that "Every boy and girl over fourteen years of age may, when the war is over, be able to say proudly, 'I had my part in winning the war.'"[6]

Despite these exhortations, authorities in both wars realized that American children may not perceive actual enemy danger as would children living in an invaded nation. In fact, the possibility of the United States itself being attacked in World War I was nearly non-existent; in World War II it was slim. To encourage American children's belief that the war really could reach the doorsteps of Anytown, USA, government leaders established a propaganda campaign mainly for children. They worked closely with any entity associated with children. This most obviously meant working with the schools, the establishments that could reach out most reliably and ubiquitously to children. But it also meant working with organizations for children, with children's media, with industry, with churches, and directly through government advertising and posters. Nearly all of these were only too happy to help out, in fact establishing their own pro-war campaigns that sometimes veered from Washington's official line. By the end of World War II, however, the campaign for the children's war grew into a highly unified and usually efficient machine designed to transform children into combatants of the home front.

How authorities produced a wartime world for America's children in some ways differed between the two world wars. In some ways it was similar. But in both cases, the outcome was the same: many millions of children enthusiastically marched to the colors of the home front, fervent patriots of their government at war, believers in the cause of Uncle Sam without question, "the army of school children."[7] Children were mobilized, became metaphorical soldiers, their classroom their citadel, their weapon an education into the values of war.[8] War became their lives, filling much of their school time, most of their waking hours, and perhaps some of their dreams. In World War I France, drawing children into a life permeated by war Audoin-Rouzeau called "framing childhood into the war."[9] While this research from a United States perspective reflects some constructs as employed by Audoin-Rouzeau, the author hesitates to call what was presented by authorities to American children "framing," because it suggests media framing theory. Framing theory in communication research examines what publications choose to emphasize, and what they choose to ignore.[10] Publications examined here possibly could have chosen to emphasize war as a disaster, could have opposed the government's call for children's service, could have counseled negotiating peace as an alternative to total war. They did not. While a tiny few publications circulating to a very few children did oppose war, they are of interest mostly to researchers considering press censorship and control. As far as America's children were concerned, no one framed the war in any way contrary to the U.S. Government's demands in favor of total victory. Interest here is how these groups implemented this frame through public and private life of American children.

Framing theory also hopes causal relationships can be established between what media disseminated, and how audiences subsequently reacted. While finding such relationships is always difficult in contemporary media research, it is even more difficult studying historical events. Surveys were not available during World War I; World War II surveys show some indications, but certainly are not sufficient to posit causal relationships—if they even are sufficient today, an ongoing controversy. Instead of considering American children's induction into the world wars as framing, a somewhat loaded term among communication scholars, this author looks from a perspective of historical research at the war world that authorities wanted a child to know, and how they constructed that world. At school, at home, at work or at play, a child's life became infused with military vocabulary and values. In this way, American children of the world wars grew up experiencing what might be called the militarization of childhood. The author became interested in studying the militarization of American childhood during world war based on his research of the World War I era. Particularly, he was interested in the steps, or perhaps the slide, that the United States has taken from a country of strongly pacifist and isolationist traditions and limited war capacity before 1914, to a country that spends more on its military than the rest of the world put together, and has seldom hesitated to use that war-waging capacity. The country began the twentieth century steeped in historic values opposing military intervention as a way to solve the world's problems, or to bring American ideals to foreign peoples. "She has abstained from interference in the concerns of others," said John Quincy Adams in an 1821 speech. He declared the United States wished freedom for everyone, but, "She is the champion and vindicator only of her own."[11] Yet in 1917 she abandoned that policy to join World War I. "That departure not only spelled the abandonment of nearly a century and a half of American diplomatic practice," observed historian David Kennedy, "a commonplace observation to which I offer neither dissent nor elaboration. It also compelled the United States, as almost never before, to measure itself against Europe."[12] The interwar attempt to return to isolationism could not be sustained, Steel wrote, as World War II fascism "destroyed the illusion that America could barricade herself from the immoralities of a corrupt world." But as he added, "It also provided the means for the dramatic growth of American military power, which made the new policy of global interventionism possible."[13] Americans became used to expecting that power to produce victories.

War historians sometimes observe that in fighting a war belligerent nations eventually turn to tactics used by their enemies, in direct violation of their own stated values for which they are fighting. This has patently been the case during the world wars, for all belligerents. In World War I, fighting ostensibly to construct President Woodrow Wilson's world safe for democracy, the government harassed, jailed, and even deported hundreds who tried to exercise free speech, and progressively stripped civil rights from its black, Native American, and other minorities. In World War II, Allies responded to Hitler's civilian bombing runs with a response so ferocious it approached death statistics of genocide. The practice seems to have continued. United States military power has become the big stick behind foreign policy in many more recent wars, big, small, and often tragic for countries so embroiled. The killing of women and children in My Lai, the torture of prisoners in Guantanamo, are just two of the more famous incidents in which the military power of the United States has been used in ways opposed to the country's bedrock values.

How did the United States become a frankly, even proudly, militaristic nation? Why has the voice of pacifism shrunk from a once strong and respected guide for American society to a marginalized, almost non-existent peep from the fringes? To help respond to this question we can take many roads through United States political, cultural, and diplomatic history. This author has chosen to walk a path with the nation's children, through two generations who grew up in a militarized childhood to accept a militarized society.

What is a "militarized generation?" Can we even define a "generation?" Strictly speaking, of course, a "generation" doesn't exist. People are born every year. The Baby Boomers are supposedly those born between 1946 and 1964, the bookends defined by a birth rate increase and a birth rate drop. It does seem that those of that time period have in general a different view of the world. The World War II children did not protest the Korean War. But the Baby Boomer generation not so militarized had plenty to say about Vietnam. Many historians who like to investigate the past through generations will look toward a defining experience of a group of children, an event they shared that was so pivotal to their development that it defined their view for the rest of their lives. Obviously, the total wars of the twentieth century were defining events for the children who lived through those eras. Those still alive to remember the experience of total war consider themselves to be a separate generation. "They cite the cheerful volunteerism of almost all the nation's children during World War II as an experience that made their age cohort unique."[14] These generations of children forged as soldiers of the home front became the leaders who built the United States we know today, a world leader in affairs military.

### Militarization of Childhood: Death and Its Denial

The value of military ideals and training as a way to develop character has its basis in the nineteenth century.[15] The idea of manliness, of purification through the cleansing power of war became an attractive theme among young Europeans in the early twentieth century, despite an inkling of just how horrible a modern war could be. As there had been no general war in Europe since 1871, it might be thought that Europeans flocked so gladly to the colors in August 1914 because they had not understood the hideous effectiveness of modern war machines. But by 1917, people in the United States certainly knew the truth. Nevertheless, these same themes found their way into the propaganda serving to militarize American childhood. Children's publications were filled with tales of heroism and sometimes ultimate sacrifice, the deed made for a cause more noble than the loss of one man. The adventure of the soldier, the excitement was emphasized, the manliness of a soldier doing his duty for his country. As a California state board of education vice president reflected:

> Our boys were becoming 'molly-coddles,' we were told—a soft, selfish, pleasure-loving, joy-riding generation. We were told that there were too many women teachers in our schools and that in consequence the youth of the nation was suffering from 'feminization'—whatever that is. Today the crisis that is 'sifting out the hearts of men' has banished doubt; it has proved that our high-school and college boys are patriots and potential heroes."[16]

This theme was carried on, perhaps rather less enthusiastically, into World War II. In the mass media certainly, although exhortations from government or other authorities that war could prove manly virtues became much less prominent. Other virtues, however, could still come from war.

The emphasis of manly themes in publication and pronouncement suggests this story of children in war is a story of males. This is mostly true; leaders of American societies focused on those who would become future warriors and after that, future leaders. Women during this period seldom became either. The needs of half of the twenty to thirty million American children were addressed often as an after-thought, or under the presumption that they might apply to boys and girls equally. Even less likely to be addressed were special needs of minorities. African Americans, Native Americans, Hispanic Americans, or Asian Americans among other minorities were mostly invisible to those in the groups which established principles for the militarization of American childhood. *The Crisis*, an adult publication for black Americans, did publish a children's issue once a year during World War I, in October. Content of these issues did not address wartime issues for children, however. As well, no consideration was made for children with disabilities. Because sources addressing these groups of children during war are so meager, this is inevitably if not happily mostly a story of regular white boys.

Ways to help children face death, or to better understand death, also were rarely addressed in either world war. In World War I, the matter of death as applied to older boys who could foresee the possibility of military service was taken relatively nonchalantly. Valor and heroics were what was important. Authors writing about presentation of World War II to children looked back upon the experiences of World War I, often for observations of things gone wrong. Writing in 1943, a Yale education professor noted some educators

> Would point to ample evidence from the last war showing that many made

an excellent adjustment to impending death by viewing it nonchalantly. Many others dismissed moment-to-moment anxiety concerning it by adopting a fatalistic attitude. Still others relieved their tensions by jesting about it. Few gave the full implications of the situation serious attention.[17]

This attitude of denial, or really more an attitude of belief that death was an honor for such a noble cause as a world war, can be borne out in the actions of young Americans who volunteered to fight in France in 1914, when the United States was still neutral. Malcolm Cowley, a Harvard University student who volunteered for an ambulance brigade in France, explained, "The war created in young men a thirst for abstract danger, not suffered for a cause but courted for itself; if later they believed in the cause, it was partly in recognition of the danger it conferred on them. Danger was a relief from boredom, a stimulus to the emotions, a color mixed with all others to make them brighter."[18]

World War I authorities and media did much to encourage this attitude with their portrayal of heroics and idealistic soldierism. Death was possible, but in a noble sense of adventure, manliness, feeling (ironically) truly alive in mortal danger: "That chance to live life most free from stain/And that rare privilege of dying well."[19]

As *American Boy* admonished in February 1918, "Boys, Get Into the Fight!":

Shut your eyes and you can see trenches. Great gashes in the ground, dug with awful labor by blistering hands. In them, helmeted heads of men moving cautiously through mud, among rats. Beyond, tangled masses of barbed wire. Then, No Man's Land. Then—the enemy. Back of the trenches, enormous guns pouring shells, trying to drive the soldiers out. *Boom–z–zing–crash*—and many men are hurled to death, or maimed, or blinded. Their comrades crawl over them. They go "over the top." They feel the sting of the bullet. Their flesh is torn by bayonets. Yet they go on, on. You can see it, can't you—and hear the deafening noise of battle and the groans of the wounded, dying men?[20]

This is death described, to be sure, but abstractly, like watching a war movie. Common sense would say a boy would not wish to join in on such an experience, but emotions more important than reason drove the wills of many a teenage boy in World War I. Adventure, manliness, the youthful belief in immortality could serve as a start, but the sustaining reason boys yearned for wartime service was patriotism. Idealism as stated by a 17-year-old writing in *American Boy*:

I, as an American boy, am under an obligation to myself and to my country. I owe it to myself to make of myself a good man and true. I owe it to my country to do for her and die for her, as the need may be.[21]

It was not necessary for authorities concerned with fashioning a view of World War I to talk about death in any frank manner. The enormous surge of patriotism, the idealism that unified the country in 1917 United States as it did in 1914 Europe washed away any cavil to the fact that war means death, and World War I already meant death to millions. Young people, recently children or still in their teens, embraced this patriotic fervor even more than their elders. The speed of technology at the turn of the last century impressed an older world (and was actually commemorated in 1903 by a series of U.S. commemorative stamps noting fast things like cars, boats and trains). But it was truly embraced by the young. "It was a movement of youth. The celebration of modernity led more to an idea of confrontation, 'war as a festival.'"[22]

It is hard to explain the enthusiasm with which older boys of the United States joined a war they knew was hideous, unless we consider a mythical, idealistic spirit that no longer seems to exist in this century. It drowned in the mud and blood of the battles—by the time the young idealists saw their first combat, few would later report any lingering feeling of idealism and patriotism. And at least some of that would linger into World War II. While certainly the popular media reclaimed the patriotism, the idealism, the adventure of serving in World War II, the young men themselves marched more soberly onto the transports.

In his highly unusual, in fact apparently unique, consideration of death for children during the period, Yale professor Brubacher noted democracies do a poor job of presenting the certainty of death to children. In school, in church, death is something to postpone, to ignore, to discard in favor of emphasizing life. Writing in 1943, he noted that democracies had mistakenly appeased dictatorships because democracies did not hold a realistic view of death.[23] The writer contended people living in democracies did not understand that death is sometimes the preferable option. "One truly conquers death when he can say life is cheap in comparison to some great cause, when he can say that there are some things worse than death."[24] The author found some of history's greatest leaders succumbed to causes they believed more important than death."[25]

This reasoning seems closer to the ideals of some World War I devil-may-care young men than to the ideals of mostly less-blinkered World War II fighting youth. Parents during the second war were encouraged to introduce children to death by building on what children already knew. "Death insists on being noticed," another World War II author observed. "Even children's stories have their killings, while military toys displayed in show windows suggest play killing as an appropriate activity for children." Faced with such ubiquity, the frank parent needs to explain that "understanding of life and understanding of death should advance together step by step." Religions have tried to explain death, but mostly by relying on clichés, noted the author, who nevertheless offered no specific approach beyond parents' need to be calm and mature.[26]

In neither war did the rare literature addressing death for children try to be explicit or realistic. Perhaps this was partly by patriotism, partly by need to spare feelings of the more delicate. But it also may have served the need to maintain home-front morale, the belief that a war is worth fighting and can be won. To avoid despair, particularly older boys needed to know only the partial truth. Because it was they who would be mostly likely to serve. In World War II, authorities had some hard statistics to back their concerns. A 1942 *Forbes* magazine poll of high school students showed that while most were in favor of the country's participation in the war, more than half worried the Axis powers had some chance of victory.[27] While certainly not an unreasonable position, less than complete certainty of Allied victory could be considered an attitude in need of propaganda infusion. A 1943 poll of high school students showed even more concern. "One concludes that pupils are rarely overoptimistic, but that there is a strong tendency to exaggerate the dangers and hardships brought by the war. Scores on Part I, describing the present status of the war effort, are especially pessimistic, the mean being well below the estimated reasonable degree of confidence." The author added, "if military affairs go badly, censorship will conceal the truth from the people."[28] While such polls certainly showed high school students reflected a realistic attitude during a year in which the Allies struggled, authorities apparently did not consider it to be cheerful enough for kids. The author concluded there was morale work to be done among the older children. "After one year of war, the morale of high school pupils is far from perfect. About half the group are more pessimistic than is justified by our accomplishments in overcoming our problems."[29]

In both wars American authorities either encouraged, or at least did not move to challenge, boys' typical nonchalance or disbelief about the possibility of death. This could be counted on in many nations that fought the world wars, because it was what made young men eager to serve. It also was what makes many older men poor soldiers. It was not so much because a forty-year-old was physically incapable of handling battlefield conditions, because many of them were. It was the changing idea of death from youth to middle age that made the old soldier more cautious and questioning. It was therefore never in a belligerent government's best interest to encourage adolescents to contemplate mortality, and was not suggested as part of a wartime curriculum, in school or out.

It is perhaps worth considering the value of realistic death education during wartime in schools as a possible way of shortening a war. Perhaps boys so enlightened would not be as happy to fight. Of course, that also may be a formula for losing a war. The truth is that once the adolescent is in the thick of it the blinders come off. Combat soldiers in the world wars became very well aware of possibly impending death. At that point, they tried to make the war as short as possible, because the only thing they really wanted to be was not a hero, a patriot, a defender of a world safe for democracy. They just wanted to go home, and as soon as possible. "What was it about the war that moved the troops to constant verbal subversion and contempt?" wrote Paul Fussell about World War II. "It was not just the danger and fear, the boredom and uncertainty and loneliness and deprivation. It was rather the conviction that optimistic publicity and euphemism had rendered their experience so falsely that it would never be readily communicable."[30]

The talk of heroics and patriotism and duty and sacrifice—that was the myth made for the home front, people who had no idea of what a battlefield was like (even if they read about one), and yet needed official nurturing to keep producing war materiel, and naive young men with adventure on their minds.

In this sense, the militarization of childhood really became a way to groom children for war. The grooming process played upon the adolescent boy's attraction to honor and to adventure, and downplayed any idea of suffering or mortality, which is far from most adolescents' thoughts to begin with. Teamwork, the fun of working with other children in an effort for a cause, pleasing parents, being active, getting out of school, doing something that seemed important—these made war more acceptable. Children could find in a war a really fun way to bond with others in the games of collecting scrap, selling bonds, picking milkweed pods, knitting scarves, or marching around with wooden stick rifles. This makes a war less scary, chops it down to size, makes it actually an attractive pursuit to children of the home front. The ugly verities of actual war were seldom indicated to children, or even much to adults, although certainly in World War II some journalists did try to avoid sugar-coating in the adult media. But by the time young men realized the shocking brutality and crazy stupidity of a world war, it was too late, and they were stuck with doing what they could to survive the experience in one piece, mentally and physically. Heroics were for children's imaginations and preachers' eulogies.

*Young children during World War I were encouraged to act like soldiers and be prepared for future service. (St. Nicholas, June 1918, page 739.)*

## War and Manly Values

During the world wars, many people believed war could be a good thing for society in general, and for children in particular. The positive qualities of a soldier have been admired certainly in the twentieth century—and even before. One can look back to the noble sentiments attached to the heroic soldiers who fought for Napoleon, and their gallant depictions by Romantic era painters such as Jacques-Louis David, or the U.S. Civil War soldier idealistically battling for his version of America. The *ésprit* of the hero, the discipline of the men in battle, the precision of obedience, the loyalty of teamwork, the honor of courage, the courage of patriotism—humble service for a cause greater than a man: all these echo through the literature of war as a noble pursuit through centuries and continents. The truth is rather less ennobling. Napoleon dealt with mass desertions, breakdown of discipline, plunder, stupidity and dishonor. World War I's pathetic human rats lived in mud and blood and rotting pieces of flesh. But World War II was the worst. When World War II reporter Marguerite Higgins was given permission to visit the European theatre in March 1945, she was shocked at what she saw:

> Cities ruined and stinking. Dead bodies everywhere, some mangled or torn apart, the American and German equally awful. 'More shocking were the wounded, many her own age or younger. Some were blinded, others cruelly disfigured.' The faces of the Allied soldiers which she had expected to register a degree, at least, of satisfaction over their victories were only 'weary' and 'bitter.'[31]

Were the high school boys who were to come into the military told the truth about total war in the twentieth century? Of course not. But who was? Even today, who really knows the truth of the battlefield beyond the men (and now women) who fight there? The reality is that in both world wars the U.S. Government was extremely concerned about home-front morale. Total war demanded the energies of a whole nation, the children not exempt, and if the literal truth about combat zones were told, it was feared morale would plummet and the country would lose. The years leading to both world wars saw in the United States a strident debate between the two p's, that is, supporters of pacifism versus those of preparedness, who believed war was sometimes necessary, perhaps even desirable, and the United States must militarize to stand ready for a fight.

"Be prepared" would seem to echo common sense, in fact so common it became the motto of the Boy Scout Movement. But common sense does not always apply to war—perhaps it never does—and at the turn of the last century a strong movement argued against preparedness. As applied to military affairs, preparedness compels a nation to spend a considerable amount of its revenue and its human capital preparing for war, even if a war is not imminent. The United States in 1914 had seen no good reason to harvest enormous swaths of its treasury preparing for the kind of vast armies, enormous field guns and dreaded battleships defending the big powers across the pond. England sparked an arms race with Germany over its Dreadnaught class of battleships; Germany threatened France with its divisions of well-trained military backed by the most advanced ordnance on the planet; Russia threatened Germany with its army of conscripts less well-trained, but considerably more numerous and supposedly more brutal. France threatened Germany with its perennial revenge talk for losing in 1871. Everyone in the Old Country seemed, at the least, extraordinarily well spoiled for an extremely bestial fight.

But not the United States. Its entire army of 128,000 men represented barely more than one-fourth of those killed during the first months of World War I alone (400,000). America had little artillery, no airplanes, and no draft. In fact, one reason Germany confidently resumed unrestricted submarine warfare in 1917, knowing full well Washington would likely respond with a war declaration, was that its military advisors presumed the war would be over by the time an unprepared America geared up for battle. They were right, almost. It took a good year for doughboys to hit the trenches, but during that time the Allies managed to hang on.

But before 1917 those U.S. leaders who most aggressively promoted a United States military buildup received only mild support. Pacifists argued that military preparation in peacetime was worse than costly; it was counterproductive. It not only did not guarantee peace, but practically guaranteed war, because nations backed by arsenals are more likely to fight. Look at Austria-Hungary, backed by Germany—it was Vienna that precipitated the war in the first place. When an apparently isolated incident in Sarajevo cascaded into general war during the summer of 1914, pacifists who maintained that preparedness meant spoiling for a fight seemed to see their baleful predictions come true. But the belligerent nations didn't see it that way. Every country believed it was fighting a defensive war for its very survival. Patriotic nationalism propagandized the position that had only their nation been even more prepared, it would have won the war before a grisly stalemate ground its way through lives of hundreds of thousands of young men.

Many in United States at the war's beginning did originally see a logic in those who argued that preparedness spoils for war. The country remained steadfastly neutral during 1914. But attacks on United States ships, worry over security of loans made to allies, effective British propaganda, and some actual atrocities and brutality from the Germans, encouraged a slide in public opinion from neutrality to favoring the preparedness advocates. Former president Theodore Roosevelt, in particular, raged against President Woodrow Wilson for not immediately jumping into the war. General Leonard Wood promoted camps to help businessmen prepare personally through military training on weekends. Reflecting business interests, the U.S. Chamber of Commerce Committee on National Defense in 1916 issued a report calling for universal military training.[32] President Wilson moved to build a larger armed force, but too slowly for many advocates. The National Security League, supported in particular by East Coast Superpatriots, grew to a powerful foil for anti-preparedness groups such as the American School Peace League. The security league promoted enormous demonstrations in favor of preparedness, particularly in New York and Chicago. Explaining the movement to children, *St. Nicholas* magazine noted accurately that the spectacles pulled the strings of patriotic emotion, as opposed to the more rational arguments of the anti-militarists.

> The main purpose of most of these demonstrations has been to awaken interest in the subject of preparedness. In all parts of the country there are large numbers of people who feel that we ought to have a larger army and a stronger navy.... That the demonstrations have done much for the cause of preparedness cannot be denied. But they have done something else: they have aroused the American spirit and have kindled the fire of genuine patriotism.[33]

While the preparedness debate rippled through government and pressure groups, the central focus argued that human beings as much as piles of ordnance must be prepared. And the human beings most likely to need preparation were children, the pool from which the future is drawn, in war and in peace. The schools became "a battleground in the struggle over militarism in American society."[34] Proponents saw in those who opposed preparedness a group threatening the masculinity of American boys, particularly as most elementary school teachers were women. "Manliness" was presumed to be lacking in American boys, presumed to mean an education advocating peace. It left them physically weak and bereft of "vigor." Declared one naval officer, "women tutelage is to do violence to that most precious possession, his masculine nature.... He will never recover. He goes through life a maimed man."[35]

Several states, most obviously New York, proposed to remedy this danger through defining preparedness as military training beginning as young as twelve. Physical education teachers, who before the war had struggled to establish credibility for the field, made what they thought was a logical connection between physical fitness and military preparation, and so became the greatest educational proponents of preparedness in the schools. One of the more restrained of these wrote in 1918 that physical drills and athletic competition could form a "plan to accomplish this preparedness through a method of training that will not taint coming generations with the desire to test their skill in the vocation of killing."[36] But even as preparedness advocates were winning their battle and teachers who opposed bringing military affairs into the schools slunk into silence for fear of their jobs or worse, some authorities continued to question the evolving value. "'Preparedness' is one of those mysterious words, hypnotic in its influence. Prepare! Prepare! is the cry of the time," wrote an Oregon legislator. "Prepare for what? It should mean preparedness for a life of usefulness, and the question is this: Do our schools give our children a workable basis for life?[37] A state normal school president observed that before the United States entered the war preparedness was so unpopular in the schools that some teachers actually forbade marching and singing martial songs. But when war was declared, the United States, children included, jumped enthusiastically to join their government in wartime patriotism. They apparently had been well prepared: "When the call came to arms, who were the first to join the colors? The young men from the halls of learning—high school, normal school, college, and university."[38]

Pacifists in World War I included socialists who in the early twentieth century formed a voice strong enough to be heard in Congress and state capitols.

Moreover, Wilson initially was concerned that the "hyphenated Americans," those immigrants recently come through Ellis Island often to escape European poverty and militarism, would balk at a call to patriotism for their newly adopted country. This turned out not to be the case, but it did not stop the government from launching an enormous propaganda campaign (the word at that time having no negative connotation) aimed at adults as well as children. The few pacifists who did not acquiesce to a spiral of silence found themselves harassed, threatened, or jailed.

After World War I ended, anti-preparedness forces reasserted their viewpoint as the United States fell back into its pre-war isolationism. By 1920, U.S. armed forces that had grown to two million men serving in Europe shrunk to 204,000. American educators reflected the country's bleak disillusion in seeing that not only did World War I not end all wars, it didn't solve much of anything. If that war seemed pointless, teaching peace might be a better answer, and interwar educators joined the nation in rejecting the kind of alliances that might only lead the United States back to the battlefields. Americans disillusioned with the outcome of World War I strongly supported moves to avoid "foreign entanglements," and in 1935 Congress passed laws to formally resurrect neutrality. Only with the threat of a second world war did President Franklin Roosevelt act to re-establish a potent military, and again, not without opposition. Peace education stayed popular—until December 7, 1941.

While martial training again was proposed for the schools, this time the U.S. military came out against it, proposing instead an emphasis on literacy, science, and fitness. But some authorities believed a lack of preparedness in the 1930s actually made World War II possible, as it emboldened Hitler and allowed Germany to remilitarize. And teachers found themselves to be one of the scapegoats. An angry response from an army officer to a letter of sympathy from a teacher for his son missing in action blamed educators: "I wish you to know that maybe if you and a lot of others like you had not preached pacifist doctrines for so many years at the high school, there might not have been a war and we might have had a trained army and an adequate air force." Interwar educators defended themselves, arguing that teaching peace had little to do with the forces that drove the world to a second general war. A North Dakota teacher wrote, "Let's all share what blame that we deserve for being unprepared for war. To imply that education should shoulder a major share, however, is evidence of a circumscribed, entirely un-American, spirit.[39] Calling anti-pacifists "social defeatists," a Chicago educator observed, "The conditions which gave rise to the present conflict have no relation whatsoever to the nonmilitant peace education of the past twenty years. And now—while we are in the very midst of war—we must educate for peace more vigorously than ever before."[40] He added, "There can be no such thing as 'militant democracy.'" But there was. There still is. If preparedness means carrying permanently one of Theodore Roosevelt's big sticks, then the United States has become a Teddysonian democracy.

Had it not been for the shock of December 7, 1941, that debate over isolationism might have continued, but by the time the date had gone to infamy the country had no doubt it would have to mobilize for a second total war. Three days after the war declaration Byron Price was asked to lead the Office of Censorship. Franklin Roosevelt declared, "All Americans abhor censorship, just as they abhor war. But the experience of this and of all other nations has demonstrated that some degree of censorship is essential in wartime, and we are at war."[41] The press did not complain. As in World War I, nearly every media outlet in the country squarely stood behind, or in fact became a partner with, the government in promoting its wartime requirements.

### Hiding the Hideous

One of them was to censor the most gruesome stories and photos from the fronts as possibly troubling to morale, and in any case, journalists self-censored images they believed their readers did not want to see. After all, they had loved ones in uniform. And no one wants to hear how one of them might have really died: not in a noble charge against a fearsome enemy, but flat as flagstone, run over by one of your own tanks in another debacle of the supposedly precision-inspired planning of the U.S. Army.[42] Reality was ugly, and war was supposed to be, well, worth waging for a higher calling, such as Franklin Roosevelt's "Four Freedoms."

The truth is that the controllers of reality were right. The home front plainly did not want to hear what war was really like. In a rare exception to the anodyne rule, in World War I the Committee on Public Information sought to comfort families whose sons had become doughboys with a 1918 film entitled "When Your Soldier Is Hit." But as Mossé discovered, it contained "too much horrifying realism, and alarmed rather than reassured audiences."[43] In World War II, authorities ever sensitive to mistakes from the first total war did let escape some frank stories. Before Pearl Harbor, *Life* magazine's photographers captured fairly shocking images. As a family magazine circulating to millions of American homes, children undoubtedly happened upon these images, but after December 7, 1941, the government moved to censor *Life* and newsreel footage.[44]

It later relented, believing as Winston Churchill had said that morale could be steeled if the home front were shown the war as it really was, "blood, sweat and tears." But showing some of this, one World War II child reported, gave her "terrible nightmares."[45]

Even toys should not be too graphic about war's realities. In 1938 Gum, Inc., produced a set of chewing gum cards entitled "The Horrors of War." These were clearly reminiscent of Goya's horrifying prints, "The Disasters of War," produced a hundred years before. The 1930s cards for children were frankly explicit in war illustration and description. "The cards could never be marketed today. Scenes showing dogs eating dead bodies, body parts flying through the air, hangings, mutilation, and decapitation."[46] Outraged parents could be perhaps mollified that each card included the words, "To Know the Horrors of War Is to Want Peace." This children's toy is rare today, and such realistic depictions of war were nearly unique in America during the world war period. But the cards were apparently popular among children, who sometimes it might be admitted particularly relish playthings that produce parent outrage.[47] Noted is that on the cards the Japanese were always depicted as the barbarians.[48]

If the truly hideous nature of the wars was mostly hidden from children, it was not because American authorities hoped to hide the wars themselves from children. Actually, this was not always quite true. Throughout the era the government, schools, organizations and media brought the war to the kids, but before World War I some voices doubted that wisdom. William Fayal Clarke, editor of *St. Nicholas Magazine for Boys and Girls*, one of the most prominent children's magazines during the World War I era, included nothing about the war before March 1915. He noted, "for the younger children of its audience, this magazine has felt a natural desire, and was in duty bound, to protect them as far as possible from any intimate knowledge of the horrors which war always carries in its train and of the suffering which, since 1914, has surpassed any similar record in human history."[49] This reflected the position of the magazine's founder, Mary Mapes Dodge, who declared that a children's magazine should be "a pleasure-ground where butterflies flit gayly hither and thither," and that "snakes of immorality and vulgarity never transgress the pages."[50]

Actually it was the children themselves who wanted to see snakes; *St. Nicholas* was most interactive of children's magazines during this period, offering regular rewards to readers who wrote letters and short articles. These readers began choosing the war as a topic at least as early as March 1915, when *St. Nicholas* that month featured a letter from a Winnipeg, Manitoba, reader, who said she was in England to be near her father and brother fighting in the war.[51] Later 1915 letters emphasized the wish for peace, theme of a children's writing contest in June 1915, and emphasis of the first non-reader generated material regarding the war, in July: "When our own American boys and girls think of the numberless boys and girls in Europe whose fathers go out to battle and never return—that is surely an incentive for every one of you to strive to the utmost to cultivate and maintain a peaceful mind toward all. It is something worth trying for."[52] In September the editor, bowing to obvious demand from readers for those snakes, inaugurated a new feature, "The Watch Tower," which digested war news of the month.[53] Other children's magazines, however, did not try to shield children from war-related topics, and were actually fairly graphic about their presentation before the United States joined the conflict.

## War as a Way of Childhood

As the United States became unable to avoid war in 1917, and again in 1941, it was clear to those who wished to reach the nation's children that the inevitable could actually be of some benefit. In fact, it could do quite a lot for American children, very little of it negative. The idea that war could be an excellent way to build character at home particularly resonated among educators and government leaders in World War I. This was a crisis; those who wanted to see change in society were determined not to let it go to waste. Leaders of the Progressive movement during World War I, in particular, hoped to use the war as a way to advance their educational goals. Strongly pro-war political leaders, such as Theodore Roosevelt, thought the war could bring the American immigrant salad bowl closer into the melting pot, and children could play a critical part in making that happen. Others just thought some old-fashioned military virtue could serve to improve children grown lazy and self-centered. "Without seeming pessimistic, one may truly say that the average modern child had become self-centered," declared Henry Davidson, chairman of the World War I Red Cross War Council. "The next generation is learning lessons of responsibility and honest service."[54]

In fact, a war could be excellent education for youth in many ways. Ideals included:

War as a way to habits of sacrifice.
War as a way to physical fitness and toughness.
War as a way to knowledge of geography and world affairs.
War as a way to self-discipline.

War as a way to patriotism.

War as a way to Americanization.

War as a way to serve parents, community, and country.

War as a way to build courage.

War as a way to build loyalty.

War as a way to encourage habits of conservation and thrift.

War as a way to build obedience to authority.

War as a way to teach duty.

War as a way to teach useful skills.

All these were present in children's programs of both world wars, although priorities and methods of transmitting these values to children differed. But before authorities could build character through a prism of wartime virtues, they had to meet a child where he or she was at. And that meant dealing with a child's fear.

Number four of the Four Freedoms that guided Americans during World War II, Freedom from Fear, was particularly applicable during that war. The others, Freedom of Speech, Freedom of Religion, and Freedom from Want, could wait until later, but fear—nothing might be more fearful than a world war. While older children could handle war, young children were thought to be especially vulnerable. They had seen their parents' response to Pearl Harbor, shock and disbelief that a foreign power would attack the United States at home. The war was no longer fought in the abstract, but really could directly reach the home front, or so it seemed. Authorities set up air raid drills in schools across the country, despite the tactical reality that no enemy plane could reach the continental United States. "Even in places like Janesville, Wisconsin, where sirens went off in air raid drills, and blackouts, and so the nights were 'punctuated with fear.'"[55] In March 1941, *Life* magazine published a photo story designed to show how parents may deal with children's fears of war, particularly as they responded to the becoming ubiquitous air raid drills. Noting the government had addressed childhood fears by employing psychologists to write a booklet for parents,[56] the [unsigned] *Life* article observed, "The need to educate children against fear—the springhead of all psychic trauma—has already released a flood of advice from child-guidance experts and well-meaning amateurs." However, the government-produced material emphasized bringing the war to the children in a manner reflecting their habits of play. "Stressing the sound psychological fact that the unfamiliar is the most fearful, the booklet recommends that war's grim realities be incorporated into family life as rapidly and as casually as possible."[57]

Photos showed an actual family from New York, "Mr. and Mrs. Eugene Mott, Queens Village, Long Island." The caption noted, "Seven-year-old Billy and four-year-old Evelyn are learning to face whatever may come as a game, for war is being made a game in their home right now. By joining in the play, the Motts are also fostering the sense of family solidarity which is a child's greatest strength."[58]

Other authorities believed the best way to reduce fear might be to keep children busy. That could also lessen the possibility for juvenile delinquency, as in both wars authorities knew from experience in England that a war declaration distracts parents and often draws them away from home, leaving children at loose ends. A well-known educator advised:

> If we can be calm and assured, if we can face whatever comes courageously and confidently, they will be courageous and strong in their turn. That is our chief concern for the duration then, because if we win the war and lose this generation of children to illness, weakness and despair, we need not have fought it. Plan to keep these children occupied at home, in school, and in the community, and protect them from the worst effect of the war—fear.[59]

The idea of forcing children to participate in air-raid drills against a far-fetched risk of attack became more controversial as the shock of Pearl Harbor receded and the reality of scaring children for no reason became more concerning. Some authorities believed these drills to be good training, but others thought it was a waste of time at the least, at most, detrimental. "Reports from many schools all over the country" showed students coordinating air-raid drills,[60] while new classes for "air raid wardens" invaded school curricula.[61] The National Education Association recommended that parents teach children about blackouts and set up air-raid shelters.[62] Air-raid drills in the elementary schools two or three times a week were in some communities bolstered by issuing each child a metal information tag, dog tag style, in case they were killed or injured. This apparently brought the war too close for comfort of some children, who became terrified of nearly non-existent danger.[63] By 1943, however, authorities began to wonder whether air-raid drills and blackouts were doing more harm than good, pointlessly scaring young children about an attack that will never happen. "I am concerned about the emotional effects of widespread preparations for meeting air-raids," said one professor of education. "To a child preparation means impending action. I doubt the wisdom of extensive air-raid drills and obvious precautions in communities very unlikely to experience raids."[64]

In World War I, conversely, no authority expressly addressed the need to

Some parents were concerned that their children loved to dress up and play war. World War II educators were divided over the psychological benefits of war play, but consensus favored the presumption that play relieved fear and gave children something to do. (Parents Magazine, July 1942, page 26.)

calm childhood fears. This may have been because child psychology had not developed into maturity as a research-based discipline. Or it may have been because the United States was not attacked on the home front. The ships at sea sunk by German submarines did not persuade home-front authorities to coordinate extensive air-raid drills, as aerial bombing was in its infancy; it was hard to find a credible war threat to actual lives of American home-front children in 1917-18.

But during this war, as in the second, children were encouraged to confront general anxiety about the war by making it part of their games. This also was addressed expressly in the *Life* magazine how-to for parents. Photographs emphasized the importance of making the war a game as a way to make it less fearful, and more acceptable:

Evelyn and Billy, wearing miniature Churchill suits, huddle under the dining-
room table to play 'air-raid shelter.' If they are ever in a real shelter, they will
think it's fun.
Billy and his father stage a naval battle on floor of the living-room. Playing
with war-like toys often helps little boys to release their hidden anxieties by
acting them out.[65]

Children in both world wars replayed the battles through an enormous variety of games, some made up, some based on manufactured items. The practice
of bringing war into the miniature world of a young child extends to at least
the eighteenth century, when boys could be encouraged to learn martial ideals
through a collection of metal soldiers. During the world wars millions were
produced, along with games and toys to depict nearly every piece of equipment
and battle a child could reduce to the language of play. On the plus side, argued
a professor of education during World War II, "Probably there is some validity
in the concept of catharsis; the child is doing something about his concerns.
Certainly it does no good to forbid such activities. Their harm is in the great
restriction of activity resulting from constant preoccupation with them."[66] Many
parents disagreed, although authorities found little to worry about in war toys,
and sometimes encouraged war games in school. Writing for a prominent magazine of the World War I era, an author who attended a toy show observed of the
many war toys and games for sale:

Feeling, impulse and idea are so welded together in a war complex in his im-
pressionable mind that for the rest of his life fighting seems to him a necessity,
war 'as inevitable as death.' I came away from that dingy, antique hotel feeling
that I had been present indeed at the sowing of the dragon's teeth even if for
ten or twenty years we wait for the crop to come up.[67]

World War II authorities generally supported war play not only because
parents were powerless to stop the kids anyway, but because it could replace
childhood fear and tension with action. One author warned, however, "we must
keep in mind that every time a child's toy gun kills a Jap or his submarine sinks
a Nazi boat he has impressed upon his character by way of his muscles and his
ears and his eyes and his sharp heart beat and his quick breathing that the surest
way out of difficulty is to destroy the thing you fear."[68]

Mossé considered war toys as a way of "trivializing the war," making it less
fearful, less menacing, and so more acceptable to children.[69] This, of course,
was precisely what American authorities wanted to do, but for reasons not so

sinister: they hoped familiarity could assuage fear within the world of a child. In any case, as parents know, if you do not allow your children to have the toys they want, they will make those toys themselves. During the world wars, sticks became rifles, trees became fortifications, and no one wanted to be the "Hun," the "Jap," or whatever other enemy children most learned to loathe. Games will be played, and the aggressive nature of children will frighten parents regardless,[70] although the politics of channeling this into a more conscious militarization of childhood deserves further consideration.

## Patriotism to Build the Ideal Child

Worry of authorities that they would have to address a child's anxiety and fear over war seldom was addressed in 1917-18, and began to shrink after 1943. It became obvious that the nation's children were not going to be bombed—although not completely obvious, as that did indeed happen one time, in 1945. Bomb-packed balloons from Japan floated near Bly, Oregon, killing six curious children who chose to investigate. This was the only fatal raid by air in the continental United States during World War II. Despite the earlier frenzy of drills that by this time had waned, this actual incident was censored, not so much to stay panic among children as to avoid giving Japan information on success of their unusual weapon.[71]

Of more lasting interest during both wars was not a concern over children's physical safety, but a focus on children's moral development. A child no longer fearful could be encouraged to play a wide variety of roles in wartime that could both help the country and help the child. Qualities that war could engender generally fell into four categories: acquisition of skills, improvement of health and fitness, development of civic spirit, and enhancement of moral character.

The hub around which all these virtues fell was patriotism. Wartime patriotism could drive the child, sometimes indolent, often cranky, to motivate herself or himself toward the goals authorities would hope to develop. Patriotism was particularly a helpful beginning, because it sprang from emotional, and not rational sources. Children were presumed to be driven by emotions. "Fortunately the feelings and emotions can be utilized for useful ends as well as evil ends," observed an author writing for elementary school educators in World War II. "A moderate, reasonable and wise appeal to these emotions can be properly used in the schools. Patriotism is an emotion."[72] World War I authorities similarly suggested patriotic appeals, "primarily to the imagination and to the emotions."[73] Patriotism was an emotion also widespread among the country's adult population, and in both world wars probably formed the single most significant force driving the country into war. The strength of World War I-era superpatriots such as Theodore Roosevelt and General Leonard Wood who, under the general heading of "preparedness," hoped to thoroughly militarize the schools and the country before 1917, was resisted fairly successfully by groups such as the American School Peace League. The league, organized by Fannie Fern Andrews in 1908, found support at the highest levels of government. Federal Bureau of Education commissioner Philander Claxton invited Andrews to advise the office on international peace studies and pacifist literature choices. League efforts spread to Europe as well before the war. In fact, in 1914 French and English governments presumed international pacifism was such a force that it might blunt appeals to the colors. That turned out to be a straw in the wind compared with the appeal of nationalism.

Nationalism, the idea that members of a race or historic class of people care about their identity as a separate state, was presumed in the early twentieth century to be a mostly spent force in world affairs. It is the wellspring of patriotism, both based on emotional feeling of independent rights and gratitude for one's country. Nationalist force today has proven over and over to be capable of cruelty to the point of genocide. Mossé's examination of the last century's incredible violence grew from his "concern with modern nationalism and its consequences."[74] Comparisons can be made regarding each world war's ghastly fests of human extermination, but both grew in their own momentum beyond anything initiators expected, black hurricanes destroying millions of lives in ways more hideous than anyone could imagine—or would want to, even today. Patriotism as the engine of morale sustains the home front, and feeds men to the battlefields to make continuation of war possible. World War I, as many Germans believed by 1939, was not lost on the battlefields. The German army had not disintegrated. The German home front had. Hitler was able to exploit this and rebuilt an über-patriotic military state to disastrous end. What American authorities knew in 1941 was that the war was going to be won only if home front support could be maintained. And that demanded a searing level of patriotism from old and from young.

No one could question the extremes of adult patriotism exhibited by those whose charge was to influence children during either war. In fact, to exhibit less than those extremes was to risk censure, harassment, jail, even physical danger. In World War I, teachers who remained neutral concerning patriotism could be fired, as ten were in New York City,[75] of hundreds in many incidents across the nation. In World War II little evidence exists showing many were fired for

flaccid patriotism. But patriotic fervor certainly drove authorities in their atten-
tions to children, as home-front morale was now clearly known to be a critical
factor in sustaining total war. In World War I many educators were commanded
to sign a guarantee of their patriotism, and to teach it. As the National Education Association itself heard, "It is the sacred obligation of the schools to instill
the love of country into the hearts of the growing generation, when the roots of
habit, and therefore character, sink deep into the plastic mold of youth."[76]

But that was preaching to the choir. Nearly everyone was perfectly patriotic
during both wars, and pleased to bring the sacred fervor of patriotism to children. Patriotism as the queen value was never in serious debate. Encouraging
the feeling of duty and love to one's country had long been a central goal for
a variety of authorities. The founder of *St. Nicholas*, considered the best children's magazine of the era, declared in 1873 that "love of country" would be one
of her goals.[77] A wellspring of patriotism among its readers demonstrated that
these goals had been achieved, or probably reflected in the patriotism children
learned in the home, because the editor noted writing contest entries "show our
young artists to be fairly bristling with patriotism, as we all ought to be about
this time, and so the editor wishes for the loyal Leaguers a joyous and 'glorious'
Fourth."[78] This was before World War I began. When the United States entered
the war, editors reminded all children to read Wilson's speech, "a historic utterance, nobly voicing the true patriotism of the American people in this world crisis, and worthy to rank with the immortal messages of Presidents Washington
and Lincoln."[79] The Committee on Public Information urged primary school
teachers to enhance patriotism and Americanism by teaching the "Flag Salute":

I give my head
My hands,
And my heart,
To God and my country—
One country,
One language,
And one flag.[80]

Patriotism was described during World War I in religious terms, a "sacred"
duty. This was as close as authorities came to presenting war to American youth
by way of religious words and metaphors. In both world wars, American children were presented with a program thoroughly secularized, unless perhaps "patriotism" or "love of country" could be considered a religious ersatz in a country
bound by religious variety. Despite the occasional reference to a generic "God,"

as in the poem above, the near-universal refusal of authorities to bring religion very far into war for children smartly contrasts with the experience of children living in European belligerents. World War II researchers found children separating war adversaries into religious metaphor: "They never talk about the British fighting against the Germans but of a conflict between God and Hitler.[81] Mossé observed that in Europe Christian ideals of morality were co-opted for nationalistic goals, and became in symbol and blessing part of the war myth experience.[82] Audoin-Rouzeau found evidence in his research of children in World War I France that Catholic authorities in particular tied religious virtue to war, bringing the Christian ideal of Jesus' sacrifice to the soldier who does the same for his country.[83]

The few authorities who found themselves uneasy with the overtones of racism and hatred behind United States patriotism saw little tolerance for their viewpoint. E. M. Robinson, director of the Boy Scouts of America, who was Canadian, in 1917 incautiously let drop the remark that Scouts "needed to learn the difference between patriotism and jingoism." When the group altered its federal charter to deny membership to anyone not an American citizen, Robinson had to resign.[84] The Boy Scout Movement in the United States clung to a stern nationalistic fervor far after that power waned in other areas of American life, and played it out through patriotic suspicion of the slightest disloyalty, even into the 1930s.[85]

But other authorities in World War II in many ways tried to temporize the white-hot rhetoric of World War I, including calls to patriotism. In particular educators worried that too emotional a patriotism would again have its flip side in the kind of jingoism that marked the last war. While certainly many pop-culture authorities reheated the old emotionalism, others urged a revised patriotism with restraint. World War II educators, for example, expressed the underlying presumption that children would be patriotic only in passing, and worried of its excess. "The best teaching of patriotism avoids the teaching of hatred," cautioned an assistant in the federal education department. "It is well for us to say we will not teach hatred even for our enemies. It might be a quite different problem to keep hatred from creeping into the minds of children."[86] The natural patriotic emotions of children should be channeled to creative work, music, art, drama and other programs. Fortunately the feelings and emotions could be utilized for useful ends as well as evil ends.[87]

Patriotism as the linchpin emotion could maintain its strength among children (and most adults) during these wars because its appeal reached beyond reason. Confident that they could rely on this quasi-religious, "sacred" virtue, authorities built an entire system for character development using war as a sourcebook. By militarizing a child's life in school and out, authorities could mold a character in three areas most coveted in the ideal citizen:

Physical and mental toughness.
Moral and civic competence.
Professional and practical skill.

### Healthy, Fit, and Ready to Fight

War would provide the most obvious base in physical and mental toughness. One of the more surprising things authorities learned on establishing the Selective Service (draft) in World War I was that many American boys were weak and sick. This came as a shock to those in government and education, because they had presumed American children were robust as children ought to be. In a 1918 address to the National Education Association, a U.S. Education Bureau representative said the government had no idea Americans were so unfit. In 1917, 34 percent of those considered for military service were rejected as "physically unfit." Of those accepted, a large portion "were lacking in the strength, endurance and general organic power necessary for intensive military training.... Here then are two facts: a large amount of rejection for physical defects, much of which could have been easily remedied in school years, and a large amount of undeveloped physical capacity, all of which could have been developed during school years." This development would have to take place before high school, however, as in 1916 only 15 percent of seven million boys reached high school.[88]

Attempts to improve physical fitness in both sexes beginning in World War I lost ground after a brief post-war burst of enthusiasm. From a high of thirty-six states requiring physical education came the Depression, and phys ed was declared a frill.[89] Again in World War II, authorities who worked under the presumption that children were now fit were shocked when draft examiners found fitness to be generally low. Leonard W. Rowntree, medical director of the National Selective Service, speaking at a National War Fitness Conference sponsored by the American Association of Health, Physical Education and Recreation in 1943 (theme: "Victory Through Fitness"), reported that before Pearl Harbor, already half of two million candidates were rejected for physical deficiencies. Standards were lowered in 1942. Still, it stood at one-third rejections. Even among the presumably strongest at age eighteen to nineteen, 25.4 percent were rejected. Older men quickly became physically unready for the army: by age thirty-six, 70 percent failed to meet army standards, and by forty-five, 80 percent failed. "The lesson that war teaches is that we must not take health for granted in times of peace. We must plan for it, work for it, and teach for it."[90] An aviation medical officer declared,

> In trying to organize an army for World War I we were surprised at the great number of potential draftees who could not meet the physical qualifications for military service. Nevertheless, this experience apparently did not make a lasting impression because we failed to put into effect any comprehensive plan for bettering the health of the population in general. The draft eligible population of today probably isn't better off than it was in 1917 and 1918.[91]

A lack of mental ability was also found to be common among draftees, and considered part of a boy's physical training. Rowntree declared that physical fitness included mental fitness, but while physical standards could be measured in things like situps and pushups, standards of mental fitness were less clear. Dr. Arthur H. Steinhaus, chief, Division of U.S. Office of Education School Health and Physical Recreation, offered several guidelines. In addition to being "reasonably free from nervous instability," a candidate "should know when and how to eat, and he must provide satisfactory evidence that he successfully regulates his bowel movements without recourse to medication in any form."[92] Exact nature of such evidence was not specified. Neither was the mental toughness called upon by numerous writers in World War I, although that such toughness was necessary, and apparently lacking, was presumed among American children. One author did note that physical fitness had as its base proper nutrition, and that the gardening that children were encouraged to undertake for victory could also improve habits of healthy eating. Finally a New York University authority speaking to the NEA laid it plainly on the line:

> We have developed into a sedentary people. We, more than any race that has ever survived in history, spend more time in overheated rooms. We have become habituated to living on refined foods, almost predigested foods. Our white flour and our breakfast foods are not the food of champions, nor are white sugar and an excessive amount of fats. Our exercise habits have been a disgrace. Our children have been indulged in limitless ways. We put in bus lines to ferry them to school, when they should walk—within a two-mile radius.[93]

## The Virtue of Sacrifice

These words, we must remind ourselves, were written in 1942! If good health and fitness could offer a base for the second and third of authorities' wartime goals for children, even more useful to parents and society might be the ever-obedient child, always cheerful, ready to serve, "morally straight to help their country to the full in time of war, as well as in time of peace," as President Franklin Roosevelt wrote in the Boy Scouts of America 1942 report.[94] To build qualities such as courage, thrift, obedience, duty, loyalty, self-discipline and knowledge, is required, to begin with, sacrifice. Authorities asked repeatedly for sacrifice from children who, many suspected, had sacrificed too little during peacetime. In declaring that American children had become self-absorbed, the World War I council chairman of the Red Cross found a solution in war service. "War has laid its hands upon American children as well as those in Europe—they are taking the responsibility seriously, as is shown by the readiness to sacrifice leisure time and candy money to the success of school war work."[95] The establishment of the Junior Red Cross could encourage children to work their way out of selfishness by volunteering under the general Red Cross umbrella. Woodrow Wilson provided to this new group his usual letter of support, while the junior director added, "President Wilson in a proclamation has summoned them to the colors, the red, white and blue—blue of truth, white of purity, and the red of sacrifice and service."[96] The red of sacrifice was a metaphor for the blood shed by soldiers fighting for children. As well-known educator Angelo Patri admonished in World War II, "Rationing isn't sacrifice. When a young man gives up his future, offers his life in pledge of our cause, he is making a sacrifice."[97]

But if authorities such as Patri did not consider rationing to be sacrifice, children surely did. Sacrifice to American children militarized for wartime needs could be taught as a metaphor: children themselves did not experience actual combat or dislocation. Instead, authorities emphasized sacrifice in three areas: loss of favored foods (specifically sugar), loss of spending money, and loss of free time. Such sacrifices were generally thought to build character as well as help the war effort. On the other hand, authorities only obliquely mentioned a fourth area of loss, if at all: that a father or brother might die. Death was almost never presented in any realistic way to the wartime American child (nor to adults, for that matter). Mourning the death of a loved one became the unspoken ultimate sacrifice for many children, particularly in World War II. Death of a loved one could be explained only through stories of heroism, bravery, and noble courage.

But authorities working in the child's world of the home front shifted the meaning of sacrifice from the demoralizing possibility of true loss to the presumably uplifting opportunity of trivial loss for patriotic good of the nation.

Food shortages and substitutions became a palpable way American children otherwise far from the battlefields could actually feel a personal loss, even if insignificant in comparison to those in combat. Writing about a twelve-year-old nephew in 1919, an author in the *New Republic* noted, "Self-sacrifice is not a matter of poems and sermons and history, it is the daily news." Still, when the abstract became a real loss to the child, ideals were harder to maintain. "The weakest spot in Billy's war program is food conservation. He does not readily respond to the sacrifice of sugar."[98] Other tangible ways children were expected to build character through sacrifice required denial of money and time for the war effort. In both wars children were recruited as a sales army to aggressively market war bonds among parents and friends, but that expectation sacrificed only some free time. More was asked: children were expected to buy bonds themselves. It did not matter if a child had only a dime or quarter to spend; he or she could accumulate savings stamps toward purchasing a bond. As highly touted campaign after campaign siphoned their money into government IOUs, children found that sacrifice also meant dwindling of small pleasures. "Individual contributions of pennies, nickels, and dimes have been made at a tremendous sacrifice of the luxuries of childhood—the ice cream cone, the stick of gum, and the movie show."[99] On the plus side, giving up money for war bonds could help children appreciate "the terrific costs of modern war."[100]

With less money, children might also find less to do. But sacrifice of time could mop up roaming children and put them to work collecting scrap, sending packages to the troops, knitting garments, delivering messages, or helping with household chores to free parents for their own war work. Whether authorities believed such wartime sacrifice could ultimately be a good way to develop childhood character depended on how the sacrifice fell on children. United States religious leaders did not develop the ideal of death as sacrifice for human salvation, common among Catholic authorities in France. But some clergy did believe sacrifice could build character. "Out of sacrifice come many blessings," affirmed Rev. Hugh F. Blunt, Church of St. John the Baptist, Cambridge, Massachusetts.[101] Schools could build sacrifice as a virtue, "with the ideals of service and self-sacrifice actuating our people."[102]

### War Work and Military Drill: Viable Alternatives to School?

Secular authorities hoped wartime sacrifice of time, money and small plea-sures could build in children the self-discipline, thrift, and community spirit so beneficial in peacetime. As an undercurrent to building character, the sacrifice of free time also might serve to blunt the danger of juvenile delinquency. Ameri-can authorities knew Britain had experienced a rise in delinquency during both world wars. War demands pulled parents out of homes and left the scamps too often with unsupervised time easily diverted into trouble-making. Children could be put to work, in paid agricultural or industrial jobs, and so kept off the streets. American industry experiencing burgeoning demand and a shrinking labor pool thought this a fine way to build character and help the nation's busi-ness at the same time. In fact, during World War I, whenever a labor gap was found, children seemed to be the most obvious sources on which to call. But child welfare advocates who had long fought for limits to child labor did not think suspending the law under an argument of wartime expediency constitut-ed character building. "The welfare of the child had been the last thing consid-ered," noted one legislator in 1917.[103] But a salary was attractive, and so children in large numbers opted for this kind of sacrifice instead of going to school. In 1918 the federal government weighed in by reminding employers, "Neither the patriotic desire to serve immediately nor the attraction of high wages should be permitted to draw children from school to work."[104]

But if children working for pay was not considered a character-building sac-rifice, children working for nothing was all right. Authorities didn't consider limits on volunteer work, by age or in hours on task. Children were expected to prefer the reward of patriotic sacrifice over that of remuneration. Children cer-tainly did respond massively to volunteer opportunities. Yet problems in both world wars keeping older children in school when they saw good-paying wartime jobs were there for the taking led authorities to repeatedly plead with the coun-try's adolescents to stay in the classroom. Between 1940 and 1944, the number of adolescents in school dropped by 1.25 million. Most left to take jobs, raising the number of working teenagers from 1 million to 2.9 million. In 1943 alone, of 4 million high school students present in class in the spring, only 3 million returned in the fall, the rest finding more tangible rewards in war industries.[105]

Sacrifice as a base on which to build other qualities of character could be used as necessary to exhort children to better behavior. From World War I juvenile media a common approach was to invoke the power of guilt. Noted an editor of a boys' magazine, "If you are willing to work and sacrifice to bring victory to her in this just cause, then you are an American. If you are not you are a traitor."[106] Presuming prompt attention gained from this shameless approach to juvenile motivation, authorities could now work on building other positive qualities difficult to instill during peacetime. Courage, determination, discipline, duty, loyalty, obedience, patriotism, teamwork, thrift—bringing military values to children's lives could help to perfect a long list of qualities society would admire in the coming generation. Progressivism, the ideological force for change in early twentieth-century America, by World War I had infiltrated political thinking to the highest reaches of government, from Woodrow Wilson to education commissioner Philander Claxton. Optimism that reason and education could change the world mirrored efforts of Progressivist educators who worked to move the nation's classrooms from relaying on formal methods commanding rote memory of traditional subjects to engaged classrooms learning through community involvement and freedom to explore. What better way to foster this than through the involvement of wartime needs at a community level? A problem with extending this ideal through opportunities opened by wartime expediency was that many Americans who distrusted new educational standards thought the sought-after values could better be taught through a lens of strict military discipline and drill. The battle over the mind of the child during this war was not so much about if childhood should be militarized, but how. "Dispersed through more than 100,000 school districts, [schools] lent themselves to a kind of ideological guerrilla warfare."[107]

World War I idealism smashed on the shallows of post-war disillusion. By the eve of World War II Progressivist educators were thrown on the defensive. How to teach values through a wartime prism became less a matter of educational philosophy, and more a matter of practical training. Politicians blamed Progressivism—unfairly—for a spike in juvenile delinquency during the 1930s, and thought virtue could better be taught through military regimentation and military schools. Concluded one historian of the era, "Army generals were blaming Progressive education for desertions, AWOLs, incompetence in the ranks and anything that smacked of 'softness' or ill discipline."[108] This attitude fed into the enthusiasm behind bringing children into the war by militarizing childhood during World War II. While Progressivism had taken a hit, in effect, authorities during both wars still hoped the supposed superiority of military values could offer children of the home front a guide for character.

To teach loyalty to one's country, community or school, authorities emphasized, teachers or others concerned with child welfare had to prove their own loyalty. In World War I particularly, this presumption developed into a series of harassments and intimidation threatening careers and safety of anyone even slightly perceived as being neutral. Loyalty oaths and tests ended careers and ruined reputations, and loyalty itself became academic subjects in schools.[109] Teachers deemed fit to impart the virtues carried by a wartime display of perfect loyalty and unquestioned patriotism in many districts walked on the thinnest of eggshells; the slightest crack of disloyalty could lead to immediate dismissal, and lingering shame. Pacifism, a powerful positive force before 1917, became treason. In one of many examples from New York, a state particularly extreme in its wartime exuberance and implacable intolerance, Mary McDowell, a New York City teacher of eighteen years with a pacifist Quaker background, was fired for "conduct unbecoming a teacher."[110] After the war, a Chicago teacher in 1919 wrote of the irony of teaching democracy in American schools that operated in such a manner. "We want to make American democracy a beacon light for the rest of the world," he wrote, but "our school system is an autocracy—autocratic in every phase of its organization."[111]

Discipline and obedience could be learned through drills: "The discipline of military drill can be made to tend to many other kinds of discipline. Obedience to all school regulations, to all civic laws, to all right customs, to all fair codes of youthful ethics, can be instilled along with the ardently adopted war discipline of which they are going to hear so much at home as long as the war lasts.[112] School athletics could be excellent preparation for war, teaching "the necessity for discipline and teamwork."[113] Patriotism must become part of the curriculum, as the NEA emphasized in its 1918 platform, and from there could flow other values. "But how are you going to teach them? Certainly not by a little morning lecture on the moral virtues. Most certainly not! Example is better far than precept and thirty children at least watch you every day and see your every word and motion. Are you living and moving as a patriot every day?"[114]

Authorities in World War II found less character-building potential in militarizing childhood, but neither did they generally question qualities of character that war could bring to children. Whether actual drills and school military training could bring these qualities, however, was a matter of debate during World War I, even more so during World War II. "If we look beneath the surface, we find that military patriotism may be no deeper and no more lasting than military obedience," warned the NEA in 1917. "We must not confuse excitement with patriotism, the showy exhibition with real love of country."[115] In fact, while World War II government and educational authorities were certainly convinced that war could build character in children, they tempered their enthusiasm in knowing that the experience of World War I proved to be only of passing success. Warned the NEA in 1943:

> Character education, in school and outside of school, is certain to be affected
> by the impact of the war on the lives of young and old. On the credit side, the
> war may be expected in most cases to promote such good qualities as valor,
> industry, thrift, self-sacrifice for a lofty cause, and devotion to the common
> good. The schools should take full advantage of the impetus provided by the
> war to cultivate with increased vigor these virtues in the young.
> However, war also brings hazards to some of our cherished ethical, religious,
> and spiritual values. Such humane sentiments as mercy, tolerance, and good-
> will are apt to be supplanted by malice, revenge, and hate. It is the continuing
> duty of teachers to encourage and exemplify the highest ethical traits and to
> cooperate with the home, the church, and other character-building agencies.[116]

Nevertheless, even the more skeptical educators during World War II
agreed that the influence of war on educational attempts to teach values could
not be all bad. "If the war brings about a more general recognition of the value
of such education, it will not be wholly detrimental to secondary education in
this country."[117]

While authorities in education and government debated the ways to teach
values through militarized curriculum, editors of juvenile media presented a
picture less nuanced: character was forged through military experience. "It is no
place for 'mollycoddles,' but there is no better place for manly boys who have
the 'real stuff' in them. That's the kind we want and welcome," wrote Secretary of the Navy Josephus Daniels in a letter to boys published in July 1918 *St.
Nicholas*.[118] The editor of *American Boy* opined confidently, "It is evident that war
and war-time conditions are having a big influence on boys. A large number of
contestants told how they had gained in the past year a realization of the true
meaning and importance of patriotism, sacrifice, thrift, education, work and
preparation for national service, as a result of the war."[119]

Those who promoted establishing a skills-based curriculum of formal military training in the schools, based on drills, firearm skills, marching and athleticism, faced strong opposition before both wars. Pacifists and others argued
that such education merely militarized the schools into warrior classrooms that
groomed their male charges for fighting. Any useful skill learned through military drills could be learned in less warlike ways. After the United States actually
declared war in 1917 and 1941, however, opponents of formal military training
sunk into silence, as many schools around the country opted for martial curriculum. Related to this was the possibility of also teaching children the skills

of making bombs. Shortly after the United States entered World War I, the possibility was raised of converting school metal shops into munitions factories. But equipment could not easily be converted to such a use. "A department store, a clothing factory, a library, or an office building would be about as fit for such a purpose as a school building. The same may be said for the use of our schools as hospitals."[120]

Less controversial, however, were the practical skills children might acquire through infusing less military-specific but still patriotic wartime spirit into their learning in school and out. Such skills gained through wartime needs could be useful in peacetime, advocates argued. Practical and vocational learning had already been part of Progressive attempts to reform American education at the turn of the last century. Reformers hoped to see more hands-on learning in the classroom, and more practical skills put to use in the community. Prominent Progressivist educator John Dewey said learning practical skills on the farm could "conscript the national enthusiasm for athletics to national usefulness, reap the advantage of organized effort with its moral and educational results..." and "develop constructive patriotism."[121] As well, some authorities hoped a war-based training program for children would help level class differences. Speaking to the NEA in 1942, Kansas Governor Payne Ratner declared, "The war has taught us the tragedy of having too many trained for white-collar jobs, too few trained for vocational tasks."[122] World War I authorities hoped teaching farming skills might encourage sedentary city adolescents to gain new appreciation for rural youngsters who spent their days in the fields. One of many such formal programs set up during World War I introduced New York City boys to farm work as a way to fill labor shortages during the harvest.

The usefulness of boys learning farm skills became so promoted in World War I that a popular booklet, *Farm Craft Lessons*, was written by University of Illinois Dean of Agriculture Eugene Davenport to help teachers on farm training camps set up to educate on agricultural matters, "the boys subjected to military discipline."[123] A variety of camps and programs set up around the United States hoped to create a new army of skilled farmers. Success was limited at best.

Less ambitious were efforts of authorities to offer both boys and girls the chance to learn skills related to practical home making. It was presumed such activities could be of actual help to the soldiers, while at the same time offering valuable skills-based training. Practical instruction should begin in early adolescence, stressed a New York professor of vocational education, targeting children aged twelve, and should emphasize skills useful during wartime. "I stated that every teacher of manual training, sewing or cooking should be think-

ing in terms of mobilization service.... I said, furthermore, that any teacher of
sewing who was not thinking in terms of Red Cross, and of mending, darning,
and repairing, was as far away from the service idea as she possibly could be."[124]
The educator emphasized, "We are going to sew now for the Red Cross because
it is war time. Later we shall sew for institutions in our community."[125] The first
issue of *Rally* (October 1917), published for Girl Scouts and leaders, included
instructions for knitting sweater sets for soldiers. Canning clubs encouraged
conservation skills; boys would pick fruit while girls would work over the hot
cook stove, a gendered division of children's skills-based instruction reinforced
during both wars. Skills girls could learn through wartime service included the
expected work in knitting; skills boys could gain included carpentry, by making packing boxes, hospital night stands, potato mashers, chests, "peg legs," or
puzzles, and checkerboards to entertain troops in France. No evidence can be
found indicating what children might have thought while working on artificial
limbs, but as one writer noted of her nephew, "Billy's attitude is that going to
war is part of the game."[126]

Skills training not only was encouraged within the schools, but also offered
through a variety of volunteer and other organizations, particularly the Red
Cross, 4-H, and during World War II, FFA. Quasi-military training camps were
set up to help teach wartime skills for girls as well as boys. The idea of training
camps dated from before World War I; at first businessmen interested in being
prepared for war joined the movement on free weekends, but after 1914 camps
were extended to accept high-school age adolescents of both sexes. Describing
one such camp, the National Service School in Chevy Chase, Maryland, a female participant noted that while military drill was part of the routine, it served
only to organize participants more efficiently. "It is needless to say that the discipline of drill is excellent training for anyone," emphasized the participant, who
added that training activities included "first aid, hygiene and home nursing,
dietetics, surgical dressing, knitting and sewing, wireless and Morse telegraphy,
and signaling; all of which are most useful in any condition of life."[127] While
skills-based training thought useful in wartime was strongly gender-specific, occasionally children would cross over. In one case, a boy learned to knit: "Carlyle
Streit, twelve years old, has knit a regulation sweater for a 'Sammy' in France—
knit it all by himself. Carlyle is distinguished among them because he is the only
boy who 'got away with it.'"[128]

While World War I skills training emphasized crafts, World War II children were less likely to provide a mountain of wooden or cloth articles for
troops. Girls continued to knit for Red Cross stocks, but skills training more

often emphasized technical and vocational abilities useful to industry and military. Adolescent boys in World War II could learn pre-induction technological skills at school—and thereby counteract the American child's tendency to be woefully unprepared in science and technical education. In particular aviation was emphasized, as authorities believed the country was alarmingly unready for a war to be determined by fighters in the sky. The movement to train boys as aviators early in the war reached almost hysterically into even the elementary schools, as one educator noted, but "it would be about as silly to study airplanes as a separate subject for elementary school children as to study 'tanks,' battleships,' or 'long-range guns' as separate subjects."[129] Agricultural skills could also be valuable, but the idea of taking a city kid to the farm did not see the kind of enthusiasm authorities gave it during the earlier war. Instead, children already familiar with rural life were encouraged to develop their skills toward wartime needs. The 4-H movement's "Feed A Fighter" program during World War II produced poultry, dairy, and produce to fill a food shortage as men left the farm for army. But usually in World War II children were not called on to sharpen manual skills beyond their ability to collect scrap, squirrel away stocks of waste paper, peel metal foil from gum wrappers, pluck pods from milkweeds, and milk adults to buy more war bonds.

### How Children Can Make Better War

The wide variety of practical things children were asked to do as part of the home-front army appealed to authorities who believed war could make a better child, and certainly a less troubled child: troublesome free time could be mopped out of an idle mind, while fear could be scrubbed away through business projects. Critics muttered darkly about a return to a world in which exploited children shined shoes, hawked newspapers, delivered parcels and generally worked like small dogs doing what adults did not want to do. Laws had made most of that illegal for the under fourteen-year-olds, but volunteer work could skirt those laws. Franklin Roosevelt declared that asking children to collect some scrap or tend a garden shouldn't harm them much, and moreover, war work could give them a "sense of involvement."[130] That said, some states ignored the law when convenient; of the three million children working part time in 1943, some were as young as twelve.[131]

Whether this frenzy of knitting socks and mufflers, scrounging for scrap, and hawking war bonds could have much practical value was less certain. Some authorities who advocated putting children to work did not expect their efforts to be of great consequence, but at least would keep them out of mischief and give them an opportunity to feel like they were contributing. Children wanted to do something, to do their bit, at least a little bit, for the war that so preoccupied their parents. A 1942 survey of seven hundred boys did indicate they wanted to play a role in the war.[132] And so they were given tasks with the affirmation that it would be of great service to the war, even if authorities privately did not believe children could do much. At the beginning of America's involvement in World War I, noted the Red Cross director, no one thought of "mobilizing the children" for real work. "As the months followed each other, however, there were more and more little girls knitting wristlets, helmets, and sweaters, and doing it about as well as their wonderful mothers did. There were little girls marching to the chapter rooms and working there like troopers as long as anybody."[133] Perhaps children really could make war in their role as troops of the home front. Keeping children busy for the war perhaps could do more than improve their character, keep them out of trouble, and allay possible fears. "Boys," a writer in St. Nicholas noted, "your part is not a small one! It is vitally important. The service you can render now in preparing for the service you will surely be called upon to render in a few years is precious to the nation."[134] And while girls would not be called upon for military service, they hardly escaped the call to do their duty as home-front warriors. "Girl Scouts, you must help to win the war," admonished Mary Stevick "at the request of Mrs. Hoover" in the Rally. "You are young but your work can be telling and effective."[135]

How telling? How effective? Authorities anxious to prove the value of children taken into war work made considerable efforts to tally the contributions of the juvenile home front to the war effort. Juvenile publications featured long lists of children's groups around the country doing their bit for the war, from knitting scarves to passing out sandwiches to passing soldiers. Wartime tallies from volunteer organizations seemed to indicate the effort was paying off. The Red Cross after World War I reported its junior members in just four months delivered 225,000 refugee garments and 4,000 items to furnish convalescent homes. "Most of this valuable supply work for the Red Cross was done by the children as a part of their school work."[136] Boy Scouts reported collecting "a hundred carloads" of fruit pits for use in World War I gas masks.[137] In 1942, according to its annual report, Boy Scouts collected 10.5 million pounds of aluminum in 11,369 communities, of a total collected by all agencies of 12 million pounds. They also collected 300 million pounds of waste paper and 30 million pounds of rubber. A 1944 scout report asserted the boys had collected enough milkweed floss to stuff 1.5 million life jackets, while a 4-H report asserted its members in one Illinois county alone had collected five tons of milkweed floss worthy of 1,100 life jackets.[138] The swamps and ditches of America apparently became a favored outing destination for World War II children, many of whom still remember fondly their efforts in milkweed pod collecting. As informal government propagandists, Scouts placed 1,607,500 posters in 1942, growing to a million posters a month by 1944.[139] Boys and girls of 4-H during World War II "produced or preserved enough food to care for a million fighting men for three years"[140] The FFA reported in 1942:

77,018,762 pounds of scrap metal collected.

30,606,875 pounds of paper collected.

2,767,821 pounds of rubber collected.

605,949 pounds of rags collected.

$44,530 in war bonds purchased by state associations.

$1,541,479.38 in war bonds and stamps purchased by local chapters and individual members.[141]

In World War I no tally was kept on the number of children who bought war stamps and bonds, noted a 1919 NEA report, but of the 20 million pupils in U.S. schools at that time, "practically all" bought some.[142] In 1943 a report to the NEA by U.S. Commissioner of Education John W. Studebaker poured together the superlatives:

The 30,000,000 children in 1943 participated in a wide variety of war effort community work. In the past year (1942-43), the schools were responsible for $300,000,000 worth of war bond and stamp sales; more than 1,500,000 tons of scrap collected, thousands of garments made for Red Cross, millions of "recreational articles" for armed forces; sponsored 1,000,000 school and home victory gardens; through Victory Farm Volunteers recruited several hundred thousand high school youth for farm work; produced 600,000 scale models of airplanes requested by armed forces; collected tons of scrap paper and waste fats; canned and preserved thousands of quarts of home-grown fruits and vegetables.[143]

This certainly seems like quite a contribution, and as the Boy Scouts boasted, "Scouts have continued to carry out war-service projects, long after the novelty was worn out and the tasks became tedious."[144] But it is difficult to determine the tangible significance of these efforts of home-front children toward winning wars fought on such an enormous scale. Both Roosevelt in World War

II and Wilson in World War I formally issued proclamations of gratitude for children's work. A more skeptical historian noted, "The truth is that besides serving or war work, there really was little most people could do to help win the war."[145] Regarding war bond sales, we can compare reported sale figures of children to totals sold. By 1945 half the U.S. population (85 million Americans) had purchased war bonds, for a total of $185.7 billion.[146] If we presume as Studebaker reported that $300 million per year of those sales came from children who purchased bonds and stamps themselves and peddled more to adults, it would total $1.2 billion. This is a tiny fraction of the total, although the Boy Scouts reported its members alone had sold, or "been responsible for" the sale of much more, $1.8 billion.[147] It is difficult to verify accuracy of such reports, but even allowing a liberal interpretation of reported figures, total sales from the children's home front would seem not very significant.

World War I Liberty Bonds sales totaled $21 billion.[148] While again it is hard to determine what percentage of this total can be credited to children, the Boy Scouts did report their members sold bonds totaling $147,876,962—still a tiny percentage of the total. But authorities during that war pursued children as sales agents more aggressively than they did in World War II. Unlike World War II's more restrained appeal to children, in 1917-18 widespread contests were promoted as a motivation to youngsters, often by shaming the slackers, to contribute till it hurt, and hurt some more. As the government-produced *National School Service* urged, "The chief means by which teachers can arouse interest and enthusiasm in the sale of Liberty Bonds by their classes is through group competition. There are a great many devices that may be used to this end."[149]

In contrast, World War II authorities, so often basing their decisions on perceived mistakes of the last war, believed that collecting bond sales through a system of guilt and peer pressure at school would do more harm than good. "One rule: avoid without exception the use of competition in promoting valuable work among the children," wrote an education professor from Northwestern University. "Buy stamps for the real reasons, not to win banners. Schools that set up cooperative enterprises, rather than competitive ones, gather more scrap, everyone is happy with the results."[150]

If it is difficult to measure tangible contributions to the wars from the children's home front, it is even more of a challenge to evaluate the intangibles. Children were exhorted to patriotic displays of public speaking and marching in parades, encouraged to bring government propaganda home, and to generally avoid vexing war-preoccupied parents with their childhood concerns. Certainly World War I authorities had highest expectations that children could be puny yet powerful propagandists. The media at the dawn of the last century consisted mostly of printed products; while movies were popular, and recordings available, radio was in its infancy and other media still far off. Authorities tried to influence a country splintered on lines of race, class and immigrant status by calling on the one institution that reached pretty much everyone: the schools. In particular immigrant children could bring wartime messages to parents whose language was not English and whose experiences made them fearful of government. But children could be used for more than this informal infiltration into the intimate family setting. They also could publicly advocate wartime needs through word and deed.

By words children could develop public speaking skill through participation in the Junior Four-Minute Man program. The program grew out of the World War I Four-Minute Man campaign established by the Committee on Public Information, in which community leaders were encouraged to give brief patriotic speeches describing wartime needs to audiences at movie theaters or at other events. Adolescents became a second wave of speakers mostly encouraging audiences of adults or other children to buy war bonds and stamps. Based on topics as assigned by teachers who received ideas from government bulletins, noted George Creel, "Both boys and girls were eligible and the winners were given an official certificate from the government, commissioning them as Four Minute speakers upon the specified topic of the contest."[151] Extent of participation seems to have been broad, although results obtained cannot be specifically determined. An NEA report asserted that in some cases children in public settings could be more persuasive than adults. But public speaking required formal commitment of teachers and schools, who needed to organize and motivate children to write and present. A less formal intangible way children could contribute to war fever and war fervor relied on youthful energy and easy identification with emotional virtues of patriotism in action. The action was marching, the venue a parade. "The American people are very fond of making use of school children for purposes of parade and exhibition whenever occasion calls for spectacular appeal, whether of war, worship, or festival," noted a California education commissioner in 1917."[152] On the other side of the country, the children marched as enthusiastically to frequent calls for participation in parades for preparedness, war bond sales, Selective Service registration, or patriotic celebrations. "To stimulate patriotism, the NYC school board set up children to participate in parades, such as one on April 19, 1917; with only three days' notice, 25,000 school children in NYC participated in the "Wake up America" parade."[153]

Authorities in World War II, however, showed less enthusiasm for using children as a way to reach adults. The Junior Four Minute Man program was not revived. Parades could feature children, but should not substitute for exercises more useful to developing the child instead of exploiting him to motivate adults. In a 1943 letter to Commissioner of Education Studebaker, U.S. Secretary of War Henry L. Stimson seemed to reflect general opinion of authorities showing lukewarm support to children's participation in parades. "Properly conducted military drills and parades do have their place," agreed Stimson. "Whenever possible, both should be included in the curriculum; however, if this is not practicable and a choice must be made, physical education is considered the more important."[154]

## Notes

1. W. Linwood Chase, *Wartime Social Studies in the Elementary School* (Washington, DC: The National Council for the Social Studies, 1943), 12.

2. July 1917, 771.

3. Arthur R. Dean, *Our Schools in War Time–and After* (Boston: Ginn and Company, 1918), 3.

4. Frederick H. Lewis, "New Citizenship Responsibilities," *Education* 64, no. 2, (1943), 113.

5. Chase, *Wartime Social Studies,* 6.

6. *National School Service,* November 1, 1918.

7. *School and Society,* September 12, 1942, 199.

8. *Education for Victory,* March 3, 1942, 1; *School Life,* October 1, 1918, 13; *School and Society,* Sept. 12, 1942, 198; *School and Society,* May 29, 1943, 615.

9. Stéphane Audoin-Rouzeau, *La Guerre des Enfants 1914-1918* (Paris: Armand Colin, 1993, 2004), 1.

10. Katherine Miller, *Communication Theories. Perspectives, Processes, and Contexts,* 2nd ed. (Boston: McGraw Hill, 2005), 275.

11. John Quincy Adams, "John Quincy Adams on U.S. Foreign Policy," Speech July 4, 1821, *The Future of Freedom Foundation,* http://www.fff.org/freedom/1001e.asp.

12. David M. Kennedy, *Over Here. The First World War and American Society* (Oxford and New York: Oxford University Press, 1980), vii.

13. Ronald Steel, *Pax Americana* (New York: Viking Press, 1967), 4.

14. Robert William Kirk, *Earning Their Stripes. The Mobilization of American Children in the Second World War* (New York: Peter Lang, 1994), 56-57.

15. George L. Mossé, *Fallen Soldiers. Reshaping the Memory of the World Wars* (New York and Oxford, Oxford University Press, 1990), 22.

16. Mrs. O. Shepard Barnum, "The Obligations and Opportunities of the Schools during the War." National Education Association, *Addresses and Proceedings,* Vol. 55, *Fifty-Fifth Annual Meeting, Portland, Oregon, July 7-14, 1917* (Washington, DC: NEA, 1917), 1162.

17. John S. Brubacher, "Education for Death," *School and Society,* August 22, 1943, 137.

18. Malcolm Cowley, *Exile's Return. A Literary Odyssey of the 1920s* (New York, Viking Press, 1956), 41-42, 46-47. Quoted in Robert H. Bremner, ed., *Children and Youth in America. A Documentary History. Volume II: 1866-1932* (Cambridge: Harvard University Press, 1971), 98.

19. Philip M. Flammer, *The Vivid Air. The Lafayette Escadrille* (Athens: University of Georgia Press, 1981), 5.

20. *American Boy,* February 1918, 30.

21. Third prize letter, Jean M. Olmstead, 17, Massachusetts, *American Boy,* February 1917, 28.

22. Mossé, *Fallen Soldiers,* 55.

23. Brubacher, *Education for Death,* 138.

24. Ibid., 139.

25. Ibid., 140.

26. Sophia L. Fahs, "When Children Confront Death," *Parents' Magazine*, April 1943, 34.

27. *School and Society*, November 14, 1942, 461.

28. Lee J. Cronbach, assistant professor of psychology, State College of Washington, Pullman, "Pupil-Morale after One Year of War," *School and Society*, April 10, 1943, 416–417.

29. Ibid., 419.

30. Paul Fussell, *Wartime. Understanding and Behavior in the Second World War* (New York and Oxford: Oxford University Press, 1989), 268.

31. Antoinette May, *Witness to War: A Biography of Marguerite Higgins* (New York, no pub., 1983), 80-81. Quoted in Fussell, *Wartime*, 12.

32. *The Nation's Business*, April 1916, 15.

33. S. E. Forman, "The Watch Tower." *St. Nicholas*, August 1916, 933.

34. Susan Zeiger, "The Schoolhouse vs. the Armory. U.S. Teachers and the Campaign Against Militarism in the Schools, 1914-1918." *Journal of Women's History* 15, no. 2, (2003), 150.

35. Admiral F. E. Chadwick of the U.S. Naval Academy, Quoted in Zeiger, 159.

36. F. L. Kleeberger, "Athletics and the War Game." *School and Society*, May 1918, 542.

37. Mrs. Alexander Thompson, member, Oregon Legislative Assembly, "Preparedness—a Veneer or a Fundamental–Which Will Our Schools Give Our Children?", National Education Association, *Addresses and Proceedings*, Vol. 55, *Fifty-Fifth Annual Meeting, Portland, Oregon, July 7-14, 1917* (Washington, DC: NEA, 1917), 69.

38. J. H. Ackerman, president, State Normal School, Monmouth, Oregon, "The Normal School as an Agency for Teaching Patriotism," National Education Association, *Addresses and Proceedings*, 1917, 61.

39. Colonel William G. Schauffler, Jr., commanding officer of Geiger Field in Spokane, Washington, quoted in Carl G. Miller, "Editorial: Comment on the Old 'Peace Preachers'" *Education*, October 1943, 128; Russell Tooze, High School, Bismarck, North Dakota, "A Teacher's Point of View." *Education*, September 1945, 62.

40. Robert R. Hume, "Peace—the Great Challenge." *School and Society*, January 17, 1942, 76.

41. Ross F. Collins and Patrick S. Washburn, *The Greenwood Library of American War Reporting, Volume 5: World War I and World War II* (Westport, Conn., Greenwood Press, 2005), 250.

42. Fussell, *Wartime*, 268.

43. Mossé, *Fallen Soldiers*, 148.

44. William M. Tuttle, Jr., *"Daddy's Gone to War." The Second World War and the Lives of America's Children* (New York and Oxford: Oxford University Press, 1993), 153.

45. Tuttle, *"Daddy's Gone to War,"* 154.

46. Jack Matthews, *Toys Go to War. World War II Military Toys, Games, Puzzles and Books* (Missoula, Montana: Pictorial Histories Publishing Co., 1994), 4.

47. Gisela Wegener-Spöhring, "War Toys in the World of Fourth Graders: 1985 and 2002," in Jeffrey Goldstein, David Buckingham, and Gilles Brougére, eds., *Toys, Games and Media* (Mahwah, NJ: Lawrence Erlbaum, 2004), 33.

48. Matthews, *Toys Go to War*, 4-5.

49. *St. Nicholas*, July 1917, 771.

50. Andrea McKenzie, "The Children's Crusade: American Children Writing War." *The Lion and the Unicorn*, 31 (2007) 89.

51. Signed Muriel Anderson, 476.

52. Jane Stannard Johnson, "What Motion-Pictures Are Telling the Boys and Girls," *St. Nicholas*, July 1915, 846-847.

53. *St. Nicholas*, September 1915, 963.

54. Henry P. Davison, *The American Red Cross in the Great War* (New York: Macmillan Co., 1919), 104.

55. Tuttle, "Daddy's Gone to War," 6.

56. Children's Bureau, U.S. Department of Labor, *To Parents in Wartime* (Washington, DC: GPO, 1942). The pamphlet cost 5 cents.

57. "Children in War. They Can be Trained Not to Fear," *Life*, March 30, 1942, 68.

58. Ibid.

59. Angelo Patri, *Your Children in Wartime*, 5.

60. Chase, *Wartime Social Studies*, 26.

61. H. M. Lafferty, "Education during War: Matriarch or Hussy?" *School and Society*, November 7, 1942,

439.

62. Educational Policies Commission, National Education Association, and American Association of School Administrators, *What the Schools Should Teach in Wartime* (Washington, DC: NEA, January 1943), 20.

63. Kirk, *Earning Their Stripes*, 16.

64. Howard Lane, associate professor of education, Northwestern University, "The Good School for the Young Child in Wartime," *Education*, February 1943, 354.

65. *Life*, "Children in War," 68.

66. Howard Lane, associate professor of education, Northwestern University, "The Good School for the Young Child in Wartime," *Education* 63, no. 6, (1943), 355.

67. Elise Clews Parsons, "The Dragon's Teeth." *Harper's Weekly*, May 8, 1915, 449.

68. C. Madeleine Dixon, "When Play Goes Warlike," *Parents' Magazine*, July 1942, 27.

69. Mossé, *Fallen Soldiers*, 139–140.

70. Wegener-Spöhring, "War Toys," 31.

71. Carmen A. Prioli, "The Fu-Go Project." *American Heritage* on line, http://www.americanheritage.com/articles/magazine/ah/1982/3/1982_3_88.shtml.

72. W. Linwood Chase. *Wartime Social Studies*, 17.

73. Quoted in Kennedy, *Over Here. The First World War and American Society*, 55.

74. Mossé, *Fallen Soldiers*, v.

75. Stephan F. Brumberg, "New York City Schools March Off to War. The Nature and Extent of Participation of the City Schools in the Great War, April 1917-June 1918." *Urban Education* 24, no. 4, (1990), 454.

76. John F. Sims, President, State Normal School, Stevens Point, Wisconsin, "Patriotism in the Schools," *National Education Association, Addresses and Proceedings, Vol. 55, Fifty-Fifth Annual Meeting, Portland, Oregon, July 7-14, 1917* (Washington, DC: NEA, 1917), 170.

77. Karen L. Hamilton, "St. Nicholas at War: The Effects of the Great War on a Prominent Children's Magazine, 1914-1919" (Master's thesis, University of Minnesota, 1972), 4.

78. *St. Nicholas*, July 1914, 849.

79. *St. Nicholas*, May 1917, 642.

80. *National School Service*, September 1, 1918 (Volume 1, No. 1), 10.

81. Anna Freud and Dorothy T. Burlingham, *War and Children* (New York: International University Press, 1944) 181.

82. Mossé, *Fallen Soldiers*, 25.

83. Stéphane Audoin-Rouzeau, *La Guerre des Enfants* (Paris: Armand Colin, 1993, 2004), 52.

84. David I. Macleod, *Building Character in the American Boy. The Boy Scouts, YMCA, and Their Forerunners, 1870-1920* (Madison: The University of Wisconsin Press, 1983), 181.

85. Macleod, 183.

86. J. Cayce Morrison, "The Teaching of Patriotism," *Education*, February 1943, 284.

87. Chase, 17.

88. W. S. Small, "Physical Education in the High School in the Present Emergency," *School and Society*, Sept. 7, 1918, 282–283.

89. Strong Hinman, "A Health and Physical Education Program for Elementary Schools." *Proceedings of the Eightieth Annual Meeting of the National Education Association, June 28–July 3, 1942* (Washington, DC: NEA, 1942), 164.

90. Col. Leonard W. Rowntree, *Education for Victory*, June 1, 1943, 3.

91. Major Edwin R. Elbel, Army Air Forces School of Aviation Medicine, Randolph Field, Texas, *Education for Victory*. March 3, 1945, 15.

92. *Education for Victory*, Sept. 12, 1944, 12.

93. Jay B. Nash, "Health and Fitness in Wartime," Proceedings of the Eightieth Annual meeting of the National Education Association, 1942, 162.

94. "Report of the Chief Scout Executive," *Thirty-Third Annual Report of the Boy Scouts of America, 1942*. House Document No. 17, 78th Congress, First Session (Washington, DC: GPO, 1943), 10.

95. Davison, *The American Red Cross in the Great War*, 103.

96. "For Country and Liberty." *St. Nicholas*, November 1917, 24.

97. Angelo Patri, *Your Children in Wartime* (Garden City, NY: Doubleday, Doran & Co., 1943), 14.

98. Woolston, "Billy and the World War," 92.

99. *National School Service*, September 1, 1918, 10.

100. W. Linwood Chase, *Wartime Social Studies in the Elementary School*, 6.

101. *Education*, January 1944, 292.

102. "Use of Schools in War Time." *School and Society*, April 6, 1918, 404.

103. Mrs. Alexander Thompson, member, Oregon Legislative Assembly, "Preparedness—a Veneer or a Fundamental—Which Will Our Schools Give Our Children?", 1162.

104. *National School Service*, October 15, 1918, 5.

105. Richard Polenberg, ed., *America at War: The Home Front 1941-1945* (Englewood Cliffs, NJ: Prentice Hall, 1968), 140; Geoffrey Perrett, *Days of Sadness, Years of Triumph. The American People 1939-1945* (New York: Coward, McCann & Geoghegan, Inc., 1973), 370.

106. "Friendly Talks with the Editor. "America or—" *American Boy*, June 1918, 3.

107. Kennedy, *Over Here*, 53.

108. Perrett, *Days of Sadness*, 359.

109. Zeiger, "The Schoolhouse vs. the Armory. U.S. Teachers and the Campaign Against Militarism in the Schools, 1914-1918," 167.

110. Ibid.

111. Frances E. Harden, teacher, Stewart School, Chicago, Illinois, "A Plea for Greater Democracy in Our Public Schools," National Education Association, *Addresses and Proceedings, Vol. 57, Fifty-Seventh Annual Meeting, Milwaukee, Wisconsin, June 28-July 5, 1919* (Washington, DC: NEA, 1919), 391.

112. Margaret S. McNaught, commissioner of elementary schools, California, "The Elementary School during the War." National Education Association, *Addresses and Proceedings*, Vol. 55, Fifty-Fifth Annual Meeting, Portland, Oregon, July 7-14, 1917 (NEA, Washington, D.C., 1917), 167.

113. W. S. Small, *School Life*, August 16, 1918, 12.

114. James Duncan Phillips, "Teaching Patriotism." *Education*, February 1918, 445.

115. *School and Society*, March 31, 1917, 385.

116. Educational Policies Commission, *What the Schools Should Teach in Wartime*, 22.

117. Ibid., 7-8.

118. Josephus Daniels, "A Message to the Boys of America." *St. Nicholas*, July 1918, 785.

119. Editor's note, *American Boy*, April 1918, 46.

120. Dean, *Our Schools in War Time,—and After*, 5.

121. Quoted in Dean, *Our Schools in War Time—and After*, 235.

122. Payne Ratner, "Education and Democracy." National Education Association, *Proceedings*. Vol. 80, Eightieth Annual meeting, Denver, Colo., June 28-July 3, 1942, (Washington, NEA, 1942), 57.

123. H. W. Wells, "Boys' Working Reserve," National Education Association, *Addresses and Proceedings*, 1919.

124. Dean, *Our Schools in War Time—and After*, 120.

125. Ibid., 12-13.

126. Woolston, "Billy and the World War," 92.

127. Miriam Warren Hubbard, "The Soldier-Girls at the National Service School," *St. Nicholas*, April 1917, 519-520.

128. "A Dozen Boys Who Do Things. All Making Good at Their Hobbies," *American Boy*. February 1918, 12.

129. Charles K. Arey, "Aviation in the Elementary School Science Program," *Education*, October 1942, 96.

130. Kirk, *Earning Their Stripes*, 80-81.

131. Sylvia Whitman, *Children of the World War II Home Front* (Minneapolis: Carolrhoda Books, 2001), 22.

132. Ibid., 81.

133. Davison, *The American Red Cross in the Great War*, 93-94.

134. Edward N. Teall, "A Letter to the Boys of America." *St. Nicholas*, October 1917, 1066.

135. Mary Stevick, "Save Food and Serve Humanity." *Rally*, March 1918, 6.

136. Davison, *The American Red Cross in the Great War*, 99.

137. U.S. Congress, First Session, House Document No. 17, *Thirty-Third Annual Report of the Boy Scouts of America, 1942* (Washington, DC: GPO, 1943), 70.

138. U.S. Congress, First Session, House Document No. 125, *Thirty-fifth Annual Report of the Boy Scouts of America, 1944* (Washington, DC: GPO, 1944), 2; Franklin M. Reck, *The 4-H Story. A History of 4-H Club Work* (Chicago: National Committee on Boys and Girls Club Work, 1951), 272.

139. U.S. Congress, *Thirty-Third Annual Report of the Boy Scouts of America, 1942*, 65; U.S. Congress, *Thirty-Fifth Annual Report of the Boy Scouts of America, 1944*, 4.

140. Reck, *The 4-H Story. A History of 4-H Club Work*, 271.

141. Future Farmers of America and U.S. Office of Education, *Proceedings of the Fifteenth National Convention of the Future Farmers of America, Kansas City, October 26–29, 1942* (Washington, DC: U.S. Office of Education, 1942), 65.

142. National Education Association, *Addresses and Proceedings*, 1919, 49.

143. John W. Studebaker, "Contribution of Education to the War Effort." National Education Association, *Proceedings*, Vol. 81, Eighty-First Annual Meeting, Indianapolis, June 27–29, 1943 (Washington, DC: NEA, 1943), 70–71.

144. U.S. Congress, *Thirty-fifth Annual Report of the Boy Scouts of America, 1944*, 3.

145. Kirk, "Earning Their Stripes," 80.

146. "U.S. War Bonds," U-S-History.com, http://www.u-s-history.com/pages/h1682.html

147. U.S. Congress, *Thirty-Fifth Annual Report of the Boy Scouts of America, 1944*, 4–5.

148. "Who's Who. William Gibbs McAdoo." FirstWorldWar.com, http://www.firstworldwar.com/bio/mcadoo.htm.

149. *National School Service*, September 15, 1918, 15.

150. Howard Lane, "The Good School for the Young Child in Wartime," *Education*, February 1943, 355.

151. United States Committee on Public Information (George Creel), *The Creel Report. Complete Report of the Chairman of the Committee on Public Information* (New York: DaCapo Press, 1972, reprint of 1920 edition), 26.

152. McNaught, "The Elementary School During the War," 166.

153. Brumberg, "New York City Schools March Off to War," 456.

154. *Education for Victory*, December 1, 1943, 14.

# 3

## EDUCATION AND PUBLIC POLICY

**A**uthorities by the first decades of the twentieth century had become greatly concerned with welfare and education of children. Partially this concern grew out of muckraking-era journalists who documented the heartbreaking work conditions under which children were exploited. The explosion of immigrants hoping to make a new life in the United States reached 12 million between 1870 and 1900, many of them coming with no jobs or even English language skills. As immigrant parents were forced to work long hours in horrible conditions for bare sustenance, so were their children expected to help. Many children at the turn of the last century had no free time; if not in school they would be expected to sell newspapers, gather rags, shine shoes, make deliveries, or do tedious jobs for adults whose time was deemed more important. Documentary photographer Lewis Hine was one of many who recorded abuses of child labor in America, leading to laws for child protection and limits on child labor. With the coming of war, however, child advocates feared those eager to employ children as cheap laborers would find an argument to turn back the era, just as the movement was winning wider appeal of American opinion.

### Child Labor and School Attendance during World War

In declaring a "Children's Year" in the very midst of war, beginning April 6, 1918, the United States Children's Bureau warned employers that it would not relax child labor standards for presumed wartime exigencies. Declaring, "three years of war reveal to us the fact that children are the chief sufferers," an advocate speaking to the National Education Association added, "The children under six are to be given particular attention in our national crusade. The 'forgotten army' includes four million children from three to six years of age in our country."[1] *National School Service*, a government-sponsored publication of George Creel's Committee on Public Information, reminded readers in 1918 that child labor laws forbade children under fourteen to be employed in "war work," and added, "Neither the patriotic desire to serve immediately nor the attraction of high wages should be permitted to draw children from school to work."[2] World War II authorities found it necessary to repeat the same message, as children were drawn away from school into paying war jobs. Declaring that "their right to schooling should not be scrapped for the duration," the U.S. Children's Bureau in 1942 issued *A Charter for Children in Wartime*, declaring, "no boy or girl shall be employed at wages that undermine the wages for adult labor; none under fourteen years of age shall be part of the labor force."[3] Authorities time and again reminded children to stay in school, and admonished teachers to do all they could to keep them at their desks. U.S. Commissioner of Education Philander Claxton, speaking of the National Child Labor Committee's planned 1918 designation of Child Labor Day, observed, "We must not permit ourselves to forget that this is a war waged by the adult population of the country, and that for both the present and future welfare of the country its burdens must not be permitted to fall on the shoulders of the children."[4]

Educators and government leaders set a tone that was echoed repeatedly in juvenile publications with more flair, if less finesse. "While it's on our mind we might as well say that in our opinion a boy who *can* go to school and won't go to school, or a boy who *can* master his studies and doesn't master them, is as much of a slacker as the man who tries to dodge the draft."[5]

Repeated and increasingly anguished calls to employers demanding they not rob the schools of their youth, as well as to youth to not rob themselves of their education, became necessary not only because employers were so ready to exploit. Children themselves wanted to be exploited, if it meant cash in the pocket as opposed to the perhaps less compelling joy of volunteer patriotic service. While authorities were exhorting children to stay in school and out of the workplace, at the same time they were asking children to fill every spare moment with a wide range of volunteer work, invariably declared necessary to help win the war. Children were asked to motivate themselves for patriotic duty through such tasks as growing and harvesting food, scavenging and collecting scrap, milkweeds, or peach pits, canning produce, knitting scarves, building furniture, mailing letters to the boys, taking care of children, typing and filing, the whole list. Many of these did not seem to offer a great mental challenge to youthful energies. Some seemed to stretch the definition of war utility for the dutiful boy or girl serving in the home-front reserve. Peeling foil off gum wrappers for scrap drives might seem to a kid less than crucial, or collecting kitchen grease, but nothing was so minor that authorities thought it beneath a child's free-time allocation. Girls asking some local authorities for volunteer war work were given clerical jobs, or opportunities to supervise day-care centers and swimming pools, orphanages and hospitals.[6] Was this really of much help to the boys overseas? Authorities offered the plausible argument that girls in these activities could free their mothers for work in war industries. But it seemed like an exaggeration to call such things "war work." At least knitting mufflers for the troops seemed to directly benefit the men at the front.

If a proposed job were at worst mind-numbing repetition, at least many young people would prefer cash to sometimes tiresome patriotic credits, pins, medals, certificates, or stripes on a uniform. Between 1940 and 1944, two million children aged fourteen to eighteen were added to the employment roles, for a total of 3 million, compared to pre-war total of 872,314. In fact, while many of us today presume accepted wisdom that during the world wars women took the place of men at the front, actually children worked in numbers as great. While children under sixteen could not according to the Fair Labor Standards Act in World War II work in war industries, they could work in many support roles such as farmhands, busboys, pin-setters in bowling alleys, waiters, caddies, delivery and messenger workers, and bakers.[7] Children under fourteen were forbidden to work at all, based on hard-fought yet modest federal child labor laws passed during the World War I era. After September 1, 1917, every child under fourteen was entitled to protection from labor in mill, cannery, workshop, factory or manufacturing establishment; between fourteen and sixteen no child could work more than eight hours a day, more than six days a week, or after 7 P.M. or before 6 A.M. No child under sixteen could work in a mine or quarry. This concerned Julie C. Lathrop, first director of the federal Department of Labor's Children's Bureau, who spearheaded the battle against child labor. "It is not too much to say that the first effect of war is to threaten all such standards," she said. It may suspend or destroy them all, so that now in the beginning it is exceedingly important that we should face squarely the risk before us and determine whether such laws are necessities or luxuries."[8]

But reference to laws against child labor hid the whole story. By the 1940s, still, three-fourths of states allowed children as young as fourteen to leave school

if they could find a job. During the world wars plenty were available, as employers themselves canvassed the schools with offers more attractive to adolescents
than day after day of perhaps dusty lectures in stuffy classrooms. Every state
allowed children sixteen or older to leave school for the real world, although
authorities hoped they would not. And while federal law did not allow children
under fourteen to work, with a few exceptions such as newspaper carriers, the
law was regularly ignored. Ten- to twelve-year-olds found after-school and night
jobs in bowling alleys, pool rooms, and all-night greasy spoons. Older children
could fill their nights with full-time jobs, then sleep by day in their classrooms.

Industries decimated by wartime shortage of adult or older adolescent em-
ployees asked for "temporary" suspension of child labor laws to allow youngsters
to take on jobs. In World War I, "It was even seriously proposed to change the
child-labor laws so as to capitalize the labor of children in factories to a greater
degree than ever before. A mighty protest went up all over the land against the
proposed child-labor legislation, and the victory of child conservation so tardily
won is made permanent."[9] "Don't close the schools; use them to maximum capacity," suggested Interior Secretary Franklin K. Lane in 1918.[10] President Wilson added his encouragement: "So long as the war continues there will be constant need of very large numbers of men and women of the highest and most
thorough training for war service in many lines."[11] Federal authorities reminded
teachers, "Neither the patriotic desire to serve immediately nor the attraction of
high wages should be permitted to draw children from school to work."[12]

Again in World War II, industries facing shortages hoped to capitalize on
the reserve of eager children by arguing child labor laws should be suspended
as part of the wartime emergency. While bills to that effect were introduced
in Congress and many state legislatures, they failed.[13] The U.S. Government
maintained a clear message that states should not consider closing schools for
work. Franklin Roosevelt, in an October 12, 1942, radio address, did encourage
children to consider volunteer and part-time jobs, but "this does not mean closing schools and stopping education." The NEA noted the president's statement
did not apply to elementary schools, which were to maintain a normal school
year. As for high schools, war service could be an integral part of classroom
education. Students could be moved more quickly through school and into war
industries, even if this meant keeping the schools open in the summer. Schools
should not be closed to allow students to find jobs.[14] Even Paul V. McNutt, serving as chairman of the federal War Manpower Commission, echoed the message, urging children with summer jobs to come back to school: "The opening
of school this fall is your 'D-Day' in the struggle for a better world."[15]

*World War I propaganda directed at adolescents urged a "draft" for school, as authorities worried too many would find more attractive paid jobs doing war work. (American Boy, September 1918, front cover.)*

Repeated pleas to students to stay in school, while providing organized opportunities for patriotic work as volunteers during free hours, produced a mixed message, however. One, the top goal of all patriotic Americans was to win the war. Two, the country faced dire labor shortages threatening the war effort. A society retooling for total war really did need children in the labor force, and so authorities faced Hobson's Choice of wanting children to stay in school while at the same time knowing they really were needed for work. Aggressive recruiters in the schools could bring strong arguments of patriotism and duty to the already strong argument of salary. Hundreds of thousands of older children apparently read through the dilemma of authorities, and so moved from patriotic penniless volunteer to patriotic paid employee. Many joined war industries in the summer, and did not return to the classroom in the fall. Younger ones obtained permits to work, and slept through or skipped day classes. "The comparatively high wages which will exist during a war emergency will call them as can no course of study," observed an educator during World War I. "Families whose earning member or members are off to war, and who feel in addition the higher cost of living, will look upon their children as being a possible added source of income."[16] In St. Louis a program was established to offer financial aid to families in an attempt to keep children in school. Called the "Child Conservation Fund," the St. Louis school board asked for donations and held fund-raisers to gather a fund able to pay three dollars a week to the family of a child asking to leave school for work.[17] Reported the U.S. Commissioner of Education in 1944, "thousands of children have left school to join a gold rush. Which is a better place for children to grow up in, a factory or a high school?" In April 1943, according to federal statistics, employed fourteen- to seventeen-year-olds totaled more than a million above the previous year's figures. Violations of child labor laws jumped 197 percent between 1941 and 1944.[18] The wink-wink view to child labor law enforcement produced alarming cases of exploitation. In a 1944 report, Connecticut investigators found twelve-year-olds working seven nights a week, for a total sixty hours, in jobs as far from war service as bowling alley pin-setters. "One boy, slowed up by lack of sleep, was hit by a bowling ball and lost two fingers of his left hand." In New Jersey merchants asked the Newark authorities to close schools so children could work through the holiday season. In indicating its unanimous disapproval, Newark NEA chapter chair Bertha Parks Batt wrote, "Teachers consider the education of boys and girls of sixteen and eighteen years much more important than aiding the stores to sell Christmas presents."[19]

By leaving school children were merely following the example set by their teachers, who also in the hundreds of thousands left the classroom for more lucrative jobs in war industries. In 1918 the need led authorities to recommend local school boards hire married women—generally considered unsuitable to teach before the war. Agreed the national Parent-Teacher Association president, "Unless married women who have been teachers or who are able to teach offer their services, the education of the children will suffer."[20] By the end of World War II, one-third of the nation's 850,000 teachers had left the profession, some for military service, but many for more lucrative war work. Not surprising, noted educators: "The public school teacher is the lowest paid professional worker in the country. Bartenders, scrub women, and sixteen-year-old messengers are paid better than many a school teacher." That was in World War II. But it was little different twenty-five years earlier. Explaining the 1918 teacher shortage, the national PTA president wrote, "Boys of fourteen can and do earn as much as is paid to teachers."[21]

## War and Juvenile Delinquency

The conundrum of how to deal with school children working long hours for pay in jobs that did actually need to be done vexed authorities even more as they discovered an alternative to that work: doing nothing. It was well understood even before the United States joined World War I that wartime dislocations affected the ability of parents to stay home with their children. They found adolescents, in particular, with time on their hands and no supervision tended to get into trouble; "juvenile delinquency" was thought to be a serious problem in Britain during both world wars, and authorities tended to look to that country for guidance on how best not to repeat mistakes. It was presumed that adolescents would probably get into trouble when they had nothing to do and no supervision. Clearly, paid work could provide some supervision, but authorities were determined not to throw older children back into the gray world of deadening child labor they'd only recently managed to curb in American society. One way to keep children busy and off the streets was to provide a wide spectrum of activities more carefully organized than haphazard calls to volunteer. With government providing direction, mostly schools were expected to organize these, but private organizations, particularly the Red Cross, Girl Scouts and Boy Scouts too could put together patriotic programs for children reaching the age of adolescence. In fact Boy Scouts, organized only a few years before World War I in 1910, had mushroomed in popularity as an ideal way to train boys on the path to good character, and so became a major wartime player in the militarizing of children during both conflicts.

Still in question, however, was the actual extent of supposed juvenile delinquency. Many authorities could not even be clear regarding the definition of the term so easily bandied about between government, private organizations and parents. Worried authorities in World War I worked mostly in anticipation of troubled trends they saw in Britain. Education authorities claimed a 30 percent rise in United States delinquency,[22] but by the time they began to collect concrete information about the presumed problem in the States, the war was over. The country's participation in World War II, of course, was almost four years long as opposed to a year and a half, and so authorities had more time to see how a situation they'd witnessed in Britain was playing out at home. Part of the problem was defining "juvenile delinquency." In 1943, one author contended, "No one has adequately, as yet, defined delinquency, and there are available no national statistics."[23] Indeed, many authorities decrying supposed wartime rises in juvenile delinquency stayed circumspect about specifics. They spoke generally about girls frequenting places of entertainment near army bases, or children loitering, but some of what authorities then called delinquency may not have resulted in criminal behavior. One historian writing of World War II declared that the war did not see any spike in delinquency at all.[24] However, at least in World War II as statistics and definitions became more reliable, it is hard to refute the contention of authorities that more kids were getting themselves into trouble, serious trouble. Florida Senator Claude Pepper, writing for the "Annual Report on the Nation's Children" produced by a congressional committee, observed:

> We could remember what we had to combat in safeguarding our boys and girls in World War I. We had already seen steep increases in juvenile delinquency in England during her first year of World War II. We knew then that unless we did something about it in America, and quickly, it would happen here. It has happened, is still happening.... Arrests of boys and girls under eighteen are showing heavy increases over last year. Almost twice as many minor girls are being charged with sex offenses. Court referrals in some cities are running 50 percent higher, and the accent of all these statistics is ever more heavily on the serious cases—sex offense, burglary, car theft and alcoholism.[25]

A more precise report came from J. Edgar Hoover, director of the FBI, who described exactly what he meant by delinquency, and provided some missing statistics:

> Last year young persons under twenty-one accounted for 15 percent of all arrests for murder, 34 percent of all arrests for robbery and larceny, and 50 percent of all arrests for burglary. Arrest of boys, as compared with 1941 figures, increased 17 percent for assault, 20 percent for rape, 26 percent for disorderly conduct, and 30 percent for drunkenness—and this in spite of the fact that thousands of young men are in the armed forces or employed in full-time war jobs! On the girls' side the picture is even darker, with arrests rising almost 56 percent and offenses against common decency alone soaring to a 106 percent increase. During 1943 this upward tendency has continued.[26]

Hoover's startling statistics become a bit misleading, however, as we observe his parameters: persons under twenty-one. An eighteen- to twenty-year-old is not, and was not at that time, defined as a juvenile. Nevertheless, authorities were convinced juveniles at large during the world wars were becoming more delinquent, or certainly threatening to fall off a cliff of iniquity. Mothers and fathers working or serving could not be brought back to the home.

One solution considered during World War II was to provide federal funds to open after-school day-care centers. While private day care had been available in some larger cities since the nineteenth century, Congress for the first time became involved with the 1941 passage of the Lanham Act. The act offered federal matching funds to cover half the cost of opening a day-care center. Cost to parents for keeping a child was fifty cents a day. However, as Pepper noted, the act did not do enough to solve the problem: enough money was available to care for 180,000 children, but by the beginning of 1944 only half the centers were open. (The program was discontinued in 1946.)[27] And presumably teenagers would not be going to day-care. The most expedient solution in both wars seemed to be finding ways to keep kids busy, particularly during school breaks. Advocating farm work for city boys, a World War I educator identified an "abundance of idle energy in the well-grown but below-war-age young men, who idle away the summer days in uselessness and mischief in the vacant lots of our large cities."[28] Other authorities advocated year-around schooling.

Work, especially volunteer work, could do more than rid the country of incipient juvenile delinquents, however. It might serve to sooth the fears of younger, and the anxieties of the older. It might also buttress character in many positive ways, enhancing patriotism, duty, self-discipline, community spirit, and practical skills. Despite what the children and even parents were told, for many authorities, making a solid contribution to the war effort did not constitute the sole reason for putting children to work. For one thing, at least during World War II, younger children could learn to conserve and collect scrap as a way to keep busy and so overcome their supposed fears about the war.[29] A noted educator writing for anxious parents advised, "Plan to keep these children occupied at home, in school, and in the community, and protect them from the worst effect of the war—fear."[30] Worry that children could be psychologically harmed by their fears seemed to be a World War II concept. World War I authorities did not consider it necessary to expressly address childhood fears during war through make-work schemes. They did agree that children could certainly build character through work, and so extolled the virtues of volunteerism and sacrifice of free time. "They are unique opportunities to enrich and test not knowledge, but the supreme lesson of intelligent and unselfish service," wrote historian Guy Stanton Ford, editor of the government's *National School Service* for World War I educators.[31]

Work expected of children, then, could be divided into two forms: volunteer jobs and paid jobs. Authorities believed volunteer work was of great benefit to building character in World War I, to building character as well as psychological health in World War II, and to empowering the national home front in both wars. Concerning paid work, authorities were less certain. But it was clearly necessary to hire children to fill those empty slots, and it might keep wayward youth out of detention centers. In any case, children themselves wanted to put their energy to useful purpose, in both paid and unpaid jobs. One thing was uniformly certain: except for the first months of the country's participation in World War I, authorities did not want children to quit school.

## American Education Faces Total War

Educational leaders had fought to extend American education from its pathetic state in the early century to its less pathetic state in 1940, and did not want to see calls to total war drag the country's children back to levels of a previous generation. In 1918, only 15.1 percent of children graduated from high school; many did not attend beyond eighth grade. Only 3.3 percent went on to universities. Twenty years later high school graduation rates had reached 45.6 percent; 8.3 percent went on to universities. [32] In World War I, 4 percent of the country's armed forces had graduated from high school; by World War II, 25 percent were high school graduates.[33]

The alarming extent of illiteracy among American adolescents was emphasized beginning in 1917, when World War I inductees were tested for physical and mental fitness. The number of supposedly educated young men of military age who could not write their name shocked authorities: 40,000 in the first draft alone. About 700,000 men of draft age were thought to be illiterate, and so unfit to be soldiers, according to the office of education and interior department.[34] Authorities realized then that many inductees were immigrants who also could not speak English. But this was less so by World War II. Military literacy standards for inductees had increased to the ability to read at least at the third- to fourth-grade level; authorities were again shocked at how many men still were "downright illiterate," and so unfit for service.[35] In fact, the military in 1940 rejected 656,000 young men as functionally illiterate; of draft registrants, 350,000 signed their name with an x.[36] Mathematics and science ability tested nearly as abysmally. Despite progress, one education researcher blamed such statistics on "lack of even elementary schooling in some states."[37] It was obvious to educators that wholesale abandonment of the classroom would set the country on a postwar road to ignorance, just at a time when the world was becoming more mechanized, and more complex.

Joining these authorities was a set of voices likely to be more influential during wartime: defense and military leaders. Generals needed boys educated well enough to operate modern weapons and understand complicated tasks. It was too late to go back to basics in the barracks: the army would need to rely on teachers to whip the boys into mental shape, an army behind the men overseas. "In this total war there are many armies. Every one is vital to victory. None is greater in size or potentialities for service than the army of education," said Paul V. McNutt, administrator of the Federal Security Agency, in opening remarks to a conference of the National Institute on Education and the War in August 1942. "I know that the nation can depend on this matchless force of more than 31,000,000 teachers, pupils, and students to give their country the full measure of loyal service in its hour of need."[38] H. H. Arnold, World War II Commanding General of U.S. Army Air Forces, agreed war work was important, "but your education has top priority."[39] World War I Secretary of the Navy Josephus Daniels echoed Wilson's call for children to stay in school by observing, "With this instruction I am sure they will be better fitted for the call when it comes to them."[40] Authorities believed the schools could keep children from failing in their role to build a better postwar society.

But calls to stay in school were made for more immediate goals. Early in the country's World War I involvement authorities hit on the idea of co-opting school buildings as military recruiting stations or munitions factories. "In many secondary schools, the classes in the manual arts or vocational subjects might, with increased interest and educational value, be engaged in the production of actual war material," advocated the president of the University of Maine. "The girls could make various articles of clothing, Red Cross and hospital materials, and the boys could produce parts of munitions and various other small articles that are necessary for the equipment of our troops."[41]

While knitting scarves and banging together boxes could be done in the classrooms, it soon became obvious schoolhouses could not be easily converted into near-armories for military production. But building on their function as centers for education was another idea, that secondary schools could become vocational training centers for adolescents soon to enter war industries and military service. The extent that schools should move to emphasize development of more practical skills had been part of a larger debate before the first war. Educators and politicians critically examined the presumed tendency of teachers and principals to remain aloof from real needs of the community and the country. Traditional emphasis on memorization and study of such impractical subjects as Latin became targets of those authorities, sometimes part of the Progressive Movement, who sought to tie the school to the community as a team working together to solve practical problems. "The theory stressed the idea that the school has a social role and must, therefore, cultivate close relations with its community and become an integral part of its activities and interests."[42]

Those critical of old style rote learning in towers purportedly of ivory found World War I to be an ideal bolster to their contention that schools must modernize. By World War II, Progressive ideals were under attack from critics who thought educators went too far in throwing out the old-time discipline. But vocational and practical education as a way to ease children into the real world—and offer a trained pool for employers and generals—offered a strong argument for staying in the classroom. The ideal school could become a center for practical training of use to the military, as well as a home-front base to coordinate scrap collections, bond sales, knitting parties and volunteer fairs. "We ask that every school house become a service center for the home front," wrote Franklin Roosevelt. "Every classroom is a citadel," concluded General Brehan Somervell at a meeting discussing the role of education in World War II.[43] "Education is a weapon," announced the New York state school superintendent in a 1943 speech.[44] "Our one objective?" asked the Massachusetts commissioner of education rhetorically: "To do as well as we can in making soldiers."

In a statement that must have come as a shock to educators hoping to keep adolescents in school, Roosevelt's aide Harry Hopkins advised, "quit high school entirely.... A diploma can only be framed and hung on a wall. A shell that a boy or girl helps to make can kill a lot of Japs."[45] Libraries could play a support role as centers of propaganda, "converted into arsenals for national defense, as war information centers, as sources of technical information for industrial defense workers and students."[46]

In his second inaugural speech just before the country joined World War I, Wilson threw his administration's support behind a bill to offer more support to development of vocational education in schools. Educators hoping to expand practical education into the country's secondary schools were pleased that his support and wartime expediency would make successful proposals that had repeatedly failed before. The Smith-Hughes Act, passed in 1917, offered federal matching grants to secondary schools interested in developing vocational education programs for students aged fourteen and up interested in farm or industry. Noting such bills introduced before the war were defeated, a New York professor of vocational education in 1918 observed, "Perhaps the measure would have met the fate of its predecessors if war had not been declared." As part of the wartime mood strongly in favor of preparedness, however, the bill passed "almost unanimously."[47] A war department education specialist speaking to the NEA in 1918 berated American educators for their ivory towerishness, asserting, "war has shown that our national unpreparedness was due in great measure to the fact that American education had almost no relation to the needs of modern life."[48]

Vocational education as it developed in secondary schools would have a more general goal of training adolescents for practical jobs, or a more specific goal of training boys for military service. The latter was particularly considered necessary, as authorities adamantly reminded the country that its immediate goal was to win the war. World War I authorities asked the country's teachers to sacrifice weekends and holidays in efforts to train children for war work, to convert every home economics kitchen, every metal shop, every sewing room, every back garden plot, into a lab for wartime vocation training:

> Every teacher of manual training, sewing or cooking should be thinking in terms of mobilization service, and that any teacher of manual training who was conducting his course of models, instead of thinking and working in terms of food production or industrial war services, was absolutely out of touch with the needs of the day.[49]

In 1942, the American Association of School Administrators in a San Francisco Convention adopted a resolution that schools in wartime ought to "provide through the development of local school systems for training for defense industries."[50] The NEA expanded on what this would mean:

> Vocational objectives should be closely related to war service for both boys and girls. No able-bodied boy should graduate from high school in wartime without specific pre-induction training; the entire high-school population should receive occupational guidance and training culminating either in employment or in specific plans for further education.[51]

Courses that did not directly benefit the war effort—at least the war effort as authorities conceived it to be—ought to be put off, thrown out for the duration. "Courses should be changed or modified to suit industrial manpower requirements and emphasis of instruction should, when necessary, be redirected along proper channels," advised the director of the federal Office of Education vocational division. "It is not to be expected that industry will change its methods to fit into the qualifications of young men and women who are trained by the schools. It is rather to be expected that the schools will instruct them in the light of industrial requirements."[52] The governor of Kansas, speaking to the NEA, concluded succinctly, "the classroom must be geared into the war effort.

Education must get into the production line."[53] Some coursework specifically targeted farming skills, particularly in World War I, as authorities (and some farmers) panicked in expectation of feeding an army and a world at war without sufficient manpower.

World War II agricultural authorities also valued farming skills, but did focus attention on elaborate programs to bring city youngsters to the fields as was done in World War I. In fact, often targeted as a vocational skill critical to the adolescent boy in World War II was aviation. The United States joined the war almost helpless in the air, blamed on neglect and policy, while the German Blitzkrieg and Battle of Britain persuaded government that this war would be won by the airman. The country had to catch up, and fast. The schools were called to help. "Both services [army and navy] have expressed their need of recruits who understand the airplane, its flight, and its workings" noted the editor of *Education*, a commercial publication not officially connected to the government.[54] Earlier in the war, children were asked to learn aviation by building airplane models of practical use to soldiers in learning to spot enemy aircraft. The government-sponsored *Education for Victory* affirmed the military needed 500,000 airplane models for training, and that the best people to build them were school children. "The model plane project is valuable for boys who participate because, as expressed by one instructor (1) it gives a boy an opportunity to render practical service to the armed forces, and (2) it teaches accuracy and thoroughness of craftsmanship." Even girls have shown interest, the report added.[55] In fact, so high was the interest in making models that only nine months later the program was terminated; the goal of 500,000 models had been met.

What else was needed? Certainly, declared authorities in 1943, it would save the army time if training in the high schools were offered in auto mechanics, telephone/telegraph linemen, medical technician and radio operators.[56] Beyond that, authorities not always certain concluded wartime society would dictate. In any case, not needed was freedom of choice: what the children wanted to do didn't matter. "These decisions cannot safely be left on the basis of individual student preferences," concluded an NEA commission. "They are national questions. They require some estimate of nationwide needs, resources, and training facilities and a national policy to guide the training programs."[57] This highlights a general observation that authorities during the world wars almost never sought opinions of what children ought to know or ought to do from the children themselves.

Not everyone agreed during World War II that aviation training was of use to every child, or that even an intense stress on vocationalism was the best answer to a wartime question of how schools ought to educate children for war. "The line pursued by some educators is somewhat as follows," wrote Charles K. Arey, an author of science books for secondary schools. "'It is a function of the schools to help in producing pilots, mechanics and factory workers to fill the pressing need for them....' While this argument undoubtedly has validity for the secondary school, from which under present conditions many students will proceed into airplane factories or into the armed services, it seems a little far-fetched when applied to the elementary school." The author contended a free-standing course in aviation would make as much sense as one entitled "Tanks" or "Battleships."[58]

Other educators worried that authorities had forgotten the importance of humanities and social sciences. Considering what he called a "rebellion against the humanities," the Reverend Hugh S. Blunt wrote, "Judging from our present educational tendencies, the little girls will be reading books on 'the phase theory of electronics and atmospheric pressure in wind tunnels.' We have retired a long way from the Three Rs."[59] A naval reserve officer writing in the *School and Society*, admitted educators felt pressure to abandon traditional studies not only from authorities, but from parents, and children themselves, who complained, "But I want to fight. There's no place for Charles Lamb, or Ben Jonson, or Plato right now. What I want is a crack at a Jap." While he agreed popular opinion during the war maintained that the only useful education was "the kind that enables a man to pull a trigger, fly a plane, or navigate a ship," he worried that practical courses would crowd out traditional work. "Canteen feeding, air-raid wardens, evacuation procedures—courses like these are competing for customers with standard time-tested offerings in history, literature, science, philosophy.... Ignorant experts or thinking men and women, which will it be?"[60] The purported superiority of taking practical classes taught by military staff was questioned by one principal, who observed that many teachers themselves were starting to lose confidence in their own methods, and wondering if they should adopt those of the army. "In the first place, the very nature and purpose of the public school is so vastly different from that of the army school as to permit no comparison," he argued. "The army school is designed for teaching to a group of highly selected adults one specific area of specialized knowledge or a specific pattern of skills." It is training for adults, he noted, not children. "'On the other hand, the primary function of the public school, and of the elementary school in particular, is to provide a long-time environment in which the child has opportunity to grow up into the kind of person we wish him to be."[61]

A World War I English teacher pointed out that emphasis on vocational education could have a less obvious consequence; it could divide children by class into those who were encouraged to learn vocational skills and those who were encouraged to learn more traditional subjects, so creating a blue collar vs. white collar work force. "If we are to escape the slow hardening of society into layers, vocational training must be kept in close touch with the other work of the schools. In a democracy it is not sound training, from childhood, to place the mechanic in one group and the professional man in another."[62]

### Reaching the Homes: The Child as a Government Agent

But while authorities were generally encouraging new courses in mechanics, agriculture, engineering, construction, and perhaps bandage-rolling and evacuation science, government leaders in particular wanted to bring war to the school children for reasons much more fundamental than how-to. Authorities particularly during World War I realized that more than any individual, it was the child who could reach most intimately into the home, and to the adults that could not be reached by any mass medium. Children are malleable, particularly younger ones. They are easily persuaded by authorities tying a patriotic message to appeals to excitement and emotion. "The American people are very fond of making use of school children for purposes of parade and exhibition whenever occasion calls for spectacular appeal, whether of war, worship, or festival," observed one California educator. "In the second place, school children are themselves sensitive to every form of excitement among their elders and are sure to imitate in play what they see and hear on the street and at home."[63]

Schools were happy to encourage such propagandistic displays of enthusiastic youth, who would advocate preparedness, Selective Service registration, bond sales, or military census in a public attempt to persuade adult spectators to join the movement. Less publicly, children could bring these ideas from the school to the dinner table or the living room floor. No door-to-door solicitor could persuade like the guilt-inspiring pleas of a child to her or his parents. No law or officer could be as effective. Observed one contemporary educator, "It is the children's convictions which take effect not only when as children they carry word to their parents but also when they come out of childhood into adult life."[64] In New York City, recorded in 1918 minutes of the Board of Education, one scamp supposedly went on a hunger strike after her father refused to buy a bond. "So I did not eat my supper, though my father and my mother begged me to eat; and I went to bed. In the morning my father said, 'Nettie, eat your breakfast.' But I said, 'No; I am an American. You will not buy a bond; I cannot eat.' Then my father said to my mother, 'Go, buy a bond.'"[65]

Part of the significance of this anecdote is in the statement, "I am an American." In 1918, many in New York City were not. In World War I, 70 percent of the city's 900,000 children in public schools were foreign born, or children of immigrants.[66] Immigration to the United States in the two decades before dwarfed levels before or since. Between 1900 and 1910, 8,795,386 immigrants arrived to the United States; from 1911 to 1920, another 5,735,811 arrived.[67] In 1910, 14.7 percent of people living in the United States were foreign born, the second highest percentage in history (the largest was 1890, 14.8 percent). While in 1910, 87.4 percent of these were listed by census as being from Europe, many of those were from southern and eastern Europe, regions whose customs were considered more foreign to the United States than those from northern and western Europe. (Immigration laws passed in the 1882 kept the number from Asian countries at a tiny level, one tenth of one percent in 1910.)[68]

The high percentage of immigrants fanning through the United States, with their own customs, communities, churches, and foreign-language press, troubled many more established Americans. Some feared the American melting pot was more closely a salad bowl, and the socialist and even anarchist politics and supposed refusal to adopt American customs might fracture the nation's unity just as it was emerging into a world power. At the time of a peak of German immigration (one million 1881-1885), Emma Goldman arrived from Lithuania to become one of the country's outspoken anarchists. In 1886 the Haymarket Square bombing in Chicago killing seven and injuring many more was blamed on anarchists; eight were arrested, seven executed. In 1901 President William McKinley was assassinated by another Eastern European immigrant, self-described anarchist Leon Czolgosz from Poland. In 1903 Congress passed an immigration act to deny entry to those who, at the turn of the last century, were feared as strongly as were feared Muslims after the 2001 World Trade Center attacks. The country was primed for a concern that should war come, the country could unravel. President Wilson joined his usual nemesis, former president Theodore Roosevelt, in worry over a country with so many "hyphenated Americans," that is, immigrants. Roosevelt famously declared that those "squabbling nationalities" would be "the one absolutely certain way of bringing this nation to ruin."[69] An answer, Roosevelt and his many powerful supporters contended, was to bring Americanization to the immigrant population. Americanization was a word that suggested many things to patriotic citizens, including pressuring immigrants to show their patriotism by buying war bonds, learning English, denouncing the country's enemies, declaring their support for the Allies, and if possible, trying to bleach out any slight stain of affection for their Old Country. Conservative preparedness groups such as the National Security League shifted their campaigns after April 1917 from preparedness to "100 percent American-ism," seeking "to ensure conformity of opinion by stifling descent."[70]

And in that children could help. They could bring the message of Ameri-canization to the immigrant home, becoming a small infiltrator into the sanc-tum of the possibly under-patriotic adult. "It is generally agreed that the nation is facing no graver problem than that of assimilating the million or so of non-English-speaking aliens in the country," wrote an Ohio educator.[71] "There is a story told of a Chicago immigrant mother, suspicious and distrustful, who when asked to sign a food pledge card said: 'I sign nodings, my man he say I sign nodings'; and slammed the door in the face of the distributor of the cards," recounted an unsigned editorial in the first issue of CPI's *National School Service.* "But when her little daughter brought the same card from school and said, 'But Mama, my teacher says it is all right'; the mother replied: 'Vell, if your teachers say it is all right, then I sign.'"[72]

Observed a New York City English teacher speaking to the NEA, "The abid-ing transformation is wrought on the foreign-born adult through his children in the public school."[73] "By all means he [the school principal] should inform pupils of the meaning of the war, that they in turn may carry word to their parents," in 1918 advised Arthur R. Dean, who in addition to his role as Colum-bia University professor of vocational education served as supervising officer, Bureau of Vocational Training, New York State Military Commission. He re-minded educators, "such work is not always limited to districts where people are foreign born."[74] U.S. Treasury Secretary William G. McAdoo was more specific:

> Every girl and boy, especially every little girl and every little boy, is, or ought to be, the boss of their mothers and fathers; and I know that if you make a patriotic appeal to your mothers and fathers to save money and lend it to the government to help our gallant soldiers and sailors who are fighting to save our liberties and our country, your mothers and fathers will listen to you and take your advice.[75]

Recruiting school children as propagandists to spread government ideology is, of course, nothing new. As public education became widespread, politicians worldwide turned to the schools to establish and promote government doctrine. Third Republic France before World War I established mandatory public educa-tion, and through the schools transmitted its version of democracy. But in the United States, authorities faced a dilemma peculiar to public education as it was established by United States law and custom. France controlled schools through federal government authority, and so could dictate curriculum and hire teachers whose loyalty was unquestioned. American schools were independent. One hundred thousand local school boards in forty-eight states dictated teacher hires and classroom content. Authorities could not be sure teachers were uniformly patriotic. They could not tell school boards what to teach. In a land whose mass communication consisted primarily of publications sent in the mail, they could not even easily reach local principals and teachers they hoped to influence. As David M. Kennedy noted, "The decentralized character of American education meant that the struggle to control teaching about the war had to be waged in countless local actions, in communities scattered across the country."[76]

Despite the challenges of local control, schools were considered the best way to reach and so draw together the American people, hyphenated or not, in a big country geographically and culturally divided. Possibly there could be no single better way to emulsify the salad bowl of 1917 into one nation, indivisible, than to devise a plan to band the schools into working together. The question was how to coordinate the remote many into the patriotic one. To begin, the Committee on Public Information was called on to coordinate efforts of a variety of public and private groups. The CPI as avowed propaganda division of the federal government may have given Commissioner of Education Philander Claxton pause; at the beginning of the war he "resisted all attempts to propagandize in the schools, and he encouraged the nation's teachers to maintain their normal educational program."[77] But early in the last century propaganda was still evolving, and did not have a negative connotation. CPI director George Creel, a former newspaper reporter, reflected Wilson's hope that the propaganda bureau would be a force for good in America—a way to counter German evil by encouraging patriotism through thrift, health, duty, sacrifice, and civic virtue. "The CPI reflected their naive faith in the integrity of the American government and its leaders and in the power of ideas to transform men and society," concluded Vaughn in his CPI history. Such values could hardly conflict with those of education. Claxton realized the need to reach local schools, and so in February 1918 authorized the CPI to create a bulletin for schools under direction of Guy Stanton Ford.[78]

Ford was University of Minnesota graduate dean when called to become director of the CPI Division of Civic and Educational Publications. The historian had no formal background in elementary/secondary education, but as a respected scholar of national stature became the voice of education through the CPI. Speaking to the NEA, he called the CPI "a war emergency national university."

Denying it was attempting either repression or censorship, he claimed in June 1918 that already twenty-five million pieces of literature had been distributed to the schools. These brochures of the CPI's War Information Service included such titles as "The War Message," "The Great War," "American Interests," "The Government of Germany," and "The President's Flag Day Address." "This is the sort of thing that the government sends out and desires you to have," advised Harvard professor Albert Bushnell Hart, a noted historian of the era,[79] although one educator at the time did call the blizzard of publications from the government "vast and confusing."[80] But that was just the beginning. Emphasizing the importance of using children to reach American households, Ford said, "The teacher is enlisted in this war, and more and more the morale of the nation and the thinking in its homes will be determined by what she knows and teaches in this supreme crisis." The schools, along with the CPI, "have a great common war task to make an Americanized, nationalized American nation."[81]

Ford and Creel aimed many CPI publications at schools, but needed still was a way to directly speak to teachers and principals. The answer as proposed by Claxton's office was a weekly newsletter. This could respond to the NEA's request for a national clearinghouse to centralize propaganda flooding the schools. The *National School Service*, subtitled "Published by the Committee on Public Information," Volume One, Number One, was issued September 1, 1918. While Ford was official editor, the publication was mostly edited by J. W. Searson, a Columbia University English professor.[82] The first issue argued (in an unsigned editorial), "The study of the war should form a part of the school course," and offering specific ways the curriculum could be adjusted to do that. Based on a booklet offered to the schools, a sample curriculum for grades three and four might include:

(1) Stories of War Incidents.
(2) Celebration of Special Holidays.
(3) Handicaps of German Boys and Girls.
(4) Why the United States Entered the War.
(5) What the Government Has Accomplished in the War.
(6) Our Soldiers and Sailors.
(7) How Children Can Help.[83]

Other issues emphasized teaching methods and topics the government hoped children would ingest, and repeat at home. One of these was distinctly different from those proposed by education authorities: hate. Information given to instruct children included strongly anti-German material and stories of German atrocities obviously designed to appeal to emotional outrage. The CPI included quite a few during the short life of the *National School Service*, these with a particular slant toward children. One such example, entitled, "Sell Your Children or Let Them Die. The Cold-Blooded Prussian System as Revealed in Poland, Belgium, and Serbia," described a proclamation of Germany to Poland that mothers send their children to Germany for education, to be paid 150 marks ($37.50) for a boy, and 100 marks ($25) for a girl. "The obvious purpose of the German government," the article continued, "was to exterminate the Polish population and to repeople the land with Germans."[84] While enemy atrocity stories were commonplace in adult media and can be considered one reason the United States declared war, World War I commercial publications aimed at children used few, and children did not seem to respond well to them. It is hard to escape the presumption that *National School Service* planted such material with an eye to reaching parents through complicity of children. While Claxton feared a disreputable CPI propaganda blast into the schools, denied by both Ford and Creel, the reality was that material did sometimes dip into that category.

Did this material reach an intended audience of parents in the homes? It is uncertain. Vaughn noted the publication was distributed to teachers, and not directly to children.[85] While the bulletin did not end until May 1919, CPI released it from its control about a month after the war ended, with the December 15, 1918, issue. In that issue Ford wrote that the *National School Service* was circulated to 600,000 teachers: "The war and the deeper meaning it has attached to America and to American citizenship have crowned the teacher with new dignity and given to the schools a new importance."[86] The figure of 600,000, given a wartime CPI run of fourteen weeks from September 1 to December 15, would total 8,400,000 issues distributed. However, Creel himself reported slightly more than half that actually were distributed: 4,251,570.[87] It is difficult to say how many issues actually reached parents; probably few, although certainly it was read by teachers anxious to formulate lesson plans loyally reflecting authorities' goal of Americanization.

## Teaching and the Taint of Disloyalty

But what about the extent of that loyalty? This second central question also could not easily be answered considering that 622,000 teachers (75.4 percent female) worked for local school boards independent of central influence.[88] Authorities in Washington could not directly control local teachers in an American educational landscape habitually distrustful of federal meddling in local schools. Government concern was reasonable. Pacifist strands within schools had been woven tightly throughout American education by such formerly popular organizations as the American School Peace League. It boasted branches in forty states, and an extensive school peace literature and study program. Socialists, whose opposition to a "capitalist war" was presumed, had been represented throughout school districts, particularly those of the Upper Midwest. "Even this great body but two short years ago had for its slogan the peace idea," a speaker reminded NEA members in July 1917, "and so strong was the sentiment and so far-reaching was its influence that many a teacher felt that it would be a disloyal act to have her children sing a martial song, or even to have them march in any of their exercises."[89]

At the war declaration, most teachers, like most Americans, declared themselves to be unstintingly patriotic. But authorities as late as a year later felt it necessary to remind them. "The teachers of the youth of America should be of outspoken loyalty," wrote one university president in a professional teachers' magazine. "No teacher should be employed for whom an apology is necessary. Every teacher should be a citizen of this country. Those of foreign birth should be so completely naturalized that all trace of the hyphen has been removed."[90] States and local governments were left to assure this loyalty as they wished. Many moved aggressively to do so, particularly targeting teachers whose loyalty could be most obviously questioned. Pacifists and socialists, even those who nearly fell in prostration below their superintendents' desks to declare their love of war and country, could be suspect—to keep their jobs they might be fibbing. New York State in particular watched meticulously for signs of prevarication. Declaring that no dissent of any kind could be permitted, the New York School Board required teachers to sign a pledge, to "declare our unqualified allegiance to the government of the United States of America, and pledge ourselves by word and example to teach and impress upon our pupils the duty of loyal obedience and patriotic service, as the highest ideal of American citizenship."[91]

The idea that such rule-oriented "obedience" ought to be the "highest ideal" obviously struck some educators as ironic. "The only way we can train citizens for democracy is through democracy, but our school system is an autocracy—autocratic in every phase of its organization," wrote a Chicago teacher in 1919, after the war had ended.[92] During the war such public criticism led to swift retribution. One rare teacher who complained in public about military training concluded, "As socialist and Quaker teachers in this city have been dismissed for expressing their opinions please permit me to sign myself A Socialist Teacher."[93] In fact, three Jewish socialist teachers were fired from New York's DeWitt Clinton High School for attempting to maintain neutrality in their classes, out of ten sacked throughout the school system.[94] Another case involved a woman named Mary McDowell, openly Quaker and so pacifist. She was fired after eighteen years of New York City teaching for "conduct unbecoming a teacher."[95] Even Fannie Fern Andrews, founder of the American School Peace League, excised the P word in favor of war values, changing the group's title to American School Citizenship League. Andrews volunteered for the CPI, helping the government in its hunt for the not-quite-loyal in education.[96] Many of her former supporters were appalled, and distanced themselves from her efforts, quietly. While we have no national statistics regarding World War I teachers fired for insufficient patriotism, probably such cases were uncommon, given a social climate in which any whiff of mere neutrality could be dangerous. In fact, the cases cited in New York represented a tiny percentage of its 22,000 public school teachers.

Also concerning were teachers whose subject was German. Declaration of war, and the alacrity in which the country fell into line behind its leaders, had in its emotional flip side the reflexive loathing of anyone or anything German. This came as a catastrophe to the legions of American immigrants from German-speaking lands, to their influential German-language press, to their cultural practices borrowed from the Old Country. It came as much of a disaster to German language teachers. Observing the national "revulsion" against teaching of German, one educator advised, "It is very important, however, that the teachers of German in our secondary schools and colleges be men and women of undoubted loyalty. This will mean that in general they will not be of German blood or if of German blood, far removed from the Fatherland."[97] This was difficult, as many of those who knew German well enough to teach were indeed of German extraction. During their peak years of immigration between 1880-1895, 1,850,610 Germans had immigrated to American shores, by far the largest percentage of immigrants during that period.[98] They formed an important and influential minority. The New York school board admitted as much, as it eliminated German from the public schools, observing, "The effective teaching of German must...be done by teachers of German origin, and it is a question whether at this crisis this is for the best interests of the pupils who are to be trained in the study of Americanism."[99]

Claxton originally took the rational approach that German should remain in the schools. "The fact that we are now at war with Germany should not, I believe, affect in any way our policies in regard to the teaching of the German

language in our schools," Claxton protested. "The United States is at war with
the Imperial Government of Germany and not with the German language or
literature.... We can not as a people afford to put ourselves in the attitude of
regarding as evil everything about any people with whom we may happen to be
at war."[100] But Claxton faced powerful adversaries determined to extirpate the
tainted language, and school board after school board moved to ban German,
including some of the largest. Referring to one of the most well-publicized decisions, in Chicago, a Kansas educator wrote, "How, then, may we best contribute
to the restoration of reason? Certainly not by argument. Passion is not wont to
yield to argument. The proper attitude must be cultivated above all by a sensible
and discreet attitude on the part of the teacher himself."[101] The author admitted
students themselves were refusing to sign up for German. Many did so from
patriotic irrationalism as reflected by communities and their school boards, but
beyond that, children who persisted in German study hazarded harassment and
accusation. The inevitable result for German teachers who had no students left
in their classrooms was lay-off, unless they could be accommodated in other
departments.

The Americanism authorities wanted children to bring to their homes obviously did not include German language and culture. It did include specific
patriotic subjects, or patriotism as a subject itself. The New York school board
prescribed it to every child beginning at age eight. "War studies" courses came
to the schools by way of the CPI, as "'Patriotism, heroism, and sacrifice' were
made the themes of the suggested study plan for elementary school children."[102]
One authority did suggest the burden of teaching patriotism along with everything else a teacher was asked to do might seem difficult. But actually, "There
is nothing mysterious about patriotism. It is made up of the homely old virtues
that everyone knows all about." Those virtues included honesty, courtesy, courage and obedience—the same virtues required of a soldier. "Obedience is exacted
from soldiers to the last hair's breadth. Obedience to laws and reverence for government are the essence of civilization. Require as much from your children."
But how can a conscientious wartime teacher teach such virtues? "Certainly not
by a little morning lecture on the moral virtues. Most certainly not! Example
is better far than precept and thirty children at least watch you every day and
see your every word and motion. Are you living and moving as a patriot every
day?"[103]

While such soldier's virtues were widespread parts of suggested World
War I school curriculum, absent were such virtues as tolerance and freedom of
speech. Disloyal was to question or discuss. These qualities were not included

in the NEA's "war platform," approved at its 1918 national convention. In fact, the document sustained local school board efforts in its demands for uncompromising oaths of loyalty and patriotic teaching. Its title, "Americanizing the Adult Population," clearly portrays the role authorities expected children to play as home-front missionaries for Mars, the god of war:

> The association demands the teaching of patriotism by every teacher from the kindergarten to the university, and the employment of only those teachers who are loyal to our national ideals. It urges that all teachers as soldiers of the common good take the oath of allegiance. The association further demands that all instruction in the schools of the nation be conducted in the English language.[104]

Still, not all educators of that time publicly threw themselves gung-ho into the drive for patriotism in the public schools. Teaching patriotism to kindergarteners? One stopped for a moment to reflect on what that meant, and came up short of good arguments. "Absolutely worthless is the fad to compel children of the kindergarten, children between the ages of four and six years, to memorize and recite the pledge. According to my humble opinion, this is all wrong; the method of teaching loyalty penetrated only skin deep." In fact, even for the older children, compelling the Pledge of Allegiance, salute to the flag, and singing of the National Anthem was worth cavil: "It has in many schools degenerated into a mechanical affair. These exercises at present do not make for loyalty."[105] It is worth noting, however, that this teacher risked speaking out publicly only after the war's end. Others hoped to tie patriotism to the liberal arts neglected in the drive to wartime vocationalism. In a speech entitled "Patriotism in the Schools," the president of a Wisconsin normal school advocated "the sacred obligation of the schools to instill the love of country into the hearts of the growing generation" could be managed best "through the teaching of art and literature, of music and history, of public speaking and debating."[106]

The decision of authorities to rely on school children as a way to reach adults at home seems mostly to have been a World War I effort. Authorities in World War II apparently did not see as compelling a need. This may have been based on unusual circumstances during the previous war. The World War I fear of social disruption in a society fractured by ideological extremes was at its base a fear of an unusually high immigrant population. In the 1930s and 1940s, immigration was low, and it has never again reached the level of the turn of the last century. This does not mean the United States Government did not fear immigrants, of course. Most Americans know the sad story of Japanese-American internment. That extreme was not taken against German-Americans in 1917-18. During World War II, authorities considering what school children should take home from their wartime education did not include propaganda for the parents. They did, of course, still believe in teaching patriotism, and did often fear critical thought. "Educational philosophies and theories that do not contribute to industrial production, civilian well-being and morale, or other war needs should be discarded for the duration," argued William Loomis of the U.S. Office of Education in 1943. "The schools can do much to instill patriotic enthusiasm in potential workers for war industries."[107]

World War II authorities showed greater caution in claiming through war the benefits of patriotism and development of character. People in charge of children recalled the mistakes of World War I, and one of them was perceived to be over-emphasis on shallow virtue that would not lead to a more peaceful postwar era. "Education faces the responsibility of helping people to live effectively under the new world conditions. But our past concepts and practices in education mislead us," wrote the president of Montana State University. "The new education must give our boys and girls as well as adults a true picture of the world in which we are living. It must face human problems on a global basis. It must avoid narrow nationalism and isolationism."[108] Added another educator, "The best teaching of patriotism avoids the teaching of hatred. It is well for us to say we will not teach hatred even for our enemies. It might be a quite different problem to keep hatred from creeping into the minds of children."[109] A federally produced booklet designed to guide elementary school teachers recommended "a moderate, reasonable and wise appeal" to patriotism.[110] In particular, World War II authorities expressly and repeatedly warned against teaching hate. "As educators we hold that hate need not enter into the curriculum of the day," declared the New York commissioner of education.[111] "Should we not be resolved to try to keep their basic convictions concerning the nature of their world as healthy and unembittered and unwarped by fear or hate as possible?" asked the United States commissioner of education, speaking to the NEA.[112] In both wars, however, these more sober authorities competed against commercial media and advertisers. Popular media fed a natural tendency of children to hate the enemy as reflecting their parents and society—marbled through as it was with enemy hatred and racism in both wars.

## The Libraries

Authorities in education relied as their support centers on the repositories of American published media, and the librarians were only too happy to join in. The country's sprawl of many thousands of independent libraries—7,000 by World War II—had long focused on drawing children to their resources. But children did not always find the public library to be their most attractive after-school option. A war might help. "The war presents a great opportunity to the workers with children to stimulate an interest in history and to arouse and quicken a true sense of patriotism," wrote a World War I children's librarian in Boston.[113] The key to attracting children was to offer the kind of material they wanted to look at, as well as a central location for volunteer activities.

Originally when the United States joined World War I, libraries were considered to be possible locations for recruiting stations, but that practical role during wartime turned out to be not nearly as useful as their role as depository for propaganda. The American Library Association meeting in 1942 borrowed from Roosevelt's "arsenal of democracy" speech to explain that the country's thousands of libraries "be converted into arsenals for national defense, as war information centers."[114] Such centers would collect material of interest to readers, and motivate children and adults alike to learn more about the war and the part the United States Government played in it. "The school library has impressively demonstrated its function as materials-center for the school's war programs," noted one librarian, adding that although children's librarians were trying to acquire a variety of material, "older adolescents remain most interested in the contemporary account of contemporary affairs, and some dislike to read anything else."[115] World War I librarians hoped to attract children they admitted were more interested in war work than reading by setting up informational and patriotic war displays. But many decided to jump on the war as a good way to promote their resources. "The war presents a great opportunity to the workers with children to stimulate an interest in history and to arouse and quicken a true sense of patriotism," wrote a Boston librarian, while a Detroit librarian noted, "The newly awakened interests, the dramatic events have their unsettling effects upon the young."

Libraries could respond with exhibits explaining food conservation, Americanization, war gardens or bond sales, post newspapers and photos, or offer war-related book lists and illustrations. A Saturday wartime story hour was attended by 100 in Norwich, New York, while, "Stories of Our Allies," produced by the Philadelphia Free Library children's department, attracted 56,916 children in six months of 1917, according to library reports.[116] The St. Louis library used Rudyard Kipling's poem in a wartime setting surrounded with Allied flags,[117] the poem "The Children's Song," ending:

> Land of our Birth, our faith, our pride,
> For whose dear sake our fathers died;
> O Motherland, we pledge to thee
> Head, heart and hand through the years to be![118]

Some World War I libraries took a more active approach, presaging their central World War II role by becoming a clearing house for war-related activities as well as publications. The Sioux City, Iowa, public library served as a headquarters for children's Liberty Bond sales, by dramatically illustrating sales as a series of black lines depicting trenches. A war stamp would advance the buyer through the trench toward Berlin, indicated by a stick pin. Children reaching Berlin were given a "baby bond," a red stripe for their stick pin and a chance to again begin the figurative journey toward buying the full Liberty Bond.[119]

As for the more substantial reading available to older children and adults who wished to learn about the war, World War I libraries veered from attempting traditional neutrality to throwing away anything smacking of disloyalty. Early in the war American libraries became prime targets for those who wished to persuade Americans to join a side. The German embassy circulated a variety of pamphlets and readings arguing its case and emphasizing German cultural achievements. Also subsidized, secretly, were American writers who disliked the British, and anti-war activists such as David Starr Jordan, first president of Stanford University.[120] But German ambassador Johann Von Bernstorff had to contend with pro-German sympathizers such as the flamboyant German-born George Sylvester Viereck, who became a paid German apologist swamping America's libraries with his *Fatherland* during the neutral period. Self-styled as "America's foremost interpreter of Germany," he did much to discredit its World War I propaganda.[121]

As the country stumbled from neutrality to pro-Allies, librarians found it impossible to keep his material from being stolen. Meanwhile British propaganda countered with its own swamping of American libraries, some of its writers also secretly supported. But it was willing to be more transparent in its efforts, and so was not as discredited. After the United States declared war, most librarians happily dropped any pretense of neutrality and packed the shelves with patriotic literature supporting the Allied side. Readings considered to be pro-

German, even if philosophical or written in the German language, along with pacifist and socialist material were removed, and sometimes burned.[122] Control of children's reading was the imperative of the World War I librarian: Books could be dangerous. Clara Hunt, superintendent of the children's department of the Brooklyn, New York, Public Library, told members of the ALA that the wrong books could "reduce a child's thinking powers to pulp and make him an easy prey to the leadership of whatever form of Prussianism flourishes anywhere disguised under some other name."[123]

Librarians, like teachers, were in close contact with children and so particularly carefully scrutinized by the communities for which they worked. Few of their employers showed tolerance for anything less than extreme exhibitions of loyalty, and like teachers, librarians were fired for exhibiting the improper spirit. In one case, a Portland, Oregon, library assistant was forced to resign for "disloyalty" after her refusal to buy war bonds caused a public outcry.[124]

Librarians in World War II did not feature the overt propaganda and implicit censorship that marked World War I, but also they did not move to strongly reassert a role independent from official propagandists. The American Library Association in early 1942 set up a Committee on War Information and Education Services, chaired by Ralph M. Dunbar. In a formal declaration, the association emphasized, "Manipulations of the truth for any reason, public hysteria or indifference, overconfidence or despair, will impair the national war effort," and so promised to provide "not only trustworthy facts but reasoned interpretation."[125] This principle admirably stated seems to have been made in tacit acknowledgment of the embarrassing role as censor played by libraries in World War I. However, it must be noted the statement was made in the official publication produced by the government's Office of Education.

In June 1942 the association announced it would collaborate with Washington's propaganda office, the Office of War Information, "in an institute on war problems for librarians."[126] This turned out to be a full-fledged partnership, the libraries becoming the government's central clearing house for its materials. One Delaware school library was commended for its "constant contact with the Office of War Information and its posting of bulletins and broadsides which contribute most to the war effort. Our library has truly [word missing, "become?"] a miniature War Information Office."[127] According to a Carnegie Corporation-sponsored 1942 study of libraries, the war information office role was interpreted as depository for myriad government publications examining United States democratic principles, war questions, postwar concerns, history, politics, and biography. In addition, libraries stocked stories that could serve to inspire adolescent boys who would soon be drafted. These might help to "satisfy student urges to experience vicariously the thrill and danger of combat and to acquaint themselves more fully with the men and machinery of battle." For adolescents facing a certain call to be a warrior, libraries would supply "detailed information about the various branches of service and the requirements for admission to each."

In addition to their book collections, libraries continued to play a role common in World War I, providing a center for applications and record-keeping serving students in salvage drives, war bond campaigns, and the High School Victory Corps. In some cases they wrote and displayed service records of former students. The Victory Books Campaign sponsored by the nation's libraries encouraged children to donate books for servicemen.[128] As the Office of War Information and libraries united "to interpret OWI to libraries and libraries to OWI,"[129] it is inconceivable that material promoted for children included tales of pacifism or stories showing a war not of thrills and adventure, but of terrors and despair. That is, war as it was, and as it is. But would the boy in 1942 eager to do his part in defeating an enemy as evil as were the villains of his comic book world care to pursue the truth? And if he would not, would a librarian feel a duty to thrust the truth under his nose? Not likely, as it threatened a critical underlying motivation of authorities in promoting war to children: to maintain home-front morale.

War wasn't like the stories in the library, as soldiers found out. Libraries did not present war honestly to children, especially those who would soon join the troops. But honestly is scant motivation for anything, and particularly not for battle. Many motivating values were employed for the sake of the children in the world wars: duty, service, sacrifice, heroism, responsibility, patriotism, citizenship, obedience, loyalty, fitness, even reverence. But not honesty.

### Fitness for War

Of these virtues physical fitness became one of the most consistently supported for children during both wars. In 1917 and 1940, the military draft measured the fitness of American youth using objective standards. Such an enormous evaluation on a national scale could not be undertaken during peacetime, and so no one had a solid idea of young Americans' physical abilities. It was presumed, however, that girls and particularly boys were active enough, and so must be physically fit. The truth came as a shock: American children appeared to be budding sloths. Of 2.5 million men examined for service in 1917, 34 percent were rejected as physically unfit, 30 to 40 percent for defects that could have been corrected in childhood. Of those accepted a large number "were lacking in the strength, endurance and general organic power necessary for intensive military training. This was a surprise, as before the draft, no one knew of the state of American men." A Bureau of Education authority emphasized that many physical defects could have been remedied during school years. Those without defect still had "a large amount of undeveloped physical capacity, all of which could have been developed during school years."[130]

Specific problems cited by World War I authorities included a variety of ailments by then treatable. "Sixty percent of the rejected men owe their impairments to either ignorance or neglect," concluded a university researcher who analyzed military records. "Bad teeth; defective vision; mouth infections, with the direful constitutional effects; flat feet and other foot deformities—reflections of faulty shoes; improper posture and muscular impairment; hernia; malnutrition following chronic infections such as tuberculosis, hookworm, etc.—all more or less preventable or curable—were among the chief causes of rejection." He emphasized these diseases were preventable, as well as "various specific infections, notably those of childhood." Less related to poor childhood fitness and hygiene were tuberculosis, typhoid, and venereal disease.[131]

What to do? School fitness training and health screening could save children from becoming vigor-challenged adults, while forming a healthy pool of young men ready to serve the country's military. New York State served to provide a model, in 1916 passing the Welsh-Slator Bill requiring three hours' training, both physical and military, per week at school for boys sixteen to nineteen. The problem became apparent: during the World War I era only about 15 percent of the nation's five million boys that age were still in school. Such a program focusing only on the secondary schools could set up "an exclusive military class, set apart, in his capacity to be trained for national service, from the employed boy of the same years." (In 1917 the law was amended to include all boys.) In practice funding did not match legislative enthusiasm, and the policy worked "imperfectly."[132]

Other authorities realized fitness education needed to start earlier than high school, when educators could still reach all children, building good habits while remedying defects for peace as well as war. "It is the duty of national government to prescribe and enforce a progressive course of bodily training for every child in the country," said Charles W. Eliot, president emeritus of Harvard University, in a speech. "The great war teaches this, but the needs of peace also require it. No child should escape it, unless incapacitated by disease, accident,

or malformation."[133] In declaring a Children's Year beginning April 1918, the
U.S. Children's Bureau reminded the country that part of child welfare ought
to be child fitness. "The same tidal wave of interest in physical education for
the higher grades has at last swept over the land for the children of kindergarten age," observed a New York kindergarten supervisor.[134] However, apparently
neither she nor Eliot brought background in physical education to their declarations. Eliot actually opposed team sports at Harvard, declaring in particular that
a sport such as hockey requires teamwork, and "I have no use for a game that
requires that."[135]

W. S. Small, Office of Education hygiene specialist, noted, "The physical
and moral values of both gymnastics and athletics are well understood, but both
lack comprehensive and unifying motive.... The philosophy of athletics is the
philosophy of play, and the philosophy of play is the philosophy of instinct—a
philosophy that is not comprehensive enough to serve as a sole basis of physical
and moral education.[136]

But the weight of Eliot's prestige alone must have encouraged physical education instructors. Health and physical education before World War I were not
taken seriously, and opinions of its instructors generally held little repute within
the educational establishment. The war gave new prestige to the field. Teachers
of sports and physical education were buoyed by their close liaisons with advocates of school-based military training for preparedness. Good health became a
duty, and those whose teaching responsibilities covered that area became leaders
for a larger cause. "Health is taken out of the field of merely personal concern,
and made a duty one owes to the nation," wrote the CPI-published *National
School Service*. "If we are to be a strong and worthy nation, we must be strong
and worthy individually."[137] Small described specifically what was expected of
boys: "An intensive and varied program of physical training under discipline
to develop strength, endurance, muscular skill, alertness, cooperation under
leadership, and the other physical and social qualities essential alike in military
or civil pursuits." But what about girls? "Everything I have asked for the boys I
ask for the girls. Racially the educated vigor of woman is more important than
that of man."[138]

While authorities during World War I had not developed specific measures
for the health and fitness they were seeking, states responded anyway by imple-
menting new programs to make children more healthy and fit. In 1918 and the
years after thirty-six states passed laws requiring physical education in school,
and thirty-seven passed laws requiring medical inspection of children.[139] The
definition of physical education varied, however, depending on what authorities

dominated.

Considering athletics as a way to universal fitness in both peace and war, proponents pointed out that competitive sports could not only make a boy more fit, but could instill an ability to work within a team, against an enemy—excellent preparation for soldiering. Military discipline, teamwork, physical skills, health and happiness could come with sports competition, playing a game as a quasi-military contest. "The organization and promotion of athletic competition conducted with participants arranged and maneuvered in military formation are becoming universal in the American army training camps," observed one educator in 1918.[140] World War I Secretary of War Newton Baker agreed, "It plays an important part in developing the youth of the day, and the beneficial results may be seen from our experience with the training camps.... I was amazed at the ease with which these young men adapted themselves to military life."[141] Secretary of the Navy Josephus Daniels, a frequent contributor to educational and popular magazines exhorting the healthful values of military service, agreed, but only if boys were more aggressively encouraged to participate. "Americans in general are not participants; they are 'fans,'" he observed, concluding that this emphasis on spectator sports had "vitally injured the physical development of the students of American high schools and universities for it has bred a race of vicarious sportsmen."[142] "If we have athletes, we shall never be without soldiers," concluded a West Point military training instructor.[143]

Presumably an acute awareness of fitness woes during World War I, followed by numerous attempts to improve children's fitness and health, would have left authorities more confident a generation later. They were—until they again discovered the truth on instituting a draft in 1940. Children still were not fit; authorities still fretted the consequences. The drift during the interwar period away from military values had as a consequence a renewed disdain for physical fitness education and its proponents. The Great Depression of 1929 spelled the end of "frills" in school curricula, and particularly targeted was physical education. "School budgets were slashed and many programs were wrecked," concluded a Kansas administrator in a 1942 report.[144] Despite this, again the apparent sloth among youth took authorities by surprise. At a national NEA "war fitness conference" of 1,200 health and physical education leaders meeting April 1943, Colonel L. G. Rowntree, chief of the medical division of the U.S. Selective Service, explained the problem directly: "We are accustomed to regard ourselves as a healthy, vigorous nation—full of rugged young men in the pink of physical condition. But what are the facts? They are disappointing.... [ellipses in original] In the first two million men examined, one million were rejected for physical and mental defects or educational deficiencies."

In fact, added Rowntree,  many of those inducted "are totally unprepared for military life. It takes weeks to bring them into the physical condition necessary for military training. This means weeks of wasted time and effort which could be avoided, if every young man now in high school would engage in physical activities."[145] Jay B. Nash, a New York University professor of education and chair of the university's physical education, health and recreation department, blamed American society for caring little about the physical well-being of its youth. He called the diet and exercise habits of American children a disgrace:

> We have carried spectatoritis to an excess never before witnessed.... In one cross section selected from the highest 13 percent according to scholarship, some 60 odd percent could not chin themselves three times and over 40 percent could not chin themselves once. Eighty percent had remediable defects. Only a smattering of these young men would have been accepted by the Army, practically none by the Air Corps.[146]

Brigadier General Joe N. Dalton, speaking on the NBC-radio "Army Hour" on April 11, 1943, called the pathetically low fitness of American boys an issue "of tremendous importance." Others both in the military and out laid blame on "progressive education" in the schools for failing to keep children fit. Lieutenant Franklin R. Fielding, Navy liaison to the U.S. Office of Education, added the government expected girls planning to enter the military to be fit as well.[147]

In response, to begin with, authorities decided to encourage children to walk more by taking their bus seats away: the Office of Defense Transportation in 1942 forbade school buses to carry students who lived within two miles of school.[148] Adolescent recreation was recast to a more challenging standard. "As preinduction preparation, adolescents were to be made tough. Commando tactics were introduced to the play of adolescents," observed a YMCA national director in 1944. Youth groups such as the Y, the High School Victory Corps, and boys' clubs "had high school boys scaling walls, running obstacles, swimming under water under covering substituting for burning oil, and wrestling and boxing."[149] Encouraging victory gardens and farm work also could keep younger children busy in fitness-building ways, while less bookish work and more childish play might bring youth to at least a respectable level.

But authorities quickly admitted that piecemeal responses could not remediate millions of unfit children. The situation was thought to be worth more serious study. A long (unsigned) article in the U.S. Office of Education-sponsored magazine *Education for Victory* lay blame on local school districts and taxpayers who have "verbally emphasized the importance of correcting health defects and developing physical fitness but have too frequently failed to provide needed funds or to put into practice beliefs advocated." What local districts seemed most to care about, the critic noted, was high school athletics, "while doing nothing for the other 90 percent of students." The report did note that boys enrolled in high school phys ed programs had increased slightly, from 43.8 in 1942 to 50.1 percent in 1943, and girls enrolled from 42.2 to 46.7 percent. But it was uncertain if this was significant. Meanwhile, it was noted that of the 273,000 teachers who left the profession between 1941 and 1943 for war work or service, "a large number" were phys ed teachers.[150]

To find a fast and efficient way to deal with flabby children facing a wartime need for fitness, authorities realized they would have to consider what no one had been able to establish during the last war: just what is good health? What is physical fitness? And, at least as established by the military, what is unhealthy and unfit? World War II military statistics produced the most specific health-related reasons for 4-F Status, that is, the men who were rejected outright. In order of prevalence, they were: "1. Diseases of the eye. 2. Mental deficiencies." The report added that for African-Americans, number one was "mental deficiencies," two was "diseases of the eye," and three was "syphilis."[151] In 1942 of the 30 percent rejected, bad teeth and eyesight accounted for one-third.

How could schools address such deficiencies? Perhaps they couldn't. A child development specialist argued that if the major causes for rejection were "defective teeth, then poor eyesight and a number of other handicaps not easy remedied or even preventable by present-day knowledge," then neither fitness training nor military drill in the schools would make any difference. As for "neurological disorders and personality disturbances," the author contended these begin in early childhood and also cannot be addressed by physical or military training. Moreover, the author added, a "large reason" for rejection was illiteracy, "due to lack of even elementary schooling in some states," and physical training could do nothing about that.[152]

In 1944 a physician took another stab at setting standards for good health in children. Dr. Arthur Steinhaus explained, "He should know when and how to eat, and he must provide satisfactory evidence that he successfully regulates his bowel movements without recourse to medication in any form," along with being "reasonably free from nervous instability."[153] Measurements of "good health" for children remained a nebulous concept open to a variety of interpretations. Authorities interested in fitness moved to define what could more easily be measured and more quickly be remedied in children and adolescents. While

World War II authorities did not establish precise measurement scales generally for children's well-being, they did find more success setting scales for physical fitness. In 1943 *Education for Victory* proposed, "A person is said to be physically fit when he is free from handicapping defects and disease, follows good health practices, and has the knowledge, skills, strength, endurance, and will to do effectively the maximum tasks of the day."[154]

However, this still provided no precise scale. In July 1944, the publication lamented, "The importance of physical fitness is heavily emphasized in this publication, more in total than any other topic.... It is difficult, however, to find a place where specific measures of physical fitness are indicated."[155] A month later, a staff member of the University of Pittsburgh physical education department offered a specific scale of what children were expected to do to be called fit. Based on a 450-boy sample and targeted to male adolescents, it indicated these averages as adopted by the High School Victory Corps:

Sit-ups, straight leg, each completed at 2-second cadence. Average should be 31-39; top level is 89-95.

Hanging half-lever, hang from a bar and raise legs straight out. Average is 12-18; top level is 40-46.

Leg lift, lie on floor and raise legs to 90 degrees. Average is 21-36; top is 63-94.

Forward bend, a straight-knee toe-touch. Average is 96-123; top end is 199-201.

Bank twist, lie on back with legs at 90 degrees, twist to touch the legs to each side. Average is 17-34; top end is 67-112.[156]

Another standard was set in New York City for boys in the Junior Commando Program: pick up and carry own weight 100 yards; chin 10 times; running broad jump 16 feet; run a mile in six minutes.[157] *Education* reminded readers that one military definition of "poor coordination" in children was "cannot climb a rope, carry a burden equal to their own weight, or vault out of a trench the height of their chests."[158] While the age of children expected to meet these high standards was not indicated, obviously elementary-age children could not do these things, and probably early adolescents were not ready. Regarding these standards, *Education* noted children fifteen and under "should not be stimulated or urged to achieve the levels of performance in strength and endurance attained by trained soldiers."[159] No standards for younger children or girls were presented.

Daily physical fitness classes were set up in many schools, particularly for high school boys presumed to be soon of draftable age. In Washington, D.C., high school boys and girls participated in five periods of physical fitness weekly; the boys added army calisthenics.[160] *Education* recommended a program "directed definitely toward the conditioning of high-school pupils for service in the armed forces and industry and agriculture." In addition to a daily phys ed class, students should spend at least ten hours a week participating in sports, as well as "road work, hikes, weekend journeys, camping, hard physical work such as plowing, cutting wood, or digging dirt, and similar activities."[161] Considering these children were also expected to attend their classes, volunteer for scrap and war bond drives, and perhaps work part-time jobs, sleep appeared expendable.

Some World War I physical educators and coaches advocated sports as good not only for lifetime physical fitness, but for building physical skills useful to warriors. Their proponents resurfaced in World War II to talk up athletics as a solution to unfit children, who could be trained in an environment ideal for military needs. "Rugged sports" could meet strength needs better than the agricultural work often touted as a way to keep children fit. A football coach (unnamed) was quoted as saying, "You can't get any better training for the armed services than football."[162]

But critics continued to question athletics as a basis for physical fitness. One noted that well-known coaches were given high-ranking commissions when joining the military, while boys in service were given time off to practice. However, boys in football programs become exhausted, neglect their studies, become injured. Is the "ruggedness of football" the most desirable physical training for fitness at home and at the front? Asserted a writer from a Kansas teachers' college, "That in itself is doubtful."[163] Other authorities recommended using athletic facilities not for competitive sports, but for fitness training. *Education for Victory* recommended a football field be configured for children's fitness drills, setting up stations for shot put, leg lift, softball target throw, chinning bar, rope climb, running high jump, bar vault, rings, and one military option, "grenade throwing." For boys boxing and wrestling might be two useful sports to include, but teachers were "discouraged from promoting judo and other extremely hazardous or unsportsmanlike activities."[164] Another stressed swimming, proposing that Japanese troops had been successful in some battles because they were able to swim carrying full equipment.[165]

## The Virtue of Military Drills

But the debate over whether competitive sports made fitter children spilled into a larger issue, the single most controversial one regarding expectations of children during both wars: should children be required to undergo military training? This was related to sports because many of those promoting military drills in schools were coaches and physical education instructors. Those were most logical choices to teach such classes. In New York, phys ed instructors were targeted for orientation as military drill leaders through classes of the National Guard Schoolmens' Battalion; by 1917, 3,000 New York boys were trained under the public schools' Athletic League.[166] Physical education historically has had ties to military service; in fact, until modern times it was presumed that the only children who needed fitness training were those grooming for an army career. Before the United States joined World War I, proponents of school military training campaigned under the banner of preparedness, their leaders reflecting some of the nation's most famous, powerful and well-regarded. Those opposing were, of course, the peace groups, along with some religious and political groups and other writers. But when war came, it was too late to prepare; the country needed boys ready to go, and they were going to find them in the high schools. One might presume, then, that the debate over military training at the secondary level was over. It was not.

While everyone realized the older boys might be drafted—and maybe the younger ones too if the war lasted long enough—the question remained: were military training and drills the best ways to make them fit to serve? Proponents noted the positives. In addition to gains in physical fitness, children could learn through training military values such as promptness, industriousness, truthfulness, obedience, courage, mental strength. In short, it could make a boy into a man, and who would not want such quality of character in American manhood? Military training could cast character for a lifetime. Those in favor saw it as no less than a miracle solution to myriad physical and mental challenges of childhood. "From the standpoint of public health and national efficiency there can be no doubt of the prime importance—nay, absolute need—of a universal system of hygienic exercise and military drill to make our citizens what they should be mentally, morally, physically," argued a physician in a 1917 *New York Times Magazine*, "and to instill into them that pride of country and love of native land without which no nation can continue to flourish and command the respect of the world."[167] Military training might prepare a generation of adults for national service, whether it be war, or natural disaster at home. Both girls and boys should participate beginning at age sixteen: "For men, daily military exercises, and for women organized calisthenics, gymnastics, or a modified military drill."[168]

Even elementary school children could participate in an informal way. "The discipline of military drill can be made to tend to many other kinds of discipline," argued the California elementary school commissioner. "Obedience to all school regulations, to all civic laws, to all right customs, to all fair codes of youthful ethics, can be instilled along with the ardently adopted war discipline."[169] In 1917 the NEA adopted a resolution declaring, "Military training should be universal and compulsory and directed by the national government, and at its expense, and given by expert instructors provided by the national government." Affirming the training could be adjusted to age groups to encourage "health, strength, vigor, alertness, endurance, self-reliance, and self-control," the resolution also emphasized that such training should be taken during summer vacations, and not during the school year.[170]

The resolution was a disingenuous marvel, notably approved at the height of war fever three months after the war declaration. In fact, it clearly calls not for school-based military training, but for summer camps operated by the federal government. This is obviously not what proponents meant by compulsive military training in schools. In fact the NEA was dead set against military training and drill in schools, but emerged from prevarication only after the New Jersey Report.

The New Jersey Report was prepared based on experiences of other states requiring in-school military training, most obviously New York. That state during World War I was most prominent in its control of education by superpatriots determined to enact in implacably pro-military agenda. The 1916 state law requiring adolescents to bear practice arms in drills became an experiment closely watched by other states. New York Commissioner of Education John H. Finley in particular argued against such a law. "It seemed to me that it was perfectly impracticable, and would have been futile even if it had been practicable. Moreover, I thought it was psychologically bad. I opposed it with all the strength I had, and others with me."[171] While that bill passed anyway, Finley did agree with a provision of another that allowed some boys to undertake vocational training as an alternative. Nevertheless, he was correct in his prediction that a military training requirement was impracticable; most New York adolescents could think of things they'd rather do than go to after-school army drills. Because they were excused if they could provide an excuse, many did. "In some schools the majority of the students find they have engagements that always fall during the drill period," reported *School and Society*. "In the DeWitt Clinton and

Stuyvesant high schools it is stated by the military instructors that there appears to be a concerted effort on the part of many pupils to avoid drills."[172]

New York City school board minutes reported dismal statistics, compliance of more than half in only four schools, and many children refusing to wear school-purchased uniforms. In April 1918 a school board determined not to let its authority be undermined by obstreperous adolescents toughened its punishment for non-compliance, to no less than expulsion.[173] It is uncertain how well that worked. Obviously authorities in New York followed the one rule nearly universal to the story of America's wartime policies toward children: they never asked the kids. In fact, before the war the scattered opinions we can find from children regarding required military training indicated a fair number did not like the idea, although an early 1917 writing contest in *American Boy* indicated only 18 percent of its readers were against the drills.[174] Those who wrote to this publication may not have represented average adolescents, however. City children also tended to vote with their feet regarding high-profile programs designed to train them into agricultural work.

New Jersey looked to its neighboring state, undoubtedly, in preparing a well-publicized study on the value of military training in public schools. In the report commissioned by the state and presented to the governor in February 1918, the state's Commission on Military Training in High Schools determined such training to be a waste of time. Conclusions of the report found no good reason to bring military training into the schools, contending it does nothing positive to inculcate values such as obedience and patriotism, leads to "undesirable social distinctions," cannot properly train students for the life they will lead as adults, and tends to encourage students to drop out of school. What is more, while military drills might in some cases offer some physical benefits, they are not as efficient as physical fitness training, even for boys destined for the draft. "Military training in high schools has been proposed, not because it is wise, but because it is easy to use the machinery of the school system for the purpose."[175]

It was clear to the commission that not only did military training and drills do a poor job of developing physical fitness; it did equally a poor job of developing the much-vaunted virtues thought to come from a career as a warrior. Obedience, for example. "Obedience to military authority is generally unthinking. It is often blind and superficial, not real," according to the report. "It is obedience under restraint. When this is removed, laxity in discipline often follows.... It is a psychological fallacy to suppose that obedience to military authority, indeed, obedience exacted under any peculiar circumstances, may automatically be translated into the general habit of obedience." The report goes on to generalize that, in fact, military training doesn't help children learn any of the qualities of character ascribed to it by proponents. "The same may be said of such qualities as alertness, promptness, industry, truthfulness, etc. It is by no means capable of demonstration that those who have had military training, or been subject to military discipline, are superior to other citizens in the possession of those qualities."[176] Not even patriotism, the queen of good character as promoted by training advocates? Drawing heavily from the New Jersey report, the NEA's Committee on Military Training concluded, "we find that military patriotism may be no deeper and no more lasting than military obedience.... We must teach our pupils to make the passage from love of country to love of mankind, love of humanity, a transition which civilization teaches us to make, but which the spirit of military drill can not make, but rather tends to prevent."[177]

The New Jersey report, its unequivocal conclusions widely quoted, emboldened the NEA to add its weight of opposition to military training for children. In March 1917 its leaders formally declared their opposition to military training, and recommended members adopt a similar stance. "If it is necessary for us to resort to force, we are compelled to say, as we have said, that the obligation of military preparation should be borne by those who are capable of it, and that the age of those should be not less than nineteen."[178] The NEA considered specific military drills in both elementary and secondary schools as a separate issue, but was no less opposed. In formulating its decision, the association examined another state, Massachusetts. That state also set up a Special Commission on Military Education to examine three years of required military drills for children in a number of that state's cities. The Massachusetts report concluded, "The overwhelming weight of opinion from school teachers, military experts, officers of both the regular army and the militia, and the general public is against military drill. It is generally agreed that the military drill which a boy receives in school is of little or no advantage to him from the point of view of practical soldiering."[179]

The NEA observed that military training for children was not required in any European nation, and even Switzerland, often cited as a model, began training at age twenty. In the United States only one state, New York, required it, and there it did not work well. The NEA concluded, "it is an educational and moral offense to snatch him from the natural life of boyhood and place him in what ought to be a man's job, and thus expose him to the risk, if not certainty, of mental and physical injury."[180]

These reports from nationally prominent groups encouraged other authorities to heap scorn on advocates of military training and drill. "The value of wooden-gunism is questionable," conceded a member of the New York State

Military Training Commission.[181] "The word 'military' implies the business of killing one's fellows through organized effort and, for many reasons, should not be used in connection with training in the lower schools if results can be accomplished without doing so."[182]

The issue returned to dormancy during the interwar period. But detractors had not killed it. The menace of a second world war again brought to the surface advocates of compulsory military training and drills for children. Those voices were at first stifled as they were before the country joined World War I. But after the attack on Pearl Harbor authorities realized they needed to build an enormous army. Boys were unready. As military leaders deplored the state of their raw recruits, voices for vicarious service in the schools again caught imagination of the public. A brigadier general directing U.S. Armed Forces military training, Walter L. Weible, was quoted in the *New York Times* as castigating the schools for neglecting their duty. "He stressed the mental and physical inadequacy of youth trained under the present educational system," reflected Captain Albert R. Brinkman shortly after the war ended. He added those Americans who claimed required military training in schools were merely "spoiling for a fight" now had changed their mind, "suddenly and quite emphatically changed to some kind of program for compulsory military training."[183]

But World War II authorities more clearly tried to separate the idea of military training from that of military drills. Drills were considered to be regimented series of movements designed to enhance physical fitness while encouraging obedience to authority. Military training encompassed a broader range of educational goals, including understanding of the war and why the United States was fighting, the country's principles of democracy and values of freedom, as well as military tactics and specific skills, notably those related to mechanical, electrical and aviation specialties the military needed. At the war's beginning, advocates of military drill as a way to enhance physical fitness in children found that viewpoint universally opposed by nearly everyone in charge of anything. Education Commissioner Studebaker declared them to be pointless. Even the military itself declared opposition. Secretary of War Henry L. Stimson in a letter to Studebaker said that while military drills might have their place, if finding a place for them in a school curriculum were not possible, a program of physical education was preferable. Theodore P. Bank, chief of athletics and recreation, special service division of the U.S. Army, agreed military drill in school was not a substitute for physical conditioning programs.[184] By this point school physical education and military drill were presumed to be separate curricula—something not at all clear during World War I.[185] Should a school wish nevertheless to introduce military drills, they would get no tangible support from the military. It was "impossible at this time to supply equipment or to detail officer personnel as instructors in high schools," the education office Wartime Policies Commission reported, and so instead the commission recommended other practices for promoting health, discipline, and instruction desired by the military forces."[186] No suggestion was made to train civilian teachers to teach drills, as was done in World War I.

While military drill for children was supported lukewarmly at best, even by the military itself, the more comprehensive ideals of military training became a leading debate throughout World War II. In its November 1944 issue, *Parents' Magazine* opened three full pages to argument. Supporters represented the country's most prominent people in civilian roles, including Eleanor Roosevelt, wife of the president; Eddie V. Rickenbaker, World War I ace and president of Eastern Airlines; Charles Seymour, president of Yale University; and George Gallup, whose poll indicated that as early as 1939, 63 percent of Americans supported military training. Eleanor Roosevelt explained that long-term peace in the world would be impossible unless nations were able to enforce it, and that military training could prepare a generation of youth for that role. Rickenbacker said training provides physical and mental benefits, as well as vocational skills for anticipated post-war shortages. Seymour repeated an argument often made during both world wars, observing, "We cannot afford, after this war, to risk our freedom, as we have in the past, through shortsighted unpreparedness." Lucy J. Dickinson, president, General Federation of Women's Clubs, pulled out the old idea of self-discipline authorities had worked to discredit a generation before, noting, ""One year of intelligent discipline would be a valuable gift for a young person."[187]

That idea was considered by the editor of *School and Society*, William C. Bagley, who noted Progressive ideals in the schools over the past generation were blamed for a public perception that discipline in the schools had been neglected. "While educationalists, in general, show no disposition to accept compulsory military training as a corrective of this neglect, they apparently recognize that something must be done to offset the criticism." Bagley said an Educational Press Association poll indicated the number one problem educators would have to face was "how to meet intelligently the demand for compulsory military training in the United States." While most educators polled were opposed to such training in the schools, the poll indicated they favored "an enriched, expanded public-school program which will build strong bodies, develop good citizens, implant skills, form good habits—traits needed both in war and in peace." Whether that would be adequate satisfaction to the "militarists," however, concluded the editor, "remains to be seen."[188]

Their view was opposed by an array equally as outspoken, although perhaps not as eminent. Opponents included Harry Emerson Fosdick, prominent New York minister; Oswald Garrison Villard, liberal journalist; Norman Thomas, socialist and pacifist. Considering it a "step away from democracy and toward war," Fosdick wrote, "compulsory military training will not solve the problems of our youths' physical unfitness, illiteracy or unemployment." Villard said, "We cannot give to our government complete control, whether for one or two or five years, of the bodies and minds and the thinking of our youth without paying a very heavy price." Thomas considered such a program to be conscription into the military, that it would lead to enormous expense of keeping a large army, and lead to incentives from those who profit "to fan the hate and fear necessary for the indefinite support of so costly a military system." The NEA added its weight to opinion against military training, president F. L. Schlagle stating, "Permanent conscription and powerful armies, as every student of history knows, have frequently threatened or destroyed civilian freedoms and blocked the path to popular government."[189]

Unresolved in the debate, however, was a specific designation of the age in which a young person should be ready for compulsory military training. It seemed clear that some of those debating were speaking not of school children, but of adults over eighteen. Such compulsory military service, as opposed to military training in school, clearly was the focus of detractors such as Thomas, and perhaps the idea of those in support as well. Also not clear was the definition of military training. Was it conscription, a draft of school leavers? Or was it education, a set of classes for adolescent boys? Or boys and girls? Perhaps because the debate remained somewhat unfocused, post-war policies remained unresolved. But one thing was sure: kids in school were no longer marching around with wooden guns.

## Notes

1. Elizabeth A. Woodward, supervisor of the Brooklyn, New York, Free Kindergarten Society, "The Children's Year and the Opportunity of the Kindergarten for Conservation Work in Congested Cities," National Education Association, *Addresses and Proceedings, Fifty-Sixth Annual Meeting, Pittsburgh, Pennsylvania, June 29–July 6, 1918* (Washington, DC: NEA, 1918), 131.

2. *National School Service*, October 15, 1918, 5.

3. U.S. Children's Bureau, *A Charter for Children in Wartime*, (Washington, DC: Children's Bureau, 1942), 3; in Robert H. Bremner, ed., *Children and Youth in America. A Documentary History. Volume III: 1933–1973* (Cambridge: Harvard University Press, 1974), 355.

4. *Education*, December 1917, 244.

5. "Slackers." *American Boy*, November 1917, 3.

6. Nena Wilson Badenoch, "Victory Volunteers," *Parents' Magazine*, June 1944, 21.

7. Elizabeth S. Magee, "Impact of the War on Child Labor," *Annals of the American Academy of Political and Social Science*, November 1944; in Bremmer, ed., *Children and Youth in America*, 360.

8. Julie C. Lathrop, "Shall This Country Economize For or Against Its Children?", National Education Association, *Addresses and Proceedings, Fifty-Fifth Annual Meeting, Portland, Oregon, July 7-14, 1917* (Washington, DC: NEA, 1917), 77.

9. Frederick E. Bolton, dean of the College of Education, University of Washington, Seattle, "Maintenance of Standards in All Schools as a Necessary Element of Preparedness," National Education Association, *Addresses and Proceedings, Fifty-Fifth Annual Meeting, Portland, Oregon*, 82.

10. "Use of Schools in War Time." *School and Society*, April 6, 1918, 404.

11. *School Life*. Official Organ of the United States Bureau of Education, August 16, 1918, 4.

12. *National School Service*, October 15, 1918, 5.

13. Gertrude Folks Zimand, "Checking Up on Child Labor." *National Parent-Teacher*, June 1943, 11.

14. Educational Policies Commission, National Education Association and American Association of School Administrators, *What the Schools Should Teach in Wartime* (Washington, DC: NEA, 1943), 24-25.

15. *Education for Victory. Official Biweekly of the United States Office of Education Federal Security Agency*, August 3, 1944, 3.

16. Arthur R. Dean, *Our Schools in War Time—and After* (Boston: Ginn and Company, 1918), 150-151.

17. Jennie Hildebrandt, "State News. Missouri," *Child-Welfare Magazine* (PTA magazine), August 1918, 276.

18. John Studebaker, "Parents, Be On Your Guard!" *Parents' Magazine*, January 1944, 27.

19. Elbert K. Fretwell, chief scout executive, *Thirty-fifth Annual Report of the Boy Scouts of America, 1944* (Washington, DC: GPO, 1944), 41.

20. "President's Desk. The Need of Teachers," *Child-Welfare Magazine* (PTA magazine), September 1918, 2.

21. Raymond Nathan and B. P. Brodinsky, "What's Next in Education," *Parents' Magazine*, January 1945, 87; "President's Desk," [no author], "Lack of Teachers Another War Problem," *Child-Welfare Magazine* (PTA magazine), October 1918, 34.

22. Bessie Locke, "Kindergarten Extension," *Child-Welfare Magazine* (became PTA magazine) May 1918, 173.

23. James Lee Ellenwood, "Growing Up in Wartime." *Parents' Magazine*, April 1943, 29.

24. Richard Polenberg, ed., *America at War: The Home Front 1941-1945* (Englewood Cliffs, NJ: Prentice Hall, 1968), 40.

25. Senator Claude Pepper of Florida, chairman, Special Sub-Committee on Wartime Health and Education, "Annual Report on the Nation's Children. Priority for Young America," *Parents' Magazine*, January 1944, 26.

26. J. Edgar Hoover, "Juvenile Delinquency—a National Problem." *National Parent-Teacher*, September 1943, 4-5.

27. Pepper, "Annual Report on the Nation's Children," 26; "Child Care," Law Library, American Law and Legal Information, http://law.jrank.org/pages/5170/Child-Care.html.

28. *Education*, September 1917, 57-58.

29. *Education for Victory. Official Biweekly of the United States Office of Education Federal Security Agency*, April 15, 1942, 8.

30. Angelo Patri, *Your Children in Wartime* (Garden City, NY: Doubleday, Doran & Co., 1943), 5.

31. *National School Service*. Published by the Committee on Public Information, September 1, 1918, 7.

32. U.S. Census Bureau, *Historical Abstracts of the United States. Colonial Times to 1970* (Washington, DC: GPO, 1975), 379, 383.

33. I. L. Kandel, *The Impact of the War upon American Education* (Chapel Hill, NC: University of North Carolina Press, 1948), 39.

34. Philander P. Claxton, "Educational Recommendations of Government," *Child-Welfare Magazine*, (PTA magazine), April 1918, 146; Franklin K. Lane, "Parent-Teacher Associations Aid in Abolishing Illiteracy," *Child-Welfare Magazine* (PTA magazine), August 1918, 261.

35. Harold Spears, principal, Highland Park High School, Illinois, "The Curriculum Movement Helps the High School Face Total War," *Education*, February 1943, 359.

36. I. L. Kandel, *The Impact of the War upon American Education*, 41.

37. Lawrence K. Frank, chairman, Society of Research in Child Development and author of *Human Con-*

*servation*, "Shall We Have Compulsory Military Training After the War?", *Parents' Magazine*, November 1944, 157.

38. *Education for Victory*, September 15, 1942, 1.

39. *Education for Victory*, August 3, 1944, 3.

40. *School Life*, August 16, 1918, 4.

41. Robert J. Aley, "The War and Secondary Schools," *Education*, May 1918, 630.

42. I. L. Kandel, *American Education in the Twentieth Century* (Cambridge: Harvard University Press, 1957), 127.

43. *School and Society*, September 12, 1942, 197–198.

44. George D. Stoddard, "The Weapons of Education," *School and Society*, May 29, 1943, 615.

45. Leroy Ashby, "Partial Promises and Semi-Visible Youths: The Depression and World War II," in Joseph M. Hawes and N. Ray Hiner, eds., *American Childhood. A Research Guide and Historical Handbook* (Westport CT: Greenwood Press, 1985), 505.

46. "Libraries and the War," *School and Society*, January 17, 1942, 64.

47. Dean, *Our Schools in War Time–And After*, 53.

48. James P. Munroe, member, advisory board, Department of War Committee on Education and Special Training, "Education after the War," National Education Association, *Addresses and Proceedings, Fifty-Sixth Annual Meeting, Pittsburgh, Pennsylvania, June 29–July 6, 1918* (Washington, DC: NEA, 1918) 197.

49. Dean, *Our Schools in War Time–And After*, 120.

50. *Education for Victory*, March 16, 1942, 33.

51. Educational Policies Commission, National Education Association, and American Association of School Administrators, *What the Schools Should Teach in Wartime*. (Washington, DC: NEA, 1943), 8.

52. William P. Loomis, "The Needs Students Must Fill—for Industry," *Education*, October 1943, 82.

53. Payne Ratner, "Education and Democracy," National Education Association, *Proceedings of the Eightieth Annual Meeting, Denver, June 28-July 3, 1942* (Washington, DC: NEA, 1942), 57.

54. Carl G. Miller, "Editorial. The Educational Stew Is Boiling," *Education*, March 1945, 37–38.

55. *Education for Victory*, April 15, 1942, 13.

56. Educational Policies Commission, *What the Schools Should Teach in Wartime*, 10.

57. Ibid., 9.

58. Charles K. Arey, "Aviation in the Elementary School Science Program," *Education*, October 1942, 95-96.

59. The Rev. Hugh F. Blunt, pastor, Church of St. John the Evangelist, Cambridge, Massachusetts, "Reclaiming Education," *Education*, January 1944, 292.

60. H. M. Lafferty, lieutenant, U.S. Naval Reserve, "Education During War: Matriarch or Hussy?", *School and Society*, November 7, 1942, 339-340.

61. George H. Deer, principal, laboratory school, Louisiana State University, "GI Methods for Children's Schools?", *School and Society*, February 17, 1945, 106-107.

62. Sara H. Fahey, Teacher of English, Seward Park School, New York City, "How the Public School Can Foster the American Ideal of Patriotism," National Education Association, *Addresses and Proceedings, Fifty-Fifth Annual Meeting, Portland, Oregon, July 7–14, 1917*, 56.

63. Margaret S. McNaught, commissioner of elementary schools, California, "The Elementary School during the War," National Education Association, *Addresses and Proceedings, Fifty-Fifth Annual Meeting, Portland, Oregon, July 7–14, 1917*, 166.

64. Dean, *Our Schools in War Time–and After*, 48.

65. New York City Board of Education minutes, 1918a: 1169, in Stephan F. Brumberg, "New York City Schools March Off to War. The Nature and Extent of Participation of the City Schools in the Great War, April 1917-June 1918," *Urban Education* 24, no. 4 (1990), 459.

66. Ibid., 444.

67. Harvard University Library Open Collections Program, "Immigration to the United States 1789-1930, http://ocp.hul.harvard.edu/immigration/dates.html.

68. U.S. Census Bureau, *Region of Birth of the Foreign-Born Population: 1850 to 1930 and 1960 to 1990*, http://www.census.gov/population/www/documentation/twps0029/tab02.html. Immigrant population dropped to a record low of 4.7 percent in 1970; in 1997 it was 9.7 percent.

69. "Quotes, Sayings and Aphorisms by Theodore Roosevelt," http://www.theodore-roosevelt.com/trquotes.html.

70. Robert D. Ward, "The Origin and Activities of the National Security League, 1914-1919," *The Mississippi Valley Historical Review* 47 (June 1960), 58.

71. Parke R. Kolbe, The Municipal University of Akron, "War work of the United States Bureau of Education," *School and Society*, May 25, 1918, 607.

72. "Why the War Should Be Studied In Schools," *National School Service*, September 1, 1918, 5.

73. Fahey, National Education Association, *Addresses and Proceedings, Fifty-Fifth Annual Meeting, Portland, Oregon, July 7-14, 1917*, 51.

74. Dean, *Our Schools in War Time—and After*, 312.

75. William McAdoo, *National School Service*, September 15, 1918, 1.

76. David M. Kennedy, *Over Here. The First World War and American Society* (Oxford and New York: Oxford University Press, 1980), 53.

77. Ibid., 55.

78. Stephen Vaughn, *Holding Fast the Inner Lines. Democracy, Nationalism, and the Committee on Public Information* (Chapel Hill: University of North Carolina Press, 1980), xii-xiii, 99.

79. Albert Bushnell Hart, "The Lesson of the Obligation of Citizenship," *Education*, June 1918, 752-753.

80. Kolbe, "War Work of the United States Bureau of Education," 607.

81. Guy Stanton Ford, "A New Educational Agency," National Education Association, *Addresses and Proceedings, Fifty-Sixth Annual Meeting, Pittsburgh, Pennsylvania, June 29-July 6, 1918*, 207-208.

82. Vaughn, *Holding Fast the Inner Lines*, 100.

83. *National School Service*, September 1, 1918, 6.

84. *National School Service*, October 15, 1918, 4. We can't help but note the irony of the story given what we know about World War II. The CPI, usually with British propaganda complicity, launched atrocity stories later proven to be untrue. But not all of them were.

85. Vaughn, *Holding Fast the Inner Lines*, 103.

86. *National School Service*, December 15, 1918, 8.

87. United States Committee on Public Information [George Creel], *The Creel Report. Complete Report of the Chairman of the Committee on Public Information 1917: 1918: 1919* (New York: DaCapo Press, 1972, reprint of 1920 edition), 16.

88. 1916 statistics; U.S. Census Bureau, *Historical Abstracts of the United States*, 375.

89. J. H. Ackerman, president, State Normal School, Monmouth, Oregon, "The Normal School as an Agency for Teaching Patriotism," *Addresses and Proceedings, Fifty-Fifth Annual Meeting, Portland, Oregon, July 7-14, 1917*, 61.

90. Aley, "The War and Secondary Schools," 629.

91. In New York City Board of Education, in Brumberg, "New York City Schools March Off to War," 446.

92. Frances E. Harden, teacher, Stewart School, Chicago, Illinois, "A Plea for Greater Democracy in our Public Schools," National Education Association, *Addresses and Proceedings, Fifty-Seventh Annual Meeting, Milwaukee, Wisconsin, June 28-July 5, 1919* (NEA, Washington, DC: 1919), 391.

93. "A Socialist's Views on the Student Army Training Corps," *School and Society*, November 23, 1918, 632.

94. Brumberg, "New York City Schools March Off to War," 447-468.

95. Susan Zeiger, "The Schoolhouse vs. the Armory. U.S. Teachers and the Campaign Against Militarism in the Schools, 1914-1918," *Journal of Women's History* 15, no. 2 (2003), 167-168.

96. "Fannie Fern Andrews," *The ABC-CLIO Companion to the American Peace Movement in the 20th Century*, Swarthmore College Peace Collection, http://www.swarthmore.edu/Library/peace/CDGA.A-L/andrews.htm.

97. Aley, "The War and Secondary Schools," 631.

98. *Historical Abstracts of the United States*, 106.

99. New York City Board of Education Minutes 1918a, 702, in Brumberg, "New York City Schools March Off to War," 454.

100. Philander P. Claxton, "The Retention of the Teaching of German in the Public Schools," a letter to Dr. Robert L. Slagle, president of the University of South Dakota, March 12, 1918, published in *School and Society*, March 30, 1918, 374.

101. T. W. Todd, Washburn College, Topeka, Kansas, "German in Our Public Schools," *Education*, March 1918, 532.

102. Kennedy, *Over Here*, 55.

103. James Duncan Phillips, [identified as "the popular and efficient treasurer of the Houghton Mifflin

Company"], "Teaching patriotism," *Education*, February 1918, 444–445.

104. *School Life*, August 15, 1918, 10.

105. George Wittich, supervisor of physical training, public schools, Milwaukee, Wisconsin, "Loyal Citizens a Product of Physical Training," National Education Association, *Addresses and Proceedings, Fifty-Seventh Annual Meeting, Milwaukee, Wisconsin, June 28–July 5, 1919*, 316.

106. John F. Sims, president, State Normal School, Stevens Point, Wisconsin, "Patriotism in the Schools," National Education Association, *Addresses and Proceedings, Fifty-Fifth Annual Meeting, Portland, Oregon, July 7–14, 1917*, 170.

107. William P. Loomis, vocational division, U.S. Office of Education, "The Needs Students Must Fill—for Industry," *Education*, October 1943, 82.

108. Ernest O. Melby, "The Responsibility of Educational Leadership in These Times," *Education*, February 1943, 330.

109. J. Cayce Morrison, assistant commissioner for research, state education department, "The Teaching of Patriotism," *School and Society*, Oct. 3, 1942, 284.

110. W. Linwood Chase. *Wartime Social Studies in the Elementary School. Curriculum Series No. 3* (Washington, DC: The National Council for the Social Studies, 1943), 17–18.

111. Stoddard, "The Weapons of Education," 615.

112. John W. Studebaker, "Seventy-Five Years of American Education," National Education Association, *Proceedings of the Eightieth Annual Meeting, Denver, June 28–July 3, 1942*, 48.

113. Alice M. Jordan, in Wayne A. Wiegand, *"An Active Instrument for Propaganda": The American Public Library During World War I* (New York and Westport, CT: Greenwood Press, 1989), 46.

114. "Libraries and the War," *School and Society*, January 17, 1942, 64.

115. Helen L. Butler, American Library Association, "The School Library in Wartime." *School and Society*, Sept. 18, 1943, 220.

116. Wiegand, *An Active Instrument for Propaganda*, 46–47.

117. Melanie A. Kimball, "From Refuge to Risk: Public Libraries and Children in World War I," *Library Trends* 55, no. 3, (2007), 460.

118. "The Children's Song," The Kipling Society, http://www.kipling.org.uk/poems_childrensong.htm.

119. Wiegand, *An Active Instrument for Propaganda*," 60.

120. Ibid., 13-14.

121. Niel M. Johnson, "George Sylvester Viereck. Poet and Propagandist." University of Iowa Special Collections, http://www.lib.uiowa.edu/spec-coll/bai/johnson2.htm.

122. Wiegand, *An Active Instrument for Propaganda*," 6.

123. Quoted in Wiegand, *An Active Instrument for Propaganda*," 48.

124. Ibid., 55–56.

125. *Education for Victory*, March 3, 1942, 15.

126. "The ALA Allies Itself with the OWI," *School and Society*, Oct. 24, 1942, 376.

127. Dorothy Marshall and Bertha Pippin, "The Victory Corps in the Wilmington High School," *Education*, October 1943, 122.

128. Butler, "The School Library in Wartime," 218.

129. "The ALA Allies Itself with the OWI," 376.

130. W. S. Small, U.S. Bureau of Education, "Physical Education in the High School in the Present Emergency," address before the Department of Secondary Education, National Education Association, July 2, 1918," *School and Society*, September 7, 1918, 182.

131. John Sundwall, University of Minnesota, "University Physical Education and Efficiency," *School and Society*, November 2, 1918, 512.

132. Dean, *Our Schools in War Time–and After*, 167.

133. Charles W. Eliot, "Educational Changes Needed for the War and the Subsequent Peace," *Education*, May 1918, 656.

134. Woodward, "The Children's Year and the Opportunity of the Kindergarten for Conservation Work in Congested Cities," National Education Association, *Addresses and Proceedings*, 132.

135. "Eliot Against Basket Ball." *The New York Times*, November 28, 1906, n.p., http://query.nytimes.com/gst/abstract.html?res=9C03E1DE1331E733A2575BC2A9679D946797D6CF.

136. W. S. Small, Annual Report of the Commissioner of Education, Department of the Interior, quoted in *Education*, March 1917, 461.

137. *National School Service*, September 1, 1918, 13.

138. Small, "Physical Education in the High School in the Present Emergency," *School and Society*, September 7, 1918, 182-183.

139. Strong Hinman, assistant superintendent of schools, Topeka, Kansas, "A Health and Physical Education Program for Elementary Schools," National Education Association, *Proceedings of the Eightieth Annual Meeting, Denver, June 28–July 3, 1942*, 164.

140. F. L. Kleeberger, "Athletics and the War Game," *School and Society*, May 1918, 543.

141. Newton D. Baker, address before National Collegiate Athletic Association, quoted in F. L. Kleeberger, "Athletics and the War Game," 543.

142. Josephus Daniels, quoted in Kleeberger, "Athletics and the War Game," Ibid., 544.

143. Captain H. J. Koehler, quoted in *School and Society*, March 31, 1917, 386.

144. Hinman, "A Health and Physical Education Program for Elementary Schools," 164.

145. Quoted in Belmont Farley, "War-Fitness Conference," *School and Society*, June 12, 1943, 674-675.

146. Jay B. Nash, "Health and Fitness in Wartime," National Education Association, *Proceedings of the Eightieth Annual Meeting, Denver, June 28–July 3, 1942*, 162.

147. Harold W. Kent, "The Needs Students Must Fill—for the War Department," *Education*, October 1943, 80-81.

148. Raymond Nathan, "Our Schools Mobilize," January 1943, 62.

149. Roy Sorenson, "Wartime Recreation for Adolescents," *The Annals of the American Academy of Political and Social Science* 236 (1944), 147.

150. *Education for Victory*, July 3,1944, 7-8.

151. Rowntree, quoted in Farley, "War-Fitness Conference," 675.

152. Lawrence K. Frank, chairman, Society of Research in Child Development and author of *Human Conservation*, "Shall We Have Compulsory Military Training After the War?", *Parents' Magazine*, November 1944, 156-157.

153. *Education for Victory*, September 4, 1944, 12.

154. *Education for Victory*, September 15, 1943, 17.

155. *Education for Victory*, July 3, 1944, 7.

156. *Education for Victory*, August 21, 1944, 5, 18-20.

157. Nathan, "Our Schools Mobilize," 62.

158. "A Physical Education Program for Every School," *Education*, October 1943, 86.

159. Ibid.

160. Nathan, "Our Schools Mobilize," 62.

161. A Physical Education Program for Every School," *Education*, October 1943, 84.

162. Major Edwin R. Elbel, Army Air Forces School of Aviation Medicine, Randolph Field, Texas, *Education for Victory*, March 3, 1945, 16.

163. Edwin J. Brown, Kansas State Teachers College, Emporia, "Football in a War Program," *School and Society*, February 2, 1943, 20-21.

164. *Education for Victory*, September 14, 1943, 19.

165. Nathan, "Our Schools Mobilize," 62.

166. Brumberg, "New York City Schools March Off to War. The Nature and Extent of Participation of the City Schools in the Great War, April 1917-June 1918," 451.

167. Hugh H. Young, Johns Hopkins University, "Military Training Would Make Us a New Race," *The New York Times Magazine*, January 7, 1917, 30.

168. James P. Munroe, member, advisory board, War Department Committee on Education and Special Training, "Education after the war," National Education Association, *Addresses and Proceedings, Fifty-Sixth Annual Meeting, Pittsburgh, Pennsylvania, June 29–July 6, 1918*, 197.

169. McNaught, "The Elementary School during the War," 167.

170. National Education Association, *Addresses and Proceedings, Fifty-Fifth Annual Meeting, Portland, Oregon, July 7-14, 1917*, 775.

171. John H. Finley, speaking April 27, 1917, quoted in *Child-Welfare Magazine* (PTA), June 1917, 293.

172. "Military Training in the Schools," *School and Society*, December 29, 1917, 762-763.

173. New York City Board of Education minutes, 1918a: 346, in Stephan F. Brumberg, "New York City Schools March Off to War. The Nature and Extent of Participation of the City Schools in the Great War, April 1917-June 1918," 452-453.

174. "The *American Boy* Contest. Compulsory Military Drill in the School," *American Boy*, January 1917, 28.

175. "Report on Military Training in the Schools of New Jersey," *School and Society*, February 17, 1917, 197.

176. Quoted in *School and Society*, March 31, 1917, 383.

177. *School and Society*, March 31, 1917, 385.

178. *School and Society*, March 31, 1917, 383.

179. *School and Society*, March 31, 1917, 384.

180. *School and Society*, March 31, 1917, 381.

181. Arthur R. Dean, *Our Schools in War Time–and After*, 309.

182. Kleeberger, "Athletics and the War Game," 542.

183. Albert R. Brinkman, Fort Ord, California, "Compulsory Military Education in the Post-War Educational Program," *Education*, September 1945, 65, 67–68.

184. Farley, "War-Fitness Conference." 675.

185. *Education for Victory*, December 1, 1943, 14.

186. *Education for Victory*, June 1, 1942, 6.

187. "Shall We Have Compulsory Military Training After the War?", *Parents' Magazine*, November 1944, 16–18.

188. W. C. B. (William C. Bagley), "Should a 'Must' Discipline Be Made a Feature of American Education?", *School and Society*, February 17, 1945, 101.

189. Ibid., 18, 156, 158.

# 4

## MOBILIZING KIDS FOR THE HOME FRONT

If total war demanded service from all groups of society, it also suggested organizing groups into military-style divisions. Cadets, corps and armies would help to militarize children in both world wars, by organizing and coordinating war work. In extending war metaphors into childhood, authorities emphasized drawing from the "army of school children" in their "citadels" of the classrooms. Education was "a weapon," directed by a "great army" which would be "mobilized" on the "home front."[1] These troops not ready for real battles were nevertheless ready for real support work, in fact, essential. "The stark fact facing parents as America enters the grimmest phase of war is this: We cannot gain victory without the labor of youth," declared an author writing in *Parents' Magazine* in 1943. In World War I, labor shortages brought "a hysterical demand for the service of children.[2] Supply met demand, as many children wanted to do something, and hoped to be recruited. "Five million school children mobilized into an army with officers and privates and sergeants—with drill and hard work and great rewards and splendid service," wrote the PTA's *Child-Welfare Magazine* in 1918 (unsigned). "What child is there on the face of the globe who would not be proud and eager to be one of such an army? Have the schools in your district begun to organize?"[3]

Efforts began ad hoc in many communities, or organized by private non-profits such as the Boy Scouts or Red Cross. But authorities soon determined in both wars that children could be most easily herded into more efficient war activities through a centrally coordinated structure. If children were an army, the

metaphor could be extended to erect a military-like structure for their deploy-
ment. Most of the divisions of this structure were of a military nature: School
Garden Army, Boys' Working Reserve, Junior Industrial Army, Student Army
Training Corps (World War I); Junior Commandos, Paper Trooper Program,
High School Victory Corps, School Garden Service (World War II). Through
these officially sponsored groups, administered mostly through the schools,
children could serve patriotically in ways authorities might find most expedient.
And because they were mostly administered through educators, these youthful
troops on the home front could learn the value of discipline, physical work, and
vocational skills that might have been denied them in the classroom. These
divisions could be structured to reflect similar separations in the military. The
World War II High School Victory Corps, a federal umbrella designed to coordinate wartime activities in the secondary schools, set up five divisions based
on student interest and wartime need. In World War I divisions particularly
addressed programs to send children into food production: New Jersey's Junior
Industrial Army was organized into three specialties to send boys to training
camps under military discipline.[4] In fact, of the jobs children were expected to
do, food production was deemed most important during the 1914-1918 war, and
significant during the 1939-1945 war. But World War I authorities sometimes
approached their mobilization for agricultural work with enthusiasm beyond
common sense. World War II authorities tapped common sense, at the expense
of enthusiasm.

### Bringing in the Sheaves: Children and Wartime Food Production

After the United States joined the war in April 1917, fear grew that America
would face food shortages, for two reasons. One, the States would be expected
to feed its strife-riven Allies along with millions of calorie-craving warriors at the
front. "We were told bread wins more wars than bayonets and bullets," noted
the University of Washington dean of education. Authorities in World War II
looking back to the previous war agreed, "Food was a critical problem in 1918
when the country was responsible not alone for feeding itself, but for sending
food to the European countries."[5] The second reason food production lagged
was less obvious: brigades of adults had thrown down their plowshares to join
the war effort. Not necessarily as soldiers; loyalty to country may have driven
many a World War I recruit, but loyalty to money drove many more. As munitions industries burgeoned to supply a growing American Expeditionary Force
moving into France, demand for workers drove wages beyond what farmhands

could make on the land. Seasonal laborers could find greener employment in factories. Noting that the shortage of workers could not be blamed on the draft, a New York professor of vocational training wrote, "workers are offered steady employment in munition and textile plants.... This resulted in an unprecedented rush of children between fourteen and sixteen to obtain employment certificates, and a clamor from those below fourteen to be allowed to leave school and go to work."[6]

State authorities in 1917 faced an apparent critical shortage of people to take in the harvest, just at a time when food stocks would be most necessary. Readily available, as usual, was America's army of children. "We have on the one hand the pressing need for labor on the farms—a need which always exists but which has become acute in present war conditions," declared an unsigned editorial in *Education*, "and on the other hand an abundance of idle energy in the well-grown but below-war-age young men, who idle away the summer days in uselessness and mischief in the vacant lots of our large cities."[7] Just how to quickly recruit such an idle army of twenty million kids was, however, the challenge. Within days of the April 6 war declaration advocates were clamoring at the schools to let children leave to tend crops. State school superintendents were besieged with demands to give school credit for the children who left for farm or other work. Some advocated simply closing the schools to divert an entire population of youngsters into patriotic service, but authorities refused to declare an educational hiatus, arguing restraint. "If we had been taught to think, there would not have been the recent hysterical appeal which was sent out some weeks ago to close the schools so that the children could be sent to the farms," argued a speaker at the National Education Association July 1917 convention.[8] Progressive educator John Dewey warned, "Random efforts not coordinated in a general scheme for the utilization of school children in large units will be foolish, misdirected effort."[9]

The U.S. Department of Labor immediately jumped to the task of coordinating a random storm of demands against children's school time by establishing the Boys' Working Reserve. Structured as a quasi-military voluntary work group for adolescent boys, the reserve aimed to answer concerns of chaos by giving participants a plan best suited to the country's needs. The reserve "has for its purpose the mobilization of the youth of America to avert the dangerous shortage of labor in the United States, especially on the farms," reported the government-sponsored *School Life*. According to its director, labor department official H. W. Wells, authorities sought cooperation of the country's high schools to identify and recruit for the reserve from the estimated 500,000 boys sixteen and older.[10]

It counted on teachers extolling benefits in class, based on a labor department series of pamphlets. Its three divisions, agricultural, industrial, and vocational, would not only answer the country's wartime labor shortages, but would keep older children from abandoning the classrooms for lucrative war work. "It has the double aim of preventing boys from abandoning school to enter industry merely for the sake of the high wages, and also, in case of boys who have entered industry for legitimate causes, of affording them the opportunity of continuing their education," explained a writer in *School Life*.[11] The agriculture division did not face such a problem, the author contended, because boys can do the work during summer vacations.

This conclusion apparently did not take into consideration the pressure to release students early or allow their late return for farm seasons that spanned wider than summer vacations. But the reserve could have benefits beyond contributions to the country's war effort. Reflecting the view of authorities that war work could build a child's character, the author declared that the quasi-military format of the reserve's farm work camps could build "a deep sense of personal and individual responsibility with an ability to give and take orders, and a new realization of the vital, national need of a rigid harmony of cooperative effort." Health would improve through compulsory drills and medical exams. "Furthermore, the semimilitary discipline in the farm training camps is performing a valuable groundwork for the boy's education by reducing his irresponsibility and increasing his sense of values." And finally, the reserve would produce better soldiers, would "render the boy better fitted for a call to the fighting ranks when he comes of age."[12]

By 1918, according to the U.S. Office of Education, 210,000 boys were working on farms, although whether these were all members of the reserve was not specified. *School Life* bragged, "It is conservatively estimated that members of the Boys' Working Reserve have produced sufficient food to supply the whole American Expeditionary Force of 1,300,000 men in France for a year."[13] After the war's end, authorities believed the experiment so successful that the Department of Labor called for keeping this "registered army of patriotic youth" mostly for farm work. A set of summer camps, "in which camps the boys are subjected to military discipline," could counteract the "demoralization" of summer vacation. It would offer a centralized way to build character and groom future soldiers, as the Boys' Working Reserve "is the only organization that affects the whole public-school system in the Untied States."[14]

But the idea of setting up camps for farm-bound city boys was hardly exclusive to the U.S. Government. In fact, many states considered such programs, and a few East Coast States actually tried them. A New York City group called the Bureau of Educational Experiments tried setting up camps to attract city boys who could fan out daily to work on farms. In New Jersey, educational authorities built their own reserve based on the pattern from Washington. Called the Junior Industrial Army, the group also was separated into three divisions. These differed from those of the national group, most obviously because they also addressed the volunteer contributions of girls. The divisions, agriculture, home gardens and girls' service, offered opportunities to both girls and boys in two divisions. The agricultural division still was reserved exclusively for boys. Unlike the age-sixteen cutoff of the national reserve, New Jersey's version reached down to age fourteen. "Nearly 60,000 boys and girls are registered in the Home Gardens Division, and canning and Red Cross sewing have been started by the Girls' Service Division," wrote an author identified as a member of the New York chapter of the National Child Labor Committee. "The work of the Agricultural Division is most significant, because for this activity children have been excused from attending school."[15] The New Jersey program allowed any boy over fourteen, in good health and with parents' permission, to leave school for agricultural work either on his home farm or elsewhere. "Boys thus employed are not considered 'absent' from school, but 'excused,' and they receive full credit for the school work which they would have done during this time."[16]

New Jersey authorities established three work programs for children wanting to work on farms. Farmers were identified based on application to schools or principals, on advice of friends and relatives or on the educators themselves asking around. By summer 1917, 6,332 New Jersey boys were working on farms, and another 2,722 were waiting for work; 51.1 percent were under sixteen; 2.4 percent were under fourteen.

The most ambitious of the three programs was on-site boys' camps set up to offer room and board for the entire summer to boys who would travel from the camp to work on designated farms. One example of such a camp, set up using a fairground, was adjacent to the Grant B. Schley farm at Far Hills. Called the Froh-Heim Farm Club, fifty-eight boys from three New Jersey High Schools were recruited to join the program. Ages varied from fourteen to twenty, although "the average age of the boys is sixteen, and the average weight 137 pounds." Rutgers University provided two farm specialists to direct the boys. Life in camp resembled military training, with about nine hours six days a week devoted to farm work:

Their daily program is as follows:
4:45 Colors.
5:00 Breakfast.
6:15 Inspection of bunks.
6:30 Drill.
7:15 Farm duty.
11:00 Lunch (served in the field).
12:00 Farm duty.
5:00 Recall.
5:30 Dinner in uniform.
6:15 Drill.
6:45 Sunset.
7:00 Recall.
8:30 Taps.[17]

Boys also were expected to pick up camp chores, although a cook was hired to serve meals. They received free room and board, plus one dollar a week spending money. "Any profits remaining after the initial outlay is met will be divided among the recruits." Boys were expected to stay for the entire farm season, which extended to mid-October.[18] What kind of boys were likely to join a camp program like this one? The wealthy ones, "chiefly the sons of moneyed people who have given up their usual summer holidays in the mountains or at the shore to be of assistance in the present crisis." The author admitted that as the boys had no farm background, they found the work to be hard, but the camp style was similar to a boys' summer camp, and participants enjoyed the spirit of camaraderie.[19]

The author declared this program to be successful, although writing during summer 1917, it seems apparent the program had not yet ended its first season. Not as successful, it seems, were the state's other two programs. A second experiment replaced the on-site work camp with fifty-two boys quartered in a high school building. Receiving twenty dollars a month plus room and board, these boys traveled daily to farms. But without the extensive system of training offered in the on-side camp, boys could not be of much help. Farmers were supposed to pay boys for their work, but many declared city kids were not worth $1.80 a day. Furthermore, program directors did not check to see if farmers needed boys before sending them to work sties. "As a result many of the boys are working on the estates, mowing lawns, pruning trees, and trimming shrubs—praiseworthy tasks, to be sure, but hardly a proper substitute for school work."[20]

A third approach left the boys at home to be hired out as day laborers. But without supervision, the author observed, farmers could easily exploit children as laborers. In one such example, a fifteen-year-old found work on a truck farm; "He was slight in build, weighing only 113 pounds and with no previous farm experience; nevertheless, he worked from five in the morning until eight at night, with about an hour and a half off at noon, doing chores and picking strawberries. For these tasks he received, in addition to his board, two dollars a month, the equivalent of $.002 an hour."[21]

While the author did note many boys who joined the program "left school with the distinct idea of serving their country," the attractions of a workaday world paying real money in some cases won over that of chalk and textbooks. "The opinion of several of the farmers interviewed, however, was that many of the children left school, not because of a desire to work, but of a dislike for school," the author noted. "'I know a boy,' said one farmer, 'who was expelled a month ago, and when this chance came along they took him back on trial. It helped him a lot, for he's not in school and so can't get into trouble.'... The granting of school credit under these circumstances is open to abuse. 'This [program] helps a lot of boys to graduate,' one farmer sagely remarked."[22]

Farmers generally seemed to be less enthusiastic than authorities. A boy eager to leave school for farm work "was not balanced by an equally eager response on the part of the farmers," who didn't think city kids could handle the work, or hired only because it looked like an opportunity for cheap labor.[23]

As ambitious was a farm work scheme set up about the same time in New York. The New York City school board encouraged boys to join one of eight farm camps set up around the state, and promised "farm work during such time as the public schools of the city are in session [would] be considered as equivalent to school work." Participation was as brisk as it was in New Jersey; by May 9, 230 boys were working and, according to school board minutes, beginning to break down "the skepticism now existing among many farmers" that city boys could not cut it on the farm.[24] Commenting on New York's program, that state's commissioner of education said, "The only objection to this scheme, as I see it, is that the girls are not included."[25] In 1918 it was expanded to 2,000 boys, along with four girls' camps. The program provided badges and insignias to participants, as it did for adolescent boys in the state's military training program. The commissioner emphasized that goal underpinning that state's farm cadet program was military: "All the boys, of course, will have to undergo some military instruction in order that they may be quickly mobilized."[26]

Frank A. Rexford, a teacher in New York City's Erasmus Hall High School and a farm camp program director, declared his boys were responsible for harvesting 11,000 of the 35,000 acres of participating farmers, while girls harvested

324,000 quarts of berries.[27] Rexford said his "Potato Growers' Association" of high schoolers might "fit the boys for military service, if needed." The teacher also had a broader aim, to prove city kids were as physically fit as country kids. His team would "teach the farmer that the alert city boy can and will perform agricultural tasks." To that end, ten boys were sent upstate funded by contributions by teachers and the New York *Tribune*. "At first the farmers were skeptical," but when they saw how well the boys were doing on Rexford's farm, began hiring them."[28]

This would appear to indicate New York's program was a success. But some observers possibly more objective than the city's school board secretary remained not quite convinced. Arthur Dean, supervising officer of the New York State Military Training Commission's Bureau of Vocational Training, wrote extensively in 1918 regarding efforts of his and other eastern states' efforts to set up farm work programs. He noted three of the most ambitious state programs were formulated in early 1917, even before war was declared. New York, New Jersey and Massachusetts responded to plans established by the Eastern Arts and Manual Training Teachers' Association meeting in Philadelphia, Dean wrote. These programs went beyond simply excusing adolescents for farm work. They tried to find ways to substitute farm work for academic or vocational studies at school. The idea sprang independently in Indiana and California, the author noted, and by July 1917 was established in around the country.[29] This would mean the federally sponsored Boys' Working Reserve was not a Washington innovation, but instead an effort to coordinate many state programs. In fact Dean noted the idea of a camp emerged from early efforts to find a way to get the boy from the city to the country. The boys participating in the state programs were called farm cadets.

The cadet program was somewhat different from New Jersey's in that children stayed with farmers themselves. They returned to the camps on weekends for a non-sectarian church service and "Sunday morning drill." Six camps of forty-eight boys each were set up around Long Island under a supervisor, military instructor, and squad leader. But farmers were not eager to take them on, saying "the presence of boys would 'demoralize' their regular help, and that the boys would not recognize the different vegetables and would hoe out corn as quickly as they would pigweed." Sometimes boys did show their ignorance: in one case a boy working in upstate New York proceeded to hoe out every corn plant while leaving the weeds. But most of the time, Dean contended, the boys won over the farmers' skepticism.[30] In Massachusetts, five hundred farm cadets by June were stationed at eighteen camps, with another five hundred serving from home or living with farmers. Regulations stipulated farmers must find something for the boys to do on rainy as well as sunny days, and give them a week's notice or week's pay, if they proved unsatisfactory. Pay was set at four dollars for an eight-hour, six-day week plus board, housing provided by donated army tents. One example cited, the New Bedford contingent of Coonamesett camp, 11,000 acres, arranged for two boys each housed in militia tents. The mess hall was seventy-five feet long and seventeen feet wide, catered by "two Japanese cooks."[31] In Maine the farm cadet camps were identical in construction to regular army camps, to prepare boys for military service as well as farm work.

Experiences observing cadets in Massachusetts, however, persuaded Dean to conclude that despite some success, bringing city children to work in the country was a challenge. He said a farm acquaintance found the program an uphill struggle: "Referring to the difficulty of obtaining competent boys, on the one hand, and of convincing farmers of the value of city-boy labor, on the other, he further stated that it was a difficult proposition to sell something we did not have to somebody who did not want it." Farmers' willingness to exploit children also galled him. "It made me sick at heart, on a trip of inspection to twenty-five camps, to see hundreds of boys at work picking berries under the hot sun in a service supposedly patriotic," Dean related, "and then to see the same berries, which had been sold by the growers at a price not much above that of other years, resold to the consumer at double the price of other years—and always with the remark: 'You know labor is scarce this year, and the farmers cannot get help.'"[32]

Experiences around the country generally were less intensely examined, and less intensely practiced. The cadet program saw participation limited to eastern seaboard states, the only states that formally set up boys' camps. The federal Boys Working Reserve program was actually adopted by only nine states, according to a 1918 North Dakota State University, Fargo, study. In that work, Thomas J. Smart surveyed every state school superintendent regarding participation in children's farm work programs, and decisions to grant academic credit for the participation. Thirty-two responded. The states offering formal programs included descriptive pamphlets and "carefully directed advertising campaigns" to bring farmers and children together in supervised work environments. The rest of the states saw their schools simply send out individual boys to farms as needed. State superintendents of the states offering formal programs reported, "Many farmers doubtful of the wisdom of employing city boys have been convinced of their fitness." Smart attributed that to the advertising campaigns, however. He added adolescents there may have joined because "Some states issue attractive enrollment certificates. Buttons are given to the boys which signify that they have been enrolled." The military nature of these programs also may attract some boys, Smart concluded. "In one state [not specified] they are placed on the same ranking as members of the National Guard. They are designated as 'volunteers' and provided with board, lodging, uniforms and medical attendance at the cost of the state. They are mobilized and trained by the state and may be dismissed only on furloughs. Each boy draws one dollar per working day from the state funds."[33]

Superintendents in states without formal programs tried to respond to a deluge of requests to release children from compulsory attendance so they could work, mostly on farms. "Demands were made for credit by those assisting in the production of food and those entering industries closely related to a successful prosecution of the war," Smart noted, adding one superintendent reported letters "pouring in" from around the state. Some superintendents did allow students to leave school early, and others allowed academic credit for farm work. But not as many as might be presumed. Six states reported giving no credit at all; only four states "show evidence of having placed no restrictions on the granting of credits." Others gave credit for substantial work, allowed students to make up work, or left the matter to local school boards. One of many superintendents who declared themselves wary of the idea responded, "Our state last year was not carried away by the fear that there would not be sufficient help on the farms."[34]

Concerns of superintendents were not unfounded. Dean had noted that even in the more structured programs of the East Coast, students would be eager to volunteer for farm work during the school year if it meant they could get out of school. During the summer break, however, those same volunteers often managed to find something else more compelling to do. Some farmers noted students would come to work as a way to salvage a flunking academic year. Superintendents found some students practically giddy at the prospect of getting credit for cutting class. Parents and others wrote to complain the kids were getting credit but not doing any work. "Some even boasted that they had 'gotten by' for that year quite easily." It was just a good excuse to leave school, wrote another superintendent, who concluded, "Disorganized school work, scholastic credit given for that which was not scholarship and a general lowering of the value of the school's worth in the eyes of the people."[35]

The country's state superintendents in 1918 took the matter more firmly in hand; fourteen declared no academic credit would be given for farm work. Only two kept a fairly liberal policy on credits. It was not that they disliked the idea of service, superintendents declared in the survey. Just not for academic credit. They suggested students instead consider a longer school day to make up the work, or eliminating their vacations.[36] But the truth seemed to be that farmers really didn't want townies invading their fields and pastures. As an Oregon legislator observed, "The farmers did not want untrained city boys, and city boys did not want work for which they were unfitted."[37] Demands to give academic credit for work, shorten the school year, enforce military training and suspend child labors law brought this 1917 response from the president of the Parent-Teacher Association: "The country has not come to such a desperate pass that it must enlist the children for war service."[38] Yet that viewpoint stayed far, far in the shadowy minority during both world wars.

While farm work programs were mostly an option for older children, the younger ones were not necessarily forgotten. Dean thought junior high school-aged boys would be best for picking berries based on their nimble fingers and general alertness. Most authorities, however, thought the younger kids would be more useful in less demanding roles. They could still build character by working outside with plants. If farmers sometimes saw no use for children, perhaps kids could cut out the middleman farmer. They could grow food themselves. The idea of increasing the country's food supply by reclaiming vacant lots and weedy backyards had been bounced around the Bureau of Education since at least 1914. Authorities thought children beginning at about age twelve or younger could augment their learning with vocational skills, for good health as well as character development. One easy option was to encourage classes to build gardens on vacant property around the city. The war gave new impetus to this idea, particularly as authorities feared food shortages, and so in March 1918 the bureau announced formation of the United States School Garden Army. Credited for the idea were U.S. Commissioner of Education Philander P. Claxton and Secretary of Interior Franklin K. Lane, who proffered these reasons for the program: "(a) increased food production, and (b) training of school children in thrift, industry, service, patriotism, and responsibility." Woodrow Wilson supported the garden army with a $50,000 appropriation to cover the first six months, and promised $200,000 more for another ten months.[39] Wilson hoped this army of young gardeners, targeting ages nine to thirteen, would feel closer to the battlefields by tending the garden plots. "I am sure they would all like to feel that they are in fact fighting in France by joining the United States School Garden Army," said Wilson. Lane declared the program to be an ideal patriotic outlet for younger children, even a way to inspire patriotism in parents: "There is no better way of educating the children of the country as to the meaning of this war than this, and through the children the parents."[40]

Authorities closer to the lives of young children did not so quickly rise to the level of enthusiasm reflected in Washington. "When young men are marching along the streets with banners displayed and martial music sounding, small boys will hardly be content to plant beans and tend school gardens if the purpose be not made clear to them," said the California commissioner of elementary schools. The explanation, she stressed, would have to come from the highest authorities, the president and governor. "The essential point is that the children of the elementary schools shall be as far as possible brought into an understanding partnership with the rest of the community in mastering the lessons the great war is teaching."[41] That central point did not seem to include the belief that younger children could actually contribute something tangible to home-front needs. In fact, Claxton himself said everyone would gain, even if the work did nothing for the war effort. "Even if the vegetables and fruits produced had no value," he said, benefitted would be "the land by cultivation, the children by the health-giving educational labor, and the older people by the hours outdoors and contact with the soil."[42] But that's not what children were led to believe. Like many wartime volunteer opportunities aimed at children, this one was promoted to youngsters as a way they could tangibly help the fighters across the seas. It had a hidden agenda most authorities believed to be more important: building character, sustaining morale, keeping kids out of trouble, and grooming them for a possible military future. To promote volunteer opportunities while withholding the real reasons adults wanted children to do them seems slightly disingenuous. Yet during both world wars it was standard operating procedure, just as it was almost never thought necessary to solicit opinions of the children themselves. While the extensive network of wartime work opportunities available to children during both world wars did have aims beyond practical, that does not mean authorities discounted children's work. In the case of the School Garden Army, Claxton hoped that work would also pay off in a substantial way. "If the millions of city boys and girls could be induced to give their leisure time to cultivating the thousands of acres of untilled land in front and back yards and vacant lots of our cities, towns, and villages," he said hopefully, "it would result in a substantial increase in food production and an improvement in the quality of our coming citizenship."[43]

But to launch such a program nation-wide required substantial organization. Where would authorities turn for help? The military. "The army plan of organization was adopted and has proved to be very popular and efficient," reported *School Life* (unsigned), the bureau's official newsletter. Schools were asked to organize children into companies of "garden soldiers," 150 maximum, preferably smaller. Each company would include a child designed as captain, first and second lieutenant, along with one adult to serve as a garden teacher. "The officers have been used to great advantage by many teachers in helping them on their reports, inspecting gardens, encouraging members of their company to do their full duty as true soldiers, and in arranging for exhibits, pageants, plays, etc." Officers received military-style insignia, the captain a double bronze bar.[44]

Planners did foresee problems finding teachers capable of teaching gardening, and operation funding. They recommended schools solve these problems on their own. "To care for it at this time has become a patriotic duty."[45] The PTA apparently considered these to be minor obstacles, in declaring its support for the garden army program: "Five million school children mobilized into an army with officers and privates and sergeants—with drill and hard work and great rewards and splendid service." It admonished possibly recalcitrant parents, "You will be interested some day when that boy of yours comes home with a chevron on his sleeve or your girl is made a first sergeant and wears a badge which tells the world that she is ready to do her bit for her country and her country's flag."[46] An Ohio educator declared, "The most extensive and important war activity now in progress at the bureau in the stimulation of patriotic endeavor is the creation of the Public School War Garden Army."[47] The Bureau of Education reported splendid cooperation, including testimonials such as that of Mabel J. Weeks, Waltham, Massachusetts. "I can't help telling you just what a great thing this army organization has been and is to the children," she wrote. "Last Saturday 600 to 700 of my soldiers had a splendid parade. It was long, and yet the entire distance they marched like true soldiers. My officers are helping me with garden inspection, the captains reporting at stated intervals." She said the program was not only developing a sense of responsibility, but a feeling in children that they really can help "Uncle Sam."[48]

A junior high schooler, Joe Lee Davis of Lexington, Kentucky, even composed a song for the garden army based on a popular ditty of the era:

Johnnie get your hoe, get your hoe, get your hoe;
Mary dig your row, dig your row, dig your row;
Down to business, boys and girls,
Learn to know the farmer's joys,
Uncle Sam's in need, pull the weed, plant the seed,
While the sunbeams lurk, do not shirk, get to work.
All the lads must spade the ground,
All the girls must hustle round.

Chorus.
Over there, over there;
Send the word, send the word over there,
That the lads are hoeing, the lads are hoeing,
The girls are sowing ev'ry where,
Each a garden to prepare,
Do your bit so that we all can share
With the boys, with the boys, the brave boys,
Who will not came back 'till it's over, over there.[49]

Authority enthusiasm behind America's child army wielding wee weapons on weedy lots would suggest the program was a huge success. Yet Claxton's enthusiasm did not as quickly win over some educational authorities not as closely connected to the bureau's programs. An unsigned editorial in *Education* observed the program asks for 40,000 teachers to monitor six million children aged nine to fourteen who could turn yards and vacant lots into gardens. While that "reads exceedingly well," the editorial sought to advise caution and small pilot programs. "First, where are we to find the 40,000 skilled teachers of gardening who will enter upon this service at a wage of $500 a year?" the editorial asked. "Secondly, is there any available means of commanding the services of the six million boys and girls for an hour or two a day? Suppose they would rather play ball or go a'fishing! Or, if the work is substituted for regular classroom work, are the school plants to be kept running through the long vacation?"[50]

The bureau remained undaunted. In a report a year later, it announced 1.5 million leaflets about gardening instruction had been mailed to teachers, 1.5 million children responding to the call, 60,000 acres of unproductive back yards and empty lots turned into gardens. "One and one-half million children have been given something to do during the summer; something that will help carry the burden of their country in this struggle for freedom, something that will help them to build character, and something that will appeal to and develop their patriotism."[51]

Whether the School Garden Army truly contributed a useful amount to the war effort is debatable. But authorities a generation later apparently thought it did good work. In 1942 an unsigned article in *Education for Victory* concluded the School Garden Army, "enrolling thousands of school children, utilizing and encouraging the utilization of thousands of acres of vacant land in cities, towns, and in the open country, proved a potent factor in attaining victory." World War II children had plenty of opportunity to get into the great outdoors for patriotic reasons. But expectations did not seem to match World War I's hoped-for intangibles of bringing city kids to the country. The programs this time were merely practical. In World War I, authorities tried setting up extensive programs in at least nine states, and more informal programs in many of the rest. State Farm Cadet programs and the federal Boys' Working Reserve extracted extensive energy and money from government entities and private donations to set up a network of camps designed to bring city kids to the farm. But for all the hopes, and a few declarations of success, overall the project did not meet expectations. World War II federal authorities responded with a program under the High School Victory Corps umbrella, Victory Farm Volunteers. But they did not expressly use the program to promote social virtues of sending city children to farms. Authorities were more interested in just putting kids to some sort of productive task. "The war has made this country the breadbasket for half the world," wrote a director of the U.S. Department of Labor's Children's Bureau in 1944. "If the supply of food is to be sufficient, thousands of boys and girls must work on farms to replace the thousands of adults gone to war or into war production."[52] "It is probable that adjustments in the school will be necessary because of the shortage of farm labor,"[53] agreed one state commissioner of education.

The Victory Farm Volunteer program did ask for such adjustments, requiring preparatory training during the school year. Students in the program could be called on to help with harvests during term time, but would rotate to the farms so no student would be away long from the classroom. Rotation was set at three days' farm work every two weeks. "In the summer, where possible, they live at home and are transported to their work on farms by bus. Where this arrangement is not feasible, work camps are set up, sometimes in the gymnasiums or other rooms in rural schools." Some state authorities did respond to calls asking for school closings and academic credit for farm work. "There have been occasional 'vacations' for picking cotton or apples or for 'rescuing the strawberries,'" but most school boards favored encouraging work during school breaks. Rural districts sometimes eliminated breaks during the year so students could get into the fields as early as possible in the spring. As for academic credit, authorities couldn't always say no. "Some credit is usually given," the authors, a University of Maryland College Park dean, and an NEA associate secretary, noted in 1944. "Most educators believe it has considerable value."[54] So did many adolescents. The War Food Administration in 1943 estimated 400,000 were placed on farms by a variety of agencies; another 300,000 found jobs of their own. The Children's Bureau surveyed and found what it expected, cases of youth exploitation.

It responded by setting guidelines for hiring non-farm kids, and produced a 1943 booklet, *Guides to Successful Employment of Nonfarm Youth in Wartime Agriculture*, to help farmers stay within federal law and guidelines. Within weeks 200,000 were distributed.[55]

In a 1942 radio address, President Franklin Roosevelt said school authorities should encourage children to use summer vacations or after-school time to help farmers. Possibly they could be permitted to leave school early for important farm or industry work. But he affirmed, "this does not mean closing schools and stopping education" and it applied only to secondary schools. Elementary students were expected to keep school hours as before.[56] But after-school time was still available. Younger children could plant and weed as well as contribute by collecting scrap or selling war bonds.

Authorities did not expect elementary school children to actually contribute much. "The habits, attitudes, and information that elementary-school children acquire by engaging in war service activities are more important."[57] A *Victory Garden Handbook* published by the Pennsylvania State Council of Defense emphasized in its school garden chapter that children of all ages could learn about nutrition by harvesting their own school lunches from their gardens. To organize such a garden for fifth through ninth graders, teachers or principals were encouraged to help children create a plan for a plot eight by ten feet, drawing rows on paper to indicate vegetables they would like to plant. To show harvested crops, rows would be marked on the plan with a red x. By planning, planting and harvesting, authorities suggested a child could learn a "horticultural gamut," along with practical knowledge of arithmetic, precision, manual dexterity. It could also "institute a competitive spirit in the child." Children enrolled would receive a certificate of participation.[58] The U.S. Department of Agriculture's Victory Garden program for home-front adults enjoyed considerable success, with some 20 million gardens planted. Contributions of children young and old to the Victory Garden program can be evaluated indirectly by a 1943 count provided by the Office of Education: John A. Studebaker reported the nation's schools "sponsored one million school and home victory gardens."[59] What the United States commissioner of education meant by "sponsored" is uncertain, but surely one can conclude that elementary school children offered more productive participation in America's wartime backlot garden program than authorities had expected. Despite that, a Boy Scout-sponsored poll of boys (not only scouts) featured in a 1943 publication for teachers indicated that their least favorite wartime volunteer activities, along with collecting paper and distributing leaflets, was tending Victory Gardens. Why? The boys didn't think it was doing much for the war effort. On the other hand, they reported liking actual farm work, because "It's new"; "It is interesting with lots of things to do"; and "We all went together." The poll observed that the boys' volunteer favorites often had included "the chance to work as a gang."[60]

Authorities did expect to see some tangible results from assigning older school children to real vocational tasks, including farm work. "Boys and girls gain educationally from contact with the real world of work and genuine experiences in community activity," said Studebaker. "This has been demonstrated again and again in the case of thousands of school youth who have helped on farms, grown victory gardens, carried programs of part-time work and part-time schooling, or participated in a variety of community services activities." In that year Studebaker reported the Victory Farm Volunteers program had recruited "several hundred thousand" youth for farms.[61] Speaking to the National Education Association a year earlier, Kansas Governor Payne Ratner found farm work a good way to get children out of a classroom supposedly disconnected from practical life, and into the real world. "The classroom must be geared into the war effort. Education must get into the production line. It must be in the fields with our farmers."[62]

It also might be in the smaller fields of backyards and vacant lots. The School Garden Army of World War I came back during World War II as the School Garden Service. No insignia or military structure emphasized this time. This idea of tending plants for Uncle Sam was rolled into the larger program of Victory Gardens meant for home-front volunteers of all ages. While the Victory Garden program for adults grew to be a huge part of America's home-front war effort, the aim of the School Garden Service began modestly. Teachers could help children tend gardens on school grounds, or children could tend by themselves at home or on community plots. Their harvests may not be enough to keep the troops victualed, but could help hometown folk. "The vegetables produced may be used chiefly to supplement the supplies needed for the school lunch; they may be used at home; or they may be used to supplement the food supplies of community organizations of institution." How could this help the war effort? In total war, "Every man, every woman, every child must be ready to take his place or her place," explained a writer identified as a spokesman for the Health and Welfare Services of the U.S. Federal Security Agency. "To do so requires health. One cannot expect to be physically fit, mentally alert, and ready to 'take it' unless a well-balanced diet, including plenty of fruits and vegetables, has provided that energy and fuel which is necessary to keep in top-notch condition all of the time."[63]

## Everything under One Roof: The High School Victory Corps

During World War II the School Garden Service, like most government-sponsored volunteer war job groups for children, was drawn under an immense bureaucratic canopy called the High School Victory Corps. In contrast, or perhaps in response, to piecemeal efforts to bring children into the war, this corps aimed to coordinate just about every activity youngsters might undertake for the home front, in school and out. While the program was announced from Washington by radio on September 25, 1943, it was not at its origins a top-down movement: federal authorities responded to a state groundswell of calls for help. The schools had been urging Washington to set up a way to bring together a variety of war-related volunteer activities and requests to the schools, explained victory corps acting national director Rall I. Grigsby in 1943, noting, "U.S. Office of Education's Wartime Commission undertook a general study of the problem of wartime service organizations in secondary schools early in the summer of 1942." From this study a national policy committee was organized, with representation from the war department, navy department, civil aeronautics authority, Federal Security Agency (entity under which the Office of Education operated during the war), and education office Wartime Commission.

Later that summer a group of high school principals were brought to Washington to witness the announcement of a new way to organize school children for war, the High School Victory Corps, wrote Grigsby, who served as Special Assistant to Studebaker. Authorities proposed a framework "into which can be fitted any and all legitimate demands that can be made upon the secondary schools of the nation in wartime," explained Grigsby. "By providing in a single organized program for the curricular, extracurricular and community service activities of participating members, the High School Victory Corps finds a place for every high school boy and girl anxious to do his or her part in helping to win the war." The Pennsylvania school superintendent concluded, "There is no legitimate demand which can be made upon the secondary school which cannot become a part of the Victory Corps."[64]

Studebaker was given more credit for the idea in *Parents' Magazine*. The author noted Studebaker as a young educator in Iowa during World War I had organized the Junior Red Cross. But while that was a part-time activity, "the High School Victory Corps seeks to engage the total interest of all students, in class and out." McNutt agreed, "Every high school student should regard himself as in the reserves."[65]

In organizing the federal structure, substituting for a military-style "chain of command" would be "chain of cooperation," explained Jay Deiss, an Office of Education editor and writer. The Victory Corps Policy Committee would meet monthly; half of its representatives would be from war agencies, and half from education. Chairing the committee would be Eddie Rickenbacker, World War I flying ace and president of Eastern Airlines. In his absence, Joseph W. Barker, Special Assistant to the secretary to the navy, would preside. Next in the "chain" would be the state education offices, each of which would appoint a Victory Corps director. These would receive a mimeographed *Victory Corps News Letter,* and other material suggesting ideas for the corps. Ideas would be transferred to local Victory Corps advisory committees. "This local committee may or may not include student representatives, but ultimately the suggestions for wartime cooperation are interpreted and acted upon in the light of the resources of the local high school."[66] "In this manner, Jimmy Colton, age seventeen, who a year hence may be James Colton, Private First Class, learns how he can make the best possible contribution to the war," Deiss offered as an example. "He learns why the federal government and the state government and his local school want him to continue in school and that they also want him to work after school.... He learns that he can help by putting a very large part of this war job income into the high school war bond drive."[67]

Agreed I. L. Kandel, a prominent educator, the corps insignia, uniform, parades, induction ceremonies and rituals—"all these were elements in developing consciousness of participation in the war effort." Writing shortly after the war, Kandel said, "The Victory Corps was designed as much for promoting and maintaining the morale of youth as it was to provide training.[68]

While this explanation suggests the Victory Corps was set up to coordinate and inspire, the corps that emerged clearly had a more specific goal, at least from Washington's perspective: to train and prepare future soldiers. An organization set up by a committee strongly represented by war-related departments, the Victory Corps continued to include war department representation on its National Policy Committee. The corps was, noted an army liaison to the education office, "an extremely useful means by which the War Department is enabled to speak to the schools with careful observation of the normal channels of education which obtain in this nation."[69] Speaking also at the 1942 radio announcement of the Victory Corps, Robert B. Patterson, under-secretary of war, said the army did not have enough time to train inductees. The high schools would have to help, and the Victory Corps was a way to achieve that. The corps could form an efficient way to adjust secondary curriculum to better fit the army's needs. "These pre-induction trained men, physically fit, can then step right into orientation and refresher courses upon enlistment."[70] Studebaker enlarged by saying the Victory Corps gave high schools a suggested pattern for adapting their curricula to wartime needs. Through this, "the schools have provided high-school boys with a valuable general orientation to the armed forces."[71] The Office of Education concluded simply in 1943, "The purpose of the Victory Corps is to prepare for work in the armed forces or in the home front."[72]

The idea of such an organization serving primarily as a military grooming system did not seem to mirror the original intention behind the groundswell of state support, which merely searched for some kind of federal clearinghouse managing home-front activities of minors. It also is not certain whether the Victory Corps worked very well as a nation-wide ersatz military training center. Participants were able to wear clothing vaguely resembling uniforms, white shirt or blouse and dark pants or skirt. Emblems for Victory Corps divisions would be earned through class work and community service. To wear the V emblem of the air service division, for example, a boy would take shop classes to prepare him for aviation mechanics, get a part-time job or volunteer at the air field, "and must participate in military drill or a physical fitness program."[73] This insignia program based on specified tasks appears to copy the well-established Boy Scout Merit Badge program which had proved enormously popular during this time. A pamphlet describing the Paper Trooper program explained, "Advancement in rank for attaining waste paper collection quotas or for winning school room, school or district contest, is one of the most effective stimulants to youthful effort. And here are chevrons to denote that rank."[74]

But one historian believed most Victory Corps volunteers did little actual training for war. "Ostensibly they were being prepared for war work or the services, but for the most part they were kept busy with parades, scrap drives, bond sales and calisthenics. For these activities the high schools gave academic credit."[75] A 1943 education professor feared the heavily vocational, war-related emphasis of the Victory Corps would lead students to the wrong conclusions. "Children will be exploited instead of educated through work. The glamour of the Victory Corps with its high official backing and colorful insignia will weight the values of pupils and may even warp the judgment of its promoters."[76] As the Victory Corps grew in its preoccupation with curricular matters most of interest to military readiness, the U.S. Office of Civil Defense launched a branch effort, the Junior Citizens Service Corps. Targeted were younger adolescents not yet in high school. "The major emphasis of the Junior Citizens Services Corps is on extracurricular activities, whereas the principal concern of the High School Victory Corps is curricular," explained Frank Lewis, identified as an advisor to

*The federal government's High School Victory Corps promoted physical fitness as preparation for war service. According to the original cutline on this photo circa 1942, boys in Flushing High School, Queens, New York, were required to scale an eight-foot obstacle "at top speed" to prepare for military service.*

*Library of Congress Collection.*

the junior corps. "In either case the insigne of the Junior Citizens Service Corps is regarded as further recognition rather than as competing with or duplicating that of the High School Victory Corps." The author declared that both corps will serve to impart "a feeling on the part of the students that they are truly a part of the war effort."[77] As for the girls, usually their interests were acknowledged as an afterthought. For work in war industries, girls were not exempt, explained a writer in *Education for Victory*: "Many girls are receiving Victory Corps training through trade and industrial education programs."[78]

Built as it was by the nation's top leaders, and heavily promoted throughout the nation, almost every school purportedly participated in the Victory Corps, "an overwhelming majority," according to Studebaker, speaking to the NEA in 1943.[79] "No one issues commands, but the power of 6,500,000 high school students and 334,000 teachers and principals is mobilized through the High School Victory Corps program for maximum contribution to victory," declared Deiss.[80] But while the program clearly was popular, a more careful study in 1943 sponsored by the non-governmental NEA showed participation in this voluntary program was by no means as universal as some authorities liked to presume. Responses from 1,426 school systems showed a 52 percent participation in the Victory Corps. Participation within individual states varied; high was 90 percent in Maryland and Georgia. In that latter state certificates granting participation were issued to schools only after state inspection to assure they met minimum qualifications. Minimums must have been modest, however, as non-participation totaled only 10 percent. In Washington State, on the other hand, every high school adopted the program "in a mass ceremony." Participation was more popular in urban areas: 86 percent of schools in cities over 100,000 reported participation, but only 42 percent in cities under 2,500. The study said this difference "might be expected," but did not explain why. Possibly smaller schools could not muster the teacher power to coordinate. Concerning curriculum, the study noted, "Since the Victory Corps emphasizes preparation for war duties, the basic question is: 'What changes have been made in cur-riculum emphasis?'" Based on *Victory Corps Pamphlet No. 1* advising schools to increase training in science, math, physical education, preflight instruction and shop work, the study concluded three-fourths of school districts had moved to make such changes. But making changes to curricula was not easy for some districts. Administrators complained that draft boards called for military duty just those teachers who had the expertise to cover these subjects, leaving an "acute" shortage. As well, some contended liberal arts education should not be abandoned for vocational and practical subjects directly relating to wartime needs, and tried to maintain "a satisfactory balance between cultural and practi-cal education." "Readjustment" to allow students time off for farm or industrial work was cited as a common concern.[81]

Considering that participation from state to state, and district to district, varied, so too did approaches to joining the corps. In Meridian, Mississippi, high school students and faculty gathered in a "mass meeting" to debate and approve a draft of several "basic assumptions" regarding participation. Included were: "The job of the schools in this total war is to educate the nation's man-power for war and for the peace that is to follow"; "We can lose this war on the educational front"; "Education is the backbone of the army"; "The secondary school must determine the aptitude of all students for specific war work."[82] High school promoters in Wilmington, Delaware, were more practical. A committee of faculty and students set up requirements for joining the corps: participation in a physical education program; studying courses suitable to grade and age "but also of immediate and future usefulness to the nation's war effort"; and "partici-pation in at least one important wartime activity or service of a specified type."[83]

Realizing that students might need encouragement to join, they decided that what was called for was an appealing campaign. At two student assemblies student representatives of five Victory Corps divisions— land, sea, air, commu-nity and production—appeared sporting extra-large division insignia to explain the purpose of their work. "To keep with the patriotic effect, the Minute Maids, in red, white, and blue costumes, presented a lively song and dance. People sang a Victory Corps song to the tune of 'Washington Lee Swing'":

Come one and all to join the Victory Corps,
To do your best to win this war.
Come give your pledge: to do always your share
Upon the land, the sea, at home, or in the air.
Come. Wear the VF which stands for Victory
And do your best to keep your Liberty.
Come one and all before it is too late;
It's a date—join TODAY![84]

How effective was that? "Enthusiastically humming their song, the students returned to their homerooms to fill out the Victory Corps Membership Blanks.... They took their blanks home to be signed by their parents. The initial return was 276." It is not clear if this figure totaled boys and girls, or just girls; the writers do not indicate what percentage of the students this represented. But the report did note later that 1,371 students attended the high school, which would make participation rate 20 percent. In addition to the rallies, the school displayed cases of Victory Corps insignia, posters and pamphlets, and the school library "has been in constant contact with the Office of War Information and its posting of bulletins and broadsides which contribute most to the war effort." Guidance counselors and teachers "encourage all students here to choose wisely some phase of the war effort to which they can give themselves immediately."[85]

Schools electing to adapt their curriculum to Victory Corps recommendations were encouraged to triage students by aptitudes needed for the war effort. Franklin R. Zeran, an Office of Education vocational division guidance specialist, suggested high school counselors take an "individual inventory" based on Victory Corps participation. An example came from the program in Maquoketa, Iowa. That school district issued a War Service Guidebook to each member of the Victory Corps "in which is recorded work experience, community surveys, occupational and personal analyses, and results of guidance conferences." Such an assessment could help authorities determine "A reliable record of the individual characteristics of each pupil, as they related to his usefulness in winning the war."[86] The writer did not suggest authorities should consider interests or requests from the students. In fact, a survey showed that after the first flush of war enthusiasm, many high school students and more than a few of their teachers did not join the Office of Education's sense of urgency in favor of a militarized curriculum. In a 1944 Indiana poll, the majority said "training to earn a living" was more important than training to serve in the military or war-related industries.[87]

Victory Corps supporters in 1943 reflected their disappointment that the corps had not spread as widely as they had hoped. The problem was money, they determined—money to call back retired teachers, and to train new teachers for vocational coursework favored by the Victory Corps program. In March 1943 a bill supported by a wide swath of authorities from the NEA to the Association of Secondary School Principals asked Congress to fund the Victory Corps with an appropriation of $8.5 million. But that request called to battle those Americans who for decades had fought against federal control of locally based education in the United States. Studebaker reminded detractors that the Victory Corps was voluntary, advisory, coordinated by local or state officials. He reminded congressional leaders, "The Victory Corps is simply a plan which in this time of national peril and of national effort creates a nationwide framework of organization into which schools may, if they desire, fit their various existing local student war organizations."[88]

Some politicians were not impressed. The Victory Corps had already been taken to task for relying on a quasi-military structure; in Ohio, for example, the corps languished as critics said the system of insignias appeared to build an organization not unlike the Hitler Youth. The large contingent of Americans averse to school-based military training said the Victory Corps surely seemed designed to remake youthful minds to a military standard. This viewpoint was taken up by a prominent literary spokesman in 1943. "Membership in the corps is voluntary, but somehow the word 'Victory' leaves a boy or girl little choice in the matter, I should think," reflected author E. B. White in *Harpers*. "High-school children in uniform are somehow a symbol of defeat, not victory. Adolescence is the time for the shedding of authority, not for the habit of obedience."[89] Others even complained about the corps' exercise program of group calisthenics, saying it was "designed to foster regimentation."[90]

Congress faced growing resistance from a fraction of its consistency fearing any kind of federal meddling in local education, and so failed to bring the bill to a vote. The setback subdued Studebaker's enthusiasm. Without congressional assistance, participation decayed to 70 percent in the larger schools by 1943, and 30 percent in communities of fewer than 2,500. In summer 1944 an Office of Education committee advised Studebaker to abandon the Victory Corps newsletter and Victory Corps section of *Education for Victory*, which he did. The corps had begun too late, reflected historian Richard Ugland, and moreover, top military leaders were not as supportive as they might seem to have been; inductees who could not read, write, do arithmetic or even pass a few basic fitness tests needed help a lot earlier. "Officials at the Office of Education often appeared more enthusiastic about preinduction training than even the military," concluded Ugland. "It was the educators' way of having a prominent spot in the war effort."[91] Writing in 1948, a prominent educator observed, "The organization and its plans received a great deal of publicity for a year or so, but no general report to indicate the extent to which it was adopted by the high schools or its effectiveness was published."[92]

Of those high schools that did join the Victory Corps, most apparently preferred self-coordinating their volunteer programs. High school-aged children in general found volunteer activities harder to find as they climbed closer to adulthood. Many selling and scrapping campaigns were aimed to those children more easily motivated by busy work, aged nine to fourteen. "They provided a sense of worth, an identification with the war effort and purposeful activity," wrote a YMCA national leader in 1944. "However, again the fifteen- to eighteen-year-olds were not involved in these service activities to any considerable extent. The bulk of the opportunity went to those under fifteen." He blamed statistics showing an increase in wartime juvenile delinquency at least partly on the country's failure to fill older adolescents' free time. "The High School Victory Corps provided for community service as part of the program for high school youth, but most high schools limited their participation in the Victory Corps program to the recommended curricular changes."[93]

### Scrapping for Uncle Sam

Authorities usually looked to the Victory Corps specifically for direction to militarize curricula for the nation's 6,387,805 secondary school students in World War II. But the Victory Corps' goal was larger, "designed to rally people to their wartime tasks."[94] In that purpose it is hard to say the corps failed. Many adolescents, particularly the younger, did themselves responded by joining in large numbers the many service opportunities loosely sheltered under the large Victory Corps umbrella. Some were strictly volunteer; some paid a little. Most were tedious tasks adults declined to do. The jobs kids were asked to do showed similarities during both wars, and included making things, collecting things, delivering things and selling things. Many Americans who were children in World War II particularly remember participating in the country's vast drives to "bring in the scrap" in an attempt to fill wartime shortages. Authorities presented this as an ideal activity for the younger child in both wars. A best age might be twelve or thirteen, but younger children certainly could have a go as well. It could fill their free time, help the nation, build team virtue, and not incidentally do a job adults might find beneath them. Children will be efficient and tireless, wrote a well-known educational author, because "Collecting is a child's instinct. During the war, when we are searching for worthwhile work for children, this instinct can well be used for the good of all concerned."[95] Every child beyond the toddler stage, advocated an author in PTA Magazine, needs to find an activity to feel he or she is doing something for the war effort. Four- and five-year-olds could collect paper, metal, and rubber, and "clean their plates to conserve food." Children six to eight could also make scrapbooks for soldiers and save pennies for war bonds. Ten pennies would buy one war stamp; 1,875 pennies would buy one war bond. The pre-teens nine to eleven could make ashtrays, checkerboards and jigsaw puzzles for soldiers in hospitals, collect playing cards for the men, sell and buy war stamps and bonds, and "learn about Democracy."[96]

Enormous numbers of children participated, according to statistics supplied by the Office of Education, as well as private groups such as the Boy Scouts and Future Farmers of America (FFA). Studebaker announced that "the 30 million children in 1943" collected more than 1.5 million tons of scrap.[97] But 30 million was the country's entire population of school children, making it doubtful his number was based on an actual count of participation. In addition to canvassing door to door and rummaging through dumpgrounds for rusty car parts, tin cans, cast-out copper and aluminum, World War II children sacrificed old toys, peeled foil off gum wrappers, dragged in tires, salvaged fats and grease, hoarded rags, and in the fall fanned out to the ditches to collect milkweed pods. Milkweed floss could substitute for kapok in life jackets, but had to be bagged from wild plants, because three years' time was necessary for cultivating milkweed. "The nation is absolutely dependent on the school children of America for the collection of a sufficient supply of milkweed pods to meet military needs," wrote Education for Victory.[98]

Children received a small payment for the pods; in fact, children generally received small payments for their scrap collections. The money may not have served as personal motivation, however. It seldom actually reached their pockets: children generally were compelled to donate it to their school or a relief agency, or contribute to war bonds sales. But children were motivated by rounds of competition, with patches or certificates for those who collected the most scrap. While comics and other popular culture promoted such competitions, some educational authorities in World War II did not want to aggressively support the kind of games that drew World War I's children embarrassment and hard feelings for not keeping up with those children who gained more from luck than from pluck. Howard Lane, a Northwestern University associate professor of education, claimed cooperation could collect more scrap than competition.

Working for awards and certificates should not be emphasized. "One rule: avoid without exception the use of competition in promoting valuable work among the children. Collect scrap. Buy stamps for the real reasons, not to win banners."[99] Elementary school pupils might be harmed by classroom competition and goal-setting that "make for dangerous pressures and possible harmful results."[100]

Others pointed out the country was reverting to the same exploitive situation common in the past, when children worked jobs adults did not want to do, while teachers dropped the three Rs from their classes to free up time for scrap drives. But as Roosevelt himself declared the need for children to collect, critics lay low to avoid charges of being unpatriotic. The truth was that competitive games worked. Authorities looking for ways to motivate children found the tactic irresistible, and promotions in children's popular media offered their own competitions.

Yet it soon became clear enthusiasm for repeated scrap drives might be wearing thin. In a poll of boys as early as 1942, several hundred thought collecting paper was pointless, while other children tired of repeated slogans and wondered why enormous mountains of scrap sat on the school grounds for months without pickup.[101] In the survey boys concluded, "They didn't need it," "Couldn't see how it was important," or "It wasn't doing much for the war."[102] Authorities responded as they knew how during the world wars, by regaling propaganda with exhortations including new flashy posters, more patriotic flyers, and innovative promotions. One such promotion was the Paper Troopers, launched later in the war by the Salvage Division of the War Production Board. Emery W. Balduf, chairman of the advisory committee for school salvage programs, explained paper was short not only because the army used five million of the seventeen million tons produced yearly, but because wood pulp to produce paper waned as its work force left for service or munitions industries. "Most of the schools throughout the country have already responded nobly to the urgent appeals to save and collect paper," he observed. "Some of them, however, have put on only 'one-time' drives. These need to be repeated—again and again." The salvage board's goal, he added, was to address "the necessity of finding some way of keeping most of our 30,000,000 school children—at least those who are too young to hold defense jobs—active in this work during the summer vacation period."[103]

Solution of these authorities was as might be expected, another patriotic scrapping squad for children. The Paper Trooper program launched fall 1944 gained momentum through cooperation from the Office of Education, along with the American Newspaper Publishers Association and Conservation Committee of the Waste Paper Consuming Industries. In this program children could earn a blue and yellow arm patch of the Paper Trooper for collecting a quota of paper set by their school. Chevrons went to those children earning above the quota, and for the outstanding paper collectors, the chair of the War Production Board would mail signed certificates of merit. Competition was encouraged, certificates also going to "the leading schools in communities where the schools compete with one another." Benefits could go beyond awards, addressing the "psychological injuries" of children during wartime. "School children with fathers or brothers in the services share their mothers' worries and inner tensions," observed Balduf. "But the child who collects waste paper so that supplies can be shipped to his soldier father or brother overseas experiences a relief from tension because he is doing something positive."[104] There was also the money factor; salvage dealers might pay for paper. In Minneapolis, for example, Longfellow School reported amassing $1,613.75 to pay for twelve school projects.[105]

According to a pamphlet issued for schools or others hoping to launch a Paper Trooper program, authorities responded by setting up a plan based on successful local efforts around the country. In common was the need to emphasize the importance of the children's efforts, and the prestige of joining a federally sponsored group. "Many productive waste paper salvage programs give pupils an opportunity to join a distinguished corps, group or army, as members of which they are publicly identified as aiding in important war work," the pamphlet observed, and so the johnny-come-lately Paper Trooper program would be no exception. Besides the military-style ranks, "the name has a resemblance to the name paratroopers, those daring raiders dropped from the sky behind enemy lines, and should, therefore, have a tremendous appeal to pupils." While appealing most to the boys' spirit of "fighting adventure," the emblem "will appeal to the girls too."[106] War Production chairman Donald M. Nelson reminded adults that children needed to help increase scrap paper collection from the current 542,000 tons a month to 667,000 tons. Studebaker could of course be counted on for support. In a letter to state school superintendents, however, he did refer to apparent criticism that paper collected from past campaigns had sometimes languished waiting for collection. "I have been assured by the salvage division of the War Production Board that the current campaign is national in scope and that there will be no 'backwash' of paper collected, as in 1942." Blame for the paper clutter that demoralized some collectors was shifted to local administrators, who were urged to "clear with their local salvage committees or the state salvage offices before undertaking waste paper collections."[107]

The specific manner in which salvage campaigns were conducted can be presumed from a description of authorities who suggested approaches for the Paper Troopers. As this was launched during the last full year of World War II, and described as a campaign based on the best programs around the nation, it probably reflected the approach of many such children's salvage campaigns during the war. To begin, propaganda: teachers were asked to start from a base of "immense publicity" for the drive by incorporating it into class lectures. Some examples: "Dramatics—Classroom or assembly skits that dramatize the story of waste paper and the war. Science—The processes of preparing waste paper for further use. Shop Work—Construction of a paper baler. Economics—The functions of paper in modern society."[108] With children so motivated in the classroom, paper drives could be set up in two ways, depending on city size. Larger cities were divided into quarters based on high school districts. Each district was subdivided into blocks under a block captain, who directed collectors. On a Thursday before the weekly pickup, children from each district visited every home to remind them to have their scrap paper ready for later pickup. The Milwaukee School District also provided handbills to leave with residents. On Saturday morning, children assembled at "Control Center" (the school) to fan out for scrap paper. Those households that failed to leave paper at the curb were again called upon by children. For the rest, children collected and bundled the paper, and hauled the bundles to the corner, where a salvage truck picked them up. A block captain rode with the truck to provide a "route book" to prove his team collected only from its designated route. This was important because competitive teams might otherwise nip into another's route to augment their load. "There is a very strong rivalry between districts and schools within a given collection district," as districts were paid and awarded for the amount of paper they collected.[109]

A second method was particularly popular in smaller cities, and more informally organized. Children were asked to collect scrap paper on their own, and bring it to the school. High-scrappers received prizes, and super-scrapping schools received banners, in addition to salvage money. Motivation schemes differed. In one example, a county organized all its schools to designate each child as a "commando." Various ranks were assigned to key scrappers. As they delivered salvaged paper or other scrap, they advanced in rank. Children in one small town received awards and cash prizes. In another example, paper industry sales people gave pep talks to students. "It has been found, however, that such talks and the discussion of the waste paper situation by the teacher must be repeated from time to time with new notes of interest added."[110]

During summer vacations it was more difficult to organize children, al-though thought no less important to continue scrap drives. Adult supervision was also more difficult to secure. Yet authorities affirmed children should not be set free for the summer. By continuing their work, children could develop "competence as youthful citizens," and, as authorities feared rising delinquency, "minds occupied with constructive projects give little thought to mischief."[111]

How well did the Paper Troopers do? In one example, Balduf reported Chi-cago elementary pupils collected an average of one million pounds of waste paper a week, sold to scrap dealers. "Half the money goes to veteran's welfare charities, the other half back to the schools in proportion of what they col-lected."[112] None, apparently, stayed in kids' pockets. A thirteen-year-old named Jack Lighthart, Maywood, Illinois, "came to national attention in February for having collected one hundred tons of waste paper by pony cart last year." His achievement was covered by radio and newsreel crews. In Massachusetts the Ab-ercrombie School of Greenfield "won the city-wide Waste Paper Salvage Contest award and flags by collecting 497.89 pounds per pupil. The average for thirteen schools was 83.40 pounds per pupil."[113]

Other youth groups reported seemingly enormous amounts of all kinds of scrap collected, making it hard to avoid concluding that the children's ef-forts did do some practical good, despite the opinion of many authorities that this was of secondary interest. Those who remembered their childhood during World War II did not generally know for sure what benefit their collecting work had on prosecution of the war overseas. But they did agree that it built virtues of character and teamwork, and they remembered fondly the spirit of patriotism and group achievement. "If young people could have that kind of mutual goal now I believe there would be a lot less drugs, crime, etc." said one in a later in-terview.[114] It was that pride of cheerful achievement that served as glue to warm memories of the World War II children's generation.[115]

World War I children did not experience the highly organized scrapper cam-paigns so vividly recalled during World War II. In fact, World War I literature reflects scant interest to collecting scrap, and great interest in harvesting crops— a striking contrast between the two generations. But World War I children were asked to collect fruit pits and nut shells for a reason no one today might guess: they were burned to charcoal for gas masks. And Wilson himself thanked Boy Scouts for helping to identify and harvest the country's "liberty tree" of World War I for its essential uses in airplane propellers and gun stocks: walnut.[116] Of course, what was considered worth a child's time to collect reflected the state of military technology at the time. Walnut certainly played little role in subsequent wars.

At the beginning World War II children were encouraged to build model airplanes for air defense. These models served to help spotters identify Allied and Axis aircraft; 500,000 models would be needed. "The model plane project is valuable for boys who participate because, as expressed by one instructor, (1) it gives a boy an opportunity to render practical service to the armed forces, and (2) it teaches accuracy and thoroughness of craftsmanship," wrote the Office of Education's *Education for Victory*. Presented as usual by afterthought, the (unsigned) article added girls had also shown interest.[117] But children needed little encouragement to do what they already liked to do. While a half million model airplanes would seem to be quite a quantity, the program was suspended at the end of 1943, the military reporting it now had plenty of models to go around. Children jumped to model building in such numbers that by the end of that year 600,000 models had been built, a hundred thousand more than requested.[118] Why? "It's my hobby," "I always liked to do that," explained boys in a poll.[119]

Of course, America's air force was in its infancy during World War I. Children then worked more intensely to provide other products for home-front use. Especially popular among girls was food canning. Canning clubs became patriotic particularly for girls not only to encourage home conservation, but to balance the shortage of commercial canning workers who were pulled away by more lucrative munitions work or military draft. While these ag-related clubs predated World War I, they helped fulfill a need after teachers were encouraged to move to larger facilities with bigger stoves and vats. "The boys will prepare the fruit; the women and girls will can it or dry it, as the case may be. To dispose of the product is a simple matter. It may be sold and the proceeds divided."[120] Sewing for the troops too was more popular among the girls (mostly) of World War I, working often for the Junior Red Cross. They sent garments to the troops "by the hundreds of thousands," a total of 225,000 garments along with 3,000 pieces of furniture from boys sent to France.[121] One librarian observed girls seemed to do nothing but knit; they certainly didn't read.[122] But common to children of both war generations was the demand that they do more than collect and motivate: they needed to sell.

### Pitching War Bonds—and Spying for Uncle Sam

Arguably the single most pervasive way the children's army contributed to the home front during both wars was to raise money for the government. They could be expected to do this in three ways. They could lend their own money, by buying war bonds and stamps. They could encourage their parents to lend money. They could encourage everyone else to lend money.

Did the government need this money to prosecute the war? Yes, but that wasn't the whole story. World wars I and II were unlike subsequent American conflicts of the twentieth century because they were financed mostly by direct contributions from American citizens. The government enhanced wartime tax revenue by issuing bonds. In World War I, four bond drives brought $21.5 billion the government critically needed to finance the war. Treasury secretary William McAdoo favored more taxes, but faced stiff opposition, and so relied heavily on borrowing. But interwar Keynesian economic theory encouraged World War II treasury secretary Henry Morgenthau to promote a new series of war bonds for motives obvious and not so. That war brought the American economy from lingering depression to full employment, and with it a rising money supply. But rationing limited purchase opportunities. To head off inflation, the government hoped to mop up excess cash from circulation. And children could help with that, too. While an enormous advertising campaign encouraged adults to send their savings to Washington, children were enlisted to do the legwork for promotion and sales. Marketing campaigns designed for adults leaked into children's daily routines, of course, but the plan to encourage sales among the under-eighteens began with a focus on the one best way Washington could reach Anytown, USA: the schools. The government set up state bond sale coordinators who recruited local agents to enlist teachers and their school districts. Teachers would become the sales agents, schools the sales headquarters, children the door-to-door sales staff, compensated in character development. Their sales territories were described by school boundaries.[123] According to the inaugural issue of the World War II U.S. Treasury pamphlet *Schools at War: A War Savings Bulletin for Teachers*, schools were expected to follow the five points of the school bond program V-Star: "Learn, Share, Serve, Conserve, Save." It explained, "You and your students must save (a) to help pay for the war; (b) to hold prices down by not spending for scarce goods, and (c) to plan for individual futures."[124]

Authorities in World War II realized they had to set up an extensive plan on a national level to reach 30 million children, in 26,000 high schools, and 200,000 elementary schools, and through them, millions of parents.[125] To begin, the kids needed to be persuaded to give their own money. Bonds had drawbacks. Most children might not realize, for example, that the ten cents they were encouraged to invest each week on a savings stamp would buy the cheapest E

Library of Congress Collection.

*Children in both wars were exhorted to buy war bonds and stamps, and to sell them to adults. According to the 1943 cutline, these children, identified as being from the Chicago's south central district, were honored for selling $263,148.83 in war bonds, "enough money for 125 jeeps, two pursuit planes, and motorcycle." Speaking was Major C. Udell Turpin "of the Illinois War Bond Sales staff."*

Bond only after three and a half years' accumulation. Considering the pervasive advertisements encouraging children to "buy bonds now and get your new bike after the war," most might also not realize their bonds would mature long after they became adults, and that the interest rate was below prevailing market rates. But their parents might have discovered this. It helps to explain why many adults did not consider war bonds to be the best investments. The propaganda point, of course, was that patriotism, not logic, paid for war bonds. For children, that patriotism could be channeled into an activity that would teach thrift and discipline.

"Children want to help in the war effort." emphasized one educator. "The earnestness and enthusiasm with which they have participated in stamp purchases and salvage drives is proof of that."[126] Still, noted another, patience lagged as the war dragged. "Most children will only buy stamps if the campaign is regularly and constantly sustained, explained a Canadian educator writing for the U.S. Treasury publication *Schools at War*. "Spasmodic campaigning is as useless financially as it is educationally."[127] World War II authorities stressed teachers need to marble war savings stamp and bond sales throughout the curriculum, in every subject, pointing out, "students and teachers realized that war savings must be a part of classroom study if everyone was to understand what it was all about."[128]

In the elementary schools, arithmetic classes could make word problems based on the cost of savings stamps, on making change for stamps sold, and on how much military ordnance a collection of stamps or bonds could buy. Secondary school children could roll the program into every class, from shop to social studies. For example, Cranford, New Jersey, secondary schools tuned its English curriculum to bond sales by "publicizing the opening of the campaign, in maintaining and even boosting the amount sold per week, and reporting the weekly results." Sewing classes made money bags for bonds and change. Songs and dramatic skits sustained interest, "while young journalists use war savings themes for stories in the local newspaper."[129] Music was considered good motivation, particularly in the elementary schools, and so a nationwide music educators' contest drew lyrics from children around the country, such as these featured entries from Minnesota:

> Tune: "Put On Your Old Gray Bonnet"
> Wear your old gray bonnet
> With the old feather on it
> Then to Uncle Sam you can say
> Because of my bonnet
> With the old feather on it
> I can buy a bond today.
> Patricia Crose—11, Grade Six, Washington School, St. Cloud, Minn.

> Tune: "Yankee Doodle Dandy"
> Yankee Doodle came to town to buy
> a bar of candy,
> But on the way he saw some bonds,
> and said, "They'll come in handy."
> Yankee Doodle keep it up,
> Yankee Doodle Dandy
> Buy a stamp and save for bonds
> Instead of so much candy.
> Marcia Hornstein—10, Grade Six, Washington School, St. Cloud, Minn.[130]

Schools kept the reminders going by putting up posters indicating class or school progress toward bond sale quotas. Sales tables sprouted weekly in halls and classrooms to glean students' spare change. Libraries kept tallies and posted leaflets. War bonds became an ever-faithful companion throughout childhood.

Ted Barton, a possibly real fourth grader described in *Schools at War*, was reportedly convinced: "I'll buy three stamps...that means a movie and a candy bar...or fifteen cartridges for the Marines.... It meant a lot of work shoveling snow too.... It will mean these three will earn a fourth stamp when I turn them in toward a bond for 1953." The article noted, "Ted Barton, a typical fourth grader, is explaining his week's savings in terms of work, sacrifice, his country, and the future."[131]

The problem for Ted in this story was his father. The owner of a small grocery was squeezed by costs, staff shortages and rationing. No money left for war bonds. "But Ted has different ideas and he says so. As Mr. Barton puts it, 'Ted seems to have all the answers.' That's because Ted understands the how, the what, and the why of war savings. Ted is the Barton Minute Man talking to his family night after night about war savings."[132]

If many authorities admitted they expected children to contribute little to war bond sales themselves, here was evidence of the key reason the program became so ubiquitous within the schools. Children educated to the country's need for money could be the strongest peddlers within a home sanctum hard to reach in any other way. Lest a child forget to do his bit, teachers were encouraged to help children write "A Letter Home" to parents. Such a letter might read as follows:

Dear Dad and Mother,
In school we have been studying how everybody will have to help to raise the money the country needs in the Sixth War Loan.
The Sixth War Loan starts November 20. The amount of money needed is equal to $19 for everybody in the country, counting grownups, children and even babies. Of course, poor families and most children can't lend this much, so most grownups will have to lend much more. The goal suggested is a $100 bond, more if they can afford it.
Each family is supposed to figure out its own share, and buy the biggest amount it can, as a sort of New Year's present for the enemy.[133]

Bringing the word home to parents was necessary, but not sufficient. Authorities expected children to be an effective sales force able to reach every house, every adult, in every town. They brought their sales to school bond booths, possibly in hand-sewn money bags, where it would be tallied for competitions and awards. The Boy Scouts as indefatigable patriots were counted on last, to be the "gleaners" after others had collected what they could. "I am convinced that children can dig out sales which others have not been able to make," said one treasury department representative who was responsible for organizing a three-day clean-up drive for extra E Bond sales in cities and towns of Massachusetts. In Detroit, each "Junior Gallant" pledged to sell $500 in bonds; they sold nearly $10 million total.[134] In 1942-43, state-wide quotas for children "resulted in war savings investments equivalent to the cost of 39,535 jeeps, virtually four times your quota," wrote Morgenthau. The report put North Dakota's young sales force in first place, at 2,162 percent of its quota; Ohio came in last, 27 percent of its quota. No explanations for such discrepancies were offered.[135] A 1943 survey showed a child's battalion of one million bond peddlers had canvassed the country's grownups for bonds; schools were credited with selling $229 million worth during the Fourth Loan Drive.[136]

A favorite motivational scheme aiming to persuade larger groups of adults relied on public speaking skills of older children. World War II statewide public speaking contests in Missouri and Iowa on the topic of bond sales encouraged schools to compete. These speaking competitions grew out of World War I's Junior Four Minute Men, a volunteer speaker's bureau designed by that war's propaganda bureau to enlist home-front enthusiasm for the war and its financing.

The junior program sprouted from one of World War I's popular adult motivational schemes, the Four Minute Men. George Creel's Committee on Public Information devised the plan to promote America's role in the war by training a stable of speakers who could jump in at a moment's notice to reel off four minutes' worth of propaganda on a selected theme. The program became so popular that older children interested in public speaking hoped to get involved. The CPI had not expected to enroll children, Creel explained, but credited the state of Minnesota with launching the idea. The topic: buying war savings stamps. "Results were such that in March 1918, a Junior War-Savings Stamps campaign was held for the rest of the country," wrote Creel in his post-war report on CPI activities. "Over a million and a half copies of the bulletin published for this campaign were sent out through the various state war-savings stamps committees, which distributed them to the schools." Based on the bulletin, a teacher explained the subject, after which students prepared speeches of about 400 words. Competition for best speakers might be held within the classroom, according to Creel, but more often were school-wide, with parents and others attending, and open to both boys and girls. "Winners were given an official certificate from the government, commissioning them as Four Minute speakers upon the specified topic of the contest." Speakers were encouraged to promote the Third Liberty Loan in a contest April 6 to May 4, 1917. The CPI mailed one million copies of the bulletin describing preparation for this contest, to 200,000 schools.[137]

How this might effectively sell war bonds in World War I was explained by a Milwaukee federal treasury official, John Puelicher, who was a witness to such an event. Authorities had determined that residents of a rural Wisconsin farming area had not been persuaded by adults to buy bonds. The area was remote, and "inhabited almost entirely by people originally from the enemy countries." Authorities decided to try the state's Junior Four Minute Man program, offering a prize to the junior propagandist who would write and deliver the best address on the subject, "Why Buy Victory Bonds?" "To determine the winner an elimination contest was advocated. A hundred meetings in a hundred schools were held on one evening, and there was scarcely a person in that county not familiar, in consequence thereof, with the reasons for again supporting the government." Winners were reduced to ten at another series of public meetings, "and by this time the interest in the Victory Loan was intense."

At a packed town hall, decked in "flags and flowers," the final contestants followed the "Star Spangled Banner" by telling "their foreign-born or foreign-descended parents their duty to the land in which they lived and prospered. There could be nothing more inspiring.... The effort of these children sold the county's quota of Victory Loan Bonds," while they learned lessons of democracy.[138] In New York Junior Four Minute Men spread out to theatres and movie houses to offer their brief message of purchase. "A Liberty Bond may be only a scrap of paper," said Junior Four Minute Person Grace Pruschen, twelve, of Manhattan. "But it is a scrap of paper which bears upon its face the death warrant to autocracy in its last stronghold."[139]

When they weren't speaking up for loan sales, New York's children joined the rest of the country's youth in regularly combing neighborhoods to sell bonds and stamps. Parades and school programs fueled interest. "One such program, at P.S. 168, included the singing of patriotic songs, the presentation of a one-act play, 'The Light of Liberty,' a recitation entitled 'There Is No Hyphen in My Heart,' and a prayer for the president of the United States, sung by the audience."[140] Authorities encouraged aggressive competition, including quotas and wall charts. One particularly stylish artist drew a German airplane menacing the observer. Stationed around the base were cannons representing competing groups. Shells representing bond sales moved toward the plane as groups competed to be first to reach the German plane.[141] Target of the sales, certainly, began with the children themselves, in pennies or dimes toward war stamps. But the real target behind motivating children in World War I, as it was in the next war, was parents. "Every girl and boy, especially every little girl and every little boy, is, or ought to be, the boss of their mothers and fathers," wrote treasury secretary William McAdoo, "and I know that if you make a patriotic appeal to your mothers and fathers to save money and lend it to the government to help our gallant soldiers and sailors who are fighting to save our liberties and our country, your mothers and fathers will listen to you and take your advice."[142]

Teachers were asked to act as agents for loans by distributing subscription blanks for parents, and collecting pledges to give to local banks for transmittal to larger financial institutions conducting the loans. To enhance participation, teachers also needed to act as motivational speakers for their charges. How? One common way, reported the CPI-sponsored *National School Service*, was to say something like this: "Good morning, boys and girls. Does anyone want to buy a thrift stamp? No? Very well, take out your geographics and we will continue yesterday's lesson." That was not an effective approach, the newsletter stressed. Specific and personal was better:

> Good morning, boys and girls!
> Uncle Sam needs some more money this morning. When the boys went forward this morning they had to use a lot of ammunition. Besides, there were a number of uniforms badly torn when the soldiers went through the German barbed wire, and some helmets had holes shot in them, the Hun bullets just missing the soldiers underneath.
> "How many stamps are we going to buy to help make everything all right again? John wants two; Mary, one.
> John, how did you get your fifty cents?
> "I worked in the provision store on Saturday."
> That's fine! Who else wants stamps?[143]

Missing from the parade of directives issued to teachers was an expectation that traditional classroom work would survive. Guy Stanton Ford defended the time-consuming diversions from academics by arguing wartime tasks for children "are not intrusions on school work. They are unique opportunities to enrich and test not knowledge, but the supreme lesson of intelligent and unselfish service. It is the lesson you have always taught."[144] But educational authorities were not universally convinced that turning the schools into war loan offices could be all for the good. Some children in World War I suffered in a highly competitive environment in which the poor or immigrants who could not afford bonds were ostracized or coerced. Many had come to American schools to escape from a world in which children tended the crops and worked the streets instead of learning to read and write. A little practical labor might have been fine for the more prosperous children. It was a setback for children who needed to learn less about wielding a hoe, and more about mastering the three Rs.

World War II authorities did try to avoid the worst of this kind of exploitation. They were not entirely successful, given the heavy vocational slant to recommended wartime curricula and widespread public sympathy for states that ignored child labor laws. World War II authorities also tried to soften the harshest competition schemes, but schools were primed to compete for the inevitable prizes and badges. Competition worked. Still, the treasury department warned repeatedly against competitive extremes. "This is a voluntary sales program for the benefit of the individual," a treasury pamphlet reminded organizers in 1944. "To avoid making any pupil uncomfortable because his purchases are limited, the treasury department urges certain precautions: (1) Stress percent of pupils who participate rather than per capita sales. (2) Avoid class competition based on dollars and cents. (3) Publicize group accomplishments rather than the purchases of individual pupils."[145]

Treasury officials apparently were serious enough about this to actually visit schools that chose to put too much emphasis on competition: "In a few instances, where we have had specific cases, we have tried to send a representative to eliminate the element of competition." The department emphasized again that sales was not the immediate objective of the program. A treasury official (unnamed) concluded, "I think we ought to bear in mind that the real objective of the war savings program in the schools is not first the sale of stamps.... It is the understanding of why saving for present emergencies and future security and why removing surplus money from possible purchase of non-essentials will aid personal and national welfare."[146]

But such an argument could hardly resonate with children who were made to understand they were doing something really necessary for the men overseas, and not just serving as a thrifty sponge mop for inflation. In the 1943 survey, boys ranked as their most important activity for the war effort, "buying war stamps." Why? "Because they felt it worth their effort. Quotes include 'We are helping pay for the war'; and 'to buy guns for the fight.'"[147] To admit to these children that their bond sale work really served only as "character development" in disguise, or that authorities didn't actually expect much real good to come of it, might have led to mass defections of demoralized kids from the bond booths. Instead authorities in both wars publicly reminded children again and again that their salesmanship for Uncle Sam was critical, announcing contest after contest and winner after winner.

Nearly every child participated in bond sales, in both wars. The treasury department despite its official warnings against unhealthy competition must have encouraged such an approach by setting goals of "at least 90 percent of pupils to save week in and week out." It lauded a high school in New Bedford, Massachusetts, for achieving 100 percent war savings participation "by a variety of promotions."[148] Some elementary school children according to a World War II survey actually sold more than their older siblings. "Elementary schools in general, and elementary schools in the less prosperous neighborhoods in particular, are leading the war stamp parade in many cities," reported a 1943 U.S. Treasury-produced pamphlet for teachers. According to Detroit administrator C. L. Thiele, of that city's ten largest producing schools per capita, seven were elementary. A Newark, New Jersey, survey concluded, "The children from the lower part of the environmental scale put more into war stamps than their friends from more well-to-do neighborhoods."[149] This suggests children's World War II bond sales might have been a class-based phenomenon, but insufficient evidence is available for that conclusion. It did seem like children were making a difference: $300 million in sales reported in 1943 sounds like a lot. But $300 million added a small amount to the billions bought by nearly every adult in World War II. That war's bond sales totaled $185.7 billion.

Still, argument could be made then—and perhaps still can be made today—that selling door to door builds assertive children who know the value of work and the tricks of persuasion. But that was not the end of the argument, at least not in World War I. While building their work ethic, children in that war could also build their observational skills. Specifically, they could spy. Children had unique access to intimate family settings, for starters. Outside the home, they could canvass their neighbors less suspiciously than adults. Why not ask them during their bond sale work to add at the same time a quick loyalty check? Adults who declined to buy bonds, for one thing, might be presumed to be disloyal. Those who actually said something critical about the war certainly were—people were thrown in jail for such comments, around the country. Children could serve as informants.

While most schools exhorted children to man bond brigades, it is uncertain how many kids also were asked to populate informal spy rings. Probably quite a few, given the paranoid patriotism of this era. We know it happened in New York; it was described in World War I school board documents. To facilitate this, children were instructed to confront those adults who claimed they already purchased bonds. From whom? Through which bank? If that person declined to answer, the solicitor would make a note on the bond subscription form. Furthermore, the city's Metropolitan Canvass Committee advised the sales agent to report "any people whose words or actions indicate to you that they are hostile to our government in any way whatever." The state attorney general's office elaborated. "Whenever anyone solicited by you, but not subscribing for the loan, so expresses him or herself as to show a feeling of hostility to the United States or in favor of Germany in the war, the canvasser will at the time enter the world 'pro' on the card."

Later the canvasser would add to the card the substance of what the person said. "By strictly observing this rule you will greatly help the United States in dealing with the enemy alien situation."[150] The city's many poor immigrants could scarcely afford a bond, yet they could scarcely afford to turn down the youthful yet observant army besieging them from school and street. During World War II, no evidence was found that children were encouraged to finger their neighbors, although the lower rate of immigrants perhaps attenuated World War I-style paranoia.

## Notes

1. Paul V. McNutt and General Brehan Somervell, *School and Society*, September 12, 1942, 197-198; George D. Stoddard, "The Weapons of Education," *School and Society*, May 29, 1943, 615; John H. Finley, "Training for Citizenship, Mobilization of Teachers and Children. New York's Plan for Preparedness," *Child-Welfare Magazine* (PTA), June 1917, 295; "School Garden Army," *Child-Welfare Magazine* (PTA), May 1918, 171; Franklin D. Roosevelt, quoted in *Education for Victory*, September 15, 1942, 3.

2. Raymond Nathan, "Should Children Work?", *Parents' Magazine*, May 1943, 24; "President's Desk. Safeguard Childhood Years," *Child-Welfare Magazine* (PTA) June 1917, 277.

3. "School Garden Army," *Child-Welfare Magazine* (PTA), May 1918, 171.

4. Gertrude H. Folks, "Junior Farm Recruits of New Jersey," *School and Society*, August 18, 1917, 195, 197.

5. Frederick E. Bolton, *School and Society*, September 15, 1917, 301; *Education for Victory*, Sept. 1, 1942, 16.

6. Arthur R. Dean, *Our Schools in War Time—And After* (Boston: Ginn and Company, 1918), 136.

7. *Education*, September 1917, 57-58.

8. Mrs. Alexander Thompson, member, Oregon Legislative Assembly, "Preparedness—A Veneer or a Fundamental—Which Will Our Schools Give Our Children?", National Education Association, *Addresses and Proceedings, Fifty-Fifth Annual Meeting, Portland, Oregon, July 7-14, 1917* (Washington, DC: NEA, 1917), 69.

9. John Dewey, "Message to Teachers and Principals of America," Columbia University War Papers, quoted in Dean, *Our Schools in War Time—And After*, 234.

10. H. W. Wells, associate national director, United States Boys' Working Reserve of the United States Employment Service of the Department of Labor, "The United States Boys' Working Reserve," National Education Association, *Addresses and Proceedings, Vol. 56, Pittsburgh, Pennsylvania, June 29–July 6, 1918* (Washington, DC: 1918), 113-114.

11. Richard Hatton, "The Boys' Working Reserve—Its Value to National Education," *School Life*, October 16, 1918, 6.

12. Ibid., 6, 14.

13. Ibid., 6.

14. Wells, "Boys' Working Reserve," 536.

15. Gertrude H. Folks, "Junior Farm Recruits of New Jersey," *School and Society*, August 18, 1917, 195.

16. Ibid.

17. Ibid., 196–197.

18. Ibid.

19. Ibid., 197.

20. Ibid.

21. Ibid.

22. Ibid, 198–199.

23. Ibid.

24. New York City School Board minutes, 1917: 651, quoted in Stephan F. Brumberg, "New York City Schools March Off to War. The Nature and Extent of Participation of the City Schools in the Great War, April 1917–June 1918," *Urban Education* 24, no. 4 (1990), 453.

25. John H. Finley, "Training for Citizenship, Mobilization of Teachers and Children. New York's Plan for Preparedness," *Child-Welfare Magazine* (PTA), June 1917, 295.

26. Ibid.

27. Brumberg, "New York City Schools March Off to War," 454.

28. Dean, *Our Schools in War Time–and After*, 257.

29. Ibid., 247.

30. Ibid., 258, 266.

31. Ibid., 252–253.

32. Ibid., 235, 270.

33. Thomas J. Smart, North Dakota Agricultural College, "The Policies of State Superintendents toward Students Entering Agricultural Employment during the War," *School and Society*, October 26, 1918, 485–486.

34. Ibid., 482.

35. Ibid., 484.

36. Ibid., 485.

37. Mrs. Alexander Thompson, member, Oregon Legislative Assembly, "Preparedness–A Veneer or a Fundamental–Which will Our Schools Give Our Children?", National Education Association, *Addresses and Proceedings, Fifty-Fifth Annual Meeting, Portland, Oregon, July 7–14, 1917*, 70.

38. "President's Desk. Safeguard Childhood Years," *Child-Welfare Magazine* (PTA), June 1917, 277.

39. *School Life*, October 1, 1918, 2.

40. Ibid., 1.

41. Margaret S. McNaught, "The Elementary School during the War," National Education Association, *Addresses and Proceedings, Fifty-Fifth Annual Meeting, Portland, Oregon, July 7–14, 1917*, 166-168.

42. Quoted in unsigned editorial, *Education*, April 1917, 527.

43. *School Life*, October 1, 1918, 2.

44. Ibid.

45. Ibid.

46. "School Garden Army," *Child-Welfare Magazine* (PTA), May 1918, 171.

47. Parke R. Kolbe, The Municipal University of Akron, "War work of the United States Bureau of Education," *School and Society*, May 25, 1918, 607.

48. *School Life*, October 1, 1918, 13.

49. Ibid.

50. *Education*, April 1917, 527.

51. *School Life*, October 1, 1918, 2.

52. Beatrice McConnell, "Child Labor in Agriculture," *The Annals of the American Academy of Political and Social Science* 236 (1944), 100.

53. Alonzo G. Grace, commissioner of education, State Office Building, Hartford, Connecticut, "Total War and the Organization of Education," *Education*, November 1942, 160.

54. Arnold E. Joyal and William G. Carr, "Work Experience Programs in American High Schools," *The Annals of the American Academy of Political and Social Science* 236 (1944), 114-115.

55. McConnell, "Child Labor in Agriculture," 97.

56. Franklin Roosevelt, October 12, 1942, radio address, reprinted in Educational Policies Commission, National Education Association and American Association of School Administrators, *What the Schools Should Teach in Wartime* (Washington, DC: NEA,1943), 24.

57. Educational Policies Commission, National Education Association and American Association of

School Administrators, *What the Schools Should Teach in Wartime*, 5.

58. Victory Garden Committee, War Services, *Victory Gardens Handbook* (No Place: Pennsylvania State Council of Defense, 1944), 66.

59. John W. Studebaker, "Contribution of Education to the War Effort," National Education Association, *Proceedings of the Eighty-First Annual Meeting Held in Indianapolis June 27–29, 1943* (Washington, DC: NEA, 1943), 70-71.

60. "How Boys See Themselves in the War Effort," *Schools at War. A War Savings Bulletin For Teachers* (Washington, DC: Education Section, War Savings Staff, U.S. Treasury, no date, "Inaugural Issue," probably September 1943), 7.

61. Ibid., 70.

62. Payne Ratner, "Education and Democracy," National Education Association, *Proceedings of the Eightieth Annual Meeting Held in Denver June 28–July 3, 1942* (Washington, DC: NEA, 1942), 57.

63. M. L. Wilson, *Education For Victory*, March 3, 1942, 16.

64. Rall I. Grigsby, "Origin and Purpose of the High School Victory Corps," *Education*, October 1943, 73; Francis B. Haas, *Education for Victory*, September 1, 1943, 17.

65. Raymond Nathan, "Our Schools Mobilize," *Parents' Magazine*, January 1943, 32.

66. Jay Deiss, "The Victory Corps Chain of Cooperation," *Education*, October 1943, 77.

67. Ibid., 78.

68. I. L. Kandel, *The Impact of the War upon American Education* (Chapel Hill, NC: University of North Carolina Press, 1948), 92.

69. Harold W. Kent, major, United States Army infantry, "The Needs Students Must Fill—for the War Department," *Education*, October 1943, 79.

70. Ibid., 80.

71. Studebaker, "Contribution of Education to the War Effort," National Education Association, *Proceedings of the Eighty-First Annual Meeting Held in Indianapolis June 27–29, 1943*, 70.

72. William P. Loomis, *Education*, October 1943, 107.

73. Raymond Nathan, "Our Schools Mobilize," 32.

74. U.S. War Production Board, *Use the Paper Trooper Campaign Materials to Energize Your School Waste Paper Collections. A Manual for School Administrators and Community Leaders* (Washington, DC: no publisher, 1944), 4.

75. Geoffrey Perrett, *Days of Sadness, Years of Triumph. The American People 1939-1945* (New York: Coward, McCann & Geoghegan, Inc., 1973), 368.

76. L. Thomas Hopkins, professor of education, Columbia University, "The War and the Curriculum," *Education*, February 1943, 350.

77. Frederick H. Lewis, "New Citizenship Responsibilities," *Education*, October 1943, 116-117.

78. Haas, *Education for Victory*, September 1, 1943, 107.

79. Studebaker, "Contribution of Education to the War Effort," National Education Association, *Proceedings of the Eighty-First Annual Meeting Held in Indianapolis June 27–29, 1943*, 70.

80. Deiss, "The Victory Corps Chain of Cooperation," 78.

81. National Education Association, "The Nation's Schools after a Year of War," quoted in *Education for Victory*, July 1, 1943, 12.

82. *Education for Victory*, February 14, 1943, 10.

83. Dorothy Marshall and Bertha Pippin, "The Victory Corps in the Wilmington High School," *Education*, October 1943, 120.

84. Ibid., 121.

85. Ibid., 122.

86. Franklin R. Zeran, "Guidance in the Victory Corps," *Education*, October 1943, 94.

87. Richard M. Ugland, "'Education for Victory': The High School Victory Corps and Curricular Adaptation during World War II," *History of Education Quarterly* 19, no. 4, (1979), 445.

88. Ibid., 440.

89. E. B. White, "One Man's Meat. Victory Corps." *Harpers* 186 (April 1943), 499-500.

90. Ugland, "'Education for Victory': The High School Victory Corps and Curricular Adaptation during World War II," 438.

91. Ibid., 442.

92. I. L. Kandel, *The Impact of the War upon American Education*, 93.

93. Roy Sorenson, "Wartime Recreation for Adolescents," *The Annals of the American Academy of Political and Social Science* 236 (1944), 148.

94. Arnold E. Joyal and William G. Carr, "Work Experience Programs in American High Schools," *The Annals of the American Academy of Political and Social Science* 236 (1944), 113.

95. Angelo Patri, *Your Children in Wartime* (Garden City, NY: Doubleday, Doran & Co., 1943), 45.

96. Ethel Kawin, "Children Can Help," *National Parent-Teacher*, May 1942, 41.

97. John W. Studebaker, "Contribution of Education to the War Effort," National Education Association, *Proceedings of the Eighty-First Annual Meeting Held in Indianapolis June 27–29, 1943*, 70–71.

98. *Education for Victory*, June 3, 1944, 16.

99. Howard Lane, "The Good School for the Young Child in Wartime," *Education*, February 1943, 355.

100. W. Linwood Chase, *Wartime Social Studies in the Elementary School. Curriculum Series No. 3* (Washington, DC: The National Council for the Social Studies, 1943), 9.

101. Robert William Kirk, "Getting in the Scrap: The Mobilization of American Children in World War II," *Journal of Popular Culture* 9, no. 1 (1995), 230.

102. "How Boys See Themselves in the War Effort," *Schools at War. A War Savings Bulletin For Teachers*, September 1943, 7.

103. Emery W. Balduf, "Service Through Salvage," *National Parent-Teacher*, May 1944, 37.

104. Emery W. Balduf, "Paper Trooping Yields Dividends," *National Parent-Teacher*, January 1945, 26.

105. Ibid.

106. U.S. War Production Board, *Use the Paper Trooper Campaign Materials to Energize Your School Waste Paper Collections*, 4.

107. Ibid., 7.

108. Ibid., 8.

109. Ibid., 9.

110. Ibid.

111. Ibid., 11.

112. Emery W. Balduf, "Paper Trooping Yields Dividends," 24, 26.

113. U.S. War Production Board, *Use the Paper Trooper Campaign Materials to Energize Your School Waste Paper Collections*, 8.

114. Kirk, "Getting in the Scrap: The Mobilization of American Children in World War II," 231.

115. Robert William Kirk, *Earning Their Stripes. The Mobilization of American Children in the Second World War* (New York: Peter Lang, 1994), 56–57.

116. William D. Murray, *The History of the Boy Scouts of America* (New York: BSA, 1937), 125.

117. *Education for Victory*, April 15, 1942, 13.

118. *Education for Victory*, July 1, 1943, 4; Studebaker, "Contribution of Education to the War Effort," National Education Association, *Proceedings of the Eighty-First Annual Meeting Held in Indianapolis June 27–29, 1943*; 70–71.

119. "How Boys See Themselves in the War Effort." *Schools at War. A War Savings Bulletin For Teachers*, September 1943, 7.

120. Dean, *Our Schools in War Time—and After*, 125–126.

121. *National School Service*, September 1, 1918, 10.

122. Melanie A. Kimball, "From Refuge to Risk: Public Libraries and Children in World War I," *Library Trends* 55, no. 3, (2007), 460.

123. Kirk, *Earning Their Stripes. The Mobilization of American Children in the Second World War*, 86–87.

124. *Schools at War. A War Savings Bulletin For Teachers*, September 1943, back cover.

125. John W. Studebaker, "Can Our Schools Build Morale?", *Parents' Magazine*, October 1942, 15.

126. Chase, *Wartime Social Studies in the Elementary School. Curriculum Series No. 3*, 5–6.

127. Bruce Mickleburgh, Prince Rupert, B.C., "A Canadian Teacher Speaks," *Schools at War. A War Savings Bulletin For Teachers*, September 1943, 5.

128. "Ted Barton, Schoolboy, 1943. The Family Minute Man Learns His Role In School," *Schools at War. A War Savings Bulletin For Teachers*, September 1943, 3.

129. *Schools at War. A War Savings Bulletin For Teachers*, September 1943, 4.

130. *Schools at War. A War Savings Bulletin For Teachers*, September 1943, 6.

131. "Ted Barton, Schoolboy, 1943. The Family Minute Man Learns His Role In School," *Schools at War. A War Savings Bulletin For Teachers*, September 1943, 3.

132. Ibid.

133. "Pupils Can Aid Drive by Telling Families the Dates, the Quotas, the Need," *Schools at War. A War Savings Bulletin For Teachers,* November 1944, 5.

134. "Students Turn Salesmen in Hundreds of Towns," *Schools at War. A War Savings Bulletin For Teachers,* November 1944, 9.

135. *Schools at War. A War Savings Bulletin For Teachers,* October 1943, Front Cover, 5.

136. *Schools at War. A War Savings Bulletin For Teachers,* November 1944, 3.

137. United States Committee on Public Information (George Creel), *The Creel Report. Complete Report of the Chairman of the Committee on Public Information 1917: 1918: 1919,* reprint of 1920 ed. (New York: DaCapo Press,1972), 26.

138. John H. Puelicher, government director of savings, Seventh Federal Reserve District, Milwaukee, Wisconsin, "The New World and the Demand That It Will Make Upon Public Education," National Education Association, *Addresses and Proceedings, Fifty-Seventh Annual Meeting, Milwaukee, Wisconsin, June 28–July 5, 1919* (Washington, DC: NEA, 1919), 50-51.

139. New York City School Board minutes, 1918a: 1170, quoted in Brumberg, "New York City Schools March Off to War. The Nature and Extent of Participation of the City Schools in the Great War, April 1917-June 1918," 459.

140. Ibid.

141. *National School Service,* September 15, 1918, 15.

142. "Bond Sales," *National School Service,* September 15, 1918, 1.

143. "Selling Thrift Stamps," *National School Service,* September 15, 1918, 15.

144. Guy Stanton Ford, director, Division of Civic and Educational Publications, and editor, *National School Service,* September 1, 1918, 7.

145. Education Section, War Savings Staff, U.S. Treasury, *Schools at War. A War Savings Bulletin For Teachers* (Washington, DC: GPO, November 1944) 3.

146. Representative (unnamed) of the U.S. Treasury war savings staff, quoted in Chase, *Wartime Social Studies in the Elementary School. Curriculum Series No. 3,* 8.

147. "How Boys See Themselves in the War Effort." 7.

148. Education Section, War Savings Staff, U.S. Treasury, *Schools at War,* November 1944, 3.

149. Education Section, War Savings Staff, U.S. Treasury, "Elementary Schools Lead Highs in War Bond Effort," *Schools at War. A War Savings Bulletin For Teachers.* Inaugural Issue (Washington, DC: GPO, n.d., probably September 1943). 7.

150. Quoted in Brumberg, "New York City Schools March Off to War," 461-462.

# 5

## YOUTH GROUPS AND BUSINESS

The early twentieth century saw enormous growth in youth organizations to promote values and character. The Boy Scouts of America, sewn together from several boys' groups in 1910, more than doubled its membership during World War I, to 486,120 participants by 1918. It reached 2,229,653 by 1942—one third of boys in scouting's age group of 12 to 18.[1] Girl Scouts grew from 5,000 in 1915 to 12,812 in 1917,[2] despite opposition from the Boy Scouts and its competing organization, Camp Fire Girls. Future Farmers of America (FFA) grew from its beginning in 1928 to a force of 245,822 by 1942.[3] National 4-H, fused from a variety of rural youth groups, bounded from 169,000 in 1916 to 500,000 two years later.[4] The YMCA had been established in the United States many decades before, in the 1860s, but by the century's turn was sponsoring a variety of youth groups that coalesced into the Boy Scouts and Camp Fire Girls.[5] It was the age in which America discovered its youth; kindergartens grew from one (Cleveland) to one in every United States city by 1918. Also by 1918 newly established groups for youth included the National Child Labor Committee, then fourteen years old, and federal Children's Bureau, six; both fought to curb child labor following shocking revelations of abuse. The first juvenile court was established in 1907, in Colorado.[6] Authorities hoped to forge character through education, both in class and out. Much of the education out of class was built by private individuals or groups with good ideas facing a youthful generation ready to respond.

## Boy Scouts: A Battle for Martial Values

Of the private groups for youth, most popular among children in both wars was the Boy Scouts of America. The Boy Scout Movement grew from its inception in the British colonial army. Robert Baden-Powell, an officer serving in Africa, determined that army training in England poorly prepared troops for service. Training in rifle care was not enough; men needed training in self-care. Baden-Powell proceeded to pen a handbook designed to guide his men, emphasizing character development rather than military drill. "When he returned to England in 1903, he found to his surprise that the thing he had worked out for men was being adapted and used in schools for boys."[7] Baden-Powell knew an opportunity when he saw it, so gathered the best of what he found in boy training history, reading of methods used in early Britain, ancient Sparta, and Japanese Bushido. He also consulted with leaders promoting other boys' movements of the time, notably Ernest Thompson Seton and Daniel Beard.[8] These two had founded early boys' movements in the United States; Beard founded the Sons of Daniel Boone in 1905, and Seton founded Woodcraft Indians in 1902. Baden-Powell set up a system based on troops, patrols, uniforms, ranks, and activities to develop the character he thought a boy ought to have: mental toughness, discipline, patriotic fervor, service to God (but no particular religion) and country, manliness. In 1908 his book *Scouting for Boys* formally launched a movement whose popularity reached to every corner of the world. By World War II one third of America's boys had signed up.

Baden-Powell's origins and early vision behind the Boy Scout Movement defined its enormous practical success, but also its great philosophical schism during the world wars. Its popularity exploded in a world of Europe and America looking to harness the energy of boys and fasten it to a definition of character esteemed in early twentieth century society. In Europe many young men feared society was falling into decadence; society was raising a generation of boys bookish, effete, lacking in virility and a sense of adventure. Men feared becoming effeminate, maybe decadent. Decadent was opposite of a real man; it was nervous and unsteady, exhausted, and a libertine.[9] In America leaders such as Theodore Roosevelt and General Leonard Wood agreed with proponents of masculine virtues who worried too that modern life was sapping the American boy of his strength, his "manliness." Perhaps the female teachers who formed the vast majority instructing children in the schools were to blame for stripping a boy's masculine nature. "He will never recover. He goes through life a maimed man."[10] A solution might be an organization designed to build the character supposedly lacking in the modern boy of the early twentieth century.

The new Boy Scout Movement offered just such a solution. Emphasis on building manliness through camping, marksmanship, fitness, first aid, and service to community could damp effeminate characteristics while building a new and better boy. And it could keep the kids out of trouble. As the era moved away from valuing virtues of personal autonomy, authorities "were especially eager to control middle-age boys—which was what character-building often came down to in practice—and they regarded strength and virtue as vital if the rising generation of the middle class was to maintain its social position."[11]

The schism in the Boy Scout Movement also began with its original Baden-Powell conceptualization, a paramilitary group for young men. The Scouting Movement as a values-building club for boys exploded into a Western world in which pacifism still was widespread and highly respected. Anti-war groups in Europe retained so much influence in the years leading to World War I that many governments feared a general strike in case of war. In the United States, the School Peace League held sway over educators at the highest levels. Baden-Powell's movement, in contrast, built on military experience and employed a quasi-military structure. In England working-class skeptics who saw the scouts as elitist distrusted its military overtones, particularly growing popular in an already militarized atmosphere of the pre-war upper classes.[12] Scouts were "obviously militaristic" according to critics. Many supporters encouraged boys to join as preparation for military service, part of a "children's culture of war."[13] While scouting had barely been established in France by the outbreak of war, in Germany it already had become popular as it absorbed older youth movements. German youth were attracted to scouts, "the wearing of insignia, uniformed clothing and competitive sports in camp life."[14]

Some authorities in the United States interested in character-building movements for children feared the militarism of the Scouting Movement so obvious in Europe would transplant to the States. The YMCA as the longtime dominant values group for children moved to direct the beginnings of scouting so it would not fall prey to military advocates. Despite 400 summer camps and 15,000 boys participating in 1910, the Y could see a challenge from a movement less evangelical and spiritual, and more nationalistic and intense. Presumed already to be quasi-military, early scout leaders tried to head off an immediate assumption that it was transferring to America "England's boy army."[15]

Leaders hoped to distance American scouting from presumed militarism in an apparent attempt to appease the strong anti-militarism movement preceding World War I, particularly the wing of it that supported scouting. On the

other hand, leaders tried to avoid giving offense to those who thought scouting
could be the bully way to bring military values to American youth. Those who
criticized what they saw as militarism creeping into American society pointed
to the burgeoning popularity of scouting as just one example. They "challenged
head-on a security for children that aspired to place rifles in their hands and
classrooms and prepared them for war."[16] Among early founders listed on the
1916 Boy Scout national charter was David Starr Jordan, a prominent antiwar
pacifist.[17] But they faced powerful opposition. Theodore Roosevelt was most
prominent of many Americans who wanted to see the country become more
armed and dangerous. Universal military training would "Americanize" children, declared Roosevelt, who added scouting would make boys "good citizens
in time of peace and, incidentally...fit them to become good soldiers in time of
war."[18]

The early Boy Scouts of America leaders were squeezed between the desire
to keep out of the military preparedness debate and the need to keep people
like Roosevelt happy. They were able to do neither very well. Baden-Powell tried
to soften the military-style discipline structure of the scouts, while American
leaders explicitly declared it was not a movement based on military principles.
The inaugural issue of *Boys' Life*, scouting's popular magazine, published an
unsigned editorial reminding readers that the boys were to be called "peace
scouts," and the movement "is not military. There is no military meaning attached to the name scouting."[19] Scouts received no military drills per se, and
learned skills such as first-aid and camping that could be useful in peace or war.
Membership was limited to age twelve and above. In 1913 the group issued a
formal statement declaring scouting was not a military movement, but taught
"The military virtues such as honor, loyalty, obedience, and patriotism."[20] Pacifist groups were mollified, slightly. At the beginning of the war, scout leaders
reminded the country, "We are not soldiers but are trained for civic service."[21]
Still more explicitly, leaders in 1915 announced, "The Boy Scout Movement
neither promotes nor discourages military training, its one concern being the
development of character and personal efficiency of adolescent boys."[22]

At war's breakout, chief scout executive James E. West immediately reminded scouts of the movement's peaceful intentions. "All connected with the Scout
Movement here and abroad have been conscientious and firm in their purpose
in advocating universal peace."[23] To punctuate this, *Boys' Life* in November
1914 published an issue roundly condemning war and militarism. Decorated
full pages were given to well-known pacifists Andrew Carnegie and David Starr
Jordan. Carnegie, the tycoon who had donated funds for a peace palace at The

Hague, was welcomed as a "principal supporter" of the Scout Movement. "The real heroes," Carnegie reminded boys, "are those of civilization, who aid and serve their fellows, in contradistinction to the 'heroes' of war, who wound and kill their fellows."[24] Facing page to Carnegie's letter was one from Jordan, a scout board of directors member, who spoke more explicitly based on his recent trip to Europe. The rivers ran with blood of young men who had no quarrel with their adversaries, he said. "It is a soldier's business to fight and kill or to stand up against other soldiers who are forced to fight and kill. It is a Boy Scout's business to help and to save, to make this world a better place for good men and women and for boys to live in." The former Stanford University president declared that despite the war, the Boy Scouts had no intention of training boys to be fit for soldiering. "That is about the poorest use a nation ever made of its young men. There must be soldiers sometimes, even in our great republic, but they are called to fight only when some men who ought to know better have made some awful blunder." War could only bring more hate and more war, he said. "As the Boy Scout grows older he will learn that the nation which asks for the fewest soldiers is also the strongest nation."[25]

This might have been what so offended preparedness advocates such as Roosevelt, whose support of the movement couldn't have come from a more different base. "Every man of fighting age who is fit to go and allowed to go ought to go to war," Roosevelt declared in a 1917 speech to scouts. "Every man of fighting age who is all right ought to go to the front, and it will be a mighty sight pleasanter to explain to his children later on why he went than why he did not."[26] The tragedy of the war in Roosevelt's mind was that the United States did not join it sooner, and obviously pacifists such as Jordon on the scout leaders' lists did not help.

But *Boys' Life* didn't stop there. The November issue went over the top of most of the country's publications both juvenile and adult—for both world wars—in explicitly and accurately describing what soldiers were actually doing in the trenches across the Atlantic. Cyrus Townsend Brady, a well-known writer of adventure fiction, reminded boys that parades and war games may be fun and exciting. "'Being a soldier is not quite so amusing.... Into the masses the shrapnel pitches. Ranks melt away like dust before the wind, the heads of columns are cut to pieces, they fall in windrows like mowed grain, men are thrown into the air by heavier shells, regiments are annihilated, the defenders grow sick, ill, actually nauseated, by the awful slaughter." After the battle, "Nobody can help the wounded between the lines. The valley is still swept with fire. It is impossible to go there. The wounded envy the dead." Refugees flee and die, "the dead are thrust aside, the wounded are left to suffer, the weak fall by the way. Children are born by the wayside; their wailing mingles with the groaning and clamor while the great mass struggles painfully on. These are all innocent people."

And who is doing the killing?

> Who are driving them from their homes, who are killing them on the way, not willfully perhaps, but unavoidably? The soldiers! Truly a pleasant trade. It is the business of the soldier to kill and destroy; that really is his only business, that is what all his training is for; just that and nothing else. Dress-parading is a side issue.

The author reminded readers he could have written worse things about what he saw on the battlefields. "This, boys, is not war as a whole; it is just one small unimportant episode in one undecisive battle as it is being waged today."[27]

Anti-war statements were not rare in American children's magazines early in World War I, but this entire issue condemning war in such explicit terms, and sponsored by the scouts themselves, struck a nerve in preparedness advocates. Both Roosevelt and Wood had previously given their endorsement to scouting; Roosevelt was named "Honorary Vice President and Chief Scout Citizen." But in awarding such a prominent moniker to such a ferocious militarist, scouting's national board put itself in a sticky wicket when war broke out. After the November anti-war issue, Roosevelt declared scouting was "part of the wicked and degrading pacifist agitation of the past few years." General Wood resigned from the national council.[28] *Boys' Life* directors responded to the fracas by hoping to re-offend no one: between November 1914 and March 1917 not a single article addressed a theme related to war. Only one war-related advertisement appeared, and that as late as December 1916. Stories covered camping, making things, baseball, serialized adventure fiction. This was in contrast to other children's publications during this period which could not ignore the world's biggest story.

It was clear that no matter what their leaders said, scouting in the eyes of many Americans who joined the movement sounded militaristic undertones— and that might be a good thing. Emphasis on uniforms, military style, with chevrons for lance corporal, corporal, sergeant, troop battery, color sergeant and first sergeant; merit awards; participation in the orderly discipline of parades; service to society (always done while in uniform); calls to fitness, vigor, toughness, the manly virtues; work done together in teams bonded by ideals; strong appeals to patriotism and nationalism—these were the virtues and trappings of the army, or at least what people imagined the army to be. "Scouting appeals to the boy's gang-loyalty, his pride of recognition, and his feeling of worth" wrote a scout leader in 1934. "It strikes deep into the boy's natural heroic spirit of chivalry and manliness. The scout obligation is based upon a high sense of duty and honor."[29] Baden-Powell could not help but reveal in a frank moment that he hoped scouting would train boys to become military cadets for the British empire, and from there "in all colonies, we shall establish a standard and bond throughout the cadets of the coming Imperial Army."[30]

Growing pro-military fervor of World War I played into the quasi-military nature of scouting. After declaration of war in 1917 the early scout leaders who pulled back on the reins of patriotism and nationalism were forced to abandon its national council. Ernest Thompson Seton, founder of American scouting and designated "Chief Scout," did not like its growing militaristic tone. He had tried to dissuade militaristic scoutmasters who insisted on formally drilling their troops in defiance of a directive from the national board against such drills. However, the board acquiesced to some forms of drills, and scoutmasters were only too happy to interpret the guidelines in a frankly military way. A flood of patriotism swamped scouting's greatest early leaders who warned the movement needed to separate patriotism from jingoism. Seton as a non-native—he was British—became vulnerable to the growing patriotic frenzy. He clashed with lawyer James E. West, who was hired as chief scout executive in 1915. Seton could not be Americanized, and resigned. The council decreed that scoutmasters must be American citizens. "After that, nobody remained to oppose militant Americanism."[31] On Wilson's war declaration *Boys Life* joined the rest of society in gearing for and glorifying the war. Roosevelt's inspiration was lauded, and all must have been forgiven; the former president was featured extensively in 1917-1918.

In 1917 the "army" of scouts was "mobilized." What an army it was! "As a matter of fact they were, at the outbreak of the war, the nation's largest uniformed body," noted a scout leader. "They had more than twice the numerical strength of the standing army of the United States."[32] But scouts were not really comparable to an army. Were they? In the searing nationalism following the war declaration no pacifist group could dare insert such a cavil. The Boy Scout Movement quickly announced its intention to muster its non-military troops to the service of the country. "Events moved very rapidly in the spring of 1917," recalled one observer. In addition to the government, private organizations jumped to propagandizing for the colors, which "put a psychological persuasion into the situation which was hard for school authorities and school children to resist." Among those children, Boy Scouts stood out for their intensity.[33] During World War II chief scout executive West remembered it as a "national dramatization of scout service."[34] The scout army spilled into all areas of volunteer service during that war, from growing gardens to guarding the shoreline against possible dangers of enemy invasion. Under the slogan "Every scout to feed a soldier," the boys planted about 12,000 home war gardens, winning medals for good performance. They also "pledged themselves to eat cornmeal mush and corn muffins to save wheat, to eat fish and fowl to save meat, and save sugar by cutting down on candy."[35]

Scout uniforms became familiar city sights as they buzzed around on bicycles or on foot to deliver government posters and messages. The duty of messenger was formalized for Boy Scouts under a federal program creating the title of Government Dispatch Bearer. Approved boys were issued a card declaring their official status as CPI aide "to serve as a dispatch bearer for the UNITED STATES GOVERNMENT." The card displayed a boy in scout uniform running and holding out an envelope in his right hand, a stars-and-stripes emblem in the background.[36] Scouts so designated helped to distribute the snowstorm of government literature produced by the CPI and other agencies—literally millions upon millions of sheets emanating from the high-capacity presses of the U.S. Bureau of Engraving and Printing, up to 81,498,000 pieces in one single day.[37] "Washington officials claimed they reached at least ten million people through Boy Scout dispatch campaigns."[38] Scouts distributed at least 30 million pieces during World War I.[39]

As World War I scavengers, scouts were also efficient at collecting the nut shells and fruit pits that were charred and used for gas mask filters, one hundred rail car loads.[40] In a January 1919 letter to scout headquarters, Secretary of War Newton Baker asked boys to stop collecting: they had gathered enough pits for half a million gas masks.[41] As spirited was the response to Wilson's call for scouts to tramp the country's fields and forests identifying and measuring black walnut trees. The wood was particularly suitable as rifle stocks and airplane propellers—for the last big war that relied extensively on wood in ordnance. Boys returned a count of 20,758,660 board feet, enough to fill 5,200 rail car loads, according to Baker's letter of acknowledgement.[42] "'Get every available black walnut tree to market' said the forest specialists."[43] But scout leaders worried about such admonishments given the value of black walnut in peaceful trades. "While hundreds of thousands of these fine old veterans of forest and roadside must be sacrificed to the need of the hour," *Boys' Life* warned, "it is patriotism and good citizenship of the highest order to see that these trees are replaced for the benefit of future generations of Americans."[44] Fortunately for this valuable tree, the war ended before scouts could precede loggers in claiming the country's entire tally.

The image of Boy Scouts hiking through the woods to identity and count trees would match Seton's vision of scouts as campers and hikers. But scouts were more interesting to authorities as city kids who could sell things. All children were called upon to sell government war bonds, but scouts in particular organized a formal campaign under national direction from scout leaders. Early scout leader William Murray, writing in 1937, recalled scout executive West, scout president Colin Livingstone, and other scout board members jumping to offer services of the scouts as war bond salesmen for Uncle Sam. After telephoning or telegraphing scout leaders around the country and studying Liberty Loan needs, the national office drafted a promotional campaign offered to a committee of bankers coordinating loan sales, as well as the U.S. Department of the Treasury. While Murray reported enthusiastic approval, federal authorities did not at first consider it wise to allow scouts to compete with adults for bond sales. Scouts were advised to hold their bond rallies and sales promotions in the waning days of campaigns, the "gleaners after the reapers" program. Theirs became the toughest of sales jobs, selling to customers who had already bought. But President Wilson put a positive spin on the gleaners campaign, thanking scouts for their effort and noting in May 1917, "This will give every scout a wonderful opportunity to do his share for his country under the slogan 'Every scout to save a soldier.'"[45]

Scouts showed their skills by raising camps in public parks and featuring buglers to call attention to bond sales opportunities. They placed promotional flyers on windows, car windshields, and into the hands of passers-by. One scout in Omaha reportedly canvassed a neighborhood despite being sick. When asked why he looked so tired, the scout responded, "I could not stand Dad telling me I was not patriotic because I had the German measles, so I got up to sell some bonds."[46] Recalled Murray, "Their main service was to induce people to take out additional amounts and to urge those who had been overlooked." Authorities tried to keep up spirit for bond sales by dropping their gleaner demand for the fourth and fifth Liberty Bond campaigns, allowing scouts to canvass with everyone else.[47]

While scouts were expected to be patriotic volunteers, the boys did hope to receive the medals and honors that had been a motivational feature throughout the movement since its inception. During World War I, medals were awarded through the U.S. Treasury for scouts who sold bonds to at least ten people; 8,499 medals were given after the first Liberty Loan campaign in June 1917. For those who sold the more modest war savings stamps, the treasury offered the "Ace Medal" for sales of twenty-five or more, and $250 total stamps. Patterned after the French government's award to aviators, the bronze palm was awarded to scouts for each $100 in sales. The scout in each state who sold the most received a personal letter of thanks from Wilson himself.[48] For the prestigious Livingstone medal, winners sold at least 300 individual Liberty Bond subscriptions. The national Livingstone Gold Medal winner was fourteen-year-old Archie Boyd, Granite City, Illinois, 1,398 subscriptions. Silver Medal winner Heber Lee Mosby, Clarksburg, West Virginia, also fourteen, sold 915 subscriptions. Ten scouts won bronze medals for selling between 903 and 330 subscriptions. Most were fourteen or fifteen; the youngest was twelve, the oldest, eighteen.[49]

Results of these bond sales reflect some difficulty in forcing scout troops to hold back the boys as gleaners: only half the nation's troops took part in the third Liberty Loan campaign, and only 7.1 percent of all scouts sold ten or more bonds.[50] Nevertheless, the scouts managed to pour into the U.S. Treasury $147,876,962, selling 2,350,977 Liberty Loan bonds.[51] This represented 6.9 percent of the $21.5 billion in war loans sold to finance World War I. West pointed out that this broke down to $936 per Boy Scout. He added scouts also sold war savings stamps totaling $52 million, in 2,189,417 sales.[52]

The enthusiasm of scouting during World War I had a consequence beyond service: public relations. The entire nation became familiar with a movement less than ten years old. As scouts became highly visible buzzing around town in uniform, compliments began to pile. Educators, politicians and other authorities climbed on board. "The Boy Scout movement is also a high-class type of what our boys need in developing the qualities of virile and resourceful citizenship," wrote an educator in *School and Society*.[53] The National Education Association promoted scouting in every school, and the Catholic Church dropped its opposition to a group originally founded through the YMCA, a Protestant organization. Wilson's repeated support for scouting—one of the few things he and Theodore Roosevelt agreed on—came by way of several proclamations throughout the war and after. "The Boy Scouts of America have rendered notable service to the nation during the world war," he wrote in a May 1, 1919, proclamation of Boy Scout Week. "The Boy Scout movement should not only be preserved, but strengthened. It deserves the support of all public-spirited citizens."[54]

Wilson wondered, however, why only 375,000 boys of a possible 10 million from age twelve to twenty-one had enrolled.[55] In years after the war that figure would climb slightly, but still stood at only 391,382 in 1921.[56] It was difficult to know just how many boys really were joining the movement; turnover rate was so great that reported numbers could be highly inflated. Elbert Fretwell, who took over as chief executive following thirty-two years of West in that role, admitted in a 1944 report that while the movement grew quickly in World War II as it did in World War I, the dropout rate also was high. "Too many boys evidently do not have a sufficiently happy experience in scouting," he reported. "Too many boys drop out before they should." He said scouting that "tends to get too bookish, too scholastic, too much subject matter and too little activity" discouraged boys from continuing.[57] While the reported 2.2 million scouts in 1943 seems to reflect a wide swath of America's boys, it is likely that from year to year the individuals populating that total mustered in and out in large numbers.

Scouting's perceived reputation as a quasi-military training program for boys was bolstered by its interwar policies. While Americans in the 1920s began to turn away from World War I's gung-ho patriotism and embrace of military virtues, Boy Scouts of America remained a nationalistic bastion. Asserting American pre-eminence, United States scout leadership diverged from Baden-Powell's movement as the British stripped values thought too militaristic. "A suspicion of disloyalty must not remain unchallenged," the American leadership declared in a 1932 *Handbook for Scoutmasters*. "It is intolerable that a man commissioned by the national office should make an utterance or give instruction which the Scouts interpret as unpatriotic. Unless perfect loyalty of the Scout leader is established,"—he should be fired.[58]

By World War II the movement still retained a strong nationalistic appeal established during its glory days of World War I. Riding on this idealistic coattail was its old reputation as a military-readiness club for boys. World War II scout leaders did repeat their position that scouting was in no way designed as an army substitute for adolescents. West reminded government authorities in 1942 that Boy Scouts were "neither military nor antimilitary," explaining, "as an organization the scout movement is not military in thought, form, or spirit. The uniform, the patrol, the troop, and the drill are not for military tactics; they are for the unity, the harmony, and the rhythm of spirit that boys learn in scouting."[59] The phrase "neither military nor antimilitary" traces to the very beginnings of the movement, when leaders tried to appease both the nation's peace preachers and preparedness hawks. But the movement retained its searing nationalism, proud masculinity, emphasis on discipline, uniforms, and ranks, its army-style organization and its appeal to military virtues and skills. Its motto, "Be Prepared," echoed to the pro-war preparedness ideology of World War I. If this were truly not quasi-military, could it perhaps certainly be pre-military, a feeder school for army life? Indeed it could. "Of course, it is true, that the Boy Scout program is not a military-training program." West said. "At the same time there is abundant evidence that it does give the basic training for a good citizen or a good soldier. Nor is that surprising, because we know the genesis of scouting." He reminded Americans, "Most army officers of experience agree that the training of Boy Scouts is about the most complete all-around pre-induction training that can be given at that age level."[60]

National scout leaders again issued a promise to President Franklin Roosevelt that America's scout troops would stand ready for the call to service. This time it would come not only through bond drives and scrap collecting, but through programs established to prepare scouts for the battlefield. Scouting "has served and does serve as the basis for meeting the needs of wartimes," affirmed West in announcing the 1942 Air Scout program. Boys should be prepared for aviation, authorities agreed, and scouts would respond by issuing a new merit badge and accompanying 452-page *Air Scout Manual*. These would attract many of the 375,000 boys over fifteen in scouting; 20,000 sold in that year.[61] The program was offered as part of the High School Victory Corps, the government's World War II umbrella organization designed to coordinate youth mobilization for war. To blend efforts, scout leader Ray O. Wyland wrote *The High School Victory Corps and Scouting* for teachers and principals. Coordinating scouting with the Victory Corps "adds a great deal of glamour, romance, and recognition to the wartime service which our high school youth are eager to carry on"[62]

Scouting may have appealed to authorities as a way to reach out and train boys for war. Bookish and scholastic was not the draw of the scouting movement, as Fretwell observed. The movement valued action, not study, and practical results. Based on measurable goals, scouts in World War II shined in the same way they did during the previous war: in selling, in collecting, in delivering and in helping little old ladies across the street, when necessary. Immediately after Pearl Harbor, West reported, he telegraphed Franklin Roosevelt to promise "the full strength and hearty support of everyone in scouting."[63] As did Wilson, Roosevelt responded with splendid displays of enthusiasm for the movement. "Next to active military service itself," Roosevelt said in a February 1942 address to scouts, "there is no higher opportunity for serving our country than helping youth to carry on in their efforts to make themselves physically strong, mentally awake and morally straight, and prepare to help their country to the full in time of war, as well as in time of peace."[64] His words actually copied those of scouting's oath. Authorities jumped on board, proclaiming virtues of scouting as surely the highest pinnacle of a boy's quest for adolescent perfection. "If anybody knows of a better way to train a boy in manly attitudes, for selfless service, for intelligent sharing of whatever place in life he finds himself, I would be glad to hear about it," wrote one prominent educator and author. "The scout is a responsible, devoted serviceman and commands the respect of all understanding citizens.... You will be trained, taught, drilled, and shown how to be useful in time of trouble."[65] While scout leaders reminded parents that the movement's interest in getting kids outside had no connection to army camp life, the parallels were obvious to authorities. "Camping experience contributes to physical fitness and provides training in many skills and activities that are of direct military value," emphasized *Education* in 1943.[66]

World War II scouts responded mostly as authorities expected, marching into action for America and scouting national headquarters. Home-front duties were similar to those of World War I, with a spin reflecting differing needs of the second war. Boys on bikes or fleet of foot again were drafted for deliveries. In fact, in January 1942 the Boy Scouts signed a formal agreement with the Office of Civil Defense. "This outlined the basis of cooperation and set up three specific areas for Scouts. The three specific areas—assisting emergency medical units, fire watchers, and messenger service." The office's first request for messenger help reached the Boy Scouts that summer: distribution of a pamphlet issued by the Office of Price Administration, "What You Should Know About Price Control." Scouts responded by distributing 25 million.[67] Also between April 1941 and January 1943, scout leaders reported 1,607,500 posters distributed, 300 million pounds of paper collected, 30 million pounds of rubber collected, and 10.5 million pounds of aluminum collected, in 11,369 communities. Salvage was "a continuous scout project. Salvage drive for old rubber, nonferrous metals, iron and steel; also coat hangers, spark plugs for reclamation; phonograph records collected in cooperation with American Legion campaign in many cities."[68] In 1944, Fretwell reported sixty requests from Washington for scout work. "The results are shown in figures which are astronomical." Scouts collected milkweed pods for floss to make 1.5 million life jackets, distributed 1 million posters a month for the Office of War Information, grew 184,000 Victory Gardens, glued together 100,000 model planes and ships, distributed more than 18 million war pledge cards and more than 5,125,000 "Keep 'Em Flying" slogan cards for the Air Force. "More than 300,000 boys have been commissioned officially as dispatch bearers by the president of the United States and carry credentials so testifying."[69]

Scouts also sold war bonds and stamps, but this time they were not constrained as gleaners. The "Scouts-at-war minute man program" established in late 1944 aimed to award troops whose bond-buying membership reached 90 percent; 3,000 troops qualified for the award of a flag and banner. In total,

Children in both wars found motivation to serve through a wide variety of tangible incentives. Late in World War II General Dwight Eisenhower lent his image to a medal awarded to high achieving collectors of the 1945 Waste Paper Campaign; 300,000 were awarded.

Fretwell reported scouts sold $1.8 billion in war bonds and stamps. "Scouts have continued to carry out war-service projects, long after the novelty was worn out and the tasks became tedious."[70]

Maybe some scouts. But beyond the optimistic annual reports were indications that the boys in scouting were losing steam. Early zeal wore into tedium, and by 1943, 36 percent of scout councils reported difficulty persuading boys to go out on new jobs. Explained one local leader, "There are many boys who feel that some of the services requested are unnecessary." Headquarters responded with a survey of boys, both in scouting and out. Boys reported least interest in delivering handbills, tending gardens, and collecting scrap paper—it seemed not very important to winning the war.[71]

Efforts were redoubled to inspire flagging youth to hang on to their spirit of wartime volunteerism. One scouting response was to launch a new program designed to re-inspire scouts to collect the paper they disdained. A system of motivational rewards was again established. But this time was different: General Dwight Eisenhower himself was tapped to add his prestige, and the general "was kind enough to lend his name and sponsor the program." The General Eisenhower Waste Paper Campaign actually was not implemented until very late in the war, March-April 1945. Eisenhower offered a shell container with citation to high-achieving troops; 5,500 earned this award. "In addition, a General Eisenhower medal was given to 300,000 Scouts who each collected 1,000 pounds during the period of the campaign. The total amount of paper collected was 318,000. It is estimated that more than 700,000 boys from 41,000 units were active in the campaign."[72] It is hard to guess what happened to the many thousands of medals and awards given to home front youth during the world wars, but they do sometimes turn up on eBay.

In focusing only on the boys, and only on the older boys, scouting left two groups in the margins: younger boys and girls. Baden-Powell established twelve as a beginning age for scouting, partially to appease military critics concerned with exposing younger children to his militaristic system. But young boys wanted to participate. Authorities were soon persuaded that something ought to be done; "In almost every elementary school there should be a Boy Scout troop and, if possible, a Girl Scout troop," declared the NEA in 1932.[73] Response of the national council two years before was to initiate "Cubbing," later called Cub Scouts, for boys nine to eleven. The group mirrored rapid growth of Boy Scouts. In 1935 it reached 82,373; by 1942, 373,813. West said Cub Scouts could do some of the same tasks as the older boys, but said that more significant during war was its ability to build strong family bonds to build confidence and reduce childhood fears. As a home-centered program, "one of Cubbing's greatest contributions to the nation's welfare is still its capacity for strengthening family ties, and for developing in our younger citizens initiative, resourcefulness, physical fitness, and a will to serve."[74] By 1944 Cub Scouts were doing their share on the scrap runs, particularly targeting tin cans, paper and kitchen grease. "One of the most unusual Cub Scout war-service projects was their development of game and fun kits for wounded servicemen."[75]

Cub Scouts could easily be worked into the spirit and ideology of the Boy Scout movement. They were boys. For girls, it was something else. Scouting was supposed to establish and promote manly qualities. During its infancy in the World War I era some leaders feared it was the influence of females that might have been responsible for a supposed disintegration of manliness. Fearing a threat to its message of masculinity, Boy Scouts initially opposed establishment of a similar girls' group, urging girls to consider Camp Fire Girls. Camp Fire, also chartered in 1912 as a companion to Boy Scouts, emphasized domestic virtues for girls, a far cry from what the boys were doing. But they received strong encouragement from West, who said in 1912 he now had an answer to many parents who asked what was available for girls.[76]

But Girl Scout founder Juliette Gordon Low did not care for a group wearing as a uniform a long fringed fanciful Indian costume, which she called a "fantastic nightgown." Following discussions with Baden-Powell, she established in 1912 the Girl Scouts based on the British Girl Guide Movement. She adopted a uniform similar to that of the boys, and a system of merit badges.[77] Girl Scouts grew from 5,000 in 1915 to 27,195 in July 1918, to 70,000 in 1920.[78] Girl Scouts from its inception proposed a diffuse mission; on the one hand, they wanted girls to swim, march, practice drill formations and camp like the boys. On the other, Low emphasized traditional domesticity. "A typical 1917 Girl Scout manual warned girls against physically overexerting themselves through gender-inappropriate sports such as high jumping, distance running, and basketball, and it asserted that girls, more than boys, needed to learn teamwork." James West objected to the group calling themselves scouts, "fearing that if the term became feminized it would become unsuitable for boys' adventure." But the girls became well known for their work during World War I, doing the same things the boys did, and by 1930 Girl Scout membership had surpassed that of Camp Fire Girls.[79] A Girl Scout march in Boston won admiration of one reporter, who wrote, "The young girl soldiers manifested every evidence that they are just as militaristic as their brother scouts."[80] Badges were offered to girls for their work. *The Rally*, first official Girl Scout publication, reminded girls, "While this award will serve as a recognition of accomplishments, its primary purpose is to stimulate thoughtful direct effort which shall be free from the reproach of emotionalism and wasted energy, and which shall have a distinct value to those engaged in the prosecution of the war."[81]

## Red Cross Work

Of particular attraction to girls both in and out of an organized movement was work for the Red Cross. This organization founded in 1881 did not display the more aggressive nationalism and values promotion reflected in scouting. But it was a lot more popular among children. Membership in the Junior Red Cross zoomed to 11 million in World War I following Wilson's sermonistic admonition, "Our Junior Red Cross will bring to you opportunities of service to your community and to other communities all over the world and guide your service with high and religious ideas."[82] It zoomed again, to 20 million in 1945,[83] dwarfing scout membership during both wars.

But the Junior Red Cross made different demands upon children during war. Its organization primarily focused on charitable deeds organized by adults; the junior division was an afterthought that sprung spontaneously from children who were already doing Red Cross work with adults. At first no one thought of mobilizing children, wrote Henry P. Davison, chairman of the World War I Red Cross war council. "There were little girls marching to the chapter rooms and working there like troopers as long as anybody. And then some one saw them and what they were doing, and just for a kind of curious mental exercise, multiplied it by a million. The result was past dispute."[84] Spontaneously in the United States, as well as in other countries, the junior divisions emerged to organize children's efforts in a more formal manner. Red Cross authorities considered how best to reach children to coordinate Junior Red Cross divisions, and fell upon the same answer as everyone else—the schools. "That the school was the existing nucleus, the machine through which all this force flowing everywhere could be most promptly and systematically concentrated, was made clear to us from the very beginning," explained Davison. Schools were encouraged to set up their own chapters, "practically autonomous." Children contributed twenty-five cents to participate, the proceeds used to fund the chapter. And from that organization children could begin the work of the Red Cross.

Most of that work involved making things, from mufflers to money. Children during war often were tapped as sales agents, but in this case the money raised made its way not into the government's treasury for war bills, but into the charity's treasury for war aid. To begin a children's campaign, teachers might tack a motivational Red Cross poster to a classroom wall. For every quarter donated to the Red Cross fund, a small cross could be attached to the poster. "What a scramble there was for odd jobs after school! Everyone wanted to paste at least one cross." The CPI lauded this character-building self-denial: "Individual contributions of pennies, nickels, and dimes have been made at a tremendous sacrifice of the luxuries of childhood—the ice cream cone, the stick of gum, and the movie show. Some have raised money by standing on the corner with an umbrella and escorting people from car to house for five cents."[85] But washing windows and raking leaves would not carry fund-raising to the level of real money: children would move on to organize bake sales, programs and garden fund-raisers. "Perhaps it was a bazaar run by all the schools of the city, like that of the city of Minneapolis, in the year of 1917, where the stock was all made by the children in school time."[86]

As the cash gathered, Junior Red Cross children turned to making practical things of use to troops or refugees. Many items involved sewing, and this was why Red Cross was considered the ideal home-front organization for girls. Sewing had long been offered through school home-economics programs. But what girls stitched in those classes was not always so charitable. "They spend half a year making graduation dresses which they may wear before admiring parents," said one critic. "They copy the latest fashion in hats without thought as to utility or beauty.... Our girls must learn to think of other than themselves."[87] The

Junior Red Cross came to the rescue, with multiple patterns for sewn objects of value more magnanimous.

In New York State, 3,000 girls set up volunteer sewing programs funded by women's groups and based on patterns supplied by the Red Cross. Two to three hours' school time a week produced enormous variety. A Mount Vernon school was able to thread together 75 children's dresses, 149 tampon bags, 224 baby booties, 219 ward shoes, 76 hospital nightshirts, 62 crocheted trench caps, 597 slings, 19 petticoats, 14 chemises, 403 body bandages, 42 eye bandages, 12 air cushions, 77 pneumonia jackets, 50 bath towels, and 373 bathing suits.[88] It is unknown what war use could be assigned to the bathing suits. In four months of 1918, youthful seamstresses sewed 255,000 refugee garments. Boys could help, by adjusting knitting machines or packing boxes, particularly the smallest war workers: "Even the youngest kindergartner could string together the right number of buttons for a garment." But in the challenge to construct a veritable warehouse of items for the Red Cross, boys were considered most useful in the wood shop. They produced "thousands of peg legs, potato mashers, equipment chests, bedside tables, splints, etc., for the use of the United States Army."[89] Children also rolled bandages and collected "Friendship Boxes" of useful items for war refugees, made knitting needles, pajamas, packing boxes, and applicators. Handmade "gloom-chasers" for military convalescents could feature games, ping-pong paddles, checkerboards, chessmen, and puzzles. Cooking classes sent jam and jelly to hospitals.[90]

It is hard to know how much the seemingly enormous output of practical items made by children during World War I contributed to the war effort, but national statistics indicated 10 percent of that war's Red Cross production came from children. In donations children were credited with contributions of $3,677,380.[91] Occasionally Junior Red Cross children left their classrooms to scavenge and conserve. "Juniors have served as stenographers and packers, and several towns have bicycle messenger corps at the service of the Red Cross chapter." In Los Angeles, children could make $1,000 a month collecting scrap paper, old rubber boots, toothpaste tubes and broken pans for salvage. In Lenhi County, Idaho, doughty gleaners plucked wool from the trees and wire fences on the sheep ranges. Result: 400 pounds.[92]

Authorities hoped to remind parents and children that war work for the Red Cross rewarded the giver as much as the receiver. "Young America was learning from the school fund the value of money and acquiring some little skill in the business of handling it," thought Davison. "Thrift is no longer a dull personal virtue, but a patriotic service."[93] "The Junior Red Cross activities make the school children warriors of mercy, soldiers of healing, volunteers of helpfulness.[94] Concluded Wilson, "And, best of all, more perfectly than through any of your other school lessons, you will learn by doing those kind things under your teacher's direction to be the future good citizens of this great country which we all love."[95]

Such learning was certainly a good thing, considering the concern of some teachers that youthful zeal for practical war production left little time for necessary bookishness. But to voice such an opinion in public during either war risked accusations of disloyalty. While in World War II skepticism came from some "educators and laymen who fear the ultimate effects of placing the schools on a war basis," a university dean of education countered that the Junior Red Cross and other school activities "can contribute to sound educational values."[96] Still, the time commitment irked some educators. In wartime, what is a teacher? Grumbled one in Arizona:

> A teacher is a person, usually a woman, who cooperates with every known federal, state and county agency in directing boys and girls from six to sixteen in vast money and junk drives for the armed services, the national treasury, the Red Cross, and for the making of aircraft carriers, beeps, jeeps, and peeps...all of this from an imposing headquarters originally known as the schoolhouse.[97]

The Junior Red Cross stayed popular during World War II. It had grown during the interwar period to include programs in two-thirds of American schools. "You are needed badly in that busy group," advised one author of a book recommending war service options for children. "Every boy and girl counts his full weight in the Red Cross service. Don't skip it. Wear your button and attend to your job."[98] Red Cross programs and classes attracted more than 19 million children after the end of the war, in 1947.[99] U.S. Commissioner of Education John W. Studebaker, himself a founder of the Iowa Junior Red Cross during World War I, reported in 1943 that the children had made "thousands of garments" for Red Cross distribution. Red Cross children continued to sponsor programs to raise money, and continued to sew and saw for the troops. Schools added Red Cross-designed curriculum for new courses in home nursing, nutrition and first aid.[100] New to World War II were Junior Red Cross promotions for blood donors. The Red Cross estimated that during its 1942-43 peak 90 percent of its chapters included activities by its junior members.[101]

## Contributions from Country Kids

While canning and sewing became popular among female Junior Red Cross volunteers, rural youth often were left out of aggressive club attempts to organize through schools. Rural schools were small and distances were great. Pre-World War I clubs drew from a variety of movements targeting rural American boys and girls for farm and countryside activities. For country boys, "corn club" leaders hoped to build in agricultural research and book learning by offering hands-on instruction for boys not likely to learn modern farm techniques in school—if they were in school. For the girls, "canning clubs" emphasized practical knowledge for domestic chores, particularly canning fruits and vegetables. By 1911, hundreds of groups around rural America had coalesced into 4-H, the year its cloverleaf emblem was adopted. In 1914 the Smith-Lever Act promoted practical programs that helped to galvanize farm youth groups into a fast-growing national 4-H Movement. Smith-Lever brought the movement under the umbrella of the U.S. Department of Agriculture's newly created Cooperative Extension Service. County extension agents reached out to youth groups as a way to attract farmers to modern techniques.[102] Focus of the rural youth movements was naturally on food production; this fed into the wartime government's goal to produce more for military use. "Food was a critical problem in 1918 when the country was responsible not alone for feeding itself, but for sending food to the European countries," noted a 1942 government report.[103] The wheat crop was down two-thirds from the year before; the potato crop was a little more than half. Authorities believed conservation was critical, and production needed boosting. City children were called to tend backlot gardens and learn to work on farms.

But rural children were already there, and they already knew how to farm. "The extension forces of the country were an ideal army to marshal the farmers for increased food production and the entire country for conservation," and, like so many youth movements during the World War I era, 4-H was burgeoning: from 169,000 in 1916 to 500,000 in 1918.[104] In addition to collecting the fruit pits and making the peg legs, World War I 4-H boys put their own spin on war volunteerism. "To ease the demand for meats, club members learned how to can game and fish. Rabbit clubs were organized." Crop and livestock projects were expanded.[105] Some 4-Hers tried to home-process sugar from beets, a perhaps desperate effort given children's apparent disdain for the government's sugar conservation requests. Canning clubs could be pulled out of school kitchens and refitted to institutional-sized capabilities.[106]

During World War II, 4-H members ploughed rural America for scrap, fat, and war bond sales, as did nearly all American children. Home canning jars were filled, by the thousands. Older children added to that efforts to keep aging farm machinery going, and to increase production with enlarged crop and livestock projects.[107] But under the extension service, rural youth in 1942 received a special charge, with a special goal: the Feed a Fighter program. The program strongly supported by Roosevelt aimed to blunt farm labor and food shortages by mobilizing the country's 4-H clubs. In a letter to "all 4-H club members" dated February 3, 1944, Roosevelt wrote, "Members of the 4-H clubs will be among the shock troops on the food production front to give that extra impetus to the war effort so essential to ultimate victory."[108] Extension produced a chart of quotas challenging 4-H members to grow, feed and harvest with the aim of feeding one soldier. For a boy raising poultry, 500 broilers or 250 baking chickens; for "a meat-animal member" producing nine-month old steers, four; a potato-raiser, four tons; a dairy member, 2,500 quarts of milk. "A girl who tended a one-acre garden of mixed vegetables or put up 829 pints of food was also feeding a fighter." The bar was high, a soldier's appetite apparently voracious. But rural American youth proved equal to the task, according to the reports. "Measured against these standards, 4-H boys and girls during the war produced or preserved enough food to care for a million fighting men for three years."[109] Awards for high-producing youth could be from $1 to $250, delivered in the form of war bonds. The 1943 contest levels set for North Carolina 4-H members included care and feeding of 16 lambs, feeding and handling one milk cow, growing 110 bushels of tomatoes, and canning 500 quarts of vegetables. Top achievers won a trip to Fort Bragg. "The state winner in 1943 raised enough food to feed thirty-four servicemen for one year. Ninety-one thousand club members participated."[110]

Beyond local awards, 4-H clubs and Future Farmers of America (FFA) could see their food production efforts rewarded in an enormous place: the side of a transport ship. The extension service made an agreement with the U.S. Maritime Commission to allow states to name cargo ships based on youth farm group production contests. These quick-built "Liberty ships" became the standard wartime goods carriers; carrying up to 9,000 tons, 2,751 were built during World War II at $2 million each. At least four Liberty ships were named to honor 4-H and FFA: "Hoke Smith," No. 1061, and "A. Frank Lever," No. 1072, sponsors of the Smith-Lever Act of 1914; "Edwin Joseph O'Hara," (FFA member killed in action), No. 186; "Cassius Hudson," early North Carolina farm demonstration leader, No. 2373. (At a construction time of as little as four days, a lot of

Liberty ships were available for naming. Also given naming rights were groups that contributed at least $2 million in war bond sales.)[111]

As a complementary club for rural youth, the FFA was not established until after World War I. It grew from the 1917 Smith-Hughes Act, which established secondary education courses in vocational agriculture. Boys in ag classes were organized into clubs beginning in 1925 under U.S. Office of Education sponsorship. FFA became a national group in a 1928 Kansas City convention, restricted to boys until 1969.[112] Like other youth movements during the world war years, FFA expanded rapidly, to a 1942 total of 245,822, in 7,542 chapters.[113] As "warriors in overalls," FFA boys at their national convention congratulated each other for staying in the fields, and out of the more remunerative work in war industry. "America's rural population has been called its backbone," said student William James Kimball of Wisconsin. "In these days America needs a backbone."[114] In another stirring call to the duty of adolescent boys on the farm, student Kenneth Eagle of Abilene, Kansas, said he borrowed from fellow Kansas speaking contestant Albert Van Walleghan:

> The all night vigils at farrowing time will be our sentry duty; the tractors we guide along contour rows will be our tanks; the seeds we plant will be our inland ocean mines....We will regard every dead pig, every missing hill of corn, every smutted wheat head, every scrub animal, every cull hen, and every bit of wasted material and effort as being of aid and comfort to our enemies.[115]

That said, World War II-era FFA convention proceedings did not offer specific information on what FFA members achieved working the land. But they did note that in 1943 FFA had done enough to earn two Liberty ship names: "Edwin J. O'Hara, FFA member killed in action in Navy; and another prisoner of war in Germany." The group also reported in 1943 $4,889,406.48 in war bond and stamp sales, and 209,454,544 pounds of scrap metal collected. In 1942 FFA members also reported collecting 30,606,875 pounds of paper, 2,767,821 pounds of rubber, and 605,949 pounds of rags; 49,408 former members had been called to the armed forces.[116]

### God and Children Face War

But what of God? In Europe, religion during World War I permeated the military message on the home front. Christianity in its teaching of purification through sacrifice offered helpful justification to war's apologists, and sad solace to war's widows. As Mossé observed, war in Europe was attached to Christian teaching and symbolism to turn violence into a force for renewal, an uplifting experience.[117] Just as Jesus according to Christian teaching washes away an individual's inevitable sin, war washes away a society's accumulated decadence. Such a theme as played out in Europe's juvenile literature could include descriptions sometimes terrifying in their brutal details, but made acceptable as examples of Christ-like heroic sacrifice. French Catholic literature for children in particular presented the war to children in such a way, justifying it as necessary for Christian renewal.[118] Religious justification could be used to present war to children as something acceptable, perhaps desirable.

In this area the United States clearly diverged from its European allies or adversaries. Well-known sociologist Harold Lasswell wrote in 1927 that "The churches of practically every description can be relied upon to bless a popular war, and to see in it an opportunity for the triumph of whatever godly design they choose to further."[119] But this did not seem to be the American case as it related to children. Christianity and God were nearly absent from children's publications and pronouncements of authorities in both World War I and World War II. No authority suggested to children that war would be God's spiritual renewal—although some authorities did contend it could be a way through which children could return to America's supposedly forgotten bedrock values. God just wasn't part of the discussion.

Of course, the United States differed from Europe in its constitutional separation of church and state. This principle made it uncomfortable for secular authorities to consider religion in any depth as part of a militarized home front for youth. In a rare attempt, Berkeley education professor Charles E. Rugh, addressing the NEA in 1917, admitted merely mentioning religion in America is sure to "generate more heat than light." But he persevered to ask a question he felt was on the minds of many Americans: Had religion failed to prevent war? "It had been believed and hoped by many of the world's wisest and best men and women that religion had evolved enough in power and effectiveness to prevent civilized nations from going to war," Rugh, a prominent educational philosopher, told the educators. "That hope has failed, but out of the failure emerges a clear and well-defined issue between war and religion....Religion has evolved as a way of preventing and alleviating sin and suffering. Religion and war are henceforth and forever incompatible."[120]

The viewpoint apparently reflected mainstream American belief during the entire world war period, for authorities both secular and religious had little to say for children about Christianity and war. Sometimes God was evoked in a general way to justify America's decisions, as it was in all belligerent nations.

"God decreed that America should rescue civilization from the dark abyss into which this military despot of Germany had thrust it," declared Secretary of the Treasury McAdoo in a 1917 speech.[121] But McAdoo did not say children should join God's team. In his remarks directed at children, and he made quite a few of them, he evoked a spirit more secular. The treasury secretary called on children to save money, to buy war bonds in the spirit of America's colonial Patriots. "Our army had drummer boys in those days, real boys of ten and twelve, who marched as bravely and as proudly into cannon fire as General Washington himself," McAdoo lectured. "Our nation had little girls who laughed and cheered and loaded muskets for their fathers as they fired through loopholes in their cabin homes." Now McAdoo hoped children would show "that we still have in every young heart the spirit of '76."[122]

While almost no United States authorities mentioned religion specifically as a way to reach children, some in general waxed spiritual about the war. If America were secular, and religion an uncomfortable topic for public discourse, a need to motivate children through spiritual means could be tied to safer, secular worship: the religion of patriotism. "Americanism must be to us a political religion," Secretary of the Interior Franklin K. Lane told the NEA.[123] "War-modified education helps the child to train himself spiritually as the patriot and lover of his kind," explained NEA president Mary C. Bradford in 1918. "War-modified education results in a surrender of personal rights in favor of the greatest of all rights—that of free cooperation in the service of the spirit of America."[124] Rugh seemed to suggest the spirituality of patriotism in his assertion that "Nothing but a spiritualizing of the means and processes by which this war is won and nothing but a religious interpretation of our human relationship can save us from the fate of Germany."[125] In World War II Patri reminded parents that sacrifice for country was spiritual: "We must, in our turn, sacrifice, serve, give what we hold most precious, the lives of our youth, that this our country may live on in a finer, better, richer spiritual way than ever before."[126]

But to say authorities in the United States offered patriotic nationalism as an ersatz religion during these wars might be overstating. Authorities during both wars did not forget about the old-time religion, or at least paying lip service to it. NEA convention proceedings in 1942 included ten references to God and Christianity, by multiple speakers. The World War I CPI national flag salute reminded kindergarteners of God, and just whose God it was:

I give my head
My hands,
And my heart,
To God and my country—
One country,
One language,
And one flag.[127]

The newly constructed Boy Scouts of America in World War I promised in its oath to do its duty to a generic God, although at first it still wasn't able to get Catholics on board. But "God" to the scouts and to the government remained safely abstract. Some authorities suggested He should play a bigger role. Writing in 1917, a University of Montana professor blamed secular education for its failure to prevent war. "If true civilization is to come, we must breathe into our education the spirit of a joyous, living religion, a confident belief in a benevolent higher power who desires justice, decency, honesty, mercy and love to reign here on earth."[128] Charles Eliot, president emeritus of Harvard University, admitted, "It has long been supposed that no religious teaching should be given in the public schools, because in this country the churches and the state are separate," but said children needed to be taught "truth, honor, fidelity and neighborliness." To do that properly "it will be necessary to use many of the sayings of Jesus Christ and of his most faithful followers down the centuries, but none of the sayings and doings of Christian councils, synods, and hierarchies."[129] A minister pointed out that if some Americans were in favor of school military drill, they ought also to be in favor of school religious drill: "If our national salvation rests upon the compulsory military training of our youths...then the conservation of character no less rests upon the severe religious discipline of our children."[130] But no one apparently heeded such suggestions, for in World War II educators still decried the failures of secular education. "We have been careless in developing the spiritual side of our youth," said NEA president Myrtle Hooper Dahl in 1942. "Let us through living, through having faith in the power of right, faith in the integrity of our leaders and our profession, faith in the fatherhood of God and the brotherhood of man, demonstrate spiritual living."[131]

Leaders of the interdenominational Religious Education Association, ironically, had little to say during both wars regarding the wartime education of children. Writers made no righteous claims associating religion with war and patriotism in the classroom. When they did consider the war's impact on children, they bemoaned the dangers yet prevaricated on the religious solution. The 1917 association president, Francis J. McConnell, called to concern "the more eager

patriotism" building among preparedness advocates. "All talk about the good
that has come out of war must be balanced by the sober reflection as to whether
the same or even greater good might not have been achieved by other than warlike instruments," said the Methodist minister from Denver. "Moreover it is
the function of the religious leader today to protest against glorification of war
itself by glorifying its motive. War itself is the devil's own business. The men
who actually do the fighting feel thus about the war."[132] A school administrator
and minister observed, "Military training is being much exploited now for its
moral value, as well as for its need for preparedness. My own experience of it is
that with school boys, as a school requirement, it has few moral qualities."[133] A
religious publication editor accepted that military training could teach school
children virtue, "but every taint of the killing objective must be cut out."[134]

World War II Religious Education Association members acted as if the war
didn't exist for children until 1943, when a New York Jewish leader examined
its result on the city's children. He found little good to say. A documented rise
in juvenile delinquency, he contended, could be blamed on a war that implicitly
condoned violence and destruction. Even glorified it. "There is an implied sanction for aggressive action and since wars are fought and won by the matching
of aggression with aggression, ruthlessness with ruthlessness, the culture of a
nation tends to change from prohibition to permissiveness of violence," wrote
John Slawson, identified as executive director of the New York Jewish Board of
Guardians. "It has to be remembered that when the adult world is engaged in
work of destruction, children and adolescents will, in effect, engage in similar
activity, even though it may be inappropriately directed." The author could see
a few moderately good things for children brought about by war, a better job
for a parent and so a more secure home life, for example. "However, these are
but a few illustrations from a clinical experience and by no means, in even the
slightest measure, compensate for the destructive effects on personality wrought
by war."[135]

A report based on debate during the association's 1944 convention in Pittsburgh agreed the war experience could only be detrimental to adolescents. The
plethora of good-paying wartime jobs left them with "more money than they
know how to handle." A war-driven society that asked youth to grow up quickly
has encouraged "a sudden maturing in sex relations—early marriages, promiscu-
ity with service men." Morality has been skewed. "What had been taught as evil
now became a duty; human life seemed no longer to be of great worth." And
parents were less available to provide guidance.[136] In the association's only published comprehensive examination of war's effect on children, Sophia L. Fahs

agreed with other American religious authorities here who found little good to say about war's effect on children. Children are always asked to conform to adult standards, she noted, and those who quickly do so enjoy adult approval and greater security. "A war pushes to an extreme this will of society for conformity. Obedience and loyalty are virtues exalted in a war-torn world." A younger child is left confused, she contended, because the world at war seemed to have lost sight of values he has learned. "'Is my daddy shooting guns and killing people?' asks the five-year-old whose father has been to him the personalization of thoughtfulness and gentleness. How can the truth be told without the child's feeling that his daddy has not only left the physical home, but that the real parent whom he knew has somehow become a different person?" Fahs said older children responded by taking on the hate and destruction that apparently had become acceptable. "In the midst of the overwhelming destruction of this global war, with the corresponding honor which is being given to aggressive and destructive behavior, children feel the pressure to participate," Fahs wrote. "We are, therefore, finding abnormally violent expressions of aggression in children's play." As the country honored destructive behavior of its armed forces, "the pressure on the child to copy leads not only to the desire to wear the soldiers' trappings, to carry toy guns, and to point them boastfully at the unpopular boy or girl, but also to an abnormal desire to become the bully, to throw one's opponent and to destroy things." Hatred diffusing through wartime society cannot help but reach children, Fahs wrote. Adults hate the enemy and find scapegoats on which to blame the war. "With such elements pressing for power in the adult world, it is only natural that children should be showing unexpected and violent forms of hate."[137]

But what could religion do? While some religious authorities stayed strong in their condemnation of war's effect on children, they mustered less strength in their proposals for an answer through religious education. A conference of the country's Catholic bishops in 1944 in fact declared that education was the problem. "This war came largely from bad education.... Discarding moral principles and crowding God out of human life, scholars produced the monstrous philosophies which, embodied in political and social systems, enslave human reason and destroy the consciousness of innate human rights and duties."[138] But how to improve that education specifically was not clarified. Simply keeping children busy could be a start. "Such constructive activities give our youngsters a feeling that this war is truly a war of all people—themselves included."[139] "Anything that religious agencies do to preserve normal home life and to provide constructive leisure-time activity is a contribution," agreed the association in its Pittsburgh convention report.[140]

But this was by now an idea more than a quarter-century old, and already dominating the thinking of secular authorities. "The government and the schools have attempted to release this emotional urge by giving children outlet in constructive forms of participation such as gathering of scraps of metal and paper and the buying of war bonds, and countless other war activities," agreed Fahs. But she pointed out that response was inadequate. "These efforts have doubtless resulted in reducing children's urges to destroy. But these milder forms of participation do not give the kind of emotional release which many children need."[141] Still Fahs, like other religious authorities, could propose no truly transformative way for religion to pull children out of a militarized American society. "We share the belief that a good religious education should contribute toward enabling the child to find that poise and stability which he needs in this difficult world," she explained. "We should help our children to dig their roots down deep enough to touch these dependable realities." Fahs said religious leaders should resist the temptation to take advantage of war's pressure to conform as license to coerce kids to church. This wartime emotion was abnormal. "We should, therefore, seek to lessen the pressure rather than to increase it so that children may be sufficiently able to resist it to keep their thinking free." But how? "By giving him or by showing his parents how to give him an extra amount of wholesome loving and understanding fellowship."[142] It is worth observing that Fahs wrote as a leader of Unitarians, a faith regarded by many Christians as highly liberal. It is uncertain that other religious leaders would have agreed with Fahs' free-thinking approach; certainly the Catholic bishops' declaration didn't seem to suggest this. But no other writer from this association took up the challenge.

The association itself did, however, acknowledge obliquely opposition to free-thinking advocates as a way to educate children during war. In presenting a "syllabus" (no author) for discussion of wartime education, it was noted, "Christians as well as Jews recognize that they are minority groups in a secular and often hostile society. They feel the need to make clear to their youth the distinctive tenets and practices of their own religious heritage and to induct them into a particular religious community with impressive ceremonies that will call forth deep devotion." But the syllabus only asked questions; it provided no concrete recommendations for religious teaching during wartime.[143]

## Commercialism in War: Jobs for Juveniles and Toys for Tots

Those who criticized the decision of the United States to join World War I often used as justification business greed. After a few months of strict neutrality in 1914, the Wilson administration grew to fear economic recession as American commerce was barred from business deals with belligerents. Its decision to lift the freeze prompted resignation of pacifist Secretary of State William Jennings Bryan. But it pleased the nation's businesses. In principle they could trade with any belligerent. In practice British blockades made it possible to trade only with England and France. Both placed enormous orders with American firms, paying by credit. The United States Government joined the war in 1917, detractors complained, because Washington feared private businesses would lose money if the Allies did not emerge victorious. Most historians view this argument as incomplete at best, but the truth was that some businesses do profit during any war. Others do not, particularly if their goods are rationed, and they cannot easily retool for war service. Toy makers in particular found a World War II ban on metal difficult, although some did manage to convert excess capacity to war use. But private business exists for one purpose, to make money, and most American commerce during both wars did their clever best to find ways to stay profitable. Part of that job involved children.

Business reached out to children by offering products kids could buy, while dressing child-targeted advertising in patriotic finery. They also evaluated children's war-work programs from a business perspective, something most authorities didn't apparently consider. During World War I, agribusiness in particular took a skeptical look at the big push the U.S. Office of Education was making in favor of the School Garden Army. These young volunteers scoured the cities for weedy back yards and unproductive lots that might produce food to fill war shortages. It worked so well, asserted government authorities, that 60,000 unproductive acres had been turned into bountiful truck gardens.

Yet not everyone prospered, according to a report by the U.S. Chamber of Commerce. Writing in spring 1918, J. W. E. Lawrence indicated that children's war gardens not only worked, they worked too well. An overflow of produce could not be trucked to market fast enough, and spoiled. But that was not the kernel of the complaint. The problem with children's gardens seemed to be that they became too competitive with commercial business interests. Lawrence predicted "enormous areas" would be planted in spring 1918, "not only for patriotic reasons, but because of the spur of high prices on food."

Lawrence interviewed L. C. Corbett "of the Department of Agriculture," a division apart from the Office of Education which had spearheaded the School Garden Army. Corbett seemed skeptical: the kids posed unfair competition. He asked gardeners to be "sure that there will be a reasonable demand for your product without unduly interfering with the legitimate operations of established market gardeners."[144] To elaborate, Corbett described such competition in Connecticut and Rhode Island. "The home gardeners of those states spread themselves. In fact, they spread out over the local markets, flooded them with produce, and disturbed the legitimate and necessary business of the truck gardener to an unwarranted extent." He added that Boy Scouts in 1917 found one hundred free acres around Washington, D.C., worth planting in produce. But they were discouraged from doing so. The Department of Agriculture suggested the boys grow corn instead. "The result was not merely a patriotic intention but an intelligent, and patriotic service."[145] Young gardeners also drew down pesticide supplies that business relied on. "A million gardeners using a quarter of a pound apiece would exhaust our national supply." While business ought to have Paris Green (an arsenic derivative) at its disposal, children were advised, "Use a stick and a tin can. It takes more time, but it's more patriotic."[146]

If children were determined to plant produce instead of corn, the chamber promoted another option popular in rural America: home canning instead of marketing. Children needed to learn "the gospel of canning." To teach them, state agencies trained 200 demonstrators. "Each demonstrator in a given field will organize boys and girls, not in clubs, at first, but as other demonstrators," wrote a U.S. Chamber of Commerce reporter. "The best way to teach Tommy or Mary Jones that he or she can do effective canning work is by having their playmate Billy Taylor give a demonstration of his canning ability at the county fair."[147] In Kansas children were encouraged to learn cold-pack style canning through "Mother-Daughter Clubs." "The Senior Member, as she is called, may hitch up either with her own son or daughter or, if she has none available, she can borrow one from a neighbor." Five teams constitute a club, earning a free USDA demonstration. The quota: "Every member of the club has to can at least twenty-five quarts the first season, and every item must produce twenty-five quarter of fruit and twenty-five of vegetables."[148]

The U.S. Chamber of Commerce during World War II had almost nothing to say about children. But it did celebrate their ability to work hard for America's war-business interests. In the only article addressing children's issues between 1940 and 1945, the chamber's publication, *Nation's Business*, called attention to the superb work children were doing to fill labor shortages. Younger children "are busy at every opportunity," wrote Lawrence N. Galton. "They're making book ends, shelves, shoe-shining boxes for Coast Guard barracks nearby. Sewing and filling with toilet articles scores of cretonne bags for distribution to servicemen in hospitals." In addition to producing army equipment, these children were keeping their schools in good repair. "In one school, they've undertaken the long-needed job of remodeling and repainting furniture and equipment, and even making equipment needed for the lower grades." High school-aged children could get real jobs, and they did work hard, Galton asserted. California schools offered a "four-four" program, Galton explained, four hours of school and four hours of work a day. "Others from more distant localities live at adult-supervised barracks near the plant for four weeks, working regular eight-hour shifts, then go back to school for four weeks." Calling results "outstanding," Galton said in one example from a California Lockheed-Vega aircraft plant, "three high school boys could do more than five women" working at standard industry pay rates—sixty cents an hour. "'Boy power,' says Mort Bach, Vega works manager, 'has given us some of our outstanding workers and fewest employee problems.'" The boys' enthusiasm for their work led them to make games out of production goals, competing with each other as if they were on a football field. "Give youngsters jobs and you'll have fewer delinquents. Give 'em jobs and you'll have more—and often better—war production."[149]

Beyond its pronouncements regarding children in the work force, America's business authorities seemed to have little to say directly to children regarding duties in the war. They had much to say indirectly, however, through toys and advertising for them. War toy manufacturing goes back to the time of Louis XIV. During early years, authorities presumed war toys were useful because they educated children into familiarity with war. But the rise of pacifism in the early twentieth century splintered opinion among those who presumed war toys taught about war, those who countered that war toys released childhood aggression, and those parents who knew it didn't matter—children could not be denied anyway. Children played war with sticks if not allowed toy guns, and dug around back lots in fanciful foxholes if forbidden to move freely in front of mother. "Certainly it does no good to forbid such activities," decided a prominent education professor in World War II. "Their harm is in the great restriction of activity resulting from constant preoccupation with them."[150] *Parents' Magazine* agreed: "Psychologists assure us that such play is inevitable, these days, and that it is harmless. But when the child is old enough to understand that guns are aimed at targets, it is possible to enlist his interest in marksmanship, starting perhaps with brush darts and bows with blunt arrows."[151]

But the concern over children playing at war was more complicated than an acknowledgment that many children are naturally aggressive and war play is the usual outlet. The focus was on the war toy itself, the object manufactured by an adult for a child. Children denied toys may craft their own, to create a childhood subculture mirroring the world of adults. But with more realistic manufactured toys, children can closely copy the tools of the world they soon will themselves enter. They can build a practice world in a sheltered environment, as the occupational therapist builds a practice world in a clinic to prepare patients for the real one. "All the toys one commonly sees are essentially a microcosm of the adult world; they are all reduced copies of human objects," observed Roland Barthes. Freud noted children treat dolls like living people. But living people also treat other living people like dolls.[152] It was the parallel world of the child in which the war toy entered, and its effect depended not only on what the children wanted, but what the manufacturer was trying to give them.

The point of war toys historically, as noted, was educational. The kind of education expected from these toys, of course, would not reflect values of peace and cooperation. In the nations of northern Europe that dominated early manufacture of war toys, authorities showed few pretentions regarding whether "boys will be boys." French war toys were simply called "the educators for tomorrow's war."[153] Their designs emphasized patriotic spirit, and their attention to detail spurred adventurous dreams of the fighting life. Board games during World War I propagandized for their own countries, the enemies depicted as a menace while children became heroes at the role of the dice. War was a glorious and heroic game, brought down to the child's world through its re-creation as toys. Reproduced soldiers' uniforms gave children entry into inspiring battles of history, and parents often rewarded the miniature warrior in photographic portraits, a more symbolic sword substituting for a rifle.

In one example Germany, center of most war toy manufacturing before the wars, featured a detailed cannon firing rubber shot. Instructions included specific information to make the play as realistic, as warlike as possible; "(We can) start a terrible killing until only a few (enemy) soldiers remain." War toys could bring history alive—at least the bloodiest parts of it. "War was woven into the fabric of daily life in a way that was irreconcilable with war as an extraordinary and scary experience—and yet its trivialization helped people confront war, just as its glorification did," observed Mossé.[154] In World War I France, concluded one observer, everyone made war: adults in real life, children in lead (toy soldiers).[155] Toys as educational propaganda for *La Patrie* could impress themselves onto the parallel world of play created by a child in a way more suited to adult goals. The wild, counterculture freedom of child's play could be grafted to a war made accessible, familiar, less menacing. Using children's war games, "harsh adult realities of war could be made more palatable."[156] Children could play games and so put the reality of death into their world in which "bang-bang, you're dead" was only temporary. "Death seems to give them no sense of mystery and awe," observed a World War I-era writer about her American twelve-year-old nephew and his friends. "Billy's attitude is that going to war is part of the game; when you're a little boy you have to go to school; when you're older, you draw your number and are called to camp—it's all in a day's work.[157]

How much of that attitude grew from the toys that stylized the war game in miniature? How much of it emanated from just being a kid, just living in the sheltered parallel world of play? In the United States, authorities boasted little ambition in favor of using war toys for propaganda. Not that it didn't happen anyway: in both world wars, toys reflected all the glory and adventure of the war myth, and all the racism and antipathy that authorities in America officially condemned. As manufactured reflections of popular culture, toys in World War II displayed the prejudice and race hate of a society that presumed subhuman qualities of its enemies. Particularly Japanese, depicted in game and comic book as slant-eyed devils, often drawn with buck teeth and large spectacles: "Toys, books, and comics passed along the message to America's young people." One glance at racist comic book covers of World War II will affirm the kind of education manufacturers of childhood items wanted to pass to the next generation.[158] But criticism aimed at widespread manufacture of toys interpreting a wartime society's racism and hatred for young folk also was part of World War I. The Huns were the enemy, and children could slay them on tables with lead soldiers, and on streets with wooden artillery.

Whether authorities desired it or not, it seemed America's war toys played to the same propagandistic goals of their European counterparts. "Geography games, map games of parcel post or trade have been converted into war map games, games of siege and maneuver," wrote a 1915 visitor to a convention of toy manufacturers. "A game of miniature bowls, for example, has been labeled a 'siege gun' and soldiers stand in place of nine pins. The background of a puzzle game, a game of shaking little balls into little holes, had been changed from a baseball field to a battle field." The write acknowledged that authorities placed great importance on the educational value of play. They emphasized cooperation, and discouraged conflict. But war play as expected by toy manufacturers encouraged other values. "From cooperation or rivalry of a tolerant kind it is directed to the struggle that ends in elimination.... Geography and history become nothing but a story of competition and strife." The result, warned the writer, could be "sowing of the dragon's teeth even if for ten or twenty years we wait for the crop to come up."[159]

During the interwar years war toys were presumed to breed warlike adults. The Treaty of Versailles banned war toys in Germany, a "real issue" to German parents, some of whom joined campaigns to swap existing war toys for "pedagogically sound" items.[160] United States sales of war toys, which had shot up during the conflict, dropped as Americans became disillusioned with the war that seemed to solve nothing. Higher end manufacturers succeeded mostly in provoking ire by hazarding introduction of a new war toy. "When Gimbels [department store] advertised military toy machine guns, a slew of people wrote in to complain that it ought to be ashamed. Due to protests, General Foods removed cut-out soldiers from its 'Post Toasties' cereal boxes." But this doesn't tell us what the children thought. It might be presumed children themselves wouldn't be shopping in the higher-end stores. But they might buy the cheap metal toy soldiers produced by the millions and sold in dime stores such as F. W. Woolworth. In fact, these stores "were selling slush-cast 'dimestore' soldiers like crazy."[161]

America's dimestore soldiers were cheap enough for nearly any kid, and sold in most stores that featured inexpensive merchandise. Production of United States-made toy soldiers was launched by Grey Iron company during World War I, with cast iron figures about three inches high introduced in August 1917. By the 1930s Barclay of New Jersey as largest manufacturer produced 500,000 toy soldiers a week.[162] Barclay produced toy soldiers in seventy-eight poses; Grey Iron produced thirty-six. Of the Barclay line, however, only one depicted a soldier in less than ship-shape, bandaged on head and arm. Grey Iron included two indicating a mishap: a soldier on crutches, and carried on a stretcher.[163] As collectibles these poses are listed as scarce or rare, possibly because they were less popular with children. Other poses depicted soldiers in nearly every activity a manufacturer could imagine, including shooting, of course, but also wearing gas masks, driving cars, aiming cannon and howitzers, as well as activities in the rear: officers at a desk, cooks, drivers, convalescents, even soldiers writing letters. No body parts, although the soft lead some toy companies favored during this more ignorant time could be easily chopped up by boys themselves. In contrast during World War II, German toy soldiers became more explicit, including depictions of wounded, amputated, or dead soldiers.[164]

Also featured during this period were sets of picture cards, "The Horrors of War," introducing children to decapitation, mutilation, flying body parts, and other everyday battlefield experiences. The manufacturer, Gum, Inc., in 1938 depicted Italians still as good guys despite their invasion of Ethiopia. Japanese already had become barbarians.[165] The racism of these cards might shock a parent today, but given the level of violence in video games, the actions likely would not. The difference, of course, is that these cards did realistically depict what happened in war. But research into the world war period shows repeatedly that authorities worked mightily to shield children from most of war's grim realities. In fact, home-front adults too did not know the true nature of battlefield violence. And mostly they did not care to learn. But while toy manufacturers seldom tried to create realism in the horrors of the battlefield, they did try to reproduce the ordnance of the battles in exceedingly accurate detail. A Chicago toy company, Walbert Manufacturing, advertised its World War I "Sinking Battleship With Torpedo." The ship broke apart and sank when hit. Samuel Orkin sold ship models closely resembling the navy's submarine chasers, cruisers, destroyers and Dreadnaughts.[166] Toy manufacturers worked to keep up with advances in military technology by issuing facsimiles of new weapons as soon as they hit the field. "Big Dick" by Milton Bradley, a toy closely resembling the World War I-era machine gun, was "ready for action":

> I shoot thirty-six (36) wooden bullets as fast as you can turn the firing crank. I shoot true as your aim and my strong iron base keeps me from 'jumping.' For indoor war play I have no equal and will give you and your friends exciting fun storming the German breast-works you can build.[167]

Toy manufacturers during World War I worried impending shortages would cramp production. A toy manufacturers' lobbying group approached Congress to impress the need for toys during the war, but that war ended before shortages could become an issue. In World War II, on the other hand, shortages became acute. Cast iron toys disappeared first. Then those of lead, mostly toy soldiers. "Rubber bathtub toys have already vanished," *Parents Magazine* observed in a 1942 report on new holiday toys. "There are wooden and plastic ones in the shapes of tanks and battleships as well as animals and sailboats." Of the twenty-eight new toys illustrated for 1942, seventeen were military-related. Particularly popular were scooters, tricycles and wagons disguised as tanks and airplanes. Featured by reviewers was a new "mili-toy," the "Sumer Ack-Ack Gun, an exciting new mili-toy of the scooter type. Tempered Presdwood and hard wood are used in place of metal and rubber. Gun raises and lowers, a ratchet simulates anti-aircraft fire, wood shells automatically eject. $39.75."[168] In contrast, the magazine's 1941 Christmas toy guide included no war toys among the 44 depicted.[169]

Of course, many were available; possibly editors hesitated before featuring toys that some pre-war parents had found objectionable. In the years before Pearl Harbor toy manufacturers still commonly called their products "defense" and not "war" toys to mollify parents.[170] Objections dwindled after the United States joined the war, and authorities bowed to reality. "Almost every child wants a gun of one sort or another," 1942 toy reviewers admitted. "The sight of one child 'machine gunning' several of his friends, who fall down 'dead' with shouts of glee is a startling commonplace these days."[171]

Shortages and rationing of raw materials drove some World War II toy manufacturers to retool for munitions manufacturing. Some simply went out of business. The rest tried to deal with the situation by making toys from wood or cardboard. One ingenious manufacturer, according to a nine-year-old describing his Christmas presents in *Jack and Jill* magazine, could even provide paper-based sound effects: "I also got a machine gun made of strong cardboard with a strip of cardboard to pull through it to make it go rat-a-tat-tat."[172] But boys preferred realistic war toys, hard to fashion from wood. "Cardboard could provide more detail and color, but not strength. For cardboard soldiers, the market wasn't there, as it was for lead."[173]

While government enforced rationing, it did not discourage manufacturers from making toys related to the war. In fact, it encouraged some to produce toys that appeared officially sanctioned. The Office of Civilian Defense in early 1942 offered toy manufacturers the opportunity to make toys look more realistic by including one of its fifteen patented Civil Defense emblems. The insignia in patriotic colors set red pictures in the CD background of white triangle and blue circle. Pictures included ladder for the rescue squad, airplane for the bomb squad, lightning bolt for the boys' and girls' messenger service, coffee cup for food and housing corps. For the agreement, the government received a five percent royalty. Paper doll manufacturers in particular could quickly produce figures designated for home-front service. "A fascinating piece was Saalfield Co.'s handsome boxed set, 'Paper Dolls in Uniforms of the U.S.A. (#S-592). The colorful box top showed fourteen civil defense insignia and the contents included various civil defense uniforms for women." Toys were marketed in association with bond drives and local civil defense projects. They were "displayed along with articles used by air raid wardens and the Auxiliary Police, and helmets, uniforms, whistles and doctors' and nurses' kits were emphasized. New York Toy and Game Mfg. Co.'s 'Junior Air Raid Warden Set' tied right in." [174] Tie-ins included military events, the toys displayed with newspaper headlines announcing Allied victories. "The trade press and Toy Trade Association gave very detailed suggestions to local retailers as to how to set up such displays and the items to include."[175]

These and some other war-related toys did not directly supply children with playtime ordnance to make their own battles. Instead, they underscored a child's home-front duties, and advanced understanding of the war's effects at home. "The Blackout Kit" By Vernon Co., Newton, Iowa, relied for its popularity on phosphorescent tape. The Child Training Association assured parents the glow-in-the-dark tape was harmless. The "Ration Game" by Jayline Manufacturing, Philadelphia, invited players to move a wooden token shaped like a car around the game board using colored paper "ration cards" labeled sugar, coffee, gas or meat. To encourage Victory Gardens, Saalfield in 1943 issued "Uncle Sam's Little Helpers," "a particularly charming set. It had a large page of costumes for little gardeners complete with seed packets, baskets, wagons and tools. Even the family's puppy and kitten are helping."[176] Authorities encouraged children to scan the skies for possible enemy aircraft—highly unlikely, but a good way to build diligence and preparedness—and toy manufacturers were quick to help out. "Spotting" by Parker Brothers (two dollars) helped participants identify aircraft they might see. "After a while, very few kids failed to distinguish a Heinkel 111 from a B-25." And if an enemy should parachute in, children would respond based on lessons from frankly racist toys like "Rap-a-Jap" (1943). Milton Bradley's "Get In the Scrap" invited children to trace the story of their scrap drives from collection point to processing.

In fact, some of World War II's scrap collected by children consisted of toys themselves. As a patriotic war sacrifice, children joined role models such as England's Princess Elizabeth in donating metal toys to the war foundry—one reason pre-war metal soldiers today are scarce and collectible.[177] "At my father's urging," recalled a World War II child, "and much to my chagrin, some of my metal toy collection, airplanes, toy cars and pop-G-Men guns wound up in a school scrap drive for the war effort."[178]

As the country threw its resources into the war's hungry maw, parents concerned that war-themed toys would skew a child's values learned from authorities that they had little to worry about. A psychologist in 1943 assured readers of *Women's Home Companion* that "it was natural for children to imitate the wartime adult world environment." A poll of parents showed most World War II mothers agreed. Children who were surrounded by war news would want to play war.[179] War was the game, toys the tokens, and the children's world a swirl of devious Nazis, buffoonish Italians, treacherous Japanese, heroic commandoes and devoted nurses. Rules of the war game were adapted from childhood culture and adult presumptions. Less assertive children were forced to play the roles no one wanted, as Germans or Japanese. Girls generally were barred from war play; if they did manage to enter the boy's realm, they were "killed" early, or became nurses. Those who wanted to dress up like the boys were ridiculed or suspected of "immorality."[180] Still, the psychologists' best advice was to encourage play, games, and toys to make the war less threatening. For grade-school children, "The war, remote or near at hand, will give him considerable excitement and fun. Already many school children are changing their time-honored game of prisoner's base and cops and robbers to air raids and ambulance and stretcher drills and real war games." Play, along with volunteer work for the war, could help children keep busy—and children occupied were children who did not have time to worry.[181] Education professor Howard Lane believed the idea of catharsis through games had "some validity."[182] Jack Mathews, who was a child in World War II, recalled, "As children, we were totally caught up in the war, but it wasn't the war our parents knew. In our minds we created our war the way we wanted it to be—it was a game of toys and play and no one really died.... We were far from the killing and bombing, and so for most American children the war was a huge game and the war years actually a fun time. This may sound terrible but, in perspective, it is true."[183] The proliferation of war toys during both world wars and their popularity concerned some authorities who feared encouraging a war-mongering new generation. While Lane admitted the likely truth of the catharsis argument, he still considered its possible consequences for the typical boy of World War II. "He hates Japs and Germans, makes jokes about Musso-lini. In his play he murders with tommy-guns, torpedoes great ships with roaring PT boats, bombs and strafes the despised enemy with 'air-cobras.'" Lane asked, "Can children thus reared build and maintain the just, orderly and peaceful world for which we profess to fight? Unless the school takes vigorous counter measurers the results of this war are not worth the fighting."[184]

War in the world of play today is fought less with wood and plastic, and more with mice and computer screens. Toy soldier production died out in the 1960s. If children are still attracted to realism and detail, video games today can do what even the most detailed metal soldier could not. Parents know children can be aggressive; ten-year-olds talked about the "joy of killing" in a 2002 study of war toys. They were speaking of video games. But the author noted that com-pared to a 1985 study, children with access to highly detailed video games in 2002 showed that "a brutalization of both language and play behavior has taken place."[185] Just such an outcome was feared by Lane, and proposed by Mossé as children were taught to trivialize war through play. Certainly world war parents

*War toys most attractive to children captured real armaments in accurate detail. Machine guns were particularly advertised during World War I. (American Boy, July 1918, page 43.)*

who encouraged war play and bought war toys did not intend to trivialize war. But they did intend to make war less fearful to children by making it more familiar, more a part of a child's new normal. Death was inevitable, as everyone knew. And so war too became acceptable as inevitable. This in no way proves definitely that children's toys encourage a warrior's attitude. However, a significant number of children populate the armies in three-fourths of today's wars worldwide—some as young as six. How may they be recruited, how may they be trained? In playgrounds, with toys. "They even have militarized playground equipment such as seesaws that have toy automatic weapons mounted on the handles."[186]

### Advertising the War to Children

If advertising can be defined as propaganda,[187] the country's commercial interests launched big campaigns for children during both wars. Selling the prod-

uct meant selling the war. To sell the war, commercial advertisers tried to make
their products sound fun a lot, educational a little bit, and a necessary part of
every kid's play life, always. Advertisers focused on four classes of products for
children. First class of product was obvious—war toys. These were marketed
mostly in World War I, and mostly to boys. A second class of product was not
made expressly for children playing war. But it could be adapted, rifles most
obviously. The third class could not be easily attached to a wartime theme, items
such as musical instruments, fitness machines, beds, bicycles, toy trains soda, or
hair tonic. To bring these goods into a wartime setting, an advertiser needed to
construct a more elaborate argument, or build a metaphor. The fourth class of
advertisement did not sell anything tangible. It marketed an idea, an appeal directly from an advertiser to a child suggesting the child take some action for the
war. Such appeals were common from government and non-profit groups such
as the Boy Scouts. But they are not considered commercial advertisements—usually a publisher donated the space. Here instead we examine direct appeals to
children from American businesses, using advertising. They were rare—but occasionally advertisers did directly address children reflecting wartime concerns.

Most tangible was manufacturers' focus on war toys. As children during the
world wars eagerly sought out toys to remake the war in their own backyards,
toy companies could offer their help. Realism was favored, particularly in toys
that gave children the opportunity to meet patriotic expectations by modeling
military skills. Big Dick, the World War I machine gun realistically designed by
Milton Bradley, came to *Boys' Life* just in time for the 1916 holiday gift season.
Playing on the scout motto, the advertisement reads, "Be Prepared. Boys! Get
ready now for great sport all winter with a Big Dick Rapid Fire Machine Gun...
demolishes toy forts or knocks over toy soldiers at a distance of fifteen feet." The
manufacturer claimed it had already sold 50,000 units at $2.50, the "Big Dick
Brigade" that every boy would want to join.[188]

Competitor A. C. Gilbert Company widely advertised its own realistic machine gun: "Note all of the features shown in the picture—they're just like the
machine guns used by all the armies of the world."[189] Advertising emphasized
virtues not only of gaining practical familiarity with military ordnance, but also
enhanced patriotism as children at play learned military tactics. "Here's the toy
that has made the biggest kind of a hit with patriotic boys—the Gilbert Machine
Gun. Built like and looks like the real rapid firers used by the U.S. Army....
Magazine for twelve (wooden) cartridges...Price $3.00."[190] Advertising for this
toy developed more aggressively by 1918, the advertiser calling boys to realistic
war adventures:

> Now, boys! Let 'em have it! There they come, boys! They're getting ready to make a rush. Steady, machine gun squad No. 1! Get their range! Now! Fire! Ha! that got 'em. Now form for attack! Double time—march!
> Fun! Gee! You can have the best fun you ever had with a Gilbert Machine Gun and a machine gun squad of boys to operate. It's almost like the real machine guns. It fires ten shots a second from a magazine into which you load clips of cartridges. The bullets are wooden ones and won't hurt anyone but you can fire the gun just like a real one.[191]

The company reminded boys, "You can get up the machine gun squad yourself and be its corporal. Every boy ought to learn military tactics so that he will have experience and be ready if his country has to call him."[192]

Milton Bradley again countered with its Big Dick, now up to three dollars: "American boys, attention! I never miss fire. I shoot thirty-six (36) wooden bullets as fast as you can turn the firing-crank.... For indoor war play I have no equal and will give you and your friends exciting fun storming the German breast-works you can easily build."[193] The advertiser suggested children remind parents of the upcoming Christmas season, because "If you are a real live American boy you will want me." Realism also was emphasized in other toy ordnance such as model tanks. "Look, Boys! You can build this tank with Meccano Toy Engineering for Boys," the advertiser announced. "The 'tank' shown above is a perfect working model of the wonderful machines which crawl over trenches and shell-holes, knock down trees and houses, and climb right over them."[194] The American Toy Company co-opted army jargon to sell its models, the text accompanying a drawing of a boy placing pieces of metal similar to an Erector Set: "Boys wanted for the 'American Army.' Good pay in lots of fun—excellent mental training—recruiting stations at stores in your home town." Approach of this advertiser, however, unlike that of the machine gun manufacturers, suggested its possibly more peaceful intention: "'Armed' with an American Model Builder outfit, each boy makes thrilling conquests not in destruction, but in construction."[195] Still, the child illustrated was building a cannon.

Advertisers also emphasized games and puzzles as educational tools to teach children about the war. "Trench. The Great War Game. Every Boy Should Play It Now," suggested a manufacturer (unnamed) in summer 1918. "Instructive, Interesting, Exciting.... Take It With You On Vacation."[196] But these were toys directly related to the war. More often during World War I, and most of the time during World War II, toys and other products marketed to children did not have an obvious war-related connection. Advertisers created one. Things sold to boys that might plausibly become of military use included rifles, obviously, but also building blocks, models, bugles, cots, flashlights, and bicycles. Bicycles could offer a more serious purpose than kid transportation, as children were encouraged to deliver and canvass for the government war effort. "One boy in 1918 is worth three boys of 1914," asserted a tire company ad in 1918. "This is especially true of a boy who has a bicycle or motorcycle. Put a boy awheel and he not only has more speed and promptness but more ambition and reliability.... United States Cycle tires are *good* tires."[197] Fisk Bicycle Tires encouraged boys to join up: "Fisk Club boys are doing their bit. They are not old enough to go to the front—but they make themselves useful and their labors in bicycle patrols... an excellent training in discipline and character-building that develops manly and honorable young men."[198]

Play block construction could prepare children for the task of building military fortifications, emphasized F. Ad. Richter and Company, New York: "Every real boy likes to play at war. He can have the time of his life with the wonderful 'Fortress Sets' of Anchor Blocks.... A boy can build all kinds of modern fortresses with them, put soldiers in the forts and have real battles. They are full of interest. They educate and instruct."[199]

Bugles could easily slide from scout to soldier, as the Grand Rapids Band Instrument Company told boys: "Regulation army bugle. $5.00. The depot quartermaster, U.S. Army, has ordered thousands of this model for the new army. They are finished to harmonize with the khaki uniform." Gold Medal Camp Furniture Manufacturing, Racine, Wisconsin, could also boast of sales to the army in the hundreds of thousands: "You want the same comfort and conveniences in camp that the government provides for the army and national guard."[200] A model train could teach military construction: "Ives Trains and Toy Railroad Systems help prepare you for work that Uncle Sam may need you to do later. You learn simplified civil engineering by laying the tracks, installing the switches, building stations, planning tunnels and setting signals. Best of all, it's great fun—the kind you like."[201]

Of course, advertisers who could make the most natural transition to wartime themes sold rifles. Shooting in particular was a popular sport among American boys during wartime, and magazines reflected a gun culture in their advertising, promoting rifles for boys who wanted to practice for future war service, or for patriotic readiness. Air rifles might be a good start. Accompanying an illustration of two boys, one in uniform, watching passing troops while holding air rifles, the ad reads, "We all thrill with pride as we see young America nobly responding to the nation's call. The Military Daisy follows the latest military lines, with carrying strap and rubber tipped bayonet. $3.50." Sterling Air Rifles

Advertisers used the war to sell unrelated products during both wars. This toothpaste advertisement appeared on the back cover of American Boy, *September 1918.*

emphasized their obvious role in war preparation: "Captain Ready, as a boy, had a crack squad equipped with Sterling Air Rifles. He knew what it meant to present arms, to right fours, and to double quick. He's now a captain and because he had this foundation it helped him to get this commission."[202] Moving from air rifle to .22 caliber, Remington encouraged older boys to join a government junior marksmanship program and win medals and honor. "Uncle Sam generally does things *right....* Get started *right* by reading the four Remington Right booklets for boys, telling everything you should know."[203] Competing rifle company Winchester set up its own shooting team. "In these times when military affairs are of such vital interest," the advertisement noted, every boy wants to learn more about rifles. The Winchester Junior Rifle Corps was the answer. "The age limit is eighteen.... If neither you nor your chums owns a .22 caliber Winchester, you can buy one for a very reasonable sum from your dealer—who has as rifle to suit every boy's pocketbook."[204]

Other advertisers trying to tie unrelated products to the war argued an indirect connection. These borrowed military routines that could be transferred to the home front, or constructed metaphors. Fitness and sports could be good military preparation. The S. B. Davega Company of New York suggested, "Boys! Prepare for WAR! Build yourself up—train at home. Become the best developed boy in your town. Combination Exerciser, Muscle Builder and chest Expander Outfit for $1." Wilson Sporting Goods suggested ball games might be imitation war games. "Boys! Uncle Sam is Watching You. Play, play, play. It's up to you boys—to keep alive America's games and sports. That's the best way you can help your Uncle Sam." The sporting goods company reminded boys, "To play your best—to get the most out of the game, you must have the right equipment. The best equipment for any game or sport is that which bears the Wilson trademark."[205]

Other advertisers struggled to find a way to attach their product to war with propagandist glue. Parker Pen Company emphasized its pen was favored "by general to private, by rear admiral to seaman." That made it "the best pen for our brave Boy Scouts, the future defenders of the nation."[206] Eastman Kodak suggested, "Make your gift to those at home, a Kodak, that they in turn may make light hearts and happy faces by sending a continued Kodak story of that home to the brave lads, somewhere in France." Menzies Shoe Company of Milwaukee proposed, "Join the army of American boys. All you have to do is to climb into a pair of American Boy Army Shoes." [207]

A few advertisers for children tried a more sophisticated technique to tie their products to war. The literary technique of metaphor in wartime advertising began during World War I as an effort to turn the war into an image, in this case something home-front children could identify with.[208] Toothpaste, for example, could become a military code, the code for good teeth. In one full-page ad, Colgate included a facsimile of the entire code with this explanation: "Every boy should know the message of Colgate's Dental Cream.... You know how soldiers and sailors benefit from good teeth, and that they must have good teeth in order to pass the physical examination."[209] Gardening could easily become a metaphoric battle: "War on bugs. Insure your garden with Imperial spray outfit for $2.00.... You can do no more patriotic act than to enlist in the war on the bugs."[210] A breakfast food producer reached for a more far-fetched war metaphor in its puffed cereal manufacture: "These Are Guns That Send Out Joys. There are guns in our mills which boom every minute, to send out airy grain foods which taste like bubbled nuts.... Puffed Rice. Corn Puffs. Puffed Wheat."

After eating cereal launched their way by the guns of the breakfast food makers, children could even go fishing, knowing they still served a military need:

> Here is a way you can fight and be a real help to Uncle Sam—while you are having lots of fun. Every solder must have plenty of meat and plenty of wheat. There is not enough meat and wheat for everybody. Soldiers must come first. Others must go without.... During your vacation the healthiest thing that you can do is to take a 'Bristol' Rod and a Meek Reel and go out on the streams and lakes and fish. Bristol Steel Fishing Rods Are Patriotic Tools."[211]

But perhaps the most ambitious attempt of any world war advertiser in a publication for children, both for product and theme, can be credited to Overland Car Company. It offered to sell its Model Eighty-Five Four as a patriotic duty to help children keep fit for service; $895. "Do your bit—but keep fit—The car of the hour. The times demand alertness—energy—efficiency," the advertiser contended. "Have an automobile. It will enable the whole family to do more each day with less fatigue. With it you can speed up your work—gain time for play—and reach your playground quickly—without fatigue."[212]

World War I commercial advertisers who presented a message to children without obviously selling a product were uncommon, but did illustrate more directly messages commercial authorities wanted children to hear. Those messages mostly admonished kids to the same duties other authorities were asking of them. "Boys, these are war times. You must pitch in and 'do your bit' just as well as the grown-ups," preached one manufacturer. "You must mix work with fun this year. A little more work and a little less time for play will be good for your health." While most of this advertisement's text advocated development of virtue through war work, it did remind boys that to get all this work done, "you'll need a Wagner Auto Coaster—the wagon that serves every purpose of work and fun."[213]

A clothing manufacturer, Keynee Company, reminded boys to obey: "Patriotism means doing your best...obeying the government's orders on the spot and to the last ditch."[214] But an unusual 1918 advertisement sponsored by Elgin Watch Company, while trying to sell nothing tangible to younger children, did propose a volunteer service, something different from growing gardens or selling war bonds. The idea was couched in children's language using an illustrated mouse in uniform. "Serve America First! A Letter from Captain Tick-Mouse," suggested the title. "Will you help us? Will you help us catch the slackers? Will you come with me and do some real detective work for your Uncle Sam? Do this and you'll be helping to win the war!" Children could learn more specifically in a free book, *Captain Tick-Mouse and His Adventures in Secret Service*, available in jewelry stores. After reading that, apparently, youthful spies could also work surreptitiously for Uncle Sam.[215]

During World War II, commercial advertisers in publications for children studied here rarely addressed readers directly with messages not tied to a specific product. Bell Telephone was an exception. This advertisement in *American Girl* called on supposedly chat-happy adolescents to free the lines for more important work. The ad below lays on the guilt about as heavily as it can, repeating "all my fault" no less than three times. Appeal to guilt was rare among commercial advertisers trying to sell products through children's magazines. It was, however, a favored tool among editors of those publications.

> It's All My Fault! Mother missed a Red Cross meeting, an important one, and it's all my fault. I was talking to Sally on the telephone yesterday. I guess we talked a long time because I told her all about the party. And after that I called Mary. That's why the Red Cross people couldn't get Mother in a hurry. Our line was busy, and it's all my fault.[216]

Unlike the lively competition to advertise war toys in World War I, World War II children's publications studied here curtailed war toy ads. This may have been necessary as shortages more severely pinched this war's toy manufacturers, although toys of wood and cardboard remained generally available. *Boys' Life*, however, published few toy advertisements during this war, as did *American Girl*, its counterpart for Girl Scouts. (In World War I, *The Rally* for Girl Scouts contained no advertising, and advertising was removed from most of the *St. Nicholas* issues consulted. *Jack and Jill* also contained no advertising.) A few advertisements did propose toys directly related to wartime needs, notably airplane models: "Mego Models for spotting the enemy planes. 6 for only 50 c. Learn to identify German, Jap, and Italian planes instantly by building them."[217]

Toy BB guns could help younger boys prepare for the real thing, as Daisy advertised with an illustration of a boy, a soldier, and Uncle Sam holding rifles: "Presenting the new Daisy defender! 1000 shot military model. Looks like a real army gun."[218] But World War II advertisers primarily expanded on efforts to use military life as a way to sell products unrelated to war. This was done mostly by writing familiar commercial items into a militarized framework. The back cover

Coca-Cola ad below included a full-color drawing of military men relaxing, and apparently enjoying the life of war:

> Have a Coca-Cola—As You Were. A Way to Relax on a Battleship. Where ever a U.S. battleship may be, the American way of life goes along, in sports, humor, customs and refreshment. So, naturally, Coca-Cola is there, too, met with frequently at the ship's soda fountain. Have a 'Coke' is a phrase as common aboard a battle-wagon as it is ashore. It's a signal that spells out We're Pals. From Atlanta to the Seven Seas, Coca-Cola stands for the pause that refreshes—and has become the symbol of happy comradeship.[219]

By tying battlefields to playgrounds, advertisers made their products seem more patriotic, and at the same time made war seem less alien. If the soldiers were drinking the same soda as the kids, if they could relax with their chums and hang out at the soda fountain, just like at home—then war was not so different at all. As Mossé observed, "War was woven into the fabric of daily life in a way that was irreconcilable with war as an extraordinary and scary experience—and yet its trivialization helped people confront war, just as its glorification did."[220] At the same time, if the children could drink the same soda as the troops, then they too were doing a patriotic duty. Many World War II advertisers favored this theme, advancing a concept established during the war a quarter century earlier. But during this war, some appealed to young people by way of comic. Royal Crown Cola featured comic pages describing brave Americans foiling Nazis or other enemies and, as a reward, kicking back with a Royal Crown:

> Foiling Nazi Spies.... "Good work, Andy! You'll get a medal for this. You should feel great."
> "Frankly, fellows, I feel kinda shaky, now that it's over."
> "Just wait, Andy—We'll fix you up."
> "Gosh, gang—this Royal Crown Cola sure gives me a lift!"
> "You deserve it, Andy!"
> "You bet...nothing but the best tasting cola for you."[221]

Common batteries could be found at every hardware store, but also at the front: "Batteries furnish the power for portable radio communication—the link between the fighting forces. Millions of Ray-O-Vac batteries are delivering this vital power on all battlefronts right now."[222]

Advertisers during this war whose products did not seem remotely related to war, but might appeal to children, borrowed current events to sell. A candy bar could be a wartime tool, if the simile worked: "Just as a searchlight needs energy to perform its guardian duties—so does your body need energy to perform the tasks you assign," argued the copy. Illustrated was a Baby Ruth candy bar, a searchlight, and children in military dress. To add patriotic flavor, the advertisement reminded children, "Keep 'em flying. Buy U.S. Defense stamps and bonds."[223] Soap brought drama to the war effort: "Through his electric gunsight, the pilot gets a bead on his target, then blasts away with the eight to ten machine guns and cannons.... It's a tough, grueling grind, and that's why so many fliers top off the day with a refreshing Lifebouy bath.... It's the largest selling soap with our fighting men."[224]

Or a boy could join the troops during exercises by favoring a certain hair tonic: "Vitalis and the '60-second workout' for well-kept handsome hair. Soaring through the stratosphere, diving on military 'objectives,' turning out at the 'double' to meet air raid alarms—that's the exciting life of our air corps.... Yes, and Vitalis rates the credit for many an airman's good-looking hair."[225]

World War II advertisements for rifles and ammunition, again a product easily tied to war, also turned to military themes. During World War II, however, manufacturers tried more explicitly to make the connection between the war front and the home front. Remington reminded readers that soldiers really were at heart just sportsmen on a bigger hunt. An ad including an illustration of a soldier reminiscing about his hunting days back home, "The Soldier and the Ten-Minute Break," explained, "Remington's part in speeding peace is, of course, to continue to furnish Uncle Sam with military supplies.... But sometime—soon, we hope—Remington will be serving sportsmen again with shotguns and rifles." Soldier Bill began shooting rabbits at home, advertised Western World Champion Ammunition. "Life began at ten for Bill, strutting out with his first Winchester and a pocketful of Western Super-X long range .22s! Today, instead of shooting for fun, Bill is shooting for freedom—and doing a great job of it."[226] And bicycle parts saw advertising for war service in both wars. In fact, the first World War II material depicting a military theme published in *American Girl*, appearing December 1941, was an advertisement, for bicycles: "Columbia answers the call to the colors. You can be doubly proud of a Columbia this year... proud to own one of the bicycles that are playing an important part in serving America's Defense Forces."[227]

Racism was seldom a part of the appeal of authorities to children, either from government, education, or editorial sources. But in World War II it did occasionally creep into advertising targeted to children. German and Italian enemies were ignored. But Japanese were dehumanized as "Japs" with big teeth and glasses. B. F. Goodrich congratulated itself for inventing GR-S, a synthetic rubber. "You see, when the Japs grabbed nearly all the territory from which we used to get natural rubber, they thought they had us licked. But the development of synthetic rubber was the answer to Tojo—he hadn't figured on that." The illustration depicted a rubber-like man crushing a toothy Japanese midget with rising sun-like flag on chest.[228]

Whether such advertisements encouraged the pervasive racism of children that worried authorities during World War II is questionable. Movies, comics, and pop culture rained Jap racism down on children; advertisers merely reflected the tune of the times. But the efforts of advertisers to bring the war to children as less frightening, more acceptable, and so more inevitable, did add a powerful voice of commercial propaganda to the presumptions at the end of the war that led to unquestioned acceptance of the United States as the world's great military power.

## Notes

1. James E. West, "Report of the Chief Scout Executive," *Thirty-third Annual Report of the Boy Scouts of America*, 1942 (Washington, DC: GPO, 1943), 12, 16; while the author has accepted this source as most authoritative, the 1918 figure cited by Macleod, based, he wrote, on national headquarters statistics, is 377,577. David I. Macleod, *Building Character in the American Boy. The Boy Scouts, YMCA, and Their Forerunners, 1870–1920* (Madison, WI: The University of Wisconsin Press, 1983), 154.

2. R. Gorden Kelly, ed., *Children's Periodicals of the United States* (Westport, CT: Greenwood, 1984), 11.

3. *Proceedings of the Fifteenth National Convention of the Future Farmers of America. Kansas City, October 26–29, 1942* (Washington DC: FFA and U.S. Office of Education, 1942)., iii.

4. Franklin M. Reck, *The 4-H Story. A History of 4-H Club Work* (Chicago: National Committee on Boys and Girls Club Work, 1951), 147.

5. YMCA, *History of the YMCA*, http://www.ymca.net/ about_the_ymca/history_of_the_ymca.html.

6. Fred Leslie Brownlee, "The Educational Challenge to the Churches," *Religious Education. The Journal of the Religious Education Association*, October 1918, 350.

7. William D. Murray, *The History of the Boy Scouts of America* (New York: BSA, 1937), 4.

8. Ray O. Wyland, *Scouting in the Schools* (New York: Teachers College, Columbia University, 1934), 26.

9. George L. Mossé, *Fallen Soldiers. Reshaping the Memory of the World Wars* (New York and Oxford: Oxford University Press, 1990), 63.

10. Army Lieutenant Edgar Steever, *School Review* 25 (March 1917A), 145–150, quoted in Susan Zeiger, "The Schoolhouse vs. the Armory. U.S. Teachers and the Campaign Against Militarism in the Schools, 1914-1918, *"Journal of Women's History* 15, no. 2, (2003), 159.

11. David I. Macleod, *Building Character in the American Boy. The Boy Scouts, YMCA, and Their Forerunners, 1870-1920*, xvi.

12. Ibid., 139.

13. Stéphane Audoin-Rouzeau, *La Guerre des Enfants 1914–1918* (Paris: Armand Colin, 1993, 2004), 175.

14. Jürgen Reulecke, "Männerbund Versus the Family: Middle-Class Youth Movements and the Family in Germany in the Period of the First World War" in Richard Wall and Jay Winter, eds., *The Upheaval of War. Family, Work and Welfare in Europe, 1914-1918* (Cambridge: Cambridge University Press, 1988), 446.

15. Macleod, *Building Character in the American Boy. The Boy Scouts, YMCA, and Their Forerunners, 1870-1920*, 146-147.

16. Zeiger, "The Schoolhouse vs. the Armory. U.S. Teachers and the Campaign Against Militarism in the Schools, 1914-1918," 163-164.

17. *The BSA National Charter, June 15, 1916*, U.S. Code Title 36, Chapter 2, http://www.scatacook.org/ BSA-NationalCharter.htm.

18. Robert D. Ward, "The Origin and Activities of the National Security League, 1914-1919," *The Mississippi Valley Historical Review* 47 (June 1960), 56; Macleod, *Building Character in the American Boy. The Boy Scouts, YMCA, and Their Forerunners, 1870-1920*, 178.

19. *Boys' Life, Boys' and Boy Scouts Magazine*, March 1911, 35.

20. Macleod, *Building Character in the American Boy. The Boy Scouts, YMCA, and Their Forerunners, 1870-1920*, 179.

21. Murray, *The History of the Boy Scouts of America*, 101.

22. Macleod, *Building Character in the American Boy. The Boy Scouts, YMCA, and Their Forerunners, 1870-1920*, 180.

23. James E. West, "Boy Scouts in the Warring Nations," *Boys' Life*, September 1914, 18.

24. *Boys' Life*, November 1914, 2.

25. David Starr Jordan, "A Challenge! Do You Want to Fight?", *Boys' Life*, November 1914, 3.

26. Theodore Roosevelt, address to Mineola, Long Island, New York, scouts, "Fellow Boy Scouts," *Boys' Life*, October 1917, 23.

27. Cyrus Townsend Brady, "What War Is—Just One Battle," *Boys' Life*, November 1914, 7-9.

28. Macleod, *Building Character in the American Boy. The Boy Scouts, YMCA, and Their Forerunners, 1870-1920*, 179.

29. Ray O. Wyland, *Scouting in the Schools*, 29.

30. Macleod, *Building Character in the American Boy. The Boy Scouts, YMCA, and Their Forerunners, 1870-1920*, 139.

31. *Blue Sky! The Ernest Thompson Seton Pages*, http://www.etsetoninstitute.org/; Mark Ray, "Faces of the Founders," *Scouting*, http://www.scoutingmagazine.org/issues/1001/a-founders.html; Macleod, *Building Character in the American Boy. The Boy Scouts, YMCA, and Their Forerunners, 1870-1920*, 181.

32. Murray, *The History of the Boy Scouts of America*, 104-105.

33. Arthur R. Dean, professor of vocational education, teachers college, Columbia University, and supervising officer, Bureau of Vocational Training, New York State Military Training Commission, *Our Schools in War Time—and After* (Boston: Ginn and Company, 1918), 139-140.

34. West, "Report of the Chief Scout Executive," *Thirty-third Annual Report of the Boy Scouts of America*, 1942, 60.

35. Murray, *The History of the Boy Scouts of America*, 122.

36. "World War I and Public Service," *Boy Scout Stuff*, http://www.boyscoutstuff.com/Galleries/World/world.html.

37. *The Nation's Business* (U.S. Chamber of Commerce), April 1918, 29.

38. Murray, *The History of the Boy Scouts of America*, 129.

39. *Thirty-third Annual Report of the Boy Scouts of America*, 1942, 70. Another official source, Boy Scouts of America, "History of the BSA Highlights," http://www.scouting.org/About/FactSheets/BSA_History.aspx, claimed 300 million, which could be possible given the amount produced, but the author accepts the first as most authoritative.

40. *Thirty-third Annual Report of the Boy Scouts of America*, 1942, 70.

41. Facsimile of typed letter dated Nov. 26, 1918, to Colin Livingstone, signed Newton D. Baker, Secretary of War, *Boys' Life*, January 1919, 23.

42. Ibid.

43. Murray, *The History of the Boy Scouts of America*, 125.

44. "Official News. What Every Scout Wants to Know," *Boys' Life*, November 1918, 29.

45. Quoted in Ibid., 107-108; West, "Report of the Chief Scout Executive," 30.

46. "Where There's a Scout There's a Way. The President Thinks So. Boy Scouts Help Uncle Sam Raise Nearly $20,000,000 of the $2,000,000,000 Liberty Bond Loan," *Boys' Life*, August 1917, 2.

47. Murray, *The History of the Boy Scouts of America.*, 112, 114.

48. Ibid., 118.

49. "Official News. What Every Scout Wants to Know. Winners of the Livingstone Medals," *Boys' Life*, November 1918, 28.

50. Macleod, *Building Character in the American Boy. The Boy Scouts, YMCA, and Their Forerunners, 1870-1920*, 181.

51. *Thirty-third Annual Report of the Boy Scouts of America*, 1942, 70.

52. James E. West, "Report of the Chief Scout Executive, 30.

53. V. L. Strickland, Department of Home Study, Kansas State Agricultural College, Manhattan, "The War and Educational Problems," *School and Society*, April 6, 1918, 404.

54. Woodrow Wilson, "Proclamation 1520, Boy Scout Week, May 1, 1919," *The American Presidency Project*, http://www.presidency.ucsb.edu/ws/index.php?pid=24406.

55. Ibid.

56. Macleod, *Building Character in the American Boy. The Boy Scouts, YMCA, and Their Forerunners, 1870–1920*, 154.

57. Elbert K. Fretwell, "Thirty-Fifth Annual Report," *Thirty-Fifth Annual Report of the Boy Scouts of America, 1944* (Washington, DC: GPO, 1944), 57.

58. Macleod, *Building Character in the American Boy. The Boy Scouts, YMCA, and Their Forerunners, 1870–1920*, 183.

59. West, "Our Aims and Ideals," *Thirty-third Annual Report of the Boy Scouts of America*, 1942, 3.

60. West, "Report of the Chief Scout Executive" *Thirty-third Annual Report of the Boy Scouts of America*, 1942, 34-35.

61. Ibid., 38.

62. Ibid., 54-55.

63. Ibid., 28.

64. Quoted in West, "Report of the Chief Scout Executive," 10.

65. Angelo Patri, *Your Children in Wartime* (Garden City, NY: Doubleday, Doran & Co., 1943), 43, 95.

66. "A Physical Education Program for Every School," *Education*, October 1943, 84.

67. West, "Report of the Chief Scout Executive," 31.

68. *Thirty-third Annual Report of the Boy Scouts of America*, 1942, 65-66.

69. Fretwell, "Thirty-Fifth Annual Report," 3-4.

70. Ibid., 3-5.

71. "How Boys See Themselves in the War Effort." *Schools at War. A War Savings Bulletin For Teachers* (Washington, DC: Education Section, War Savings Staff, U.S. Treasury, no date, "Inaugural Issue," probably September 1943), 7.

72. Elbert K. Fretwell, Thirty-Sixth Annual Report," Boy Scouts of America, *Thirty-Sixth Annual Report, 1945* (Washington, DC: GPO, 1945), 10.

73. Quoted in Wyland, *Scouting in the Schools*, 24.

74. West, "Report of the Chief Scout Executive," 46-47.

75. Fretwell, "Thirty-Fifth Annual Report," 3.

76. Edward Marshall, "Girls Take Up the Boy Scout Idea and Band Together," *New York Times*, March 17, 1912, n.p, http://query.nytimes.com/mem/archive-free/pdf?_r=2&res=9F00E6DE1E3CE633A25754C1A9659C946396D6CF.

77. Macleod, *Building Character in the American Boy. The Boy Scouts, YMCA, and Their Forerunners, 1870–1920*, 184.

78. *Girl Scouts Timeline, 1912–1919*, Girl Scouts USA, http://www.girlscouts.org; *The Rally*, July 1918, 4; Macleod reported a 1920 figure of 20,000 members, but the author has used the Girl Scouts' figure as most authoritative.

79. Leslie Paris, *Children's Nature. The Rise of the American Summer Camp* (New York: New York University Press, 2008), 51-52.

80. Macleod, *Building Character in the American Boy. The Boy Scouts, YMCA, and Their Forerunners, 1870–1920*, 184.

81. "Girl Scout War Service Award. *The Rally*, March 1918, 1.

82. Woodrow Wilson, "To the School Children of the United States—A Proclamation," quoted in *The Rally*, October 1917, 6.

83. *Museum. Explore Our History. Youth and the American Red Cross*, American Red Cross, http://www.redcross.org/museum/history/youth.asp.

84. Henry P. Davison, *The American Red Cross in the Great War* (New York: Macmillan Co., 1919), 93-94.

85. *National School Service*, September 1, 1918, 10.

86. Ibid., 97.

87. Dean, *Our Schools in War Time–and After*, 192.

88. Ibid., 196.

89. Davison, *The American Red Cross in the Great War*, 99.

90. Sheldon Siegel, "Youth Looks at the Junior Red Cross," *National Parent-Teacher*, January 1945, 15; *National School Service*, September 1, 1918, 10.

91. *Museum. Explore Our History. Youth and the American Red Cross*, American Red Cross, http://www.redcross.org/museum/history/youth.asp.

92. Davison, *The American Red Cross in the Great War*, 97-98.

93. Ibid., 98, 103.

94. Mary C. Bradford, "Building the New Civilization, Address of the President of the National Education Association, July 1, 1918," *School and Society*, July 20, 1918, 70.

95. Quoted in Dean, *Our Schools in War Time—and After*, 210.

96. Walter A. Anderson, dean of the school of education, Montana State University, "School Supervision in Wartime," *Education*, February 1943, 329.

97. Rex Putman, quoted in Joseph Leese, "What Shall We Keep When the War Is Over?", *Education*, September 1945, 36.

98. Patri, *Your Children in Wartime*, 95.

99. Charles Hurd, *A Compact History of the American Red Cross* (New York: Hawthorn Books, Inc., 1959), 258.

100. John W. Studebaker, "Contribution of Education to the War Effort," National Education Association, *Proceedings of the Eighty-First Annual Meeting Held in Indianapolis June 27-29, 1943* (Washington, DC: NEA, 1943), 70; Harold Spears, "The Curriculum Movement Helps the High School Face Total War," *Education*, February 1943, 361; Ethel Kawin, "Children Can Help," *National Parent-Teacher*, May 1942, 41.

101. *Museum. Explore Our History. Youth and the American Red Cross*, American Red Cross, http://www.redcross.org/museum/history/youth.asp.

102. *4-H History*, United States Department of Agriculture, 4-H National Headquarters, http://www.national4-hheadquarters.gov/about/4h_history.htm.

103. *Education for Victory*, September 1, 1942, 16.

104. Reck, *The 4-H Story. A History of 4-H Club Work*, 147.

105. Reck, *The 4-H Story. A History of 4-H Club Work*, 148, 268.

106. Dean, *Our Schools in War Time—and After*, 125-126.

107. Reck, *The 4-H Story. A History of 4-H Club Work*, 268.

108. Franklin D. Roosevelt, "To All 4-H Club Members of the United States," facsimile of letter in Reck, *The 4-H Story. A History of 4-H Club Work*, 270.

109. Reck, *The 4-H Story. A History of 4-H Club Work*, 271.

110. "4-H and Home Demonstration during World War II," *Green N' Growing. The History of Home Demonstration and 4-H Youth Development in North Carolina*, North Carolina State University Libraries, http://www.lib.ncsu.edu/specialcollections/greenngrowing/essay_wwii.html.

111. "Liberty Ships Built by the United States Maritime Commission in World War II," *American Merchant Marine at War*, U.S. Merchant Marine, http://www.usmm.org/libertyships.html.

112. "National FFA Organization Records 1916-2008," *Ruth Lilly Special Collections and Archives*, University Library, Indiana University-Purdue University Indianapolis, http://www-lib.iupui.edu/special/ffa.

113. *Proceedings of the Fifteenth National Convention of the Future Farmers of America, Kansas City, October 26-29, 1942* (Washington, DC: FFA in cooperation with the U.S. Office of Education, Federal Security Agency, 1942) III.

114. Richard Saunders, Monmouth, Maine, "Food for Victory," *Proceedings of the Sixteenth National Convention of the Future Farmers of America. Kansas City, October 11-14, 1943* (Washington, DC: FFA in cooperation with the U.S. Office of Education, Federal Security Agency, 1943), 104; William James Kimball, Seymour, Wisconsin, "Warriors in Overalls," Ibid., 107.

115. Kenneth Engle, "Food Our Weapon," *Proceedings of the Fifteenth National Convention of the Future Farmers of America, Kansas City, October 26-29, 1942*, 98-99.

116. *Proceedings of the Sixteenth National Convention of the Future Farmers of America. Kansas City, October 11-14, 1943*, 57-58; *Proceedings of the Fifteenth National Convention of the Future Farmers of America, Kansas City, October 26-29, 1942*, 65.

117. Mosse, *Fallen Soldiers. Reshaping the Memory of the World Wars*, 25.

118. Stéphane Audoin-Rouzeau, *La Guerre des Enfants 1914-1918* (Paris: Armand Colin, 1993, 2004), 139.

119. Harold D. Lasswell, *Propaganda Technique in the World War* (New York: Alfred A. Knopf, 1927), 73.

120. Charles E. Rugh, School of Education, University of California, Berkeley, "Religious Education as a

Means of National Preparedness," *National Education Association, Addresses and Proceedings, Fifty-Fifth Annual Meeting, Portland, Oregon, July 7-14, 1917* (Washington, DC: NEA, 1917), 107.

121. William McAdoo, "Calls On Nation for War's Sinews," *The New York Times*, October 2, 1917, 3.

122. "Secretary McAdoo's Thrift Message," *St. Nicholas*, February 1918, 305.

123. Franklin K. Lane, "The New Americanism," National Education Association, *Addresses and Proceedings, Fifty-Sixth Annual Meeting, Pittsburgh, Pennsylvania, June 29-July 6, 1918* (Washington, DC: NEA, 1918), 106.

124. Mary C. Bradford, "Building the New Civilization," *School and Society*, July 20, 1918, 70.

125. Rugh, "Religious Education as a Means of National Preparedness," 110.

126. Patri, *Your Children in Wartime*, 4.

127. *National School Service*, September 1, 1918, 10.

128. Carl Holliday, "A Return to God in Education," *School and Society*, June 30, 1917, 767.

129. Charles W. Eliot, "Abstract of Address by Charles W. Eliot, President Emeritus, Harvard University, on Educational Changes Needed for the War and the Subsequent Peace," *Education*, May 1918, 658.

130. Stanley B. Hazzard, A.M., Mt. Vernon, N.Y., "Religion for Children," *Education*, February 1918, 474-475.

131. Myrtle Hooper Dahl, National Education Association, *Proceedings of the Eightieth Annual meeting Held in Denver June 28-July 3, 1942* (Washington, DC: NEA, 1942), 10.

132. Francis J. McConnell, "Instrument and Ends in Spiritual World Conquest. President's Annual Address Delivered at the Fourteenth General Convention of the Religious Education Association, Boston, February 27-March 1, 1917," *Religious Education*, April 1917, 91-92.

133. Rev. Frederic Gardiner, secretary for schools and colleges of the Episcopal Board of Religious Education of Philadelphia, "Private Schools. Their Special Opportunity," *Religious Education*, December 1917, 419.

134. *The Christian Register*, November 7, 1918, "Military Training," quoted in *Religious Education*, December 1918, 425.

135. John Slawson, "Wartime Delinquency and the Church," *Religious Education*, March-April 1943, 95-96, 98.

136. Isaac Landman, chairman and discussion leader, "Religious Education for Youth. Report of the Annual Meeting of the Religious Education Association, Pittsburgh, May 1-2, 1944," *Religious Education*, September-October 1944, 285.

137. Sophia L. Fahs, editor, Children's Materials, American Unitarian Association, "What Should Religious Education Do for Children in a War Torn World?", *Religious Education*, September-October 1944, 293-295.

138. William A. Scully, secretary of education of the Archdiocese of New York, "A Communication from Vice-President Monsignor Scully. Is Peace a Delusion?", *Religious Education*, January-February 1945, 2.

139. Slawson, "Wartime Delinquency and the Church," 98.

140. Isaac Landman, "Religious Education for Youth. Report of the Annual Meeting of the Religious Education Association, Pittsburgh, May 1-2, 1944," 286.

141. Fahs, "What Should Religious Education Do for Children in a War Torn World?", 295.

142. Ibid., 297.

143. "Religious Education in a War-Shocked World. A Syllabus for Local Study Groups. II. Teen-Age Youth," *Religious Education*, March-April 1945, 113.

144. J. W. E. Lawrence, "Again, the War Garden. The Patriot of the Hoe Is Being Guided by the Errors of Last Year When He Planted Not Wisely But Too Well," *The Nation's Business*, April 1918, 21.

145. Ibid., 22.

146. Ibid., 21.

147. J. Wainwright Evans, "Saving the Yield of War Gardens," *The Nation's Business*, July 1917, 14.

148. Ibid., 14-15.

149. Lawrence N. Galton, "The Kids Go to Work," *Nation's Business*, July 1944, 66-67.

150. Howard Lane, associate professor of education, Northwestern University, "The Good School for the Young Child in Wartime," *Education*, February 1943, 355.

151. Ruth Henschel Hamlin and Mary Elizabeth Marlow, "Toys New and Different," *Parents' Magazine*, December 1942, 108.

152. Margaret R. Higonnet, "War Toys: Breaking and Remaking in Great War Narratives," *The Lion and the Unicorn* 31 (2007), 117.

153. Mossé, *Fallen Soldiers. Reshaping the Memory of the World Wars*, 137.

154. Ibid., 141, 143.

155. Audoin-Rouzeau, *La Guerre des Enfants 1914-1918*, 175.

156. Marie-Monique Huss, "Pronatalism and the Popular Ideology of the Child in Wartime France: The Evidence of the Picture Postcard," in Richard Wall and Jay Winter, eds., *The Upheaval of War. Family, Work and Welfare in Europe, 1914-1918* (Cambridge: Cambridge University Press, 1988), 329.

157. Florence Woolston, "Billy and the World War," *New Republic*, January 25, 1919, 369-371, in David F. Trask, ed., *World War I at Home. Readings on American Life, 1914-1920* (New York: John Wiley, 1970), 92.

158. Richard O'Brien, *The Story of American Toys* (New York: Abbeville Press, 1990), 230-231.

159. Elise Clews Parsons, "The Dragon's Teeth," *Harper's Weekly*, May 8, 1915, 449.

160. Jeffrey Goldstein, David Buckingham, Gilles Brougére, eds., *Toys, Games and Media* (Mahwah, NJ: Lawrence Erlbaum, 2004), 19.

161. Jack Matthews, *Toys Go to War. World War II Military Toys, Games, Puzzles and Books* (Missoula, MT: Pictorial Histories Publishing Co., 1994), 3-4.

162. O'Brien, *The Story of American Toys*, 118-120.

163. *Schroeder's Collectible Toys Antique to Modern Price Guide*, 11th ed., (Paducah, KY: Collector Books, Schroeder Publishing, Inc., 2008), 403-405.

164. Mossé, *Fallen Soldiers. Reshaping the Memory of the World War*, 144.

165. Matthews, *Toys Go to War. World War II Military Toys, Games, Puzzles and Books*, 4-5.

166. O'Brien, *The Story of American Toys*, 84.

167. Advertisement, *American Boy*, November 1917, 56.

168. Hamlin and Marlow, "Toys New and Different," 107.

169. *Parents' Magazine*, December 1941, 28-29.

170. Matthews, *Toys Go to War. World War II Military Toys, Games, Puzzles and Books*, 9.

171. Hamlin and Marlow, "Toys New and Different," 108.

172. Edward Jackes, Letter to the Editor, *Jack and Jill*, June 1945, 33.

173. O'Brien, *The Story of American Toys*, 157-158.

174. Ibid., 49, 53.

175. Matthews, *Toys Go to War. World War II Military Toys, Games, Puzzles and Books*, 25.

176. O'Brien, *The Story of American Toys*, 52, 57-59.

177. Ibid., 43, 55: Matthews, *Toys Go to War. World War II Military Toys, Games, Puzzles and Books*, 25.

178. Robert Heidi, in Robert Heide and John Gilman, *Home Front America. Popular Culture of the World War II Era* (San Francisco: Chronicle Books, 1995), 24.

179. Quoted in Matthews, *Toys Go to War. World War II Military Toys, Games, Puzzles and Books*, 26.

180. William M. Tuttle, Jr., *"Daddy's Gone to War." The Second World War and the Lives of America's Children* (New York and Oxford: Oxford University Press, 1993), 138, 143.

181. Children's Bureau, U.S. Department of Labor, *To Parents in Wartime. Bureau Publication 282* (Washington, DC: GPO, 1942), 4, 12.

182. Lane, "The Good School for the Young Child in Wartime," 355.

183. Matthews, *Toys Go to War. World War II Military Toys, Games, Puzzles and Books*, vii.

184. Lane, "The Good School for the Young Child in Wartime," 352.

185. Gisela Wegener-Spöhring, "War Toys in the World of Fourth Graders: 1985 and 2002," Goldstein, Buckingham, Brougére, eds., *Toys, Games and Media, 29.*

186. P. W. Singer, *Children at War* (New York: Pantheon Books, 2005), 6, 69.

187. Garth S. Jowett and Victoria O'Donnell, *Propaganda and Persuasion*. 4th ed. (Thousand Oaks, CA, and London: Sage Publications, 2006), 145.

188. *Boys' Life*, December 1916, 35.

189. *Boys' Life*, October 1917, 28-29.

190. *American Boy*, November 1917, 31.

191. Ibid., July 1918, 43.

192. Ibid.

193. Ibid., November 1917, 56.

194. *Boys' Life*, November 1917, back cover.

195. *Boys' Life*, December 1916, 52.

196. *American Boy*, June 1918, 50.

197. Ibid., July 1918, 33.

198. Ibid., August 1917, back cover.

199. Ibid., November 1917, 46.

200. *Boys' Life*, June 1918, 53, 56.

201. *American Boy*, November 1918, 55.

202. Ibid., November 1917, 43.

203. Ibid., September 1918, 31.

204. *Boys' Life*, August 1918, back cover.

205. *American Boy*, December 1917, 41, 43.

206. *Boys' Life*, June 1918, 65.

207. *Boys' Life*, May 1918, 23; December 1917, back cover; January 1918, 28.

208. Ross F. Collins, "Positioning the War: The Evolution of Civilian War-Related Advertising in France," *Journalism History* 19, no. 3 (1993), 83.

209. *American Boy*, July 1917, back cover.

210. Imperial Chemical Co, Grand Rapids, Michigan, *Boys' Life*, June 1917, 51.

211. Ibid., May 1918, 4.

212. Ibid., September 1917, inside front cover.

213. Ibid., May 1918, 51.

214. Ibid., March 1918, 49.

215. *American Boy*, November 1917, 56; *Boys' Life*, December 1917, 3-4.

216. *American Girl*, May 1942, 39.

217. *Boys' Life*, March 1942, 39.

218. *Boys' Life*, May 1942, 35.

219. Ibid., February 1944, back cover.

220. Mossé, *Fallen Soldiers. Reshaping the Memory of the World Wars*, 143.

221. *American Girl*, October 1943, 25.

222. *Boys' Life*, February 1944, 27.

223. *Boys' Life*, May 1942, 35.

224. Ibid., 39.

225. *Boys' Life*, July 1942, 25.

226. *Boys' Life*, March 1944, 13, 25.

227. *American Girl*, December 1941, 37.

228. *Boys' Life*, May 1944, 17.

# 6

## MILITARIZING CHILDREN'S MAGAZINES

Editors of quality magazines for juveniles took seriously their role as teachers of a next generation. During World War I American publications such as *St. Nicholas* and *American Boy* spread to youthful readers around the country, and abroad. Commercial broadcast did not exist; comic books did not exist; movies still were silent. Children's magazines represented the closest thing to a national voice reaching the country's children. "The newspapers and magazines are the chief educational agencies of our country," the editor of *American Boy* reminded readers in 1918. "Widespread opportunity of reading means efficient patriotism."[1] By World War II, children's magazines faced more competition. Many titles from World War I had folded, although many others replaced them. But despite the growing power of popular culture aimed at kids through movies, radio and comics, World War II's quality children's publications retained the broadest national circulation to children around the country.

In the first half of the twentieth century, a golden age for mass circulation magazines, adults who would oversee the education of children into the country's cultural values relied as a medium on magazines aimed especially at children. Stories for children published as serials serve "as a means by which a society transmits its most cherished ideas, attitudes and values, in the hope that they will be carried on in the child," observed a scholar who researched one of the era's most prominent children's magazines, *St. Nicholas*. "It is natural then, that during periods of great conflict and change, or national crisis, such as during war, the children's literature, if it is at all responsive to its environment, should reflect these conditions."[2] A compiler of American children's magazines, R. Gorden Kelly, concluded turn-of-the-century children's periodicals "were shaped by editors' and authors' desires to entertain children but also by their wish that, grown to adulthood, those children would hold and act on certain beliefs and values."[3] Kelly's research agreed with the 1918 opinion of *American Boy's* editor, as he noted editors of children's publications made a "highly self-conscious effort to transmit their culture, their world view, to American children who would one day be charted with furthering the nation's historical destiny."[4]

In using historical techniques to examine children's periodicals during both wars, we can't measure directly the propaganda power of these private media. We can proceed from agreement of editors and scholars that they were, however, important in the life of the child, both as teachers and as chroniclers. Indirectly, we can also presume influence based on circulation, critical success, and response from readers through their letters to editors.

Based on this presumption, the author has examined four prominent children's publications from World War I, and three from World War II. Choice was based partly on availability: historians have not usually taken children's publications seriously. Nor have libraries. "Children's periodicals have not been collected regularly by research libraries," wrote Kelly, "and even the Library of Congress has not retained copies of certain types of children's periodicals."[5] But *St. Nicholas Illustrated Magazine for Boys and Girls*, originally produced by Scribner's, was considered the most important World War-I era children's magazine, and is still fairly accessible. It was established by Mary Mapes Dodge in 1873, a widely known children's author who hoped it would become "a pleasure-ground where butterflies flit gayly hither and thither.... But where toads hop quickly out of sight and snakes dare not show themselves at all."[6] At a World War I circulation of 70,000 it was considered to be the best children's magazine."[7] Edited by William Fayal Clarke during the war years, *St. Nicholas* appealed to children of all ages, featuring material for early elementary school ages through adolescence. *St. Nicholas* helped give a glance of what children were thinking through its popular *St. Nicholas* League, a competition inviting readers to submit 300-word articles and photos on monthly themes; first prize, five dollars. Motto of the league: "Live to Learn, and Learn to Live."[8] *St. Nicholas* succumbed between the wars to the trend of specialized children's magazines tied to a movement, such as the scouts. But even in World War II, the editor of a successor, *Jack and Jill*, called *St. Nicholas* a "child-magazine classic."[9]

*American Boy*, at nearly triple the 1917 circulation of the more literary *St. Nicholas*, appealed to a broad spectrum of boys from about age nine through high school. Printed in a large magazine format by Sprague Publishing, Detroit, editor Griffith Ogden Ellis emphasized action fiction and how-to features. Also part of this publication was an encouragement similar to the *St. Nicholas* League, which offered prizes to readers who wrote the best letters and brief articles.[10] *American Boy* also did not last through the interwar period, but a World War I contemporary, *Boys' Life*, grew to become the most influential American children's magazine of the century—and in fact is now in its second century of continuous publication. It was established by George S. Barton in April 1911, but in June 1912 the Boy Scouts bought the publication. It has remained a Boy Scout-owned magazine since. *Boys' Life* during the world war era grew to an enormous circulation—more than two million at its height—by promising boys a magazine brimming with masculinity. On its pages girls did not exist. Kelly found it "as thoroughly permeated with the traditional values of white, middle-class America as it is with the values of its parent organization."[11] Listed on the masthead as editor was James E. West, chief scout executive, who wrote a monthly editorial until his 1943 retirement as chief executive. His replacement, Elbert K. Fretwell, abandoned the column in April 1943.

The exclusiveness of boy power as reflected in *Boys' Life* was countered by Juliette Gordon Low, founder of Girl Scouts, in her own publication, *The Rally*. *The Rally*, however, began modestly in October 1917; its first issues were hardly more than newsletters, and its circulation only 3,000, primarily to girl scout troops. But after a 1920 name change to *American Girl*, the Girl Scout magazine grew to a 1942 circulation of 200,000, one of the era's most influential magazines for girls.[12] Both *Boys' Life* and *American Girl* counted many subscribers who were not scouts, and appealed broadly to children aged about nine through adolescence. *American Girl* editor during World War II was Ann Stoddard. Neither scouting magazine during this period, unfortunately, opened its pages to letters or articles from readers. But *Jack and Jill* did. Appealing to elementary school children during World War II, the no-advertising magazine was established by Curtis Publishing in 1938. By 1940 it was considered "the representative and most successful magazine in its field."[13] World War II editor was Ada Campbell Rose.

These prominent children's magazines became household names to millions of American children during their long runs. Editors tried to place themselves as friendly counselors who appeared once a month in the home. "As a monthly visitor in your home, *St. Nicholas* stimulates all that is best in developing minds," *St. Nicholas* reminded parents in May 1918. "*St. Nicholas* magazine will give you a bond of understanding between your boy's or girl's mind and your own. *St.*

*Nicholas* is a real magazine, as complete as any grown-up publication, but it is edited especially for boys and girls of high school and grammar school ages."[14] *American Boy's* "Friendly Talks with the Editor" addressed boys directly, as did the *Boys' Life's* monthly editorial, and Juliette Low wrote messages directly to Girl Scouts—mostly asking them to work harder on the home front. During World War II, scouting magazines seemed less interested in forging personal relationships with its readers, particularly after West, who had been with *Boys' Life* all the way back to World War I, retired. *Jack and Jill's* editor spoke to parents on its monthly Mother's Page, and also encouraged its readers to speak through letters, short articles, and pictures.

Children's periodical editors accepted in stages the challenge of educating for total war. To begin with, was it acceptable at all to encourage militarization of the American child's culture? Certainly many societies over many wars have groomed children for battle against foreign enemies. But not the United States, a nation set apart by temperament and tradition from European militarism. Moreover, before the twentieth century, no nation expected its children to actually participate in war in any extensive way, even on the home front. Just what children should do in a new kind of total war such as World War I—in scope and destruction unlike any war in recorded history—could not be easily determined. Authorities knew European children had definitely become soldiers of the home front. But the United States celebrated its presumed separateness from the iniquities of the Old World. A few prominent Americans in 1914 were calling noisily for the United States to join Europe's agony, invariably on the side of the Allies. But those who edited children's periodicals did not jump on board. In fact, most saw in the war no noble struggle at all, only pointless slaughter, and made no strong moves to militarize their pages—until 1917. After that, the debate ended. America's children would indeed be called to join battle as home-front warriors, in a pattern following that of Europe's children. Now children were no longer exempt from war duties, a historical change of social ideology.

Once World War I's juvenile periodical editors were persuaded that children could, and should, join the war, they lost no space in encouraging them to do so. In an introduction to a story about French children doing war work, authors declared that American children too could no longer be exempt from war work: "In no other war in all history have children taken so important a part as in the Great War."[15] Home-front war service was presented as more than a child's pastime; children were to be drafted into military-style obligations, a civilian army of minors, obedient, loyal and ready to sacrifice for critical war work. "Our army is at the front," explained a writer in *The Rally*, described in an editor's note as writing at the request of Mrs. Herbert Hoover. "We must be its soldiers behind the lines!"[16]

Hamilton contended that *St. Nicholas* "went from a position of neutrality to one of being little more than a tool for the communication of official war propaganda."[17] This is perhaps a slight exaggeration, considering together the World War I publications examined here, or those of World War II as well. Certainly these magazines continued to include some variety of stories, pictures, games and activities not related to the war. Yet in total coverage, the war did tend to dominate. Editors in World War I worked to legitimize the death and violence of war both rationally and emotionally. Rational explanations attempted to justify the war based on German perfidy and threats. More often employed, however, were emotional appeals, specifically calls to patriotism and duty on the positive, guilt and shame on the negative. Presuming successful persuasion, editors asked children to take action. They spun together a whirlwind of ways children could join the battle, from the boring—weeding gardens, to the exotic—raising carrier pigeons. Finally, to bolster the value of war as a possibility positive thing, editors enumerated the many ways war virtues could build fitness both physical and mental. And finally, war could be fun; war could be an adventure, a sport played on the world's greatest sporting field. A child need not feel threatened by the war that had come to his playground.

### American Militarism: A Children's Debate

At the outbreak of hostilities in 1914, the United States, along with much of Europe, had not seen major war for a generation. America did have its Spanish-American war of 1898, but that was comparatively a minor effort, its outcome settled quickly. Before that, the Civil War ended nearly a half century ago. Washington spent little on its small military, while peace movements operated with powerful authorities influential to children. The American School Peace League worked to organize the nation's teachers for pacifism. Its message resonated not only through support of the National Education Association, but all the way to Washington: organizer Fannie Fern Andrews became a special advisor to commissioner of education Philander Claxton. The league's nationwide efforts rose to a rain of books, pamphlets, endorsements, poems, pageants, essay contests, branching to forty states, and overseas. Andrews organized peace leagues in England and Ireland. France followed.[18] Truly, it seemed, the education of twentieth century children in Europe and America would be more and more based on ideology of peace and pacifism. They could find support at the

highest levels of government and business, from Claxton to Carnegie, the tycoon and peace advocate.

But those who supported the school peace curriculum faced adversaries
at least as powerful, if initially less organized. Preparedness advocates such as
former president Theodore Roosevelt hoped to see schools turn out children
ready to face an armed and likely dangerous modern world. Within the schools,
advocates of military training and education were mostly male, and often physical education instructors. Pacifism, they claimed, was "feminization of teaching," which could put the country's security at risk. They advocated preparing
children—and in fact the entire country—for possible war. In 1911, Katherine
Devereux Blake, a New York City grade school principal and women's suffrage
proponent, said preparedness advocates "are organized for war. We must be
organized for peace. They have their organization not merely in the army, not
merely in the family, but they have been cleverer than we are—they have it in
the schoolhouse."[19] The debate grew to a rage after Europe fell into world war.
Children's publications participated, and prevaricated. During the country's
neutral period, editors clearly influenced by peace propaganda moved to paint
militarism in a color bleak and fearsome. *St. Nicholas*, after nearly a year of
conspicuously ignoring the world's biggest story, in July 1915 published its first
non-reader generated material regarding the conflict. It affirmed its commitment to peace. "Doubtless if you were asked what you seriously thought was the
one thing of greatest importance to the entire world at this time, you would say
'Peace,'" wrote Jane Stannard Johnson. "When our own American boys and
girls think of the numberless boys and girls in Europe whose fathers go out
to battle and never return—that is surely an incentive for every one of you to
strive to the utmost to cultivate and maintain a peaceful mind toward all."[20]
In September, apparently bowing to the readers determined to see "frogs and
snakes" among the *St. Nicholas* butterflies, the editor launched a new feature,
"The Watch Tower." Author Samuel E. Forman, identified as a writer of civics
and history, explained the column would emphasize only great events: "You will
find that they will be of real use to you in your life; they will try to teach you
the true meaning of what is going on in the world at present; and because they
will do this, they will give you a broader and a more intelligent outlook upon
the future."[21] Appearance of this current events-based material was a departure
from the literary focus of *St. Nicholas*.

But Forman's reporting quickly became political critique of militarism. Emphasizing the human and material costs of the war—including seven million
dead—he decried the waste. "We must at the same time think of the millions of

women who were made widows, of the millions of children who were made orphans, of the millions of fortunes that were shattered, and of the millions whose
health was broken by the hardships of war." Regarding the U.S. Army, he wrote,
"Up to this time in our history we have not thought it wise to keep a large army
in times of peace," but that proponents have looked to Switzerland a model for
preparedness. If the United States had a comparable army, he noted, it "would
make us a nation of warriors, whereas we want to remain what we have always
been, a nation of workers."[22]

In October 1915, Forman showed annoyance as the war seemed to have
no chance of ending soon. "Instead of thinking of peace, the powers rallied for
another year of strife," he wrote, noting British girls were working in munitions
factories, "while in Germany, little boys and girls became farmers and tilled every foot of ground upon which vegetables or gain could be raised."[23] A photo of
German children tilling soil was included, presaging United States efforts hardly more than a year later. By 1916, Forman had become even more shocked at
the "harvest of death," making little effort to hide the toll of slaughter. Lament-
ing the sacrifice and waste, he noted the battle of Verdun in March had seen
150,000 German soldiers killed and wounded, four times that of Gettysburg.
He saw no glory in these deaths, no heroic sacrifice: "The Great War seems to
be bringing but little fame and glory to those who are fighting the battles."[24]

By fall 1916 the United States had clearly slid from neutrality to support
for the Allies fighting against Germany. *St. Nicholas* reflected this through "The
Watch Tower," as Germans had become the more pejorative "Teutons." Forman
called a "monster preparedness parade" in New York of 150,000, "a successful
effort to wake the country to the need for preparedness. That the demonstrations have done much for the cause of preparedness cannot be denied. But
they have done something else: they have aroused the American spirit and have
kindled the fire of genuine patriotism." In April 1917, obviously written before
the war declaration of April 6, Forman observed the United States seemed to
be "drifting toward war." The terminology apparently betrayed still a pacifist
bias; the pro-war preparedness advocates certainly were driving, not drifting.
Still Forman wrote of the war with disapproval, "the death dance of Europe"[25]

In May 1917 the tone changed. President Woodrow Wilson's war declaration of April was "memorably worded...promptly acclaimed," and "every reader
of *St. Nicholas* who is old enough to understand it should read it." Yet in November 1917 Forman was replaced without explanation by Edward N. Teall "of
the New York *Sun*." This columnist no longer looked so admirably at peace,
or so balefully at war. In an article entitled "A Letter to the Boys of America,"

published two months earlier, Teall wrote, "Dear Lads: These are great times for American boys. American! The word brings your shoulders back, head up, chin out, and starts a thumping under your ribs. You are not yet of military age. Perhaps you wish you were older. How proud and happy you would be to shoulder a gun and go marching away, following the flag to France!"[26] The debate over preparedness and pacifism in *St. Nicholas* had been settled.

American Boy stayed on the pacifist side as late as February 1917. Along with a readers' debate on preparedness, the publication editorialized, "As the Great War goes on we come more and more to realize what a frightful thing war is. We realize it is something we never want our country to mix up with. We don't want our young men killed and mutilated by millions; we don't want our towns and cities burned, nor do we want to burn other folks' cities." Still, the editor continued, invasion is a possibility, and so preparedness might be worth considering. "Let us have a navy that is great enough to keep off an invasion from overseas—and an army large enough to make the thought of trying the job a bit discouraging. That is the surest, safest way of keeping out of the war we dread."[27] But most stridently pacifist, and most unexpectedly so, was *Boys' Life*. The scouts' magazine had since its 1911 inception dealt with accusations from powerful pre-war pacifists that its organization was quasi-military. So strongly did it deny the link that Volume One, Number One, found it necessary to remind readers that "peace scouting" was in no way militarist. Shortly after the first battles, in October 1914, *Boys' Life* published a letter from British scout secretary A. J. Wade to James E. West, emphasizing the dreadful waste of the Dreadnaught-class battleships: "Six years ago the chief scout stated that if he were given the price of one dreadnought he would make international war impossible; with practically no funds he has established a world-wide brotherhood; therefore, it is only reasonable to assume that with funds and six years to work in he could have made the movement a real factor for peace."[28] But of all the children's publications consulted in both world wars, the single issue that most soundly condemned war, and came most closely to giving it a portrayal unfiltered by the usual gauze of heroics and nobility, was *Boys' Life*. Its November 1914 edition poured out pacifism and played out anti-war vitriol, in full-page propaganda and page after page of description. Noted pacifist and Boy Scout council member David Starr Jordan declared, "We want you, Boy Scouts, for braver things than war. We want to make men of you, strong, kind, alert, vigorous, helpful men, useful to yourselves, to your neighbors, to your country and to the world." Bringing pacifist reasoning to bear, Jordon explained:

If a nation is victorious, it has at the end the same troubles it would have had if it had been vanquished. War is a two-edged sword without any hilt, and it cuts everyone that wields it. And as bad as the sting of defeat is the curse of victory. The defeated nation wants to fight again, to revenge itself; and the victorious nation wants to fight again because it feels sure that it is strong enough to whip anybody.[29]

In the same issue, noted author Cyrus Townsend Brady described the misery in just one insignificant engagement:

Nobody can help the wounded between the lines. The valley is still swept with fire. It is impossible to go there. The wounded envy the dead. The groans or shrieks or appeals of the wounded are heard above the awful din—and most horrible of sounds, the screams of wounded horses, poor, unwitting victims of the savagery of man.[30]

Reader response to this material showed the limits of pacifist strength after the war began. Particularly this was true among supporters of scouting who, perhaps logically, thought it was good military training no matter what its founders claimed. Theodore Roosevelt and Leonard Wood declared their disgust that the official magazine of Boy Scouting would allow such material on its pages. Recriminations public and private must have cowed editors, because following the November 1914 anti-war issue, *Boys' Life* eliminated the littlest whiff of war discussion from its pages. Issue after issue ignored the world war, mentioning it not a single time between December 1914 and February 1917. No advertisements related to the war appeared until December 1916. After that hiatus, never again during the world war periods would *Boys' Life* promote pacifism. In fact, while World War II did have its early pacifists who espoused continued isolationism, the juvenile publications studied here did not take up the issue, as editors had during the last war. This issue of pacifism versus preparedness, at least in the minds of children's editors, apparently was no longer worth the debate. Preparedness had won.

As editors recast their publications to bring children into a militarized world, expected contents changed, sometimes drastically. McKenzie called *St. Nicholas* in 1918 "a war zone with little escape or diversion."[31] Other publications during both wars shifted material to take on a war slant. *American Boy* and *Boys' Life* geared their adventure serials to the war, particularly emphasizing aviation. Girls' publications emphasized duty. Many writers and editors couldn't help but become preachy, although those in World War II clearly tried to tone down the sermons.

## Explaining War to Children

In July 1917 *St. Nicholas* published a feature unusually candid in its revelation of editorial strategy. This public self-examination sought to explain, perhaps excuse, its pre-war coverage, and to defend its new pro-war stance. "No young reader of *St. Nicholas*, and no parent or teacher familiar with its history, needs to be told that patriotism has always been among the foremost of the great ideals which it seeks to cherish and inculcate," wrote the editor, presumably William Fayal Clarke. But the magazine took a month to put together, and another month to print; every older child would already know the war's events from the newspapers. It was, he argued, therefore pointless to include war news in *St. Nicholas*. "And, for the younger children of its audience, this magazine has felt a natural desire, and was duty bound, to protect them as far as possible from any intimate knowledge of the horrors which war always carries in its train and of the suffering which, since 1914, has surpassed any similar record in human history." But with the war declaration, any "right-thinking American" can only choose to support the country. "Against deliberate, unprovoked, and outrageous aggression the United States has striven with a patience never equaled by any great commonwealth and for more than two years to avert a conflict." The editor concluded children should realize their country is joining as a selfless act: "*St. Nicholas* feels it a solemn obligation to emphasize to its young folk the president's declaration that we are fighting not for any selfish end whatever, and not merely to defend our beloved land in a war that has been forced upon us, but that, in common with our brave and devoted Allies, we are to battle for liberty itself.[32]

The editor also opened its pages to a message for children from Secretary of the Interior Franklin B. Lane, "an apostle of patriotism," who explained, "This is a war against war. Someone must fight that war shall not be the one method by which peoples shall be governed. In a democracy all are for peace, but not for peace at any price."[33]

In explaining the country's decision to join World War I using Wilsonian terms, Clarke also immediately defended its decision to include children in the struggle. "And this, as all boys and girls should know, is peculiarly *their* war—a war waged for the sake of the years to come. Whether long continued or not, it will vitally affect the lives of those now in their teens, who are soon to become citizens of the Republic."[34] The idea that children must take ownership of the war extended through pronouncements of authorities at various levels, and in various children's magazines. "Why should you work for and sacrifice and love your country?" asked the editor of *American Boy*, Griffith Ogden Ellis. "First, because it is *your* country—yours. Because it belongs to you as citizens and sharers in it…. Because *your* country does more for you than any other country on earth." But in explaining why boys needed to prepare for war, the editor still betrayed a lingering pacifism that had been marbled through the magazine until mere weeks before Wilson's war declaration. "No man wishes to go to war. No man wishes to become a soldier. No man wishes to live in a militaristic country," wrote Ellis, reflecting the resolve of fewer and fewer of his readers. "But, if our land is to be kept inviolate, if Germany is not to carry out her schemes to partition us, and casually to give away Texas, Arizona and New Mexico, as Mr. Zimmerman [sic] promised to do, you must *all* be able to take your places as trained soldiers."[35]

Rational explanations for the war seemed to be the least common tool this war's editors chose to bring their juvenile readers into the military life. With a conspicuous exception. Josephine Daskam Bacon, in the fledgling Girl Scouts' magazine *The Rally*, tried to explain the reasons for war by extending it to an elaborate metaphor of a school playground. In her lengthy tale, "all the leaders of the various groups in our school-yard" have met to propose regulations to benefit the best interests of everyone. They have signed a paper promising to agree:

> Suppose that all are busily engaged with their own concerns, when suddenly a great band of older boys, who have passed all their spare time of late in drilling, exercising, shooting, and collecting suitable stones for their sling shots, rushes across the playground to fight a band of Boy Scouts. Right in their way lies the sand pile of the littlest ones.
> The mean older boys, shouting "What's a bit of paper?" trample the playground.
> They fight bravely, these littlest ones, but what chance have they? The girls are kicked, bruised maimed for life; the babies are killed; their rest house is set on fire and burned down.

Who can face the bullies? "'This has got to be stopped,' growl out the big Boy Scouts, and they leave trading marbles and get out their motorcycles and try to patrol the whole yard." Bacon concluded:

> We are not in this great and terrible war because of some little petty legal quibble. We are not in it because a ship carrying Americans was blown up…. No: we are in it, shoulder to shoulder with determined England and glorious France, because we allies, the scouts of the world, are determined that the

world shall not slip back, thousands of years, into cruelty and brutality and oppression.[36]

Bacon's metaphorical explanation apparently was noticed beyond *The Rally's* small readership; in March 1918 it reported Roosevelt wrote a letter of admiration, saying "That's a capital story by Josephine Daskam Bacon. It is admirable from every standpoint, and I wish it could be read in every schoolroom in the United States." The superpatriot National Security League ordered 5,000 copies, according to the report, and the U.S. Government's Committee on Public Information distributed hundreds more.[37]

But such rational attempts to justify war remained scarce in these juvenile publications. Shortly after the country joined World War II, James West wrote in *Boys' Life* an editorial notable for the somber determination that was widespread among authorities after Pearl Harbor. "Scouts, it is a most unhappy circumstance that we should celebrate our thirty-second anniversary under the dark clouds of war," he wrote, noting for the first time in more than a century the nation itself had been attacked. "None of us would choose war if we could honorably avoid it.... But when we are attacked; when war is thrust upon us, no people under the sun can rise to a mightier effort or greater heights of determination to crush out those things that are evil than we of the United States of America." As did those editors who explained the country's entry into World War I, West too emphasized that it was to be a war not only of adults, but of children. "Scouts," he wrote, "we have taken up the sword in defense of the American way of life and all that is traditionally worthwhile to use. We are all in this battle!"[38]

It was true in both world wars that few Americans opposed the war declarations. Those who did in World War II lay low. Those who did not lay low in World War I were hounded into silence. The pervasive bigotry in the first war toward all things German concerned the editor of *American Boy*. At war's outbreak, he pleaded with boys to take the high road. "There is no difference between a citizen born in Germany and one born in the United States. Both are citizens," he wrote. "But boys may jeer at them, or even go farther. Which would be too bad, indeed. For our citizens of German descent are among our best and most valuable, and most loyal Americans. Maybe some of them are better citizens than *you* are yourself."[39]

*The Rally* wasn't convinced. Of the publications examined here, the Girl Scout serial most squarely targeted the foreign-born as a group worthy of suspicion, and deserving strenuous effort at Americanization. Joining an "America

First" campaign, "Girl Scouts have pledged themselves to cooperate in every possible way to promote the unqualified allegiance of each foreign-born citizen to the United States; to nationalize the use of the English language; to induce the 3,000,000 non-English speaking immigrants to attend evening school."[40]

Apparently the *American Boy* editor's appeal to decency against a cacophony of hate did not have the effect he had hoped. In October 1917, again, Ellis asked, "Should boys hate all things German?" At first, said the editor, he thought, perhaps. Then he reflected some more. "Suppose you were disobedient and your dad licked you—as you deserved—and then kept on being angry with you for years. How would you like it? Would it be fair? The world will not be bettered by hatred dwelling within it. Lick 'em good; make 'em behave—then let it stop."[41] While no editor of the children's publications studied here advocated hatred of the enemy in either war, epithets such as the "Hun" or "Boche" for German did creep into World War I copy, if only occasionally. In World War II "Jap" was also considered occasionally acceptable—but not by every reader. "Again, last fall, we had a serial chapter in which one child chanted to another, 'We're after scrap to get a Jap,'" wrote the editor of *Jack and Jill* in 1944. "This very jingle has appeared dozens of times during the past two years in our mail from children." Nevertheless, with the epithet's publication as part of a serial, the editor received a complaint from one child's mother. The adult noted, "I think it is our duty as parents and publishers to be very careful not to saddle our children with our prejudices and narrow viewpoints."[42]

But sober argument was not a favored way to introduce children to their new wartime roles. Instead editors particularly in World War I spent most of the time setting children to a wartime footing through appeals to patriotism, heroism, duty, guilt, or shame. Patriotism was the emotion most easy for propagandists to tap as a way to establish legitimacy of wartime sacrifice. Writing in 1943, a prominent educator observed that the parades, the dramatizations, the slogans, the heroes, the music, the programs, and the rituals rely on the natural well of a child's patriotism. "As such they can be extremely helpful in developing all aspects of loyalty and morale."[43] Most of these editors needed only to build onto a framework already in place before the war. The Boy Scouts of America had set patriotism as its primary guiding force, an outgrowth of the strong nationalism consistently part of scouting's mission. *Boys' Life* faithfully promulgated BSA ideology. *American Boy* presumed patriotic virtue among its readers, and even the more literary *St. Nicholas* infused its pages with patriotic intent, as its founder, Mary Mapes Dodge, bequeathed. Contributors to *St. Nicholas* League complied, as noted in submissions of July 1914: "Headings show our young artists to be fairly bristling with patriotism, as we all ought to be about this time."[44] *American Girl* and *Jack and Jill* during World War II did not set a mission so obviously patriotic, but certainly said nothing impugning patriotic virtue. Relying on such a base, children's publications leaped to graft general patriotism to wartime needs. "In every July issue for more than forty years," wrote the editor of *St. Nicholas* in 1917, "the magazine has made a patriotic appeal to American boys and girls through story, article, poem, and picture filled with the spirit of an exalted love of country."[45]

In a publication which valued readers' contributions, this reserve of useful sentiment could be diverted into a propaganda tool during war. *St. Nicholas* marshaled those resources, promising, "*St. Nicholas* plans to aid the zealous young patriots who prize its pages by acting as their counselor and friend in all possible ways."[46] *St. Nicholas* editors thus seldom generated patriotic appeals through their own editorial copy. Instead, the magazine let its readers do the job. The *St. Nicholas* League directed children by setting up patriotic themes, topics such as "The Story of Our Flag," and "The Story of a Patriot." Readers responded as anticipated, in 300-word bursts of florid prose and poetry. "The league fairly glows with the ardent patriotism of Young America," observed the editor, encouraged by children such as fifteen-year-old Agnes Law, who wrote:

Bright above them waved Old Glory,
Proudly waved, o'er cheering thousands,
Flung her silken folds toward heaven—
Precious emblem of the free![47]

Other juvenile editors of the World War I publications studied here did not draft readers to craft its message of patriotism. Instead, they nearly always tied patriotism to a task. The presumption seemed to be that children could be counted on to be patriotic, needing little encouragement. More useful was to build on patriotism as a way to action for the home-front army. After the war declaration, the boys of *American Boy* wrote a mushroom of enthusiasm in favor of military camps. The editor built on this by opening the pages of *American Boy* to Secretary of War Newton Baker, who encouraged participation in military summer camps as evidence of patriotism: "In addition to the patriotic motive there are the physical benefits to be derived from the active, healthful outdoor life of a military camp."[48] Patriotism, opined the editor the next month, meant boys owned a debt to the flag. It could be paid by obedience. "Try now to think like men. For this space of time, remember that the truest patriotism you can offer is to refrain from being a drag and a responsibility on your elders."[49] The problem of "boy mobilization," the magazine emphasized in summer 1917, was to define patriotism as willingness to work to bring in the harvest: "It means boys who are patriotic—boys who take off their hats when the flag goes by and stand when the 'Star Spangled Banner' is played."[50] And that same patriotism was expected when children were asked to buy war bonds. "Let's start on the theory that every boy who reads this paragraph is a patriotic American boy. Right? Certainly!.... Buy war savings stamps. That just means, let the United States use some of your money—no matter how little."[51]

*Boys' Life* also reflected patriotism as children taking action: "Every boy, especially every Boy Scout, now has his big opportunity to prove his patriotism," the editor wrote in May 1917.[52] Boy Scout success selling war bonds resulted in a letter from Woodrow Wilson, observing the scout work "is a convincing testimonial to the value of organized boyhood for the kind of patriotic service that is worth while."[53] The *Rally* for Girl Scouts nearly always tied patriotism to the words duty or sacrifice, "in many...ways giving time and service for patriotic duty."[54] Patriotism in *The Rally* was defined through work.

Twenty-five years later, editors spoke to a new generation. And apparently this time the word these children no longer wanted to hear was patriotism. None of the World War II publications used the word. It was neither an exhortation for its own value, nor was it tied to duty, work, or indeed any other value. Why the word patriotism apparently did not resonate among World War II's juvenile editors studied here can't be known for certain. Possibly, however, the interwar backlash against patriotism that drove America to distrust World War I's more blatant propaganda gave the old style patriotic exhortations a suspicious taint. That said, these editors still asked children to do the same jobs, to be the same soldiers of the home front. "It isn't necessary for me to tell the hundreds of thousands of intelligent readers of *Boys' Life* that there are two fronts in war times: the fighting front and the home front," explained West in *Boys' Life*. During World War I, "The contribution that boys wearing the scout uniform made during those three war years was nothing short of magnificent," but this time, West was confident the boys could do even better.[55] *American Girl* wrote nothing of patriotism. It did, however, feature on its March 1942 cover a Girl Scout saluting the United States flag. If "patriotism" could not be uttered, these editors were no less patriotic.

## Duty and Duties

Closely tied in word and spirit to patriotism for these publications was the idea of duty. Working on the home front was a child's duty in total war. After its two-year blackout on war news, *Boys' Life* in 1917 finally acknowledged war by calling boys to duty: "What will the Boy Scouts of America do in case of war? They will do their duty to God and their country."[56] "What can you do?" the editor of *American Boy* asked readers. "Most of you are not yet of an age to bear arms. Many of you are. It is to those who are not that we speak. It is your duty, in so far as possible, to take the places of men who are called to the colors."[57] Work was a duty. So was "judgment and self-restraint." In World War I, American children had many duties. In fact, the entire September 1917 *American Boy* issue enumerated "War duties for boys."[58] Particularly staying in school, as boys were tempted, indeed encouraged, by parents and businesses to instead work for the war effort. "His first and highest duty is to make himself a fit and valuable citizen," the editor admonished, and the way to do this was "to stick to his school with all his heart and soul and to study as he never studied before."[59] Woodrow Wilson, several cabinet members, General Leonard Wood, a number of university presidents, and prominent politicians added their ponderous prestige to arguments supporting this particular duty,[60] as apparently some boys did not perceive the classroom as directly germane to the work of a warrior of the home front. It seemed, however, boys were doing enough, because at the year's turn the editor observed, "As the country has changed, so have you changed. The country has responded to the call of a great duty; you have responded to the call of a lesser duty."[61]

*St. Nicholas* reminded its readers of the onerous daily life children were living in England and France. This gave rise to duty for children in America: "For us in this more favored country, the call to duty is no less imperative; and we need covet no higher reward than the knowledge that we have 'done our bit,' no matter whether the task itself be great or small."[62] Obedience to the government was in itself a duty: "There lies a duty upon every group of citizens, be they young or old, to organize themselves for service, in order that, when the government has need of them they may be quickly and conveniently allocated their proper place and the government may not find itself hampered by an unorganized crowd."[63] *The Rally* made duty a central theme behind its call to girls for a wide variety of work during the war. And to prove girls were responding, the editor published reports from around the country, showing what girls who did their duty could accomplish. "Achievement has inoculated the Girl Scouts with its driving power," reported a Washington, D.C., leader. "All summer long troop after troop has kept hard at work making surgical dressings, comfort bags, knitting all soft woolly comfortables that will keep Jack Frost from nipping military noses, ears and fingers."[64] Advertisers also occasionally pitched duty from their own perspective, such as the Imperial Chemical Company, Grand Rapids, Michigan: "It is every one's duty to help solve the food problem.... You can do no more patriotic act than to enlist in the war on the bugs."[65]

World War II editors seemed more hesitant to call on their readers for duty; while they wanted children to work on the home front, duty, as a general virtue, was less often offered as motivation. If these editors talked of "duty," they meant something more specific: the duties scouts need to learn as messengers, or jobs to do while on duty at work.[66] When Farmer Green's animals in *Jack and Jill* talked of tasks they could do for the war, they asked specifically, "What is the duty of the people at home?"[67] *American Girl* suggested its readers reflect on what they could do for men on active duty.[68] Men in the service were doing their duty. But "duty" as a general virtue did not return to the editorial content of these magazines in World War II.

While World War II's editors of juvenile publications were not likely to call their readers to work on the home front based on abstract appeals to patriotism or duty, they no less called upon them to work for the war effort. Children had a job to do; lots of jobs, in fact. *Boys' Life* made appeals based on its extensive history of service during the last war. West in early 1942 called on the weight of scout tradition to spur the Boy Scouts to massive effort for the home front. The editor, who had also been chief scout executive during World War I, reminded readers, "There are some of us, and your fathers (those fathers who were scouts are among our number) who recall with pride another great war emergency, that of 1917-1919 during the first World War." Achievement this time ought to be greater, he wrote. "Already scouts have gone door to door to collect aluminum, in 10,000 communities, 315,774 scouts, collecting 10,316,407 pounds."[69] In the next month's issue, the *Boys' Life* cover illustration depicted Liberty marching, followed by a uniformed Cub Scout, Boy Scout, Marine, and infantryman, these followed by a United States flag, and identification: "Troop 12, Nassau County." It is entitled, "We, Too, Have a Job to Do." Featured inside was a Boy Scout-sponsored advertisement depicting facsimiles of a 1917 letter from Woodrow Wilson, and a 1941 letter from Franklin Roosevelt. "Once again we have a job to do," proposed the accompanying copy. "Boy Scouts in World War I made great contributions. Now it's your turn to make scouting history!... Are you ready to step out in the distinguished uniform of scouting?"[70]

In its first campaign promoting specific home front tasks for boys, *Boys' Life* in April 1942 joined the push to appropriate the natural affinity of most boys of that era in building models. The cover featured a boy with a model airplane, entitled, "500,000 Model Planes for the Navy." West wrote the models needed to be detailed and accurate. "The United States Navy is depending upon the boys of America to furnish these models, and furnish them swiftly.... I have the utmost confidence that scouts will be able to live up to this demand for perfection."[71] In fact, Boy Scouts and many other children so aptly responded to that campaign that one year later the military had to tell the children, "no more models." In May the summer garden season was launched with West asking the boys to plant Victory Gardens. In August West invited boys to a "treasure hunt," the treasure being scrap rubber. "I hope that scouts will personally visit each home in their community to give information as to what is needed."[72]

But after West's retirement as scout executive and editor of the magazine in February 1943, *Boys' Life* abruptly changed its tone regarding boys' service in the war. West was a sermonizer, encouraging boys to serve the home front in both wars. His successor, Elbert K. Fretwell, apparently did not perceive such monthly homilies to be effective motivations in 1943, as they might have been in 1917. Fretwell's first article featured a biography of Thomas Jefferson. Subsequent *Boys' Life* content de-emphasized wartime calls to service as they had been presented by West in the form of editorials. In 1944 its cover featured a $100 war savings bond, with a military jeep driving through, and photos of people behind selling bonds, headlined, "Buy One of These Bonds!"[73] Occasionally stories told of boys who were working for the war. The author of "It's a Boys' War Too" explained, "With a victory to be won American boys want a finger in it—even if it's only a little finger." Eight photos showed fingers attached to boys making hangers, wood clamps, lunch boxes, and tent pegs. But the boys were not in scout uniform. They were part of the Junior Achievement program for children.[74] For this magazine, promoting home-front work now seemed to fall instead to advertisements, some of them sponsored by the government in space donated by the publisher.

*Boys' Life* World War II companion publication for Girl Scouts, *American Girl*, encouraged war bond purchases also in advertising donated by the publisher. "Buy Bombers," the ad suggested, "with Defense Stamps! Lend your quarters for victory while you save for your Defense Bond."[75] This was part of a larger campaign by the Girl Scouts to promote service in the same way as West did for the boys—by calling readers to remember their history. "In one respect only were the Girl Scouts of the First World War a jump ahead of Girl Scouts today: they received governmental honors for their aid to the Liberty Loan drive," wrote Gertrude Simpson. While World War II Girl Scouts would not receive a similar medal for their war bond sale work, "let's look at the opportunities for service in 1942. Girl Scouts have already taken the lead in many communities in the scrap rubber salvage campaign. They've proved their worth already in Red Cross work, serving as messengers, knitters, bandage makers, and lunch servers." Also recognized was Girl Scout work as clerks, aides, and tenders of Victory Gardens. "No Girl Scout of today would blush to have a Girl Scout veteran of the last war see what is being done by the girls of 1942 to help their country win this war."[76] Girls of this war did even more by purchasing war bonds and stamps for the group's newly launched Girl Scout Victory Fund. In 1943 *American Girl* writer Claire Liske investigated girls' service to the war in Indiana. "Let's listen in on the telephone of the Girl Scout office in Indianapolis for a sample of what is happening," she wrote. It seemed the Girl Scout office was facing a deluge of requests. "'Will you take part in the youth Cavalcade of America. One hundred girls?' 'We're having a rally. Can we have thirty scouts in uniform to usher?' 'We need hundreds of ash trays for the opening of our new Service Men's Club tonight. Can the scouts collect them by that time?'.... Exciting? You bet it's exciting!" concluded Liske, although one has to wonder about the critical need to the war effort of all those ash trays.[77]

While *Boys' Life* in 1944 was winding down its appeals to service, readers of *American Girl* still were reminded to buy bonds, now moving from the ponderous to the whimsical. In a U.S. Treasury-sponsored advertisement, the space contributed by *American Girl,* a balding man with mustache is sewing. "I'm sorry I invented the pocket.... Pockets are no place for any kind of money except actual expense money these days. The place—the only place—for money above living expenses is in war bond.... Reach into the pocket I invented. Take out all that extra cash."[78]

In 1945 the government launched a new campaign aimed at children to once again scavenge for paper. *Boys' Life* did not promote this, but *American Girl* did. In another bit of propagandist whimsy unknown to the no-nonsense editors of World War I, the War Production Board-sponsored advertisement depicted sweaty, bare-chested men working artillery duty apparently in the Pacific Theater. Behind them—a girl wearing a smart skirt passes a mortar shell. "Of course, you can't pass the ammunition—but—You can see that that ammunition gets right up there in perfect condition. How? By doing everything you possibly can to use less paper and to save waste paper!"[79] In fact, World War II's girls, at least, could sometimes take the war a little less seriously, even in the dark days of 1942. "Want to be trim as a drill sergeant—bright as a polished button?" asked writer Helen Hatcher's "Glamour Drill." "Want to go marching through your day slick and smart from reveille to taps? Here's the way to do it—soldier style and double-time!" Girls could organize in the military manner by ensuring a separate hanger for each garment, a shoe rack and, of course, shelves, "with a stand for each hat. No piling one on top of the other, or that will be three days K.P. next inspection."[80] This publication aimed at World War II girls was the only one to give wartime experience lighter treatment. World War II propaganda strongly emphasized traditional gender roles; it is possible *American Girl* could sometimes favor less serious content because its female readers were not perceived to be as critical as victory. In contrast, World War I children's publication found little time for whimsy regarding children's wartime expectations. *Boys' Life* did try to motivate young gardeners by turning their chore into a battlefield metaphor. "Mobilize your forces. Get a store of ammunition (arsenate of lead, and the other poisons), get a machine gun or two (hand sprayers) and post your guards.... Overwhelmed by the suddenness and fury of the attack, the Hun of the potato patch hesitates, loses his grip, falls and dies."[81]

*Jack and Jill* aimed at younger readers, but during both these wars youth was not an excuse for home front inaction. This editor tried to reach readers less directly, preferring playful propaganda in contrast to stern calls. Its first war-related material not generated by readers offered a wartime game, "Puzzle Jingle":

> My brother Bill went in the navy today
> To do his share for the U.S.A.
> And here at home we take part too.
> This puzzle tells the things we do.
> Sister wraps bandages over our maid
> She's learning how in a class on ----- ---
> Grandad has planted a vegetable garden,
> My father is an air raid -----
> Our twins gather paper and old metal wires.
> Mom walks to the store, to save our -----
> Aunt Helen, too, is part of this verse,
> She's assisting a Red Cross -----
> I help the sailors, and soldiers in camps,
> by using my money to buy ------- ------.[82]

Young children could do a lot for the war. While World War II's *Jack and Jill* readers were not asked to meet quotas or to round up ash trays, they were asked to round up what the older children often didn't want to collect, such as milkweed floss. In a 1944 letter to the magazine, Michigan reader Ella Mae Henshaw (no age listed) wrote, "Last fall our school picked milkweed pods. The floss is used for life preservers for our armed forces. Picking milkweed pods isn't a hard job if you get right at it, and it is good sport. You can pick twenty bushels in a day if you keep busy."[83] This was the kind of thing *Jack and Jill* thought its readers could do. Collecting became the feature of a six-part fiction serial, "The Scrappies Club," over the 1943-44 holiday season. The "scrappies," as their grandfather called the group, could pick up waste paper during hikes, among other things. Why? "'We're collecting scrap to shoot at the Japs,' said Benjy. 'Bang! Bang!' said Bobby. And Carol began to say it too. 'Bang! Bang! Bang! Bang! Bang!' They said it so loudly that Grandma Tompkin put her hands to her ears. 'Mercy goodness! I'm glad I'm not a Jap,' she said."[84] But this story had a point beyond collecting scrap, noted the editor in her "Mother's Page" comments. "In this story, Mrs. Lovelace reiterates a theme that 'wars always end,'" Rose explained.

Two years is a long time in the life of a child, and, after two years of war, most boys and girls welcome the comforting thought that sometimes it really will end. And so we carry on, with the aid of writers who feel that the war is important to children—yes—but that boys' and girls' other interests, too, must be kept alive.[85]

Alone among the publications for children studied here, *Jack and Jill* twice explained reasoning behind its choices of wartime material. "How much grief and sorrow can children stand?" Rose asked rhetorically. "Here at *Jack and Jill* it is our candid opinion that young children aren't nearly so tender as most adults suppose them to be.... In considering the reactions of present-day boys and girls, as well as our own interests in the past, we don't worry too much about children's need for exclusive sweetness and light." The problem, she observed, was the parents, and so *Jack and Jill* would not resort to "blood and thunder" stories. "We are never allowed to forget that many adults who see the magazine do need protection."[86]

But *Jack and Jill* did try to bring the war to the young child's level by giving military themes lighter, more fanciful, treatment, sometimes almost sweet. Games and activities were favored. Readers in June 1942 were encouraged to cut out colorful drawings of sixteen men in uniforms, and paste them to paper for a standing collection.[87] Tommy wanted a toy tank. He had the money, fifty cents. He was looking at it through the shop window when approached by friendly soldier Paul. Tommy said he wished he could buy a real tank.

"'Why don't you?'" asked the soldier.

"Tommy laughed when Paul asked him this. A tank must cost many hundreds of dollars.

"'But you can buy a part of a tank,' said the soldier. 'That's what thousands of children throughout the United States are doing right now. They are saving up dimes and nickels and buying tanks for Uncle Sam.'

"'Oh, I know,' said Tommy. 'The government buys tanks with war stamp money.'

"'That's it,' said Paul."[88]

Corporal Charles May was drafted, not only to war service but as *Jack and Jill's* "war correspondent." For several months in 1942 and 1943 he wrote breezy stories of his experiences of army camp life, all of which took place in the United States. The army, according to Corporal May's posts, was not that scary at all, and not even too hard work.[89] *Jack and Jill* tried to add appeal to its youngest readers with war poems and songs, such as "Uncle Sam Can Count on Me":

Americans all do their share, at home and far away
To win the war. May I help too? Yes, and I know the way.
For I will buy stamps, buy stamps, to keep our country free.
I'll give the flag my very best, Uncle Sam can count on me.[90]

Bringing children into the war through rhyme, game, and song proved a popular propaganda technique aimed at the youngest readers, in both wars. World War I's small children could play anticipatory roles:

Shoulder arm! Forward march! Hep—hep—Halt!
Mark time—forward march—Hep—hep—Halt!
Toodle-oot—Boom! Boom! Soldiers brave are we!
Toodle-oot—Boom! Boom! Neighbors out to see!
Daddy send a telegram to the President;
Tell him we are ready to go when we are sent![91]

Pre-schoolers were not exempt from war work:

I cannot knit a scarf nor sweater,
Nor write a soldier boy a letter,
For I am only five, you know,
And have not learned to write nor sew.
I know, though, I must "do my bit,"
So when my mother starts to knit,

I hold the yarn, stretch wide each hand
And very, very still I stand
Until she winds it in a ball,
And never say I'm tired at all![92]

St. Nicholas reflected its World War I contemporaries in its determined effort to educate children regarding the jobs they could do for the wartime home front. This publication even launched a new department, "For Country and for Liberty," "dedicated to patriotic service such as the readers of this magazine can render." Duty, an ideal so favored by World War I editors, gave American children in particular an opportunity for selfless service. What could World War I children do? Of course, they could sell and buy war bonds and stamps, plant gardens, help on the farm, save peach pits, knit sweaters, build cabinets, post bills—for starters. But unlike the more official authorities, children's magazine editors didn't stop with the basics.

They could write letters. "Every reader of the *American Boy* should write a Christmas letter to a soldier this month—a letter that will make the fighting man who receives it feel that the boys at home are with him, and bring good cheer at Christmas time.... If he can stand it to live in a trench and dodge German shells, you ought to be able to bear up under the dangers and hardships of pushing a pen across a sheet of paper."[93]

They could send old newspapers to the troops. "These papers must be neatly wrapped and addressed to the captain of that company. Twenty papers will answer for one tent. Thus by a little consistent effort a company of men in the cantonment will receive the daily news from home, which does more to keep them happy than anything else that can be given them."[94]

They could make Christmas gifts. "Such articles as the following are acceptable: letter paper and writing pad and pencil, a pipe (not clay), tobacco or cigarettes, chocolate bars or hard candies easily packed, games such as packs of cards, dominoes, checkers or puzzles."[95]

They could mail music to the front. "These slackers are a new kind altogether—they are the 'slacker records,' and they are being drafted into service by The National Phonograph Records Recruiting Corps, 21 East 40th Street, New York City. A slacker record is one which you have grown tired of playing and which now lies idle."[96]

They could raise pigeons. "Do not be surprised—a dove may be the emblem of peace, but a carrier pigeon is a messenger of war."[97]

They could give away their dog. "Suddenly he remembered what Father had

*World War I pre-school children were not exempt from war duties. The* St. Nicholas *feature "For Very Little Folk" describes how a pre-school child can do war work by giving away toys for Belgian refugee children, or holding yarn for mothers knitting troop clothing. (July 1918, page 852).*

said that stay-at-home folk could do for their country. He looked at the flag—and then at his dog. 'Yes,' he said, with a brave little smile, 'Boko may go.'"[98]

*The Rally* for Girl Scouts in particular emphasized war service for girls, while ignoring the character development or adventure as benefits of war commonly presented in boys' publications. And for those girls who might hesitate, it pulled out the bleaker of the propaganda tools juvenile publications used to enlist children into war: shame and guilt. Children who did not do their bit faced consequences. Asking children to buy war bonds, Ruth G. Bowman wondered, "Could you, as has been your wont, stand complacent in the magnificent white arc of national hope and plan your own little pleasures, your own little joys, your own little life? Could you bear to contemplate your hands folded in luxury and idleness while thousands of hands and hearts toiled for your freedom?"[99] The vast majority of children in both wars did buy war stamps and bonds, despite their low interest rates and maturity years later. Patriotism was the wellspring, certainly. Should that fail, editors were not above psychological coercion and vague threats of future failure. "Every child who buys a thrift stamp for twenty-five cents is loaning that twenty-five cents to his country," wrote Josephine Daskam Bacon. But "any child who does not want to do this is not worthy, it seems to me, of the name American…. Any girl who cannot deny herself to this extent to help her Great Mother in her trouble, will not make, I am sure, the war nurse or ambulance driver that she wants to be today."[100]

*American Boy* tried another approach using the same tool. It imagined the shame a boy without war bonds would face. "Wouldn't it be awful to see the other fellows getting their money back from Uncle Sam—and you getting nothing—that is, nothing but the sneers of the other fellows and taunts that you had been a 'slacker?'"[101] *American Boy* found a similar way to berate readers who might have been tempted to slip away from the many volunteer service opportunities asked of children. Noting that the boys of Europe were rendering historic service to the war effort, it asked, "Do you, American boys, want to be mentioned on that page? Or do you want it to be silent regarding you? Rather let it be said that the British and French boys were wonderful, but that it was the American boys who really showed the world what boys could do."[102] Theodore Roosevelt reminded boys that every male child ought to prepare for war, and everyone ought to go: "It will be a mighty sight pleasanter to explain to his children later on why he went than why he did not."[103] Shaming youngsters who did not immediately climb onto the wartime bandwagon, of course, borrowed a page from the same chapter of adult propaganda made famous in World War I, such as the poster depicting a father and child, the caption reading, "Daddy, what did YOU do during the war?" If the century's tools of psychological manipulation through propaganda seemed appropriate for adults, they'd apparently seem equally appropriate for children. Mobilization of children for home front duty was no light matter. Particularly for some of the children themselves. *Boys' Life* in 1918 detailed one scout's work to organize mobilization of his troop. To track the boys, each scout was expected to fill out a "mobilization record": "address, telephone, nearest telephone, telegraph instrument, wireless outfit, bicycle, motorcycle, automobile, horse, attending school, all other addresses on certain days and hours, age, scout rank, special training." Some boys responded with less than due diligence, such as one Spike Tuller. who "thought he'd be smart (like he always does) and wrote on his report like this":

Home address—Where ever I am.
Home telephone—Nay, nay.
Wireless outfit—Sure we're a wireless outfit—didn't I say we didn't have a phone?
Bicycle—Wish I had one.
Automobile—My name's Spike, not Rockefeller.
Attending school—Yes darn it.

The boy mobilizer, Robert Shackly, was not amused. Telling this to his father in a letter, he wrote, "Don't you think, father, such a kid ought to be court-marshaled when it's such hard work for a patrol leader who is mobilizing his patrol? I do."[104] So did the editor. Such a smirking shirking child who failed to sell his bonds—was a murderer. "A machine gun goes empty at a critical moment. The Hun listens, turns, counter-attacks. A rush carries our hard-won trench. Americans go down, cold, stiff, full of ghastly wounds. Your sale could have stopped it—that sale you did not make. Isn't it treason? Isn't it murder?" The Boy Scouts, West added, have pledged 100 percent loyalty to the nation. There was no room for debate, no room for question: "Are you with them or against them? There's no neutral gear in Uncle Sam's tank; you must work or be junked."[105] The demand that children sacrifice free thought in a country that traditionally valued individual freedoms needed special bolster. Observed McKenzie, "Children were exhorted to sacrifice individuality for the group and pleasure for work; in essence, to take on the previous 'adult' role of responsible worker."[106] *American Boy* emphasized children had two choices: patriot or traitor. "In this country there are just two kinds of people—Americans and traitors. You've got to be with one or the other."[107]

To be a good American, a child merely did absolutely everything authorities asked of him. If he hesitated or questioned, he was the other one. "An order is to be obeyed, discipline is to be observed. That is something we are learning from the war," preached Ellis in an editorial. "If you are under the command of a man or of an organization either in this war or in a peaceful occupation, it is not for you to ask if an order be right, or if you want to obey it, or if it is beneath your dignity to do the thing. If the person who orders you has the right to give and order, obey it on the jump. Only slackers hesitate when an order is given."[108]

As an exception, *St. Nicholas* did not rely on naked guilt to motivate children. In doing that it presaged the next war. World War II editors presented as many home front jobs for children, and as strongly exhorted them to service. But seldom did a heavy blanket of shame and guilt await the slackers of World War II's children's army. They were asked to contribute, but not draped with humiliation if they chose not to. Children were presumed to be doing the right thing. Copy focused on the "are," and seldom on the "are not: "As Girl Scouts, you are doing your big share for victory," emphasized optimistically a scout-sponsored ad. "Show them how important it is by wearing your uniform with pride."[109] *Boys' Life*, perhaps because it was still edited by West, the only holdover from the World War I era, did come close to laying guilt in a scout-sponsored ad: "This war is being fought for you.... Don't betray their trust! In your own town there are hundreds of ways in which you as a scout and through your scout training can help America win this war."[110] But this implied guilt differs from World War's direct accusation. World War II's editors again presented propaganda quite different from that of their predecessors, most likely based on general distaste in America for World War I's propaganda techniques.

## War Makes the Better Boy

In common during both wars, however, was extensive material designed to be positive, to promote the attractive values of war as virtuous, educational, practical, sporting, inspiring and adventurous. The war could build numerous virtues, even surprising ones. "After all these years folks have come to appreciate what a boy can do and how valuable he can be to his country," observed the editor of *American Boy*. "It took a war to do it."[111] Learning how to fight could forge a useful attitude. "When you get to your business of life remember that you've got to fight every fight through to a finish just as you have in war," argued an *American Boy* editorial in 1918. "The successful man is the one who doesn't know when he is licked, but sticks to it till he has made his deal or put through the sale, or achieved his point."[112] War demonstrated that fight and honor could make a life worth living. "You have found out that life, carelessly lived, regardless of duty to God, your country and your fellows, is not worth while, but is ugly and leads only into swamps."[113] The military "is no place for 'mollycoddles,' but there is no better place for manly boys who have the 'real stuff' in them," Secretary of the Navy Josephus Daniels told readers of *St. Nicholas*. "That's the kind we want and welcome."[114] Manly virtues could be tested through battle, while at home children could learn the spirit of volunteerism, the rewards of thrift, and the value of hard work. Joining the Boys' Working Reserve, for example, could build "boys who are not afraid of a blistered hand or a sunburned nose, who don't mind honest toil for a living wage, even if it is not in the direction of the life work for which they want to fit themselves."[115] Saving for war bonds could enhance the good of the frugal: "No less useful is the service of the girl who evolves a consistent plan for personal thrift, who sticks to it herself and inspires others to follow."[116] Virtues of a militarized life could even extend to better diction. In her "Patriotic Resolution for Girls and Boys," Grace Williamson Willett said the war required improvements in spoken English. She asked *St. Nicholas* children to promise to enunciate more clearly, to avoid leaving final sounds off words, and "That I will say a good American 'yes' and 'no' in place of an Indian grunt ('un-hum' or nup-um') or a foreign 'ya' or 'yeh' and 'nope.'"[117]

While World War II's editors did not emphasize virtue as a wartime value, they did see benefits in skills development. Particularly in aviation. Aviation students would likely be boys, and they could use their skills both during and after war. But girls, too, could become aviators, emphasized *American Girl*. Writer Sally Knapp asked readers, Would you like to help win the war? Thousands of girls did—in aviation. Wartime aviation training could offer a service now, and a career later, in an industry expected to expand rapidly after the war. Describing the training procedure in detail, the writer noted, "Girls in aviation positions fall into two general groups: those who fly the planes and those who help others to fly." The "great majority" would be working behind the scenes, but girls too could become pilots.[118] But encouragement of girls into roles traditionally expected of boys seldom saw favor among authorities in either war. In World War I the Girl Scouts' publication published page after page laden with calls to domestic duties for wartime service. By World War II domestic duties still were featured. But aviation was a comparatively new industry. Men were not as entrenched, and famous women aviators could show how girls could dream. Girls could even join the air force—if they could weather the chauvinism. "'If she's a pilot I'll eat my wings!' exclaimed a bronzed U.S. Army Air Forces captain." But, of course, the man soon lost his appetite: "The pint-size pilot identified herself as no less a person than Mrs. Betty Gillies, squadron leader of the women ferrying pilots of the WASP, or Women Air Force Service Pilots, stationed at the Ferrying Division's Newcastle, Delaware, base."[119]

While *American Girl* promoted aviation in long practical articles describing how girls could work toward a pilot's license, *Boys' Life* let military advertising take over. Repeat air force ads boasted the excitement of a wartime flying career, and the satisfaction of working together as a team. "Teamwork Does It! In the bright sun of mid-morning a Jap convoy crawls over the Burma Road. Suddenly the look-outs yell.... The road under their wheels explodes in a splash of bomb-bursts that hurl men and trucks and Jap supplies into the gorge below."

The skill behind the attack, according to the captain, was teamwork, every man a specialist. Boys could prepare for their turn: "If you want a chance to fly on the 'greatest team in the world,' an AAF air combat crew, go to your nearest AAF examining board. See if you can qualify for the Air Corps Enlisted Reserve."[120]

Even very young children could find educational value in wartime published material. *Jack and Jill's* puzzles enhanced language skills as well as war bond sales:

In each of the puzzles on this page you change a bond into something that can be used by our military forces. In each puzzle the word is changed one letter at a time....
Bond...Bond.
Group of musicians...----
Place to keep money...----
Armored car...Tank. [121]

Authorities realized the military had its own schools. Why not use them as an alternative to civilian study? Josephus Daniels proposed the idea in *American Boy*. He admitted the navy was "largely a boy institution, as the sailor enlists at seventeen. Most of these youths have very little education when they come in, and are sent to the training stations.... They are given technical instruction and taught the three Rs and this academic instruction is continued aboard ship except when military duties make it impossible."[122]

The most obvious benefit of a militarized childhood to these publications, however, was physical fitness. It seemed logical to editors that fitness and military service were related. Statistics showed recruits in both wars were unfit; a call to a life of vigor for wartime needs might reduce the dismal number of America's youthful indolent. *Boys' Life* in World War II featured detailed articles covering fitness training for war, West asking boys to "toughen up and buckle down!" He suspected the truth was that "we have been leading a pretty soft life for a good many years past." The answer was to use the war as an excuse to turn troop meetings into exercise bouts. "Why shouldn't we make every troop meeting as nearly as we can a training center? Give scouts an opportunity to develop themselves physically, to climb, to get through difficult places." Physical skill would keep children prepared. "Every boy and indeed every girl should feel the importance of knowing how to take care of himself or herself," West concluded, in one of the rare occasions that *Boys' Life* actually acknowledged the other sex.[123]

Fitness could do more than make a strong boy; it could groom the boy for soldiering. "We mean he should learn to keep his body fit," wrote *Boys' Life* in a 1917 editorial. "He should learn to care for himself out of doors; he should learn self-reliance; he should learn how to handle a gun. If he will do these things, he will cut down by a year the time required by his country to make a soldier of him if his country ever needs him."[124] *St. Nicholas* described in detail a good way to use military values in making the fit child: the setting-up exercises. These calisthenics were developed for military recruits, but could give kids a boost in obedience, discipline, and maybe even fitness. The article's accompanying illustrations were borrowed from the 1917 *Plattsburg Manual* for military training:

> "What shall I do about the boy? He had plenty of exercise during the football
> season, but he doesn't have half enough now, especially in bad weather."
> "M-m," said Uncle John. "May I smoke here? Thank you. M-m—I have it! The
> setting-up exercises. Here, Jack, take your nose out of that *St. Nicholas* for a
> minute and fall in."
> Jack climbed out of the corner of the big leather sofa at the other end of the
> room and came to where his uncle was sitting.
> "'Slip off your jacket. There! Now assume the position of a soldier," command-
> ed the captain.[125]

Summer camps could offer fitness training, particularly those which diverted activities to those of a military nature. "There is every indication that
this year will be the greatest of all camping years, not in spite of the war but
because of it!", pointed out a writer in *St. Nicholas*. "The 'setting-up drill' and
the military drill, which are now a part of the program of every well-regulated
camp, inculcate habits of regularity, exactitude and discipline which are invalu-
able in after life."[126] In World War II, *Boys' Life* hoped to see more boys in camp;
the enemy may have been evil, but their exercise programs could give America
a framework against youthful sloth. "The Hitler youth movement and the Mus-
solini youth movement have made much for years back of the values that come
from camping and those experiences which overcome softness and make young
people physically strong and self-reliant," wrote West. Boy Scout camps could do
the same. While again reminding readers that "Scouting is neither military nor
anti-military," he said Americans could look with pride to a movement that is
giving the country "men who are physically strong, mentally awake and morally
straight."[127]

While editors did feature calisthenics, camps, and other formal exercises as
a way to keep fit as a soldier, the best choice for most children was presumed to
be something they presumably already liked: sports. Authorities in both wars
encouraged sports participation as a paramilitary substitution for real combat.
Sports could build team work, competitive spirit, strategy, speed, fitness—all
valuable qualities for warriors. Who beat Napoleon at Waterloo? asked C. Ward
Crampton, a physician writing in 1942 *Boys' Life*. Sporting school boys from the
playing fields of Eton. "Now we have our job! The Battle of the Atlantic and the
Pacific. Play ball! Let's look at our own playing fields from the war angles." Readers might not have considered this, but America's national pastime groomed
boys for war:

Baseball. What is there in our own great American game of baseball that prepares us in youth to fight as men?.... War, life and baseball are team games— everyone is for you, you are for everyone else. Now is the time to learn it. It becomes automatic. It gets in the system. It's the only way to victory. Play ball!"[128]

Tennis could be a game of military strategy: "Attack means the same with a racket as it does with an infantry squad."[129] In fact, war itself was just another game, for higher stakes. Football formations resembled battlefield formations, asserted a former football trainer, writing as an army lieutenant in 1918. "There is, also, a very close similarity in the manner in which the men are prepared for the two games; for war is nothing more than a game played for the greatest stake in the world—life itself."[130] The article was accompanied by a cover illustration of a boy throwing a football, and next to him, a soldier in gas mask throwing a grenade. Schools should not curtail athletics during the war; good soldiers must have "endurance, power applied, discipline, teamwork, on guard against stratagems, and courage," all learned through sports. "The schools and colleges should continue their athletic activities."[131]

If a battlefield was just another sporting ground, children might be tempted to presume war could be entertaining. Maybe fun. Editors agreed. War could be noble, glorious, heroic, inspiring, an adventure. The editor of *American Boy* no longer wrote of the war as a "frightful thing" after Wilson's 1917 war declaration. The war was reframed. It was now a noble thing.[132] "Glorious" had been used as a word of peace. A 1915 writer in *St. Nicholas* spoke of stories on film for children: "One glorious story now being told on the screen is the story of peace."[133] But after the war declaration, glorious joined noble as words applied to warriors. A former Boy Scout, now in military service for Britain, volunteered for a dangerous mission. "I got three wounds in doing it but I dare not go into hospital lest I should be detained there and so lose the chance of the next fight. I like to feel my three punctures smarting because they serve as a constant reminder to me of the three points of my promise as a scout." Opposition to war had become a refuge for the craven who did not recognize war's noble goals. "I was till now a conscientious pacifist, but those glorious few minutes of bombing at close quarters by a brutal enemy have made another man of me."[134] Wilson's war declaration was a "historic utterance, nobly voicing the true patriotism of the American people." Girls could not fight, but could become "noble nurses."[135] "Every one of us—man, woman and child—can do something to help bring our boys back in the glory of victory," proposed a government-sponsored ad. What? "Save our quarters and buy W.S.S. [War Savings Stamps]. Is that too much to ask for the safety of our mothers' sons?"[136]

Heroes were men who fought in war; even more were they heroic if they did not return. Andrew Carnegie had reminded boys in 1914 that the "real heroes" were not the men who wounded and killed their fellows,[137] but definition of that word, too, changed with the coming of war. As Americans become soldiers, "We shall have new heroes," wrote *Boys' Life*. "You can be one."[138] Children's editors during both wars larded their pages with serials and dramatized stories of military men finding adventure and heroism on battlefields around the world. "Every American boy is reading hero stories nowadays," explained *St. Nicholas*. "And they are the best kind of hero stories, because they are all true, and because they are about men—and boys—who are fighting now in the great war to make the world safe for democracy."[139]

Europe's children were "heroic figures in the center of a heroic epoch."[140] Children according to these stories were becoming real war heroes, such as the French girl who joined an ambulance service because, "'I want so much—oh, so much—to do something for France!'" The story ended, "'Hurrah!' The young men shouted. "'Hurrah for the ambulance-girl!'"[141] America's children, editors suggested, could also be heroic by working hard in school and out, obeying authorities, keeping fit, and buying bonds. Writing that these were "great times" for American boys, Edward Teall encouraged kids to be "soldiers in the garden army" or volunteer in other ways. "You are not yet of military age. Perhaps you wish you were older. How proud and happy you would be to shoulder a gun and go marching away, following the flag to France!", Teall wrote. But their time might come, would come. "Boys, your part is not a small one! It is vitally important. The service you can render now in preparing for the service you will surely be called upon to render in a few years is precious to the nation."[142]

World War II children's editors spoke little about the nobility and glamour of war. But they spoke a lot about heroes, particularly in the many stirring tales of wartime adventures. *Boys' Life* featured at least two in each issue, usually more. The March 1942 edition offered four: "Eagles Fly High" by Raoul Whitfield: "America's war-cry, 'keep 'em flying,' roars through this new thrill-packed serial"; "Now Is Tomorrow" by Robb White: "Duty! Service! Guts! The Navy! Empty words until you're through an ordeal— 'Well done!'"; "Rendezvous at Midnight," by John R. Hoyt: "Meet me at 10,000 feet over the objective—orders filled with danger for Art Kane"; and one story of an ancient army heroically applied to modern war, "Caesar Goes Recruiting," by I. M. Bolton: "The recruits quailed at rumors of impending disaster, but Marcus took courage—the cause was just."[143] Fretwell in *Boys' Life* wrote that children were heroes too.

Boys working on farms were "Heroes of the Potato Front." This might seem like Mark Twain comparing lightning to a lightning bug, but Fretwell elaborated, "428,000 of you dug, planted and weeded Victory Gardens at home, by troops or in camp."[144]

Given the torrent of copy in both wars swarming with adventure and heroism, it is not surprising children were not always patient while planting potatoes. "Get over that!" admonished a 1918 government-sponsored ad on space contributed by publishers. "The battles are not only on the battlefields. The war is fought by saving behind the lines. And there is one job-of-work you can do that is 100 percent man's size. Don't doubt it for minutes!" And what might that be? "You buy United States War Savings Stamps.... Stick out your chest and tell your father that here's where you get in the game with your money for War Savings Stamps."[145] World War I editors had set the tone for this material. Editors in both wars favored exciting stories of aviators, World War I's knights of the air, as fewer inspiring tales of infantry could be found. "Look up," advised *American Boy*, in another plea to inspire war bond sales. "Daring men, like the young Captain Guynemer and our own Freddie Zinn, sail through the skies, observing enemy positions, attacking enemy planes, battling against odds—doing their dangerous part to keep the Germans back."[146] "Great war stories," *American Boy* promised for 1918. "Heroes of battles in the air, in the trenches, on the sea, will tell the wonderful stories of their thrilling adventures."[147] Even work for the ambulance service was crowded with thrilling tales.[148] And finally, even the simple camaraderie of the soldiers could be fun: "The train began to move. The ambulance men sang riotously: Over there, over there, send the word, send the word over there—."[149] Adventure in war was a story of boys. Neither *The Rally* nor *American Girl* served this fare to its readers. Instead they preferred to emphasize practical but mundane things girls could do on the home front. War stories for the younger readers of *Jack and Jill* favored working at home, in addition to the fairly tame experiences of Corporal May at camp. Explained the editor, "We take pride in being able to interest our readers without resorting to sensational features."[150]

## The Enchanted World of War

Editors of the representative children's publications studied here constructed war as a mythical world children need not be afraid of. The military culture they were invited to join could be stern, would certainly require work, and sometimes would demand sacrifice. But rewards were many. Regardless of who was winning on the battlefields, children could benefit from the wide variety of virtues extracted through mobilization on the home front. They could be inspired by heroism across the seas. They could be part of the team. War was anything but frightening. It was a fine and noble thing, pretty much.

And of the destruction? Violence? Suffering? Brutality? Death? Early in World War I, before the United States joined, editors would consider frankly those questions. After April 1917, they never asked again. They never asked in World War II. Still, these juvenile publications did not deny that war included suffering and death. "Boom—z—zing—crash—and many men are hurled to death, or maimed, or blinded. Their comrades crawl over them. They go 'over the top.' They feel the sting of the bullet."[151] Soldiers could die in war stories: "Yes, it was over, but dead and wounded men were all about us, and we had lost many of our own."[152] Real soldiers could die: "Killed at Pearl Harbor! Yes, John Duncan, the strong, athletic, hearty, popular John had enlisted and gone straight into the war."[153] A field surgeon's amputation was described in detail, "the tender sensitive stumps with exposed nerves, stumps with projecting bone."[154] But death in war was part of the duty, the patriotism, the heroism; a price to be paid, and worth it. Death was incorporated into a war myth constructed by children's publications, a world noble and righteous, just and meaningful, in which the dead man was euphemized into a "fallen hero." It is not surprising editors of children's publications would do this. Euphemizing death, or not speaking of it at all, was part of the adult world too, during war—and perhaps still is today. In war, soldiers don't die. Heroes fall. They are lost. They meet their fate. If children's publications transmit adult values to the next generation, it is understandable to see them make war more palatable, more acceptable to the children—many of whom would be called to face battlefield death themselves. If war must be accepted—and Americans in both world wars accepted it almost universally—then it needs to be constructed for the home front in a way that makes tolerable its excruciating pain and sorrow. Children's editors cannot be blamed for publishing what society wanted to hear.

Or can they? What might strike a reader perusing World War I's material for children is its cheerfulness. So many things to do, so many virtues to foster—so many opportunities to celebrate. So many people to despise, including quite a lot of actual American citizens, and all of those slackers. So many ideals to discredit, including pacifism and aberrant thought in general. McKenzie argued the war propaganda of magazines such as St. Nicholas "demonstrate a fundamental transformation in defining childhood.... Children were exhorted to sacrifice individuality for the group and pleasure for work; in essence, to take on the previous 'adult' role of responsible worker."[155] Children's editors in World War II must be given credit for trying to avoid to most egregious of this sort of thing. Propaganda's buzzwords of the 1914–1918 war, words like patriotism and duty, and the reprisals of guilt and shame, were mostly banned, or at least carefully nuanced. Soldiers of World War II were heroic, yes, but world war was not quite the celebration it had been the first time. On the other hand, war on the pages of children's magazines was still an adventure, a worthy sacrifice and, well, not very scary. War became merely part of everyday life.

## Notes

1. "More Reading—Better Patriots," publisher's advertisement, *American Boy*, August 1918, 42.

2. Karen L. Hamilton, "*St. Nicholas* at War: The Effects of the Great War on a Prominent Children's Magazine, 1914–1919" (Master's thesis, University of Minnesota, 1972), 1.

3. R. Gorden Kelly, ed., *Children's Periodicals of the United States* (Westport, CT: Greenwood, 1984), xv.

4. Ibid.

5. Ibid., ix.

6. Quoted in Andrea McKenzie, "The Children's Crusade: American Children Writing War," *The Lion and the Unicorn* 31 (2007), 89.

7. Hamilton, 3; Kelly, xiii.

8. "St. Nicholas League," *St. Nicholas*, July 1914, masthead.

9. "Mother's Page, "*Jack and Jill*, April 1944, 52.

10. *American Boy*, passim.

11. Kelly, 48.

12. *The Rally*, May 1918, 4; Kelly, 17.

13. Kelly, 226.

14. Publisher's advertisement, *St. Nicholas*, May 1918, 6.

15. Mabel Louise Mountsier and Robert DeMain Mountsier, "Three Loyal Children of France," *St. Nicholas*, July 1917, 780.

16. Mary Stevick, "Save Food and Serve Humanity," *The Rally*, March 1918, 6.

17. Hamilton, "*St. Nicholas* at War: The Effects of the Great War on a Prominent Children's Magazine, 1914–1919," 2.

18. Swarthmore College Peace Collection, Swarthmore College library, http://www.swarthmore.edu/Library/peace/CDGA.A-L/andrews.htm.

19. Susan Zeiger, "The Schoolhouse vs. the Armory. U.S. Teachers and the Campaign Against Militarism in the Schools, 1914-1918," *Journal of Women's History* 15, no. 2, (2003), 150.

20. Jane Stannard Johnson, "What Motion-Pictures Are Telling the Boys and Girls," *St. Nicholas*, July 1915, 846–847.

21. S. E. Forman, "The Watch Tower. A Forword," *St. Nicholas*, September 1915, 963–964.

22. Ibid., 964, 966.

23. Forman, "The Watch Tower. The Great War," *St. Nicholas*, October 1915, 1068.

24. Forman, "The Watch Tower. The Great War," *St. Nicholas*, April 1916, 541; May 1916, 645.

25. Forman, "The Watch Tower. The Great War," *St. Nicholas*, August 1916, 933; September 1916, 1030; April 1917, 546.

26. Edward M. Teall, "A Letter to the Boys of America," *St. Nicholas*, October 1917, 1066.

27. "War," editorial, *American Boy*, February 1917, 3.

28. "Boy Scouts in Time of War," *Boys' Life*, October 1914, 30.

29. David Starr Jordan, "A Challenge! Do You Want to Fight?", *Boys' Life*, November 1914, 3.

30. Cyrus Townsend Brady, "What War Is—Just One Battle," *Boys' Life*, 9.

31. McKenzie, "The Children's Crusade: American Children Writing War," *The Lion and the Unicorn*, 96.

32. Editorial, "For Country and For Liberty. Patriotic Service for American Boys and Girls," *St. Nicholas*,

July 1917, 771.

33. Franklin K. Lane, "All for Liberty," *St. Nicholas*, August 1917, 877.

34. Editorial, "For Country and For Liberty. Patriotic Service for American Boys and Girls," *St. Nicholas*, July 1917, 771.

35. Editorial (unsigned; Griffith Ogden Ellis) "What Can You Do?", *American Boy*, June 1917, 3.

36. "Why We Are at War," Josephine Daskam Bacon, vice commissioner, girl scout council, Pleasantville, NY, *The Rally*, February 1918, 1-2, 10.

37. *The Rally*, March 1918, 9.

38. James E. West, "Strong for America," *Boys' Life*, February 1942, 10.

39. Editorial, "Perhaps Better Than Yourself," *American Boy*, April 1917, 3.

40. "Americans for America," *The Rally*, January 1918, 2.

41. Editorial, "A Harvest of Hatred," *American Boy*, October 1917, 3.

42. "Mother's Page," *Jack and Jill*, April 1944, 52.

43. W. Linwood Chase, *Wartime Social Studies in the Elementary School. Curriculum. Series No. 3* (Washington, DC: The National Council for the Social Studies, 1943), 17-18.

44. Editor's note, *St. Nicholas*, July 1914, 849.

45. Editor, "For Country and For Liberty. Patriotic Service for American Boys and Girls," *St. Nicholas*, July 1917, 771.

46. Ibid., 772.

47. Editor's note; Agnes Law, "The Flag," *St. Nicholas*, November 1917, 86.

48. Newton Baker, "The Summer Camps," *American Boy*, May 1917, 4.

49. Editorial, "What Can You Do?" *American Boy*, June 1917, 3.

50. C. H. Claudy, "Will You Do Your Bit? Here's the Way," *American Boy*, June 1917, 49.

51. "Boys! Get into the Fight!", *American Boy*, February 1918, 30.

52. Editorial, "Our Country Is at War," *Boys' Life*, May 1917, 3.

53. Woodrow Wilson, Facsimile of letter from Wilson to Colin H. Livingstone, dated 23 August 1918, *Boys' Life*, October 1918, 47.

54. Edna Mary Colman, "War Work of the Girl Scouts of Washington," *Rally*, October 1917, 8.

55. Editorial, James E. West, "The American's Creed," *Boys' Life*, February 1942, 10.

56. "If War Should Come," *Boys' Life*, March 1917, 37.

57. Editorial, "What Can You Do?", *American Boy*, June 1917, 3.

58. *American Boy*, September 1917, front cover.

59. "Friendly Talks with the Editor," *American Boy*, November 1917, 3.

60."The War Duty of Boys Is to Return to School," *American Boy*, September 1917, 18.

61. "Friendly Talks with the Editor, *American Boy*, January 1918, 3.

62. Editorial, "For Country and Liberty," *St. Nicholas*, July 1917, 772.

63. Lieutenant-General Tom Bridges, "General Bridges' Message to American Boys and Girls. May 16th, 1917," *St. Nicholas*, July 1917, 779.

64. Edna Mary Colman, "War Work of the Girl Scouts of Washington," *Rally*, October 1917, 8.

65. *Boys' Life*, June 1917, 51.

66. Editorial, *Boys' Life*, July 1942, 3.

67. Lucile Hoffman, "Farmer Green's Animals and the War," *Jack and Jill*, August 1942, 5.

68. Adria Aldrich, "Of Course You Can. Can the surplus of your Victory Garden and Help your Uncle Sam," *American Girl*, September 1942, 24.

69. West, "The American's Creed," *Boys' Life*, February 1942, 10.

70. *Boys' Life*, March 1942, front cover; 30.

71. *Boys' Life*, April 1942, front cover; 14.

72. *Boys' Life*, May 1942, 3; August 1942, 3;

73. *Boys' Life*, June 1944, front cover.

74. Randolph Bartlett, "It's a Boys' War Too," *Boys' Life*, October 1943, 8-9.

75. *American Girl*, March 1942, 35.

76. Gertrude Simpson, "Girl Scouts in Two Wars," *American Girl*, October 1942, 28-29.

77. Claire Liske, "To Be Needed Makes Us Proud," *American Girl*, February 1943, 28.

78. *American Girl*, August 1944, 43.

79. *American Girl*, January 1945, inside cover.

80. Helen Hatcher, "Glamour Drill," *American Girl*, November 1942, 30.
81. "The Second Phase of the War. The Trenches Have been Established—Defend Them!", *Boys' Life*, June 1917, 34.
82. *Jack and Jill*, April 1942, 37; responses are "first aid," "warden," "tires," "nurse," and "Victory Stamps."
83. *Jack and Jill*, September 1944, 48.
84. Maud Hart Lovelace, "The Scrappies' Club," *Jack and Jill*, November 1943, 7.
85. "Mother's Page," *Jack and Jill*, November 1942, 52.
86. "Mother's Page," *Jack and Jill*, April 1944, 52.
87. *Jack and Jill*, June 1942, 26–28.
88. Alfred Lewis, "Tommy Buys a Tank," *Jack and Jill*, July 1943, 23.
89. Charles May, "My Army Experiences," *Jack and Jill*, passim, 1942–1943.
90. May M. Hake, "Uncle Sam Can Count on Me," *Jack and Jill*, July 1943, inside front cover.
91. Jane Redfield Hoover, "Preparedness," *St. Nicholas*, June 1918, 739.
92. Mattie Lee Haugen, "Doing Her Bit," *St. Nicholas*, July 1918, 852.
93. "Christmas Letters to Soldiers," *American Boy*, November 1917; 36; "Friendly Talks with the Editor," *American Boy*, February 1918, 3.
94. Edna Mary Colman, "War Work of the Girl Scouts of Washington," *The Rally*, October 1917, 8.
95. Juliette Low, editorial, *The Rally*, November 1917, 4.
96. "Have You Any 'Slacker Records?'" *The Rally*, October 1918, 12.
97. "A Service for Girl Scouts," Juliette Low, *The Rally*, October 1917, 3.
98. Nelly Love, *St. Nicholas*, "For Very Little Folk. Billy and Boko," August 1917, 949.
99. Ruth G. Bowman, "Resolved: To Serve," *The Rally*, January 1918, 4.
100. Josephine Daskam Bacon, "Members of One Family," *The Rally*, June 1918, 1.
101. *American Boy*, February 1918, 31.
102. Editorial, "Don't Be Outdistanced," *American Boy*, June 1917, 3.
103. Speech by Theodore Roosevelt, *Boys' Life*, October 1917, 23.
104. Robert Shackly, "The Letters of a Boy Scout in War Time" *Boys' Life*, May 1917, 17.
105. Editorial, "Work or Be Junked," *Boys' Life*, October 1918, 3.
106. McKenzie, "The Children's Crusade: American Children Writing War," 96.
107. Editorial, "Friendly Talks with the Editor. America or—," *American Boy*, June 1918, 3.
108. Editorial, "Friendly Talks with the Editor. Orders," *American Boy*, October 1918, 5.
109. *American Girl*, March 1942, back cover.
110. BSA-sponsored advertisement, *Boys' Life*, July 1942, 26.
111. Editorial, "Appreciated at Last," *American Boy*, August 1917, 3.
112. Editorial, "Friendly Talks with the Editor. Fight," *American Boy*, June 1918, 3.
113. Herman Hagedorn, "You Are the Hope of the World. A Ringing Message to Youth," *Boys' Life*, September 1917, 2.
114. Josephus Daniels, "A Message to the Boys of America," *St. Nicholas*, July 1918, 785.
115. C. H. Claudy, "Will You Do Your Bit? Here's the Way," *American Boy*, June 1917, 49.
116. "Girl Scout War Service Award," *The Rally*, March 1918, 2.
117. Grace Williamson Willett, "Better Speech for Better Americans," *St. Nicholas*, July 1918, 839–840.
118. Sally E. Knapp, "Jobs in Aviation for Girls," *American Girl*, March 1943, 14.
119. Betty Peckham, "How the Women Air Force Service Pilots Keep 'Em Flying," *American Girl*, December 1943, 8.
120. *Boys' Life*, October 1944, 29.
121. Ann King, "War-Bond Puzzles," *Jack and Jill*, December 1943, 35.
122. Josephus Daniels, "You Can Go to School in the Navy," *American Boy*, May 1917, 4.
123. James E. West, editorial, "Toughen Up and Buckle Down," *Boys' Life*, December 1942, 3.
124. Editorial, "Friendly Talks with the Editor. Universal Service," *American Boy*, May 1917, 3.
125. Rodman Gilder, "Setting Up Jack," *St. Nicholas*, June 1917, 689.
126. William H. Brown, "Summer Camps and the War," *St. Nicholas*, May 1918, 31.
127. James E. West, Editorial, *Boys' Life*, June 1942, 3.
128. C. Ward Crampton, "Team Play!", *Boys' Life*, April 1942, 20.
129. Captain David B. Parker, "Tactics and Tennis," *Boys' Life*, August 1942, 24.
130. Harry Tuthill, formerly trainer of the Michigan and West Point football teams and the Detroit Tigers,

"Football and War," *American Boy*, October 1918, 10.

131. Walter Kellogg Towers, "'Athletics' Aid to War. How Training in One Helps in the Other," *American Boy*, October 1917, 13.

132. Editorial, "War," *American Boy*, February 1917, 3

133. Jane Stannard Johnson, "What Motion-Pictures Are Telling the Boys and Girls," *St. Nicholas*, July 1915, 846.

134. Robert Baden-Powell, "The Most Interesting Boy I Ever Knew," *American Boy*, January 1918, 9.

135. "The Watch Tower. The Call to Arms!", *St. Nicholas*, May 1917, 642; Margaret Dadmun, "The Girls in Khaki," *St. Nicholas*, April 1917, 520.

136. "My Boy! Will You Lend 24 c to Uncle Sam to Help Save Her Boy's Life?," *Boys' Life*, April 1918, 48.

137. Andrew Carnegie, *Boys' Life*, November 1914, 2.

138. Editorial, "Our Country Is At War," May 1917, 2.

139. "An American College Boy Who Flew and Fell in France," May 1918, *St. Nicholas*, 31.

140. Editorial, "For Country and For Liberty. Patriotic Service for American Boys and Girls," *St. Nicholas*, July 1917, 772.

141. Grace E. Craig, "The Ambulance-Girl. A Story of the French Front," *St. Nicholas*, July 1917, 789.

142. Edward N. Teall, "A Letter to the Boys of America," *St. Nicholas*, October 1917, 1066.

143. *Boys' Life*, March 1942, 5, 12, 14.

144. Elbert K. Fretwell, "Heroes of the Potato Front," *Boys' Life*, March 1944, 12.

145. "To the Boy Who Thinks He Was Born Too Late." *Boys' Life*, August 1918, 37; *St. Nicholas*, July 1918, 19.

146. "Boys, Get into the Fight!", *American Boy*, February 1918, 30.

147. *American Boy*, November 1917, 53.

148. William Heyliger and Donald Palmer, "The Recruit's Hardest Lesson," *American Boy*, February 1918, 22.

149. William Heyliger and Donald Palmer, "Into the National Army," *American Boy*, January 1918, 27.

150. Rose, "Mother's Page," *Jack and Jill*, April 1944, 52.

151. "Boys, Get into the Fight," *American Boy*, February 1918, 30.

152. Tommy Kehoe, "The Fighting Mascot," *Boys' Life*, August 1918, 8-9.

153. C. Ward Crampton, "The Making of a Hero," *Boys' Life*, June 1942, 13.

154. Surgeon-General W. C. Braised, U.S. Navy, "The Military Surgeon in War," *American Boy*, November 1917, 10.

155. McKenzie, "The Children's Crusade: American Children Writing War," 96.

# 7

## WAR AND THE MIND OF A CHILD

A challenge in writing a history of propaganda aimed at children during the world wars is finding out what the children themselves thought about militarization of their daily lives. In World War I, authorities seldom considered opinions from children regarding the effectiveness of their propaganda. Scientific polling did not exist; if it had, would authorities in 1918 have even thought of asking the children? In his study of French children during World War I, Audoin-Rouzeau also found solid evidence from the children themselves to be scanty. We can examine what authorities attempted to do, he noted, but "the real impact remains very difficult to measure."[1]

### What Did the Children Think?

Some evidence from World War I American children may be extracted from submissions to the era's juvenile publications. It must be admitted these were filtered through adult editors, who also in some cases set a theme for the children's submissions. Nevertheless, these letters might offer some evidence of how children responded to the war, and to the home-front duty expectations of authorities. Children's magazines such as St. Nicholas and American Boy encouraged their readers to write. As one of the most prestigious of children's publications from that era,[2] St. Nicholas opened its pages to young writers in keen competition to win space as part of the St. Nicholas League. The league offered cash prizes for children aged nine to sixteen who submitted the best three-hundred-word articles on a monthly theme.[3] The magazine also encouraged letters to the editor.

St. Nicholas editors tried at first to hide the war from children—no war-related material appeared before March 1915. The magazine had as a mission to offer children "a pleasure-ground where butterflies flit gayly hither and thither... and snakes dare not show themselves at all.[4] War was a snake. But some children liked snakes, and some St. Nicholas readers wanted to talk about war. The first material relating to war was generated by a Canadian reader writing a letter from England to note, "My father and brother belong to one of the Winnipeg regiments, and after war was declared between England and Germany, they came over with the first Canadian contingent."[5] This lone letter obliquely referring to the war apparently was enough to open the gates to war-related commentary from readers. April 1915 writers in the St. Nicholas League tackled the theme of "peace." Sixteen-year-old Florence Lauter Kite wrote one of several poems longing for peace:

> From warring lands we hear of grievous wrong,
> Of nations in dire need, and sore oppressed.
> Fain would we cry, "How long, O Lord, how long?"[6]

Other children from what must have been a world-wide circulation wrote of their war experiences. As the United States was still fairly neutral in spirit by this date, the editor included a letter from a ten-year-old in Austria, soon to be America's enemy. "In Vienna, everyone thinks only about the war. We saw the soldiers going away every day at the beginning, and the trains from the Tyrol were all decorated with flowers from the high Alps; the Tyrolean songs were chalked on the outside of the trains, and the soldiers sang as they passed."[7]

No editor-generated copy covering the war appeared until July 1915, an appeal for peace. In September of that year, St. Nicholas established "The Watch Tower" to make regular reports about the war. Through 1916 letters from children overseas dropped to none. Children no longer made regular appeals for peace. It is uncertain whether this represents an editor's choice, or a change in children's interests, although during this period the country's mood did move from neutrality to a pro-Allied stance, and to a more pro-war posture. Children may have reflected adult shifts in attitude toward the war. In February 1917 nine-year-old Helen A. Koch told St. Nicholas readers her tale under the league topic of "A Great Idea." A German jumped into the back seat of a French aviator's plane, "pointed the pistol at the aëronaut's head," and demanded that he fly to French lines. But the German forgot to fasten his safety belt. The aviator "looped the loop," and "naturally, when the aëroplane was turned upside down, the German officer, who was not strapped in, fell, and was dashed to pieces when he struck the ground."[8] This was a familiar and probably apocryphal World War I tale, but its matter-of-fact violence in a child's story marks a distinct change from children's peace-loving writing of 1915. Patriotic sentiment replaced pacifism in story and poem. Declared Kathryn Rose Oliver, eleven, "If I were a boy instead of a girl, and had straight hair instead of a curl, I'd be a soldier—just let me say that—and wear khaki clothes and a big brown hat."[9] The issue marked another clear shift from ignoring war, to emphasizing pacifism, to glorifying war and patriotism. As these themes dominated editorial content, so it dominated output from children. "The pages of the league fairly glow with the ardent patriotism of young America," remarked the editor in the November 1917 issue.[10] Agnes Law, fifteen, wrote:

> Proudly marched the boys in khaki,
> Bravely, swiftly, striding onward
> Toward their goal across the waters,
> There to fight for liberty.[11]

After 1917, *St. Nicholas* "indulged in openly admitted propaganda to enlist the war support and active service of its young readers,"[12] concluded Hamilton. Some of this emanated from the readers themselves. We can presume these writers were sincerely patriotic, and so reflected adult sentiment during World War I. But we can't say for certain how children felt about wartime expectations and exhortations from authorities.

Children who wrote to *American Boy* showed stronger opinions about the war, and about their place in it. This publication, too, featured writing contests for its readers, and set themes for them to follow. The debate over military drill on the eve of war apparently struck a nerve among boys. Adolescent boys were presumed to be the group that would do the drilling, and this writing contest in a prominent boys' magazine might serve as a poll reflecting the opinions of the children themselves.

"In November we asked, 'Do you want compulsory military drill in your school?'" began an editor's note. "Three hundred and forty-one readers wrote telling why they did want it; sixty-two explained why they were opposed to it."[13] This reflects a majority of 82 percent in favor of military drills. It is probable based on published debate that the favorable percentage was higher than that of the general population in early 1917, and likely it was higher than that of educators and politicians who were debating its implementation. But readers of *American Boy*, a magazine emphasizing adventure and action for boys, might not have reflected the general population; experiments in New York and other cities showed required military drills were not popular. In any case, those who supported military drills used explanations of patriotism and virtue. The letter winning first prize was written by a twelve-year-old from Illinois, George Buchanen:

> Military training develops a boy physically, mentally and morally. Physically by training to right living, clean habits, and definite athletics, such as running, hiking and military maneuvers. Right living produces right thinking and right thinking develops moral character. Military training is good for the boy; what is good for the boy is good for the man; and what is good for the man is good for the nation. Give us compulsory military training in our schools![14]

Argued fifteen-year-old Corwine [sic] D. Edwards of Missouri, "The only argument produced against the plan is militarism. But it must be remembered that militarism is a state of mind. One may be prepared and yet not be militaristic." Armand E. Cohen, sixteen, of Indiana, emphasized, "If we must have war, let us not send our youth into the field merely to furnish the stuff for camp fever and the bullets of the enemy. To send untrained youth into the field against highly trained and efficient war machines is not war; it is slaughter most cruel and inexcusable." "I, as an American boy, am under an obligation to myself and to my country," declared seventeen-year-old Jean M. Olmstead of Massachusetts. "I owe it to myself to make of myself a good man and true. I owe it to my country to do for her and die for her, as the need may be." Massachusetts was one of the states which experimented with school military drill during this era, and Olmstead said it had helped him to become a better boy. "It has taught me self-respect, implicit and prompt obedience, the spirit of cooperation under leadership, a sense of duty at all cost, and reverence for my flag."[15]

Not every boy agreed. Stewart F. Gelders, sixteen, of Georgia, won second prize for his argument against military drill, and militarism in general:

> War is the only logical purpose of military drill. Dissemination of knowledge is the first purpose of the school. War is a hindrance to knowledge and civilization and, because the titanic European struggle proves that preparation is not prevention, military drill is not properly a branch of school work.... Patriotism is spontaneous. It would die, not flourish, under compulsion. And is compulsory military drill compatible with the principles of democracy on which our government is founded?[16]

This debate came to an end, at least as reflected by letters published in these children's publications, after the United States joined the war in April 1917. Letters to *American Boy* reflected duty and patriotism as did the rest of the publication. They were channeled into these themes based on parameters set by the editor for the writing contests. The theme of August 1917 asked boys to reflect, "What Are You Doing for Your Country?" "I am wearing two buttons on my coat lapel," responded first prize winner Donald Stauffer, fourteen, of Colorado. "One is the emblem of the high school volunteers, the other a Liberty Bond button. This is because I think that no boy has a right to call himself an American boy until he has done everything in his power to help his country, especially in times of war." William S. Cunningham of Ohio (no age listed), reported he was buying a fifty dollar Liberty Bond by installments, was helping his sister with her Red Cross work, and, "I am practicing with my rifle at home to become a crack shot.... Last but not least, I am keeping myself in good physical condition so I shall be ready when it is my time to 'go across.'"[17]

Boys seemed particularly interested in preparing for war through target practice. "I just got my new rifle, and my father and I practice shooting in the basement," wrote first-prize letter winner Earl London, Waterloo, Iowa, who declared he would have been "over there" now, except he was only fourteen, "and pretty small at that.... My target is a picture of the Kaiser. I can plunk the old duffer pretty good now."[18] Harold M. Sherman of Michigan, no age indicated, offered a comforting prayer for the doughboy, who he hoped would return home a "cleaner, bigger, better man.... And, if during this terrific strife it should be God's will that you go over the top into the Great Beyond, you may die secure in the knowledge of reward for service well rendered."[19]

William F. Long, Jr., of Pennsylvania was sad that his father was in the army instead of home for Christmas, but he was "saving OUR families—homes—and the homes of the entire universe, from the hand of the murdering Hun." And in addition to saving and sacrificing, "I will try to comfort those who have received that dreaded cable gram 'Died, on the eleventh of May.'"[20] A fifteen-year-old from Salsbury, Nebraska, [sic—Salisbury?] concluded he would stay in school. "Our president has asked schoolboys to get all the education they can and do their war work after school hours. A request from the president has become a command now, so we have to obey."[21]

It is hard to verify the accuracy of sentiments as reflected by these children during World War I. One might suspect reality sometimes fell short of literary finery. One writer in the *New Republic* observed shortly after the war's end that her nephew had not been quite so noble in his patriotic response to the war. The twelve-year-old and his friends had a "marked absence of patriotic sentiment" during the war. "When a Liberty Loan orator gushes about the starry banner, they roll their eyes expressively and murmur 'Cut it out.'" But the boys loved the war's trappings, the medals, the uniforms, the parades and excitement. "With the possible exception of the beef profiteers and a few superpatriots to whom life has been a prolonged Fourth of July oration, no one has got quite so much fun out of the war as Billy and his inseparable companions, Fritters, George and Bean-Pole Ross."[22]

World War II's children did not have as many writing opportunities in children's publications as the previous war generation enjoyed. *Boys' Life*, sponsored by the Boy Scouts, and *American Girl*, sponsored by the Girl Scouts, focused on telling, not asking, and so had no pages open to letters or comments. *Jack and Jill*, however, did. The editor of this advertising-free monthly began in 1938 by Curtis Publishing encouraged children to write. Response was enormous; the editor in 1942 reported she read 1,000 letters a month. She regretted she could not print them all.[23] The writers were young; *Jack and Jill*'s material attracted an audience from barely reading to about age eleven, in contrast to the scouts' publications for pre-teens to high school age. But letters from the elementary-school children show they did think about war, and sometimes what they thought did not reflect what authorities wanted them to hear. As was also the case in *St. Nicholas* during World War I, it was the children, not the magazine's editors, who insisted first on bringing up the topic of war. "Dear *Jack and Jill*," wrote eight-year-old Ophelia Pierce Ingold in January 1942. "Our school began a month late this year because of the army maneuvers. My real home is in North Carolina. I am here because my daddy is called to the army. He is a major in the reserve corps. There is so much noise around here. The airplanes go zoom! Zoom! The army trucks go rumble! Rumble! The soldiers' feet go thud! Thud!" Two months later a nine-year-old from New Jersey reported he was making models for the war effort: "I am very fond of building airplane models. Bombers fly over our house from the navy yard training station. I like to watch them dive, and also watch them do the falling leaf. Alfred Joslin, Jr."[24]

By late spring *Jack and Jill* readers tilted full-steam into production of war-themed creations, filling the void of the editor, Ada Campbell Rose, who published in May only a puzzle using the war theme. "War Pictures. Drawn by the following *Jack and Jill* readers" included eleven names, with sketches of a plane labeled RAF dropping a bomb, a parachutist and anti-aircraft aimed toward it, a U.S. fighter plane, a tank, rifle, machine gun with "V for Victory" behind it, an antiaircraft gun, an American  submarine, battleship and airplanes, a man in military uniform, and a nurse with Red Cross uniform below the words "Give."[25] By February 1943 the children were speaking of the war in verse. "Jap" by this time having become the most hated enemy of the children's world, Peter Putnam Severson, wrote,

War Verse.
Four deadly bombs
Fell through the hatch.
Down, down, down, down
To meet the Japs.
Peter Putnam Severson, 7 1/2 years.[26]

Authorities during both wars, be they educators, editors, or childhood experts, never wrote of death in any honest way for children—if they discussed it at all, and they seldom did. Early in World War I, a few authorities did frankly try to present the horrors of war. In World War II, no one did that. Those tiny few who talked about war and death advocated mythic, patriotic, or heroic themes. But young children, when authorities allowed them to be heard, knew what it meant when death came to their own families. It was only after World War II was over that children's letters to *Jack and Jill* contained references to death, and then, only twice. It is hard to know if this can be blamed on children who did not write about death in war, or editors who censored it. But one can presume the latter, given the obvious aversion of authorities to that topic for children.

The Hero. There was a boy named Jackie Brod. He fought for a country he loved so. He's one of the many who gave his life for liberty. He gave it for a nation that will always be free. So remember this hero forevermore. And let there be peace and never again war. Shirley Brod, 13 years.[27]

A month later, twelve-year-old Sandy Dufort wrote,

My mother is a pilot and manages the Dufort Airport of Malone, N.Y. The airport was dedicated to my father, who was killed in an airplane crash a little over a year ago. He was a pilot too. My mother has a commercial pilot's rating and is carrying on my father's business. I want to be a pilot when I am big enough.[28]

While we know almost nothing about what World War II's older children honestly thought concerning death in war, we do know a little more about other topics, based on opinion polls. These did not exist in World War I. The ques-

*In World War II boys more than girls were likely to engage in war play, as might be expected. Girls who wanted to join usually became "nurses," reflecting dominant gender roles of the era. (Parents Magazine, July 1942, page 27.)*

tion of military drill during World War II expanded into a sometimes acrid debate over requiring adolescent boys (and maybe girls) to undertake a period of compulsory military training. The argument this time was based on a fear that the United States had been caught snoozing as the world turned violent. That ought not to happen again. "Washington observers predict that when World War II reaches its finale, we will not relapse into the pacifist isolationism of the 1920s," reported *Parents Magazine* in 1944. "They believe that parents will have learned that such a policy can only result in the rise of new aggressors, and the hasty training of boys in future generations to crush them. American parents, they feel, will consider this an unthinkable return for our expenditure of blood and treasure in two world wars."[29] Polls showed educators to be opposed to military training, but the general population to be in favor. This may be misleading, however, as the polls asked if compulsory military training should be required for young men, and not boys or adolescents.[30] When pollsters asked the adolescents themselves, however, respondents "were somewhat less enthusiastic about the idea." Setting the age for military training at seventeen to twenty-three, fewer than 50 percent of high school-aged children agreed. Results showed a wide split between the sexes: 58.5 percent of boys liked the idea, while only 38.5 percent of girls were in favor. Educators, on the other hand, did not reflect the general population: 64 percent were opposed to compulsory military training.[31] If we can compare these findings to the informal poll based on World War I letters to *American Boy*, we might conclude that adolescent boys did not differ in their attraction to military training during school. But experiences in New York and other American cities showed the boys did not like the training when proposed as an after-school or summer break option.

In a 1943 poll of high school students, depth of optimism was plumbed. It was found to be shallow—despite extensive propaganda both confident and patriotic. "In every school there is a morale problem, although in some places more pupils are affected than in others," reported a poll-taker from the University of Washington, Pullman. Students also worried that the home front would become gloomier, apparently due to shortages, that "all non-essential businesses will be closed." The author reasoned that the pessimism was based on misinformation—inadequate propaganda, in other words. "The necessities of the immediate situation provide an especial incentive for the schools to recognize this problem at once." Not acknowledged in this article was the truth that 1943 was indeed a grim year for the Allies, and that high school students certainly were reading the newspapers.[32]

Still, none of this tells us directly what children thought of authorities' plans to draw them into the war. In World War II, however, we do get some sense based on a poll of boys conducted by the Boy Scouts. This poll actually asked children what they thought was most fun about World War II's home-front activities. Boys nine to fifteen, not so surprisingly, reported they liked making airplane models. They also liked scavenging for rubber and metal, working as a team. More surprisingly, they also liked selling bonds. They did not, however, like putting up the government's posters, or collecting paper—these did not seem to be doing much for the war effort, they reported. "A chance to work as a gang, to do something different, to engage in something of a hobby nature—these seem to be the key to the 'fun activities,'" concluded the report. "But note that the boys are able to make a clear distinction between fun and importance."[33]

As for actual complaints about what was said to or expected from the country's children during these wars, we have almost none. Given a wartime spirit in which questioning authorities was considered unpatriotic, it is not surprising children would not say much publicly, even if they could. Sometimes they did, however—if promised anonymity. Presumptions of juvenile delinquency during

World War II angered one teen. "We're tired of juvenile delinquency," she argued. (We presume it was a she because an unidentified photo of an adolescent girl was included with the article.) She called teachers and principals who hounded students for supposed delinquency "over-vigilant." "My gosh—my little brother came home from school with a chocolate bar yesterday," she elaborated. "I said, 'where'd you get it, Bill?—they're scarce!' And he said, 'I'm a juvenile delinquent—see—I snitched it!' He didn't, of course—but it shows even HE is getting talked at too much. And he isn't even ten! I'm sick and tired of juvenile delinquency!"[34]

While we have little evidence to draw on regarding children's opinions of their experiences during the war, we do have some later opinions. Historians have surveyed and interviewed the generation of World War II children to learn more about their wartime memories. In the early 1990s Tuttle amassed a collection of 2,500 letters from World War II's children, reflections of growing up during total war.[35] These letters showed generally that the generation of children tempered by World War II propaganda remembered warmly their experiences. Working together as a team, collecting, constructing, selling, playing war games, and even denying themselves as common things became scarce—these served to bring together a generation that really believed they were working for a cause larger than themselves. "These girls and boys learned well the lesson of their country's righteousness before all nations," Tuttle found, "imbibing it in their schools, churches, and theatres. Indeed, although feelings of invincibility and moral certainty were two qualities widely shared by the school-age children, another was a sense of personal self-worth, motivated by participation in the war effort."[36] Nostalgia for a wartime childhood led some to wish the spirit would return, contending it would combat delinquency, "a lot less drugs, crime, etc."[37] Jack Matthews, who grew up during World War II and played with the toys he wrote about, recalled, "Geographic locations were fuzzy, political and ethnic causes totally obscure. We were far from the killing and bombing, and so for most American children the war was a huge game and the war years actually a fun time. This may sound terrible but, in perspective, it is true."[38] Another author writing about World War II popular culture recalled nostalgically, "I remember the intense family togetherness mixed with feelings of sweet sadness.... To a child like myself much of the home front idea of combat seemed to be more akin to play."[39] Others recalled with pride their cheerful participation in the war.[40] Still, not all of that generation remembers the home front so favorably. Tuttle found some became skeptical, claiming they were part of a "brainwashed generation...propagandized by our government and taught to hate at an early age."[41]

And what about those children whose fathers did not return from the battlefields? World War I draft boards exempted married men from service, and beginning with the Selective Service act of 1940, World War II draft boards did the same. But the government perceived the possibility that some young men were marrying to avoid war service. On October 1, 1943, the exemption was repealed. By September 1945 the Selective Service counted 6,200,000 service men as fathers; more than half in the younger age group of 18 to 25 saw active military duty. How many of those fathers died? How many war orphans were there? We do not know. "Although benefits have been paid to individual dependents, no records were kept on the orphans themselves."[42]

Based on statistics of those dependents who received veteran's benefits, we can estimate that at least 183,000 children lost a father in the war.[43] More would have lost a brother, many more a close relative. We know so little because during World War II, as during World War I, few people talked about death in war. "American families who lost a loved one generally hid their suffering," wrote a historian examining war orphans. Even the distinction of war orphan was not recognized. "What was our status? Who were we? We did not know," reflected one. "So, like society, we remained silent. We withdrew into our fears and fantasies, doing our best to ignore or accept our loss."[44]

War orphans Susan Johnson Hadler and Ann Bennett Mix, who collected orphan stories as part of the American World War II Orphan Network founded by Mix, were surprised to discover no one had considered the toll of war deaths on World War II American children. Even official records were not available. This comes as no surprise when one considers the difficulty finding collections of children's materials during the world war periods, and the general lack of interest authorities had in children's opinions. Mix and Hadler set out to collect recollections by orphans then in their 50s. Most orphans recalled little about what authorities wanted them to do during World War II, undoubtedly because they were never addressed as a separate group. But those children who faced the death of a father certainly must have felt differently about selling war bonds and collecting milkweed floss. Death became ever-present in daily thought, recalled one: "I used to kill people off in my mind so I could cope with them when they did die, and I used to expect to die young myself."[45]

It would seem, however, that at least for the war in which we have most direct evidence, most who were children in the early 1940s reported they enjoyed the home-front theater of World War II, and remember the years with fondness and nostalgia. Memory, however, is tricky—particularly nearly a half century later. Hindsight bias makes relying on interviews as history imperfect at best. People will adjust their memory of a past event based on how it turned out.[46] In fact, it's so common there is an old expression for it: looking back with rose-colored glasses.

In the case of the good folk who remember their childhood during total war, we can find some evidence of hindsight bias. The 1943 survey seemed to indicate many children weren't as happy and didn't feel as confident as they much later recalled. A good share were fearful and pessimistic. Hindsight presumptions that the kids stayed out of trouble while patriotically collecting scrap and selling bonds for the war effort also can't be supported by statistics of the era: juvenile delinquency was increasing, and authorities were worried about it. Even the fun of scraping perhaps wasn't always *that* fun: the poll of boys showed they didn't much like some of the work they were asked to do. Collecting scrap paper, in particular, failed to inspire, so much so that late in the war authorities felt it necessary to launch a whole new program in hopes it would rekindle fading enthusiasm. This is not to say that later interviews were not insightful and worth while, or that people were lying. But as a guide for what children really thought about what they were doing at the time they were doing it, the best source would be children in 1945, or 1918. And that source is no longer available.


### The Wake of World War: Savagery, Sacrifice, and Children

What we do have seems to show what we probably would expect to see. Children for the most part did what authorities told them they ought to do, and thought what authorities told them they ought to think. They were happy to have a job to do during the wars. It gave them the feeling they were doing something tangible to help, and sometimes diverted their attention from worrying about relatives serving overseas, or what might become of their own lives in a looming uncertain future. Repeat motivational schemes did get tiresome after a while. In World War II older children started to ignore exhortations to enroll in wartime-specific curriculum, and instead worked to prepare for their own future, thinking, "the conflict will not last forever."[47] Younger children reverted to the play and self-absorption you would expect from elementary-school-aged kids. But these presumptions beg larger questions, questions that can't be answered by the children themselves.

And that brings us back to the largest concern of all: death. We do not know how the 183,000 children at least who lost a father in World War II responded. Admittedly that number represents only six one hundredths of one percent of the 30 million children who constituted that generation. But it does not represent the whole spectrum of children who lost not only fathers, but brothers and relatives. A total 405,399 U.S. soldiers died in World War II; 116,516 died in World War I.[48] We have little idea what children thought about that. "Each number in the real body count represents a hole in the life of some children—a mother, father, brother, sister, aunt, uncle or cousin ripped away," a researcher of children in war reminded us.[49] The men who saw real combat—although only a fraction of those who served—witnessed what could not be imagined by people on the home front. "Indescribably cruel and insane," wrote Fussell of World War II. The second war was even worse than the worst of World War I, if that could even by thought possible.[50] What is war really like?

> Our conception of war is sanitized by images associated with words like glory, struggle, patriotism, bravery, casualties, national security, collateral damage, victory, and defeat. As those who have been there tell us, however, the real essence of real war is terror, dismemberment, disfigurement, peeing in your pants from fear, being splattered with the guts of your friends, chaos so profound you can hardly bear to recognize it for what it is. When asked, "What was it like?" one soldier replied bitterly, "It's not like anything. It just is."[51]

This is an examination of children, living on a home front that never was seriously threatened. This is not a story about the battlefields and the offensives, about the death and the brutality. Or is it? We need to be reminded, it seems, even today what war was like. And what war is like. The world in which these children lived—if not their own street, or school or scout troop—was ugly, chaotic and deadly. It was stupid, sadistic, as Fussell wrote, brutal, cruel, as Mossé wrote, and indescribable, as every soldier who actually fought must have thought. How could you describe witnessing your buddy killed by an officer's flying bloody leg? Or pooping your pants from fear? Or threading through naked body parts strewn about the battlefield? Or the flies: "With human corpses, human excrement, and rotting rations scattered across Peleliu's ridges, those nasty insects were so large, so glutted, and so lazy that some could scarcely fly."[52] Not even the bloodiest war movies drop far into the really grotesque truth, perhaps because they don't want to be held responsible for the vomit in the theaters that somebody has to clean up.

But such was mere fact in both wars, and it helps to explain why all soldiers will break down from shell shock (Post Traumatic Stress Disorder) if in combat long enough, estimated at 200 to 240 days.[53] One might be amazed soldiers could cling to sanity even that long, when the world around them wasn't remotely so. World War I perhaps people today can forget—funny helmets and bizarre gas masks, but America came out okay, except for the hundred thousand dead. World War II we think of today as "The Necessary War," "The Good War," so that "the young and innocent could get the impression that it was really not such a bad thing after all."[54] But World War II was not good. World War I was not funny. World war was evil. The children of these wars grew up in a world of evil incarnate rising from the mud and the blood and the guts of the incarnate who fought them.

Such words make disturbing reading, horrible, really. We don't want to know what really happened during the world wars, and we still don't know the half of it, in either war. But such things made even more disturbing reading during the wars themselves—for adults as well as children. Death was all around. But if it was taking place "Over There," maybe the home front could ignore it. In fact, as noted, authorities seldom concerned themselves with frank discussions about death. We return to the one rare example, the Yale University professor who asked in 1943, has the school "anything to offer on how to bear its greatest wartime peril—death?"

John S. Brubacher, an associate professor of education and philosophy at Yale, believed children living in democracies could not understand realistically the true implications of death. In modern times American educators did not teach "spiritual ruggedness," a preparation for death, Brubacher contended. "Consequently, those of sterner stuff hold that if democracy's youth should be better prepared than they are to face the possibility of death, it may well be that the schools should do something about it." During colonial times, death dogged children as an ever-present dark angel. Reminders of death infused early school books and teaching of puritanical America, Brubacher observed. But times changed. By the twentieth century, "there can be little doubt that the dominating spirit of the modern school is to teach children to live, not to die."[55] Brubacher might have expected that during war an honest discussion of death for children would have been taken up by the churches. He found American churches did no such thing. Even during Lent, when Christians talked most about death, "Easter is rather an escape from death, a rebirth." This contrasted with the Christian message of hope through dying, Brubacher believed, which could give children a way to make sense of the many killed in the war. "The prospect of life eternal should make it easy for one to walk joyfully into the shadow of death. At least the risk of death should be undertaken as optimistically as the Japanese die for their emperor. Yet such is not the case."[56]

Possibly one way to teach children during war about death, Brubacher wrote, was to emphasize the cycle of life, the autumn, the tree resplendent in its dying fall foliage. But does this metaphor really comfort young people facing death in wartime? Perhaps not. "We must still search." Socrates, Jesus and Patrick Henry believed some things were worse than death; this was an attitude worth encouraging. "These instances indicate not only that death is not the great evil that contemporary culture has come to regard it, but conversely life is rather rich when we learn to treat it with some abandon," counseled Brubacher. "There is little rollicking enjoyment in life if we are always preoccupied with living it safely."[57] He concluded, "After the severe lesson learned in this war, it would be unfortunate for democracy's schools again to become so obsessed with peace and with life as to be unable to sacrifice them readily in the future."[58]

This came fairly close to the opinion of the great militarist of World War I, Theodore Roosevelt. But the former president was more direct. In words published by the PTA-sponsored *Child-Welfare Magazine*, Roosevelt declared, "The man who is not willing to die, and the woman who is not willing to send her man to die in a war for a great cause are not worthy to live."[59] Theodore Roosevelt was a courageous man, a great president; he mourned one of his own sons who died serving as a pilot in World War I. But he never faced combat in world war.

Authorities who squarely faced the question of death in war as a children's question seemed to always return to what Mossé called the myth of war; war as something sacred, glorious, manly, a purification, a transcendence to the noble call. The myth served to legitimize and justify the appalling sacrifice.[60] But during the world wars, boys didn't appear to need such coaxing. Given a cause that seemed just, they were eager to fight. In World War I, the ease in which authorities persuaded young men to accept a call to the colors surprised even those who issued that call. World War II survivors repeat tales of young recruits anxious for adventure and in denial about mortality. And in that war they were really young—generally much younger than those who served in World War I, most of them eighteen, many still children at seventeen.

It seems true that many authorities who criticized the sad state of young people and schools before each war welcomed a coming war as a builder of manly character. Boys of high school age bought into this argument in large numbers, to build themselves into "real men" through a crucible of battle. America's youthful idealism responded to a simple call of patriotism and duty—as it surely does still. But in both world wars the American home front showed near-universal ignorance of how terrible warfare had become, how imbecilic its prosecution, how little heroism would be possible, and how hollow calls to patriotism would sound from the trenches, foxholes, and beaches drenched in lethal projectile. Yet the argument to military service as a way to make a "real man" still seems to resonate in today's world, and some of that argument does sound pretty good. The ability to work as a team, to be efficient, to have courage, to believe in honor and duty; these are among many positive attributes allegedly imparted through military training. Why these qualities can't be imparted through civilian education is a question seldom pondered and, at least until very recent years, why these qualities are not valuable for girls was also a question poorly posed.

But military training is not actual war. War is not about snappy uniforms, proud salutes, and stirring anthems. Only a fraction of American men who went through military training saw actual combat during the world wars; that still is mostly the case today. The men who actually saw combat in World War I or World War II might well ask if their experience built their "character"—that is, if they can bear to talk about their experience at all. E. B. Sledge, in one of the most honest accounts of an American soldier in World War II, admitted it required thirty-five years for him to put to paper his combat experience because, by then, "time heals, and the nightmares no longer wake me." He and his buddies, like nearly all young American men who faced the enemy in both world conflicts, fell ignorantly into the "abyss of war."[61] More recent wars fought by U.S. soldiers have left the country with veterans such as Eric Johnson, who at sixty-two still can't escape the mental demons of Vietnam combat. Of the $22 billion spent on VA disability payments to veterans of the country's more recent wars, 35 percent go to those with mental illness; one in four vets are affected.[62] Said William Manchester, who fought in Okinawa, "We were all psychotic, inmates of the greatest madhouse in history."[63] This is how real war builds manliness and character. Because battlefield experience is so alien to home-front experience, however, it is easy for civilians to believe a good battle forges a good man, especially as famous literature about noble wars and great battles is part of all recorded history, and all the world's civilizations. Authorities during both world wars did little to dissuade children from accepting this perspective. In fact, they did the opposite.

Authorities still seem to do that today. In making an almost religion of "supporting the troops," many Americans and their media send a clear message to children: war is a good and noble thing, whether it be fought in Germany or in France or in Afghanistan. Adults understand the difference between supporting a war and supporting the soldiers called to do the fighting, usually. But do children? A witness to 2010 Memorial Day parades worried they did not. "Children eight to ten years old were interviewed and were breathless and excited, as from a game," he observed. "On camera, they explained what they were doing with dutifully recited platitudes about dying for one's country. In their minds, the vague nature of war, death and patriotism were bound up in an amorphous but festive and competitive pep rally."[64] When the topic is war propaganda and its effect on American children, after a century, some themes don't seem to have changed.

It was the world war-era boy's typical idealism, his ignorance, his proud athleticism, his nonchalance or disbelief about the possibility of death that was counted on by those who declared war. That was what helped to make young people eager to serve. It also was what made many older men less satisfactory soldiers. It is never in a belligerent government's best interest to encourage youth to contemplate mortality, and during these wars it was never suggested as part of a wartime school curriculum. When *Boys' Life* during World War I published its frankly shocking account describing the death and chaos of the trenches, it faced the rage of that era's superpatriots and others who definitely did not want adolescent boys to learn about war separately from the propaganda of mythical idealism, the noble quest for the higher good. Such a discussion of death was not found again in children's publications, or in children's school curriculum, in either war. If death was mentioned, it was a lyrical death, promoted even by children themselves. "Listen to the sound of marching feet; Listen to the bugle— listen to the drum!", wrote Beatrice Caldwell, thirteen. "For that flag many a soldier will die; For that flag they're marching one and all."[65]

It is worth considering the value of more honest death education during wartime in schools as a possible way of shortening a war, as perhaps boys would not be so quick to join. Of course, not wanting to fight might be called "poor morale," and it also might be a recipe for losing a war. The truth is that once young men are in the thick of it the blinders come off and soldiers become well aware of impending doom. Soldiers in both world wars reported this. By then the only noble thought was survival. The standard greeting to new marine re- cruits in 1942 was not "Welcome, friend." It was, "You'll be sorreee."[66] People today sometimes question the decision of the United States to drop the Bomb on Hiroshima and Nagasaki, at the death of hundreds of thousands of civilians. No world war soldier in combat would have asked such a question. Beyond the not-so-honorable sentiment of revenge for Pearl Harbor, any action that might save American lives and shorten the war was an action worthy of execution.

Even destruction of entire cities. Unimaginable misery. Death to thousands of home-front children. This is savagery. But that is what war comes down to.

### Children Become Warriors: Militarization and Brutalization

Death, then, as it related to propaganda for children during these wars, relied on myth, metaphor and sentiment. Authorities really didn't talk much about death. It was an uncomfortable topic, as war orphans interviewed later pointed out, and so carefully ignored as not conducive to preservation of morale. Anyway, children did not relate to talk of death, perhaps could not, but they did relate to talk of patriotism. Like many adults, noted a researcher who studied children and politics, children crave simple symbols: flags, music, slogans, inspirational speeches, the tools of patriotism built on the foundation of nationalistic propaganda. By age ten children already have a pretty good idea of friend and enemy. "Nationalism works its way into just about every corner of the mind's life," observed Robert Coles. "The energies of the id, the instincts, certainly become connected to nationalist sentiments, if not passions. The tears, the goose-pimpled flesh, the shouts and cries of adults are not lost on children—many of whom, at school, are eager to show their own strong and deep love for their country."

Children he interviewed in 1980s Boston included one who had lost an uncle to the war in Vietnam. His mother had never forgotten; the child knew well that war meant death. Was he afraid? Did his abhor war? He was not. He did not. "It's worth dying to protect all we've got," he explained. "No wonder people try to sneak in here; no wonder they challenge us; they're all jealous, I think. You have to be careful, when you've got something good; people will want it!"[67] Considering the probability that children during the world wars were as patriotic as this one in the 1980s, we can presume the prospect of demise did not resonate as strongly for children during the world wars as did the prospect of patriotism. Probably bolstering children's attraction to patriotic calls is their natural gullibility; in a 1958 study children showed little distrust or cynicism toward government and politics, even if the interviewer tried to invoke such a response.[68]

The idea of studying children involved in war began during World War II, in a London nursery operated by the daughter of Sigmund Freud. Anna Freud observed from her experience that children seemed to take the trauma calmly, unless their parents showed great agitation. Younger children made sense of the war by personalizing the conflict: "They never talk about the British fighting against the Germans but of a conflict between God and Hitler."[69] A study of a Bristol, England, children's hospital bombed in 1941 indicated the children aged two to twelve showed little panic. None was injured. "Only five of the forty-four children he contacted had any lasting psychological symptoms that could be attributed to the raid." Children most fearful were those whose parents exhibited more emotional responses. Children who were separated from parents and moved to locations physically safer also suffered more trauma.[70] Based on such evidence, World War II authorities were confident American children would come through the war with no mental concerns, as long as they were reassured by calm parents. "In considering the reactions of present-day boys and girls, as well as our own interests in the past," wrote Ada Campbell Rose, editor of *Jack and Jill*, in 1944, "we don't worry too much about children's need for exclusive sweetness and light."[71]

Subsequent research called this comforting presumption into question. Researchers began to see symptoms of PTSD in the World War II children they had presumed were all right. The "sleeper effect" might not be observed until many years later, when adults challenged by life decisions began to display dysfunctions relating to their wartime upbringing.[72] The literature still has come to no firm conclusions regarding children during wartime. More recent studies of conflicts in many countries "showed no psychological ill effects. Furthermore, their well-being was not necessarily related to the amount of violence they had suffered, but it was related to the way they made sense of their experiences, their subjective view of events." But, added this researcher, "while it might not have made them psychologically ill, it had an effect."[73] Of course, the effect depended on the experience as well. Few American children in either world war actually experienced combat or destruction. Unfortunately, the twentieth century has offered historians a good opportunity to follow the progression of children who did, first as victims, then also as participants. Wars of past centuries may have included a few children as valets, drummer boys, powder monkeys or water carriers. But they were not expected to fight, or made deliberate targets. Engaging in battle was a man's duty, by custom, and because weapons were heavy and fighting was hand to hand. Weapons became lighter and deadlier by the beginning of the last century, and acceptable battlefields began to feature larger and larger populations of civilians. In World War I, civilian casualties totaled 10 percent. In World War II they totaled 50 percent. It has risen since. At the dawn of the millennium the majority of those killed in war were civilians: nearly 90 percent in African and Balkan wars. In the decade of the 1990s, two million children were killed in war, six million were seriously injured, 25 million were driven from their homes.[74]

Late twentieth century war so blurred the traditional distinction between combatants and civilians that often the home front as someplace relatively safe for children no longer existed. This is what Mossé meant when he examined reasons for the progressive brutalization of world societies after World War I, the greater and greater indifference to mass death.[75] His study stopped at World War II, and he hoped the 1939-45 murder on a global scale had opened the world's eyes to the idiocy of war. Alas, it does not appear to have. While the venues have shifted away from northern Europe, we find the insanity of the Holocaust repeated in multiple countries, from Southeast Asia, to Africa, to the Middle East.

We also find children to be more and more involved, at a younger and younger age. America's World War II recruiters dipped to age seventeen in an attempt to fill voracious need. But they didn't recruit young children. Germany did command its trained *Hitler Jugend* to fight, though still adolescents. Many were killed in the last months of the war, pointless deaths in a war Germany had already lost. Since that war, the age of combatants has slunk lower and lower. In three-quarters of wars raging at the beginning of the new millennium, a significant number of warriors were children. Twenty-three percent of armed organizations recruited children under fifteen; 18 percent welcomed those under twelve. Some were as young as six. The Ayatollah Khomeini's delight in the Iranian "children's sacrifice" during the 1980-1988 Iran-Iraq war led 100,000 boys to their deaths on the lines. But Saddam Hussein's Iraq showed little more concern for children under arms.[76] In 2008, fighters in the Afghanistan war included teenagers: the teen would fire a few dozen rounds at American troops, then hopefully scamper away before U.S. mortars could respond. For this the Taliban recruiters reportedly paid five dollars per adolescent.[77]

How can a six-year-old fight? Today's weapons make it easy: the AK-47, for example, weighs only ten pounds, takes only a half hour to learn. A few kids can kill as quickly as a whole regiment of Napoleon's day.[78] But the kids' regiments more often target unarmed civilians. The question is no longer how they can fight, but why. For the adolescents, soldiering might be a good solution to the motivations that have driven older boys for centuries: youthful idealism, a taste for adventure, a way to find meaning, dead-end prospects for a better life at home. "Teenagers do volunteer to fight, particularly if they are angry, if they despair of a better future, or if they believe in a cause," observed Garbarino, Kostelny, and Dubrow. "For teenagers, war may offer a chance to move forward in identity and status, to escape dead ends at home, or just to feel the excitement of change and challenge.... There are always adults ready to offer making war as a way for adolescents to find themselves."[79]

Motivation for the little ones is less certain. Babies are not born to war-mongering. But they may learn it at a young age through a militarized childhood in which martial morals are esteemed, combat is normal, brutalization is habitual, and values turn to military necessity. "For many children, war is a crucible of darkness from which they emerge bitter, angry, and distrustful. They may learn all too well the primal lesson of war: kill and/or be killed."[80] Children who grow up in a war zone, or who find themselves in a war zone, may be kidnapped for war service, and coerced to fight. They are taken away from their natural attachments to parents and stable home life, the one aspect Freud found most traumatizing to children in war. Replacing this the kidnappers force the children to rely on their military commanders for every need, from food to comfort. The price is their willingness to carry a weapon, and to use it. Intense brutalization and indoctrination mark the path to an ability to kill without concern.

Children in Mozambique, for example, were "kidnapped by antigovernment bandits and compelled to join their 'army' under the threat of death if they refuse."[81] Coercion to fight has always been a tactic in war, of course; World War I soldiers who refused to go over the top faced guns from behind as well as from the enemy. For children, coercion "may be based on physical punishment, remunerative, based on promise of material reward, or normative, based on offer or withdrawal of psychological rewards such as honors and group acceptance." Beatings are common for those who resist, or the child may be killed.[82] In Liberia, children were recruited for the National Patriotic Front's "Small Boys Unit" aged six to twenty; 20,000 children were recruited from all fighting groups in that country.[83]

Children can be militarized into soldiers through targeted propaganda and education. In Sri Lanka, the Liberation Tigers of Tamil Eelam used the formal school system. Education for those pulled from the classroom involved long periods of indoctrination. In some cases, toy guns were attached to playground equipment to develop weapon skills. Occasional beatings "socialized" children into violence. In Sierra Leone Revolutionary United Front leaders forced children to witness executions of their relatives, were fed drugs or crack cocaine, and then urged to repeat their experiences in other villages.[84]

This, for children, is what war in the twentieth century had come to. Between 1945 and 1992, the average number of war deaths per year was double that of the nineteenth century, seven times that of the eighteenth century, as children and other civilians were drawn into the vortex of militarism. Since World War II the world has seen 149 wars, killing 23,142,000.[85] We have moved a long way from the home front of world war America—from collecting peach pits to shouldering automatic weapons. America's children during these wars did not face the kind of coercion children faced elsewhere. They did not fear death as an immediate, personal threat. They were not wrenched from parents, beaten and tortured, either as soldiers or victims. Their experience was in no direct way comparable to that of the world wars' victims, or the children who have become warriors in the decades since.

On the other hand, they were among the first generation of children expected to participate directly in the enormous total wars of the twentieth century. They received the heavy propaganda, they responded to the patriotic call to convert their childhoods to a military posture. "In wartime war is the way of life," Patri explained to parents in 1943. "We must adjust our thinking and our behavior to its demands."[86] These adjustments included thinking about hate, and behaving to control fear, two wartime lessons children learned as part of their total war experience. Most authorities did not intend to teach hate. But they did intend to uphold morale, and to do that in war, you needed someone to hate. Even respectable children's magazines let slip the "Hun" and the "Jap." A New York Times Magazine article in 1942 decried the drive to teach hate, "to hate and hate and hate. Without hate we cannot win the war! Dear God, since the world began, hate and selfishness have spawned all wars." Fifty years later, Kirk's research uncovered lingering vestiges of anti-Japanese racism among the generation of World War II children.[87] Another contemporary critic worried about the consequences of presenting government-sponsored violence as acceptable. "There is an implied sanction for aggressive action and since wars are fought and won by the matching of aggression with aggression, ruthlessness with ruthlessness, the culture of a nation tends to change from prohibition to permissiveness of violence."[88]

World war, as told through American propaganda to children, was necessary and just. It was not something to fear, not something to condemn; it was a daily duty, inevitable as rain. It was something fought for patriotic goals beyond the practical needs of the heroic soldiers. Those goals involved children, children most importantly, because children were the future. Soldiers sacrificed much, and sometimes all, for that future, but for those to whom much was given, much was required. Children were expected to join an army of their own, the home front army, mobilized for a war that permeated the culture of the kids.

Their duties were myriad; their future might be drafted; their daily life certainly was militarized.

## The Militarized Generation

But what of this militarized generation? Did America's children so thoroughly mobilized for world war turn into adults who believed the answer to the world's problems could be found in combat zones? Mossé believed so. Attempts by authorities to turn war into a game, into play, into part of everyday life, "cut it down to size," made it less fearsome, so more acceptable.[89] Kirk believed so. Even if World War I's children had admitted a return to pacifist and isolationist values during the interwar years, at the beginning of World War II, they did not hesitate to support another war. War, World War I's childhood generation believed, was an acceptable alternative to compromise. "Similarly, World War II children were not silent during the Cold War. Rather, unlike some anti-war members of the generation that followed, they contributed to a bellicose anti-communist postwar near-consensus."[90] Tuttle thought so too. War's propaganda to children was intense and powerful, he concluded. "And it is only when viewing the mental structures and the wartime messages as reciprocal and complimentary that one can grasp the centrality of the Second World War to these home front children, both then and in the values and attitudes which they have carried with them throughout their lives.[91] The mind of a child is at its most vulnerable in response to the propaganda of nationalism, wrote psychologist Coles. A Belfast pediatrician who expressed shock at savage denunciations of the enemy coming from the mouths of his small patients asked, what happens to these children? Coles said the answer is observable:

> What happens to "these children" is that one day they will become the grown-ups—the ones who, as he put it so aptly, send "a signal" every day to their children, "world without end" as the religious phrase goes. These "signals," these politically energized admonitions, injunctions, exhortations, these vociferous calls upon boys and girls to say this, believe that, become in their sum an important part of the mind's house, maybe the hallway that connects the various rooms yet is never really considered to be a room.[92]

This sounds like a denunciation of authorities during the world wars, their attempts to draw children into war a travesty echoing through the rest of the century. We recognize that the messages of wartime propaganda these children received did seem to miss a point on which the nation was built. We have de-

cried the totalitarianism of wartime dictators for their control of an entire culture of communication, a single government-inspired message broadcast to the
schools, the churches, the workplaces and the media. But this certainly was
what happened in world war America as these messages were presented to children. To question or discuss the war and its prosecution by the government was
disloyal extrinsically. Disloyal intrinsically was any realistic discussion of death.

Educator Howard Lane in 1943 feared wartime propaganda aimed at children would create adults fearful and suspicious. "In another fourteen years
Johnny will vote, shortly he might become a congressman. What kind of world
will he want? To grow up in hatred, suspicion, dread and terror is to become
a vindictive, suspicious, anxious, terrified adult."[93] This seems to define fairly
well the McCarthy Era of the 1950s—hate-filled, suspicious, vindictive, fearful.
War had been busted down to a child's level, as a game, as a sport, as a toy, as
an inspiration, as a youthful adventure, with easy targets to hate. The decision
by many nations to militarize children's lives during world war has emerged
worldwide by logical yet horrifying extension into societies in which children
have become acceptable as warriors. If war is a game and a sport, kids ought to
participate. For American children, that participation was a metaphor: "mobilizing" the "army" for "battle" on the home "front" did not mean actually killing.
But to make things familiar we begin by adopting the terminology. The first step
to making war is to begin thinking like a soldier.

This all may be plausible. But it is not an attempt to blame authorities for
turning two generations of children into violent, war-happy zealots. While some
evidence seemed to indicate world war children retained vestiges of racist propaganda into adulthood, none indicated they became more violent. No matter
how much we abhor war, we have to remember facts as they were in 1917 and
1941. In World War I, United States civilian ships *were* attacked and *were* sunk.
Germany's Zimmermann Telegram *did* threaten the country. Perhaps these don't
seem like good reasons now to declare war, but people then surely thought they
were, nearly everybody. In World War II, the country actually *was* attacked. Fascism *was* evil and powerful. Again, few Americans opposed Franklin Roosevelt's
request of December 8, 1941.

Authorities in both wars thought children needed to understand why their
parents supported war, and how kid power could help America win. They worried about war's tendency to turn good kids bad, worried about school curriculum perverted by military exigencies, worried about the rise in wartime juvenile
delinquency. Particularly in World War II, authorities worried children would
become anxious and fearful. They sought to reassure and comfort. Making war

into a game was one way to do that. It may have had the consequence of trivial-izing war, but authorities certainly didn't intend that. Toys too may have brought war down to a child's world, but children themselves wanted war toys, whether or not authorities condemned the idea as war-mongering. By making war more familiar, by giving children a job to do, and by grooming them for possible ser-vice, authorities believed they were doing the best thing for America's younger generation.

Unintended consequences open the way to a larger discussion about chil-dren and the last century's decision to move the nation from mostly pacifist and isolationist to mostly aggressive and interventionist. World War II marked an end to pacifism, an end to what was once a credible option for America. Many Americans in 1941 grew to agree with preparedness advocates who argued that if the United States and its allies had more aggressively opposed fascist forces, if the country had been more prepared for war, World War II might not have happened. As we now understand the impact of the 1919 Versailles Treaty and 1930s economic depression, today we can't be so sure of that. But then the "peace preachers," as antiwar supporters were called, were thoroughly cowed by the aftermath of Pearl Harbor. The message of World War II seemed to be that if you want peace, prepare for war. The United States has done that. The country grew its forces to stand alone as the greatest military power the world has ever known. In 2010 it maintained its lead, as usual spending more than all other countries combined. President Barack Obama, often accused of cutting military spending, had by 2010 done no such thing. "Yet we persist in thinking of ourselves," concluded *Chicago Tribune* columnist Steve Chapman, "as endan-gered by foreign countries that are military pipsqueaks."[94]

In 2010 the United States was expanding into Afghanistan, a new war but an old story considering the many overseas expeditions the country had un-dertaken since 1945. Ironically, Franklin Roosevelt's famous "Four Freedoms" speech to Congress on January 6, 1941, seemed to ask for an opposite post-war foreign policy. Roosevelt said his fourth freedom, freedom from fear, "means a world-wide reduction of armaments to such a point and in such a thorough fash-ion that no nation will be in a position to commit an act of physical aggression against any neighbor—anywhere in the world."[95]

The United States found itself exempt from that principle. More than sixty years of experience did seem to show the world that preparedness at the level the United States had reached had as its consequences lots of wars, at enormous expense. The cost of the country's military budget in 2008 was $623 billion. Next closest nation in expenditure was China, $65 billion.[96] The total cost to

the United States in wars since 1945 has been astronomical. In fact, at the end
of 2009 the cost of the Iraqi War alone surpassed that of the Vietnam War in
inflation-adjusted dollars: $694 billion, compared with $686 billion.[97] Oswald
Villard in 1944 warned that to maintain a great military would tie the country
to "the most paralyzing expenditures and debt." "Militarism breeds militarism,"
warned Senator Claude Pepper in 1944. Rebutting this, Yale President Charles
Seymour reflected the reasoning that has prevailed among successive United
States governments: "We cannot afford, after this war, to risk our freedom, as
we have in the past, through shortsighted unpreparedness."[98]

Did the United States fight wars since 1945 because it was prepared to do
it, because it ought to do it—and because its new adults had been thoroughly
militarized through a propaganda that, perhaps inadvertently, glorified military
values and so accepted war as a worthwhile tool of foreign policy? Would a more
robust return to pacifism after World War II have spared some of the 100,766
Americans dead in campaigns from 1945 to 2009? Would the "we will bury you"
Soviet Union actually have done as it threatened? Or maybe those countries that
questioned United States values since the Good War would not have been as
threatening if they had not feared the immense global projection of confident
American militarism.

These questions are controversial—and perhaps not nearly as often debated
as they ought to be. A history of the country's children during world war can
hardly provide complete answers. It certainly did seem at the end of World War
II that the earth was a very dangerous place, that communism really was a threat
to democracy, and that the United States had not been adequately prepared to
confront fascism. A prudent response did seem to require building a formidable
wall of men and armaments as warranty against perils. But the practical end of
pacifism in American policy also led to multiple wars that tore the country apart
and left social scars so pervasive they would never be truly understood. Many
patriotic Americans found the purpose and prosecution of those wars to have
been highly questionable. The United States learned "what works" as shown
by World War II success, and so became a military power *par excellence*. We can
hardly hand credit for this decision to the propagandized children of world
war—finding such causation in this immense debate isn't remotely feasible. We
may be able to say this: by infusing world war into their children's daily lives,
America raised a generation to accept the principle that war works.

# Notes

1. Stéphane Audoin-Rouzeau, *La Guerre des Enfants 1914–1918*, 2nd ed. (Paris: Armand Colin, 2004), 213.

2. Karen L. Hamilton, "St. Nicholas at War: The Effects of the Great War on a Prominent Children's Magazine, 1914–1919" (Master's thesis, University of Minnesota, 1972), 3.

3. *St. Nicholas*, July 1914, 856.

4. Andrea McKenzie, "The Children's Crusade: American Children Writing War," *The Lion and the Unicorn*, 31 (2007), 89.

5. Muriel Anderson, "Salisbury, England," *St. Nicholas*, March 1915, 476.

6. Florence Lauter Kite, "On the European War—A Prayer for Peace," *St. Nicholas*, April 1915, 557.

7. Margaret Juers, "Vienna, Austria," *St. Nicholas*, June 1915, 765.

8. Helen A. Koch, "A Great Idea," *St. Nicholas*, February 1917, 374.

9. Kathryn Rose Oliver, "A Marching Song," *St. Nicholas*, February 1917, 376.

10. *St. Nicholas*, November 1917, 86.

11. Agnes Law, "The Flag," *St. Nicholas*, November 1917, 86.

12. Hamilton, "St. Nicholas at War," 5.

13. "The *American Boy* Contest. Compulsory Military Drill in the School," *American Boy*, January 1917, 28.

14. George Buchanen, "War to Build Character," *American Boy*, January 1917, 28.

15. Corwine D. Edwards, "Third Prize Letter"; Armand E. Cohen; Jean M. Olmstead, "The *American Boy* Contest. Compulsory Military Drill in the School," *American Boy*, January 1917, 28.

16. Stewart F. Gelders, "Second Prize Winner," "The *American Boy* Contest. Compulsory Military Drill in the School," *American Boy*, January 1917, 28.

17. Donald Stauffer, "Giving All He Can"; William S. Cunningham, "Doing His Bit in Several Ways"; "What You Are Doing for Your Country?", *American Boy*, August 1917, 24.

18. Earl London, "First Prize Letter," *American Boy*, January 1918, 34.

19. Harold M. Sherman, "Special Prize," *American Boy*, January 1918, 34.

20. William F. Long, Jr., "Third Prize Letter. My Resolutions for Dad," *American Boy*, February 1918, 23.

21. J. Russel [sic], "First Prize Letter. Why I Am Going Back to School," *American Boy*, September 1918, 17.

22. Florence Woolston, "Billy and the World War," excerpt from *New Republic*, January 25, 1919, in David F. Trask, ed., *World War I at Home. Readings on American Life, 1914–1920* (New York: John Wiley, 1970), 93.

23. *Jack and Jill*, May 1942, 47.

24. *Jack and Jill*, January 1942, 48; March 1942, 50.

25. Ibid., May 1942, 36-37.

26. Ibid., February 1943, 50.

27. *Jack and Jill*, September 1945, 43.

28. Ibid., October 1945, 38.

29. Raymond Nathan and B. P. Brodinsky, "Will Military Training be Compulsory?", *Parents' Magazine*, May 1944, 23.

30. Hedvig Ylvisaker, "Public Opinion Toward Compulsory Peacetime Military Training," *Annals of the American Academy of Political and Social Science* 241 (September 1945), 86-87.

31. Ibid., 91.

32. Lee J. Cronbach, assistant professor of psychology, State College of Washington, Pullman, "Pupil-Morale After One Year of War," *School and Society*, April 10, 1943, 417-420.

33. Education Section, War Savings Staff, U.S. Treasury, *Schools at War. A War Savings Bulletin For Teachers. Inaugural Issue* (Washington, DC: GPO, n.d., September 1943), 7.

34. "By a Seventeen-Year-Old. We're Tired of Juvenile Delinquency," *Parents' Magazine*, August 1944, 130.

35. William M. Tuttle, Jr., *"Daddy's Gone to War." The Second World War and the Lives of America's Children* (New York and Oxford: Oxford University Press, 1993), ix.

36. Ibid., 112.

37. Robert William Kirk, "Getting in the Scrap: The Mobilization of American Children in World War II," *Journal of Popular Culture* 29, no. 1 (1995), 231.

38. Jack Matthews, *Toys Go to War. World War II Military Toys, Games, Puzzles and Books* (Missoula, Montana: Pictorial Histories Publishing Co., 1994), vii.

39. Robert Heide, in Robert Heide and John Gilman, *Home Front America. Popular Culture of the World War II Era* (San Francisco: Chronicle Books, 1995), 23.

40. Robert William Kirk, *Earning Their Stripes. The Mobilization of American Children in the Second World War* (New York: Peter Lang, 1994), 56-57.

41. Tuttle, *"Daddy's Gone to War." The Second World War and the Lives of America's Children,* 245.

42. Calvin L. Christman, ed., *Lost in the Victory. Reflections of American War Orphans of World War II* (Denton, TX: University of North Texas Press, 1998), xx.

43. Robert William Kirk, *Earning Their Stripes. The Mobilization of American Children in the Second World War,* 3.

44. Christman, ed., *Lost in the Victory,* xviii–xix.

45. Jeff Ward, in *Lost in the Victory,* 183. Ward's father was killed on October 20, 1943.

46. Joseph T. Hallinan, *Why We Make Mistakes* (New York: Broadway Books, 2009), 64.

47. Richard M. Ugland, "'Education for Victory': The High School Victory Corps and Curricular Adaptation during World War II," *History of Education Quarterly* 19, no. 4, (1979), 446.

48. "America's Wars. U.S. Casualties and Veterans," *Information Please,* http://www.infoplease.com/ipa/A0004615.html.

49. James Garbarino, Kathleen Kostelny and Nancy Dubrow, *No Place to Be a Child. Growing Up in a War Zone* (Lexington, MA: Lexington Books, 1991), 8.

50. Paul Fussell, *Wartime. Understanding and Behavior in the Second World War* (New York and Oxford: Oxford University Press, 1989), 132.

51. James Garbarino, Kathleen Kostelny and Nancy Dubrow, *No Place to Be a Child. Growing Up in a War Zone,* 7.

52. E. B. Sledge, *With the Old Breed* (Novato, CA: Presidio Press, 1981), 144.

53. Fussell, *Wartime. Understanding and Behavior in the Second World War,* 277, 281.

54. Fussell, *Wartime. Understanding and Behavior in the Second World War,* 142.

55. John S. Brubacher, "Education for Death," *School and Society,* August 22, 1943, 138.

56. Ibid., 139.

57. Ibid., 140.

58. Ibid., 141.

59. Theodore Roosevelt, "Only Those Are Fit to Live Who Do Not Fear to Die," *Child-Welfare* (PTA), November 1918, 62.

60. George L. Mossé, *Fallen Soldiers. Reshaping the Memory of the World Wars* (New York and Oxford, Oxford University Press, 1990), 10.

61. Sledge, *With the Old Breed,* xiii.

62. *Chicago Tribune,* analysis of U.S. Department of Veterans Affairs data, "Costs Soar for Treating Mental Scars. PTSD Affecting More Veterans," Fargo, North Dakota, *Forum,* April 19, 2010, A6.

63. Quoted in Jon Zobenica, "Getting Their Guns Off," *Atlantic,* May 2010, 94.

64. David McGrath, emeritus professor of English, College of DuPage, IL, "Empty Gestures Often Equal Hollow Support," Duluth (MN) *News Tribune,* July 18, 2010, A10.

65. Beatrice Caldwell, "A Marching Song," *St. Nicholas,* February 1917, 372.

66. Sledge, *With the Old Breed,* 8.

67. Robert Coles, *The Political Life of Children* (Boston and New York: The Atlantic Monthly Press, 1986), 61.

68. Fred I. Greenstein, *Children and Politics.* Revised ed. (New Haven and London: Yale University Press, 1965, 1969), 31.

69. Anna Freud and Dorothy T. Burlingham, *War and Children* (New York: International University Press, 1944), 181.

70. Lynne Jones, *Then They Started Shooting. Growing Up in Wartime Bosnia* (Cambridge, MA, and London: Harvard University Press, 2004), 191.

71. Ada Campbell Rose, "Mother's Page," *Jack and Jill,* April 1944, 52.

72. James Garbarino, Kathleen Kostelny and Nancy Dubrow, *No Place to Be a Child. Growing Up in a War Zone* (Lexington, MA: Lexington Books, 1991), 18.

73. Lynne Jones, *Then They Started Shooting. Growing Up in Wartime Bosnia,* 5.

74. P. W. Singer, *Children at War* (New York: Pantheon Books, 2005), 4-5; UNICEF, "Children in War," http://www.unicef.org/sowc96/1cinwar.htm.

75. Mossé, *Fallen Soldiers. Reshaping the Memory of the World Wars,* 159-160.

76. Singer, *Children at War,* 6, 29.

77. Sebastian Junger, *War* (New York: Hachette Book Group, 2010), 82–83.

78. Ibid., 46.

79. Garbarino, Kostelny, and Dubrow, *No Place to Be a Child. Growing Up in a War Zone*, 16.

80. Ibid.

81. Ibid.

82. Singer, *Children at War*, 70–71.

83. UNICEF, "Children in War. Children as Soldiers," http://www.unicef.org/sowc96/2csoldrs.htm.

84. Ibid.

85. Ruth Leger Sivard, *World Military and Social Expenditures 1993* (Washington, DC: World Priorities, Inc.), 20.

86. Angelo Patri, *Your Children in Wartime* (Garden City, NY: Doubleday, Doran & Co., 1943), 4.

87. Catherine Mackenzie, "Parent and Child: Warding Off Wartime Anxiety," *New York Times Magazine*, October 15, 1942, 26; quoted in Kirk, *Earning Their Stripes. The Mobilization of American Children in the Second World War*, 108; 4.

88. John Slawson, executive director, Jewish Board of Guardians, New York, "Wartime Delinquency and the Church," *Religious Education*, March-April 1943, 95–96.

89. Mossé, *Fallen Soldiers. Reshaping the Memory of the World Wars*, 137.

90. Kirk, *Earning Their Stripes. The Mobilization of American Children in the Second World War*, 110–111.

91. Tuttle, *"Daddy's Gone to War." The Second World War and the Lives of America's Children*, 115.

92. Coles, *The Political Life of Children*, 66–67.

93. Howard Lane, associate professor of education, Northwestern University, "The Good School for the Young Child in Wartime," *Education*, February 1943, 352.

94. Steve Chapman, Chicago *Tribune*, "Obama, Wimp on Defense? That's Bull," Minneapolis (MN) *Star-Tribune*, January 15, 2010, A11.

95. Franklin D. Roosevelt, "The Four Freedoms," address to Congress January 6, 1941, *American Rhetoric. The Top 100 Speeches*, http://americanrhetoric.com/speeches/fdrthefourfreedoms.htm.

96. GlobalSecurity.org, "World Wide Military Expenditures," http://www.globalsecurity.org/military/world/spending.htm.

97. E. Barnes, "Cost of Iraqi War Will Surpass Vietnam by Year's End," *Military World*, http://www.military-world.net/Iraq/1112.html.

98. Garrison Villard, Claude Pepper, Charles Seymour, "Shall We Have Compulsory Military Training After the War?", *Parents' Magazine*, November 1944, 16–18, 56.

# Bibliography of Works Cited

## Secondary Sources

Audoin-Rouzeau, Stéphane. *La Guerre Des Enfants, 1914–1918*, 2nd ed. Paris: Armand Colin, 2004.

Bartlett, F. C. "The Aims of Political Propaganda," in *Public Opinion and Propaganda. A Book of Readings*. New York: Dryden Press, 1954.

Blue, Edna. "Children in War Time." *Nation*, May 9, 1942, 545–546.

Blum, John Morton. *V Was for Victory. Politics and American Culture during World War II*. New York: Harcourt Brace Jovanovich, 1976.

Bremner, Robert H., ed. *Children and Youth in America. A Documentary History*. Vol. 2, *1866–1932*, Vol. 3, *1933-1973*. Cambridge: Harvard University Press, 1971, 1974.

Brumberg, Stephan F. "New York City Schools March Off to War. The Nature and Extent of Participation of the City Schools in the Great War, April 1917–June 1918." *Urban Education* 24, no. 4, (January 1990): 440–475.

Cadogan, Mary and Patricia Craig. *Women and Children First. The Fiction of Two World Wars*. London: Victor Gollancz Ltd., 1978.

Chafee, Zechariah, Jr. *Freedom of Speech*. New York: Harcourt, Brace and Howe, 1920.

Chapman, Steve, "Obama, Wimp on Defense? That's Bull." Minneapolis (MN) *Star-Tribune*, January 15, 2010, A11.

Christman, Calvin L., ed. *Lost in the Victory. Reflections of American War Orphans of World War II*. Denton, TX: University of North Texas Press, 1998.

Coles, Robert. *The Political Life of Children*. Boston and New York: The Atlantic Monthly Press, 1986.

Collins, Ross F. *World War I. Primary Documents from 1914 to 1919*. Westport, CT: Greenwood Press, 2008.

Collins, Ross F. "Positioning the War: The Evolution of Civilian War-Related Advertising in France." *Journalism History* 19, no. 3 (1993): 79–86.

Collins, Ross F. and Patrick S. Washburn. *The Greenwood Library of American Reporting Volume 5, World War I and World War II, the European Theater.* Westport, CT: Greenwood Press, 2005.

Creel, George. *Rebel At Large.* New York: G.P. Putnam's Sons, 1947.

Cull, Nicholas J., David Culbert and David Welch. *Propaganda and Mass Persuasion. A Historical Encyclopedia, 1500 to the Present.* Santa Barbara, CA: ABC-CLIO, 2003.

Davison, Henry P. *The American Red Cross in the Great War.* New York: Macmillan Co., 1919.

Eksteins, Modris. *Rites of Spring. The Great War and the Birth of the Modern Age.* Boston: Houghton Mifflin Co., 1989.

Filipovic, Zlata and Melanie Challenger. *Stolen Voices. Young People's War Diaries from World War I to Iraq.* New York: Penguin, 2006.

Folly, Martin. *The United States and World War II: The Awakening Giant.* Edinburgh: Edinburgh University Press, 2002.

Freud, Anna and Dorothy Burlingham. *War and Children.* New York: International University Press, 1944.

Fussell, Paul. *Wartime. Understanding and Behavior in the Second World War.* New York and Oxford: Oxford University Press, 1989.

Garbarino, James, Kathleen Kostelny and Nancy Dubrow. *No Place to Be a Child. Growing Up in a War Zone.* Lexington, MA: Lexington Books, 1991.

Goldstein, Jeffrey, David Buckingham, Gilles Brougére, eds. *Toys, Games and Media.* Mahwah, NJ: Lawrence Erlbaum, 2004.

Graham, Irvin. *Encyclopedia of Advertising.* 2nd ed. New York: Fairchild Publications, Inc., 1969.

Greenstein, Fred I. *Children and Politics.* Revised ed. New Haven and London: Yale University Press, 1969.

Gruenberg, Sidonie Matsner and Benjamin C. Gruenberg. "Crosscurrents in the Rearing of Youth." *The Annals of the American Academy of Political and Social Science* 236 (1944), 67–73.

Hallinan, Joseph T. *Why We Make Mistakes.* New York: Broadway Books, 2009.

Hamilton, Karen L. "*St. Nicholas* at War: The Effects of the Great War on a Prominent Children's Magazine, 1914-1918." Master's thesis, University of Minnesota, 1972.

Hart, Jeffrey. *From This Moment On. America in 1940.* New York: Crown, 1987.

Hawes, Joseph M. and N. Ray Hiner. *American Childhood. A Research Guide and Historical Handbook.* Westport CT: Greenwood Press, 1985.

Heide, Robert and John Gilman. *Home Front America. Popular Culture of the World War II Era.* San Francisco: Chronicle Books, 1995.

Higonnet, Margaret R. "War Toys: Breaking and Remaking in Great War Narratives." *The Lion and the Unicorn* 31 (2007): 116-131.

Hurd, Charles. *A Compact History of the American Red Cross.* New York: Hawthorn Books, Inc., 1959.

Jones, Lynne. *Then They Started Shooting. Growing Up in Wartime Bosnia.* Cambridge,

MA: Harvard University Press, 2004.

Joyal, Arnold E. and William G. Carr. "Work Experience Programs in American High Schools." *The Annals of the American Academy of Political and Social Science* 236 (1944): 110–116.

Junger, Sebastian. *War.* New York: Hachette Book Group, 2010.

Kandel, I. L. *The Impact of the War upon American Education.* Chapel Hill, NC: the University of North Carolina Press, 1948.

Kelly, R. Gorden, ed. *Children's Periodicals of the United States.* Westport, CT: Greenwood, 1984.

Kennedy, David M. *Over Here. The First World War and American Society.* Oxford and New York: Oxford University Press, 1980.

Kimball, Melanie A. "From Refuge to Risk: Public Libraries and Children in World War I." *Library Trends* 55, no. 3 (2007): 455–463.

Kirk, Robert William. *Earning Their Stripes. The Mobilization of American Children in the Second World War.* New York: Peter Lang, 1994.

Kirk, Robert William. "Getting in the Scrap: The Mobilization of American Children in World War II." *Journal of Popular Culture* 29, no. 1 (1995): 223–233.

Kornhaber, Donna. "Animating the War: The First World War and Children's Cartoons in America." *The Lion and the Unicorn* 31 (2007): 132–146.

Lasswell. Harold D. *Propaganda Technique in the World War.* New York: Alfred A. Knopf, 1927.

Lavine, Harold and James Wechsler. *War Propaganda and the United States.* New Haven: Yale University Press, 1940.

Macleod, David I. *Building Character in the American Boy. The Boy Scouts, YMCA, and Their Forerunners, 1870–1920.* Madison: The University of Wisconsin Press, 1983.

McConnell, Beatrice. "Child Labor in Agriculture." *The Annals of the American Academy of Political and Social Science* 236 (1944): 92–100.

McGrath, David, "Empty Gestures Often Equal Hollow Support." Duluth (MN) *News Tribune,* July 18, 2010, A10.

McKenzie, Andrea. "The Children's Crusade: American Children Writing War." *The Lion and the Unicorn* 31 (2007): 88–102.

Machel, Graça. *The Impact of War on Children.* London: Hurst, 2001.

Matthews, Jack. *Toys Go to War. World War II Military Toys, Games, Puzzles and Books.* Missoula, MT: Pictorial Histories Publishing Co., 1994.

Miller, Katherine. *Communication Theories. Perspectives, Processes, and Contexts,* 2nd ed. Boston: McGraw Hill, 2005.

Mock, James R. and Cedric Larson. *Words that Won the War. The Story of the Committee on Public Information.* Princeton, NJ: Princeton University Press, 1939.

Mossé, George L. *Fallen Soldiers. Reshaping the Memory of the World Wars.* New York and Oxford: Oxford University Press, 1990.

Murray, William D. *The History of the Boy Scouts of America.* New York: Boy Scouts of America, 1937.

O'Brien, Richard. *The Story of American Toys.* New York: Abbeville Press, 1990.

Perrett, Geoffrey. *Days of Sadness, Years of Triumph. The American People 1939–1945.*

New York: Coward, McCann & Geoghegan, Inc., 1973.

Polenberg, Richard, ed. *America at War: The Home Front 1941–1945*. Englewood Cliffs, NJ: Prentice Hall, 1968.

Ponsonby, Arthur. *Falsehood in Wartime*. New York: E. P. Dutton, 1928.

Repplier, Agnes. "War and the Child." *Atlantic Monthly*, March 1917, 311–320.

Rosenberry, Jack and Lauren A. Vicker. *Applied Mass Communication Theory*. Boston: Pearson, 2009.

*Schroeder's Collectible Toys Antique to Modern Price Guide*, 11th ed. Paducah, KY: Collector Books, Schroeder Publishing, Inc., 2008.

Singer, P. W. *Children at War*. New York: Pantheon Books, 2005.

Sivard, Ruth Leger. *World Military and Social Expenditures 1993*. Washington, DC: World Priorities, Inc., 1993.

Sledge, E. B. *With the Old Breed*. Novato, CA: Presidio Press, 1981.

Sorenson, Roy. "Wartime Recreation for Adolescents." *The Annals of the American Academy of Political and Social Science* 236 (1944): 145–151.

Steel, Ronald. *Pax Americana*. New York: Viking Press, 1967.

Stroyar, J. N. *The Children's War*. New York: Pocket Books, 2001.

Taylor, Theodore. *The Children's War*. Garden City, NY: Doubleday, 1971.

Trask, David F., ed. *World War I at Home. Readings on American Life, 1914–1920*. New York: John Wiley, 1970.

Tuttle, William M., Jr. "*Daddy's Gone to War*." *The Second World War in the Lives of America's Children*. New York and Oxford: Oxford University Press, 1993.

Reck, Franklin M. *The 4-H Story. A History of 4-H Club Work*. Chicago: National Committee on Boys and Girls Club Work, 1951.

Ugland, Richard M. "'Education for Victory': The High School Victory Corps and Curricular Adaptation during World War II." *History of Education Quarterly* 19, no. 4, (1979): 435–451.

United States Census Bureau, *Historical Abstracts of the United States. Colonial Times to 1970*. Washington, DC: GPO, 1975.

Vaughn, Stephen. *Holding Fast the Inner Lines*. Chapel Hill: University of North Carolina Press, 1980.

Wall, Richard and Jay Winter, eds. *The Upheaval of War. Family, Work and Welfare in Europe, 1914-1918*. Cambridge, UK: Cambridge University Press, 1988.

Ward, Robert D. "The Origin and Activities of the National Security League, 1914-1919." *The Mississippi Valley Historical Review* 47 (June 1960): 51–65.

White, E. B. "One Man's Meat. Victory Corps." *Harpers*, April 1943, 499–500.

Wiegand, Wayne A. *An Active Instrument for Propaganda: The American Public Library During World War I*. Westport, CT: Greenwood Press, 1989.

Winkler, Allan M. *The Politics of Propaganda*. New Haven, CT: Yale University Press, 1978.

Wyland, Ray O. *Scouting in the Schools*. New York: Teachers College, Columbia University, 1934.

Ylvisaker, Hedvig. Public Opinion toward Compulsory Peacetime Military Training. *Annals of the American Academy of Political and Social Science* 241 (September 1945):

86-94.

Zeiger, Susan. "The Schoolhouse vs. the Armory. U.S. Teachers and the Campaign Against Militarism in the Schools, 1914-1918." *Journal of Women's History* 15, no. 2, (2003): 150-179.

## Primary Sources

*American Boy.* January 1917-December 1918.

*American Girl.* April 1941-December 1945.

Bernays, Edward. *Propaganda.* New York: Ig Publishing, 2005, reprint of 1928 edition.

Boas, George, "Priorities in Education." *Atlantic Monthly,* January 1943, 63-66.

Boy Scouts of America. *Thirty-Third Annual Report, 1942;* 78th Congress First Session, House Document No. 17. Washington, DC: GPO, 1943.

Boy Scouts of America. *Thirty-Fourth Annual Report 1943;* 78th Congress Second Session, House Document No. 450. Washington, DC: GPO, 1943.

Boy Scouts of America. *Thirty-Fifth Annual Report, 1944;* 79th Congress First Session, House Document No. 125. Washington, DC: GPO, 1944.

Boy Scouts of America. *Thirty-Sixth Annual Report, 1945;* 79th Congress Second Session, House Document No. 516. Washington, DC: U.S. GPO, 1945.

*Boys' Life,* 1914-1919, 1941-1945.

Chase, W. Linwood. *Wartime Social Studies in the Elementary School. Curriculum Series: Number Three.* Washington, DC: The National Council for the Social Studies, National Education Association, September 1943.

*Child-Welfare Magazine,* 1914-1919.

Children's Bureau, U.S. Department of Labor. *To Parents in Wartime.* Washington, DC: GPO, 1942.

*The Crisis,* Children's Number, October 1916, 1917, and 1918.

Committee on Public Information (George Creel). *The Creel Report. Complete Report of the Chairman of the Committee on Public Information 1917: 1918: 1919.* New York: DaCapo Press, 1972, reprint of 1920 edition.

Dean, Arthur D., *Our Schools In War Time—And After.* Boston: Ginn and Company, 1918.

*Education,* 1916-1918, 1942-1946.

*Education for Victory,* 1942-1945.

Educational Policies Commission, National Education Association and American Association of School Administrators. *Education for All American Youth.* Washington, DC: National Education Association, 1944.

Educational Policies Commission, National Education Association and American Association of School Administrators. *What the Schools Should Teach in Wartime.* Washington, DC: National Education Association, 1943.

Future Farmers of America. *Proceedings of the National Convention of the Future Farmers of America.* Washington, DC: FFA and U.S. Office of Education, Federal Security Agency, 1942-1946.

*Jack and Jill,* 1940-1945.

*Nation's Business.* December 1916–January 1919, November 1940–September 1945.

"National Crisis Demands a New Kind of Public School Teaching." *American City* 18 (February 1918): 136–138.

National Education Association. *Addresses and Proceedings, Vol. 55, Fifty-Fifth Annual Meeting, Portland, Oregon, July 7–14, 1917.* Washington, DC: NEA, 1917.

National Education Association. *Addresses and Proceedings, Vol. 56, Fifty-Sixth Annual Meeting, Pittsburgh, Pennsylvania, June 29–July 6, 1918.* Washington, DC: NEA, 1918.

National Education Association. *Addresses and Proceedings, Vol. 57, Fifty-Seventh Annual Meeting, Milwaukee, Wisconsin, June 28–July 5, 1919.* Washington, DC: NEA, 1919.

National Education Association. *Proceedings of the Eightieth Annual Meeting Held in Denver June 27–29, 1943, Vol. 80.* Washington, DC: NEA, 1942.

National Education Association. *Proceedings of the Eighty-First Annual Meeting Held in Indianapolis June 27–29, 1943, Vol. 81.* Washington, DC: NEA, 1943.

National Education Association. *Proceedings of the Eighty-Second Annual Meeting Held in Pittsburgh, July 4, 5, and 6, 1944, Vol. 82.* Washington, DC: NEA, 1944.

National Education Association. *Proceedings of the Eighty-Fourth Annual Meeting Held in Buffalo, New York, 1945–46, Vols. 83 and 84.* Washington, DC: NEA, 1946.

*National Parent-Teacher/The PTA Magazine,* January 1941–December 1945.

*National School Service,* September 1, 1918–December 15, 1918.

*Parents' Magazine,* 1941–1945.

Patri, Angelo. *Your Children in Wartime.* Garden City, NY: Doubleday, Doran & Co., 1943.

Parsons, Elise Clews. "The Dragon's Teeth." *Harper's Weekly,* May 8, 1915, 449.

*The Rally,* 1917–1918.

*Religious Education,* 1917–1918, 1940–1945.

*St. Nicholas Magazine for Boys and Girls,* 1914–1918.

*School Life,* August 1, 1918–January 1, 1919.

"Education in War Time." *Scientific American,* September 1, 1917, 152.

*School and Society,* 1917–1918, 1942–1945.

*Schools at War. A War Savings Bulletin For Teachers.* Washington, DC: Education Section, War Savings Staff, U.S. Treasury, September 1943, October 1943, November 1944.

United States War Production Board, *Use the Paper Trooper Campaign Materials to Energize Your School Waste Paper Collections. A Manual for School Administrators and Community Leaders.* Washington, DC: no publisher, 1944.

Victory Garden Committee, War Services, *Victory Gardens Handbook.* No place: Pennsylvania State Council of Defense, 1944.

Young, Hugh H. "Military Training Would Make Us a New Race." *The New York Times Magazine,* January 7, 1917, 4.

# INDEX

**A Word about the Type**

This book is set in Goudy Old Style, a choice befitting a theme of world war and the United States: it was designed in 1915 by an American. Frederic W. Goudy's classic is considered one of the most readable and legible of typefaces, a good option for children's books as well as books about children.

## SERIES EDITOR: DAVID COPELAND

Realizing the important role that the media have played in American history, this series provides a venue for a diverse range of works that deal with the mass media and its relationship to society. This new series is aimed at both scholars and students. New book proposals are welcomed.

For additional information about this series or for the submission of manuscripts, please contact:

Mary Savigar, Acquisitions Editor
Peter Lang Publishing, Inc.
29 Broadway, 18th floor
New York, New York 10006
Mary.Savigar@plang.com

To order other books in this series, please contact our Customer Service Department:

(800) 770-LANG (within the U.S.)
(212) 647-7706 (outside the U.S.)
(212) 647-7707 FAX

Or browse by series: